PROSPERING IN PRIVATE PRACTICE

A Handbook for Speech-Language Pathology and Audiology

Contributors

Deena K. Bernstein, Ph.D.
Assistant Professor, Speech-Language Pathology
Herbert J. Lehman College, City University of
  New York
New York, New York

Marlene A. Bevan, Ph.D.
Executive Director, Northwestern Michigan
  Hearing and Speech Center
Traverse City, Michigan

Joseph F. Butler, M.A.
Assistant Professor, Telecommunications
  Management
S.I. Newhouse School of Public Communication
Syracuse University
Syracuse, New York

Katharine G. Butler, Ph.D.
Professor, Communication Sciences and
  Disorders
  and
Director, Center for Research
School of Education
Syracuse University
Syracuse, New York

Patricia R. Cole, Ph.D.
Director, Austin Center for Speech, Language
  and Learning Disorders
Austin, Texas

Jeremy J. Conoway, J.D.
Brott, Conoway & Kipley, P.C.
Traverse City, Michigan

Richard M. Flower, Ph.D.
Professor and Vice-Chairman
Department of Otolaryngology
University of California, San Francisco
San Francisco, California

Dennis C. Hampton, Ph.D.
Dennis C. Hampton, Ph.D. and Associates
White Plains, New York

Rebecca F. Kooper, J.D.
NASSAU-BOCES Hearing Impaired Program
Merrick, New York

Angela M. Loavenbruck, Ed.D.
Loavenbruck Associates, P.C.
New City, New York

Mariana Newton, Ph.D.
University of North Carolina, Greensboro
Greensboro, North Carolina

Robbin Parish, M.A.
The Parish School
Houston, Texas

Carol A. Sullivan, M.S.
Sullivan and Sullivan
Garden City, New York

Robert H. Woody, Ph.D., J.D.
Department of Psychology
University of Nebraska at Omaha
Omaha, Nebraska

PROSPERING
IN PRIVATE PRACTICE

*A Handbook for Speech-Language
Pathology and Audiology*

Edited by
Katharine G. Butler

Communication Sciences and Disorders
Syracuse University

AN ASPEN PUBLICATION®
Aspen Publishers, Inc.
Rockville, Maryland
Royal Tunbridge Wells
1986

Library of Congress Cataloging in Publication Data

Prospering in private practice.

"An Aspen publication."
Includes bibliographies and index.
1. Speech therapy—Practice. 2. Audiology—Practice. I. Butler, Katharine G. [DNLM:
1. Audiology. 2. Private Practice. 3. Speech Pathology. WM 475 D966]
RC428.5.P76   1986   616.85′506   86-10828
ISBN: 0-87189-368-¹

Editorial Services: Carolyn Ormes

Library of Congress Catalog Card Number: 86-10828
ISBN: 0-87189-368-1

Printed in the United States of America

1 2 3 4 5

First, this book is dedicated to the private practitioners who, commencing with Paul Knight, broke new ground as they expanded the dimensions of the practice of speech-language pathology and audiology in the private sector. Their efforts to establish a high standard of care for their patients or clients has addressed the issue of whether it is possible to retain professional idealism in a fee-for-service setting. Those who will follow in their footsteps reap rich rewards from their pioneer efforts.

Second, this book is dedicated to a beloved husband and son both of whom willingly relinquished the computer terminal and an expanse of dining room table as the occasion demanded. To Joe and Andy, thanks . . . and henceforth, bon appetit!

Table of Contents

**Chapter 3— Legal Issues for Private Practitioners in Speech-Language
Pathology and Audiology** **47**
Robert Henley Woody, Ph.D., Sc.D., J.D.

Chapter 4— Professional Liability: Management and Prevention **59**
Rebecca Kooper, J.D. and Carol A. Sullivan, M.S.

**Chapter 5— Constraints and Commitments: An Introduction to the Financial
Aspects of Private Practice** **81**
Robbin Parish, M.A.

Preface

This book was written for practicing professionals in speech-language pathology and audiology who may be contemplating entering private practice and for those private practitioners who are interested in obtaining further knowledge regarding maintaining and expanding their private practice. In addition, those entering the field or in graduate school may learn about one of the most rapidly growing work settings in the field of communication disorders. This book will identify the parameters of private practice, focusing on those aspects most frequently overlooked or under-analyzed.

Part I is composed of six chapters whose authors identify the most critical elements of the personal and professional prerequisites to entering the private sector. The chapter authors, who have been successfully engaged in private practices for some years, systematically cover the basic precepts of such an endeavor, highlighting the organizational, economic, legal, and ethical aspects of their practices. Dr. Patricia Cole identifies the personal qualifications that are likely to be required of the full-time private practitioner in Chapter 1. In Chapter 2 Dr. Deena Bernstein lays out the pleasures and pitfalls of part-time private practice. Dr. Robert Woody, a psychologist and practicing attorney, has written extensively on legal issues for private practitioners in the health and education field. In Chapter 3, he raises important issues regarding the determination of appropriate standards for private practices within the purview of public policy, elaborates on the fundamental framework for a professional standard of care, and discusses the patient-practitioner relationship from a legal viewpoint. In Chapter 4, a speech-language pathologist in private practice, Carol Sullivan, and her co-author, Rebecca Kooper, an audiologist and attorney, reflect on professional liability issues and provide guidelines for practice that take into account the most recent court cases involving speech-language pathologists and audiologists. They emphasize the importance of preventing professional liability actions by (1) careful attention to the quality of the professional services, (2) the care and integrity of appropriate record keeping, and (3) the pro-active stance that a well-qualified practitioner must take in establishing a standard of care that meets both professional and personal goals. Chapter 5 by Robbin Parish identifies the financial principles that must undergird the efforts to begin a practice in the private sector. Constructing a business plan for successful operation of the practice is emphasized, and examples of planning failures and successes provide "real-life" relevance to the underlying themes. Chapter 6, the final chapter of this section, written by Dr. Richard Flower, deals with overriding ethical principles that guide all professionals in speech-language pathology and audiology, no matter in which service delivery system they practice. He takes note of the fact, however, that *institutional* environments may well provide a more insulated environment and hence may "shelter professionals from difficult ethical decisions." His discussion of initial and continuing professional competence merits close attention, as does the discussion of confidentiality and informed consent.

The realities of actually establishing a private practice are revealed in Part II. The first three chapters provide requisite information regarding the selection of the site for a private practice, equipping an audiological practice, and establishing successful management procedures. Written by Dr. Patricia Cole, a speech-language pathologist; Dr. Dennis Hampton, an audiologist; and Carol Sullivan, a speech-language pathologist; respectively, Chapters 7, 8, and 9 inform readers of the complex decisions that must be made in the process of initiating a private practice. All of the authors write from many years of experience and pass on to the reader their accumulated experience. Chapter 10, by Dr. Mariana Newton, who heads a univer-sity-based clinic that has successfully utilized computers, stresses that all services, regardless of work setting, are reflected in the written accounts of those services. She clearly defines the multiple uses to which computers and their software may be put by speech-language pathologists and audiologists who enter private practice.

Part III addresses the needs of the experienced private practitioner who is considering the possibility of expanding either the size or the scope of that practice. Dr. Patricia Cole addresses marketing strategies in Chapter 11. She analyzes such important aspects as fluctuations in revenue, billing procedures, control of expenses, and employee productivity and satisfaction as she stresses the need for the private practitioner undertaking expansion to develop long-range personal and professional goals. Continuing this theme in Chapter 12, Dr. Marlene Bevan, an audiologist, focuses on the variations on the theme of expansion that are of particular importance to audiologists. She discusses the need for professionals to identify themselves "as the primary provider of hearing health care and the ongoing manager of hearing rehabilitation." The entire issue of hearing aid dispensing within an audiological practice is addressed in a straightforward fashion, as the importance of strategic planning is again emphasized. A companion chapter, Chapter 14, is written by Dr. Angela Loavenbruck, an audiologist in private practice, who delineates marketing strategies that are particularly appropriate to that specialty. Speech-language pathologists, however, would do well to review her comments because many of the suggestions may be modified for use by them. Chapter 13 by Dr. Mariana Newton provides advanced information on computer applications in private practice, particularly the more sophisticated strategies that are of particular use to practitioners whose practices require refined systems for clinical and business management. From spread sheets to specialized software for patient care, she provides a framework for analyzing software needs in private practice.

The experienced practitioner will find Part IV particularly interesting, because it addresses two issues that are sometimes lost to sight among those who are deeply involved in the initial throes of private practice, wherein survival skills are the order of the day. The author of Chapter 15, Joseph F. Butler, is a telecommunication specialist who has served as owner and chief executive officer of several radio stations and who is a professor of telecommunications management. He presents a plan for utilizing the financial rewards garnered by the private practitioner, discussing both preinvestment and investment strategies. Such concepts as key-personnel insurance and retirement planning may seem somewhat distant to the new practitioner, but each needs to be taken into consideration at the appropriate time. As capital becomes available for investment purposes, private practitioners may wish to lay out a series of investment strategies that utilize current income in the short term, but also provide an analysis of long-term possibilities and practices. An investment decision flow chart, a monthly investment planning document, and a market price chart provide the reader with examples of how the practitioner may approach investment opportunities. Chapter 16, by Jeremy Conoway, a lawyer long familiar with the field of speech-language pathology and audiology, discusses a critical issue that is rarely addressed by even experienced practitioners. He notes that not only the novice but also the expert practitioner seldom consciously considers the ''life cycle'' of a business. Efforts tend to be concentrated on startup, marketing, and business operations, ignoring the most critical factor of all, the termination and/or sale of the practice. He points out that the ''ultimate return'' for the investment of energy and skill required of the private practice entrepreneur lies in the sale, or perhaps partial transfer, of the practice to others. Conoway notes that the assets of such a practice are both tangible and intangible and provides the reader with a guide through the thorny thickets of this most crucial matter. As he notes, ''The ultimate sale of a private practice in speech-language pathology or audiology is a phase of the business life cycle that should be designed and anticipated from the very beginning.''

The final section of the book, Part V, reflects on the past and provides a view of the future. Chapter 17, edited by Katharine Butler, is a compendium of the personal reflections of a number of practitioners who represent the variety of possible foci of practice: large urban practices or small rural practices; full-time practices or part-time practices; specialized practice or general practice; solo practice or large group practice; practices that involve only speech-language pathologists or practices that meld audiology and speech-language services in a combined setting; practices that provide only on-site services or practices that provide multisite services; practices that have endured for 30 or more years or those that were initiated only a few years ago. Reflected in these personal accounts are a number of the issues brought forth by the chapter authors in Parts I–IV, perhaps validating their choice of topics as being those of the most critical importance. However, what the reader may most easily discern is the satisfaction that these individuals express in their efforts to serve the speech, language, and hearing disordered clients or patients in the private sector. For the most part, they do not dwell on the downside of such practice. Although recognizing its trials and tribulations, they direct the reader's attention to the motivating force for entering and remaining within the private practice arena. These "cameos" provide insight and indelibly describe the role and requirements of those who would enter a world far different from that of the present majority of our profession. That there are real differences, real dilemmas, and real triumphs cannot be denied.

Finally, an epilogue views the future of the profession as seen from a mid-1980s perspective. Perhaps the epilogue may best be viewed for what it purports to be: an attempt to forecast that which will befall us, gazing into a crystal ball that rests on a base of facts and figures. Or perhaps it is merely a periscope, a circumscribed view of the likely outcome of today's governmental, political, and professional forces on the practice of speech-language pathology and audiology, restricted by as yet unknown rules and regulations. Some might even say it is an Alice in Wonderland foray, attempting to predict the wanderings of the private practitioner, the "dream-child moving through a land of wonders wild and new" (Carroll, 1976, p. 13).

Indeed, Lewis Carroll wrote wondrous poetry that is perhaps less well known than his famous stories about Alice. One poem, entitled "Canto VI, *Discomfyture*," expresses well the feelings of an individual who embarks on an enterprise as problematic as private practice:

> As one who strives a hill to climb,
>   Who never climbed before:
> Who finds it, in a little time,
> Grow every moment less sublime,
>   And votes the thing a bore:
>
> Yet, having once begun to try,
>   Dares not desert his quest,
> But, climbing, ever keeps his eye
> On one small hut against the sky
>   Wherein he hopes to rest:
>   (Carroll, Canto VI, *Phantasmagoria*, p. 847).

It is the hope of the editor and the authors of this volume that the reader will strive to climb the hill and will reach the entrepreneur's goal—a successful conclusion to the quest for independence and success.

Katharine G. Butler, Ph.D., Editor
Syracuse University
March 1986

REFERENCES   Dodgson, C.L. (1976). *Complete works of Lewis Carroll.* New York: Modern Library.

Acknowledgments

The Editor and authors wish to extend their deep appreciation to a significant number of individuals who have assisted in the design and preparation of this book; the clarity and the accuracy of the substance of the chapters has been enhanced thereby.

As Editor, I like to thank a number of reviewers of early drafts, among them, Dr. Bradley L. Billings, Dr. Alan Feldman, and Dr. Thomas Grimes for their reviews of a number of chapters related to audiology; Dr. Elaine Silliman, Dr. Donna Fox, Mrs. Carol Sullivan, and Ms. Lisa Breakey for chapters related to speech-language pathology; and the American Speech-Language-Hearing Association national office staff, particularly Dr. Morgan Downey, for their review of matters dealing with association standards of practice and other matters. The willingness of the entire ASHA staff to assist in the provision of information and documentation is yet another example of how the national professional association provides services to our field. Dr. Deena Bernstein, Ms. Rebecca Kooper, and Mrs. Carol Sullivan worked closely with ASHA in the development of their materials.

In addition, Kooper and Sullivan gratefully acknowledge the technical assistance and counsel given by Mathew S. Manning, Ken Locke, and Maureen A. Griffin in relation to Chapter 4. Mrs. Sullivan also gratefully acknowledges the assistance and counsel given by J. Chadwick, John Marming, and Evan Sullivan in relation to Chapter 9.

Finally, the Editor acknowledges the contributions of each contributing author, all of whom gallantly devoted significant time and effort to share with the reader the accumulated wisdom garnered over years of private practice experience. The distillation of this experience and knowledge provides a rich tapestry to be viewed by novice and expert professionals alike. In this endeavor, we have been most ably assisted by Aspen Publishers, Inc. Senior Editor, Margaret Quinlin, who has devoted much time over the past two years to bring this book to fruition.

Part I

Entering Private Practice: Some Preliminary Considerations

Chapter 1

Private Practice: Personal Prerequisites and Potential

Patricia R. Cole, Ph.D.

Speech-language pathology and audiology services are delivered in numerous employment settings. Although speech-language pathologists and audiologists in all work settings share a common goal of delivering effective evaluation and treatment services to persons with communication disorders, the demands that accompany employment vary from setting to setting. In selecting the most appropriate place to work, individuals should look at the demands, expectations, and assurances that will be a part of each job.

Over the past 10 years, an increasing number of speech-language pathologists and audiologists have entered private practice. In 1984, 8.7 percent of the American Speech-Language-Hearing Association (ASHA) members holding clinical certification engaged in private practice on a full-time basis, and 18.8 percent did so on a part-time basis (ASHA Executive Director, personal communication, March, 1985). With the decline in public funding for health and human services, more people are likely to look to private practice as a system for service delivery.

Individuals find private practice appealing for a variety of reasons. Perhaps the strongest attraction for many people is the opportunity to be one's own boss, to run a practice as one chooses without having to operate under the constraints of policies set by someone else. Some enter full-time private practice with the belief that this work setting offers the greatest opportunity for substantial financial gain, and some use part-time private practice to supplement their income. Although each of these goals can be reached, persons considering private practice should give careful attention to the risks and demands that accompany establishing and maintaining a business of this nature.

This chapter addresses many of the key points that should be considered in determining whether one is ready to establish a private practice. These include professional attitudes and skills relating to patient care, business, and public relations, as well as personal obligations and characteristics likely to affect a private practitioner. Each of these factors should be explored as one decides whether private practice is the appropriate setting to deliver services, whether the time and place are right to establish a private practice, and whether one's personal and financial demands can be met.

PRIVATE PRACTICE: WHAT DOES IT REQUIRE?

The unique demands of private practice create special professional and personal conditions that should be considered by those contemplating such a practice. Persons in private practice are not only clinicians; they are also businesspersons, public relations specialists, and administrators. Their view of their practice must extend beyond direct patient care in order for them to manage the multiple demands of business ownership. The financial and personal responsibilities may cause significant alterations in lifestyle, particularly early in the life of the practice. Therefore one should consider personal obligations and goals in deciding whether to enter into such a professional and business venture.

Professional Attitudes and Skills

To own and manage a private practice, individuals should hold certain attitudes about patient care and about the service delivery system in which patients receive care. They must have the knowledge and inclination necessary to function successfully in a private enterprise mode of service delivery.

Attitudes and Skills: Patient Care

Patient care is the core of private practice because fees for services to patients are the primary source of income for the practice. Prospective private practitioners should look closely at their attitudes, interests, and skills about patient care.

Do you enjoy working directly with patients with communication disorders? For most private practitioners, patient care is their only source of revenue for paying overhead and for personal income. Those seeking a change in employment because they are tired of working with patients are likely to find that private practice will not meet their interests and needs. Although consulting with other agencies or employing additional clinicians to provide services is possible, it is important to remember that, by financial necessity, private practitioners spend most of their time in direct contact with patients.

Most beginning private practitioners serve patients with a broad range of disabilities. Specialization is possible in some situations, but in order to have enough patients to support the practice, most practitioners work with a variety of disorders, at least until the practice is well established.

Specialization may be possible early in the life of the practice if the population characteristics in the area are such that services to a particular group are in high demand. For example, in a region populated primarily by retired persons, one may limit the practice to areas of disability common in older persons. In an area with few services for young children the practitioner may be able to build a stable practice that serves only infants and very young children. However, in most new practices, the practitioner needs to see patients with a wide range of disabilities, waiting to specialize until the practice and the practitioner become well known in the community.

Do you enjoy working with families of patients? When families seek a private practice as a source of service, a close relationship with the clinician usually is an expected part of the treatment program. Most successful private practitioners interact frequently with families of their patients, both to inform them of progress and to gain their support through home management programs. If the patient is experiencing difficulties in school, in employment, or in the home, families usually seek the clinician's advice and assistance in resolving these problems. (See Chapter 17, The Private Practice Viewpoint, for personal accounts of experienced practitioners' involvement with families of patients.) Clinicians who are not skilled and comfortable in working closely with families are likely to find that private practice is not the best work setting for them.

Can you place a relative value on the services you provide? Some families must choose between speech-language pathology or audiology services and some other service or activity for the patient or another family member. The private practitioner should be able to evaluate with reasonable objectivity the relative importance of speech-language pathology or audiology services to the individuals concerned and then to assist the family in making decisions about services. For example, for a particular aphasic patient, is speech-language pathology more important than physical therapy at a given time? For a certain child, are speech-language pathology services more important than the family's buying a piano for an older, musically gifted child? If a mother has a rare opportunity for a major promotion in her job but the promotion will require longer work hours that will prevent her from transporting her child to therapy, should she accept or turn down the promotion?

Although most speech-language pathologists and audiologists rightfully view their services as important, few are faced with helping patients make difficult choices about receiving therapy. The private practitioner should recognize that his or her services may not always be the highest priority for a given patient and family in a specific situation. Likewise, he or she should recognize when continued therapy is of the utmost importance and assist families in arriving at that conclusion.

Are you aware of your strengths and limitations as a clinician? Although private practitioners often work with a broad range of communication disorders, there are instances when clinicians are presented with a patient whose disorder is beyond their competence. Regardless of work setting, it is the clinician's ethical responsibility to seek consultation from other professionals whose expertise can assist in the diagnosis and treatment of the disorder. Because the beginning private practitioner is especially eager for new patients in order to make the practice financially stable, there may be a temptation to work with patients whose disorders are outside the practitioner's range of competence. Those in private practice should be especially careful not to let the need for patients outweigh their responsibility to work only with persons whose disorders they can manage appropriately.

Clinicians working in a rural area at times may find themselves presented with patients whose disorders they do not know how to treat, yet their services are the only ones available to the patient. Unlike those professionals in more heavily populated areas, they have no opportunity to refer these patients to persons with expertise in the area of the disability. Under such circumstances, the clinicians should contact by telephone or letter another clinician who has the necessary expertise, asking for recommendations for clinical procedures and for references for reading materials that will increase their knowledge and skills in the area of disability. In some instances, the patient may be able to make a single trip for an appointment with a professional who specializes in the disorder. Once that professional has evaluated the patient, he or she can give suggestions for treatment to the rural clinician. If the clinician regularly sees patients with a disorder type that he or she is not prepared to treat, attending seminars or workshops that address that disorder is appropriate. The schedules of seminars and workshops generally are available through local or state professional associations. Regardless of the location of a practice, it is the clinician's professional responsibility to have or to acquire the skills and knowledge necessary to provide appropriate treatment for patients one agrees to serve. (See also Chapter 4, Professional Liability, and Chapter 6, Ethical Concerns in Private Practice.)

Attitudes and Skills: Business

Most speech-language pathologists and audiologists are salaried employees and have never studied carefully the cost of delivering services. Education programs for persons entering human service professions rarely provide preparation in cost accounting or in business management. Although speech-language pathologists and audiologists want to receive reasonable salaries and benefits, they seldom feel responsible for generating the income necessary to cover their salaries. Few have ever found themselves responsible for bringing in money sufficient to pay for the overhead expenses associated with their services.

In order to be successful, the private practitioner must be able to treat the practice as a business and to accept responsibility for the financial aspects of that business. Persons considering private practice need to examine their attitudes and skills with respect to the financial and management aspects of professional practice.

Will you treat your professional practice as a business? The successful private practitioner must be able to view clinical services as a product being sold, not as a service being given away. The professional practice becomes a business. The concern for patients and the quality of care need not diminish, but the practitioner must attach a monetary value to those services and require payment for the time spent in patient care.

Few speech-language pathologists and audiologists have been responsible for setting fees and collecting payments from patients. However, at least in the early stages of the practice, most practitioners must assume partial or total responsibility for billings and collections. The owner of the practice often is required to talk to patients about fees, billing procedures, and past due accounts. Persons entering private practice should not ignore these responsibilities; they must be prepared to deal with them directly, openly, and firmly. Without an effective system for collection of fees, a private practice will experience financial distress or failure very quickly. (See Chapter 9 for information about billing and collection procedures).

Will you learn financial planning and management skills? Most speech-language pathologists and audiologists have devoted their education and employment experience to attaining the knowledge and skills necessary for evaluating and treating persons with communication disorders. Because few are prepared by education or experience to manage a business, they must acquire cost accounting, budget planning, and business management skills in order to run a successful practice. Even with the assistance of accountants and bookkeepers, the business owner needs to have a reasonable understanding of the business in order to make informed decisions about the practice.

Speech-language pathologists and audiologists sometimes express a desire to be in private practice but want to turn the financial worries over to someone else, or worse, to ignore them. Such persons likely should find another employment setting. The successful private practitioner must be a good businessperson as well as a good clinician.

Financial planning and management of a private practice are discussed in detail in Chapters 5 and 9. Readers are encouraged to consider information in those chapters carefully.

Attitudes and Skills: Public Relations

As businesspersons, private practitioners must sell their product. Doing so means finding effective ways to promote the practice in order to generate referrals.

Speech-language pathologists and audiologists across work settings express concern that members of other professions and the general public have a limited understanding of the profession and its importance. In no other work environment is this more detrimental than in private practice, where there is no built-in patient population or institutional base of support. The private practitioner must assume responsibility for promoting his or her profession and practice. (See Chapter 14 on marketing strategies.)

Are you willing to seek out referrals? Too often, speech-language pathologists and audiologists abdicate the responsibility for public information efforts to a state or national association rather than taking actions themselves to promote their professional practice. Persons in private practice cannot wait for a public service announcement to create an awareness of communication disorders and of the profession and then hope that persons in their community will find out somehow that they are there to provide needed services. Such a position is a sure path to starvation for most private practitioners.

One part of business promotion includes contacting potential referral sources, promoting the importance of speech-language pathology and audiology, and convincing them that one is a credible provider. The chances for success in private practice depend partially on a willingness and ability to generate referrals from a variety of sources. The private practitioner must take the initiative in public relations in order to build and maintain a practice. (See Chapters 11 and 12 for information on building and maintaining a patient base.)

Personal Characteristics and Obligations

In making career decisions, persons should consider their own personal characteristics and preferences along with the performance expectations that accompany a long-term professional commitment. The tasks demanded by the work setting should be ones that, by personality, one enjoys and is adept at performing. Similarly, personal obligations affect the nature and extent of commitment to professional endeavors that one can make at any given time. Potential private practitioners should examine their own characteristics and situations in making career choices.

Personal Characteristics and Preferences

As clinicians, businesspersons, and public relations specialists, private practitioners deal with many persons and situations. They must move forward in the face of uncertainty, make decisions in a timely and determined manner, be creative yet systematic, and be flexible enough to adjust to changing opportunities and demands. Some persons find these demands invigorating, whereas others find them debilitating. Individuals considering private practice should evaluate their own characteristics, interests, and abilities.

Are you comfortable taking risks? Initiating and maintaining a private practice involve risk taking. There is no assurance that one's plans, no matter how carefully made, will lead to success. Of the approximately 500,000 new businesses initiated in the United States each year, about 20 percent provide human services of some nature (dentists, speech-language pathologists, audiologists, psychologists, etc.) U.S. Department of Commerce statistics show that one-third of all new businesses fail in the first year, and almost two-thirds survive less than 5 years (Macfarlane, 1977). Failures in the first 5 years are higher in human services enterprises than in any other type of business, except for retail businesses.

Persons considering private practice should recognize the risks involved and realize that they will live with uncertainty about the success and stability of the practice, *at least* for several years. In an established practice, risks accompany expansion, whether it entails purchasing new equipment, increasing office space, or hiring additional personnel. For persons who have another source of financial support, the risks may not be as stressful. However the personal, financial, and professional investments are likely to cause even the most affluent person to sense the uncertainty and pressure for success.

Although irregular income and delayed reward may not be incapacitating, they will be present. For persons who thrive on risk taking, private practice can be stimulating and pleasurable. Those who are uncomfortable with uncertainty likely will be more satisfied and productive in work settings that provide an ensured salary and employee benefits, regular hours, and a built-in source of referrals and income.

Do you enjoy "presenting your case" to other people? Private practice owners should be assertive yet diplomatic in promoting their profession and their practice. Whether building, maintaining, or expanding a practice, practitioners who wait in their offices until others notice their presence, recognize their worth, and decide to refer patients are not likely to succeed. Individuals who not only believe in the value of their services but also can sell their product effectively are best suited for private practice.

Certain outstanding clinicians enjoy talking with patients and their families and providing direct clinical services, yet they are neither comfortable nor effective in promoting themselves and their services to other professionals or to the lay public. These persons make valuable contributions to the profession, but they probably are not well suited for working in a private practice system of service delivery.

Are you healthy and energetic? Because immediate income will depend on the number of revenue-generating hours spent in the practice, the practitioner cannot afford to have health problems that require frequent absences from the practice. Also, the mental and physical investments necessary for generating referrals during hours not spent with patients are essential to building and maintaining the practice. Especially in the early stages of building the practice, private practitioners who are handicapped by ill health or low energy levels may find that they are unable to cope with the demands of a solo practice.

Are you comfortable with changes in direction and routine? A set schedule and predictable hours and routines are rare in private practice, especially in its early stages. Because schedules often must be set around patient work or school times, practitioners may begin work before 8:00 A.M., work through the traditional lunch hour, and see patients after 5:00 P.M. Patient contact hours may vary from day to day, with the clinician's schedule dictated by the needs of patients.

Private practitioners must respond to opportunities for practice as they arise. When screening programs, teacher workshops, or other opportunities are available, practitioners need to adjust their schedules so that they can respond to these opportunities and demands. Doing so requires flexibility, good judgment, determination, and stamina.

Are you a decision maker? Many people state a desire for autonomy in their professional practice, but few have lived with the responsibilities of this autonomy. With rare exceptions, the private practitioner makes final decisions about business matters, personnel, and professional practices. The person in charge of a private practice needs the professional knowledge and experience and the personal confidence to know when to make a firm decision, when to seek counsel, and when to postpone a decision until additional information or different circumstances occur.

The luxury of being the boss sometimes is diminished by the necessity of making and implementing difficult decisions. Persons who are more adept at advising than deciding and who are most comfortable with a group consensus approach to decision making likely will work best in a position other than owner and manager of a business.

Are you an initiator of new activities? Private practitioners need to identify and respond to marketplace opportunities, create new service opportunities, and alter delivery procedures to make them more effective and efficient. If a practice is to grow, the practitioner must make things happen, and this requires taking the initiative to create expanded business opportunities. An established practice may survive by relying on old referral sources to supply new patients, but this passive approach is risky.

In order to be aware of probable changes in education and health care services, the private practitioner should monitor closely the local, state, and national policies and trends that affect such services. Public and private reimbursement policies, services for children and adults, and the creation or dissolution of private or public agencies serving handicapped persons may open the door for expanded services by persons in private practice. One of the best ways to maintain an awareness of expanded opportunities for providing services is to participate actively in local, state, and national professional associations. Through such participation, the practitioner gains access to information about public policies and may have opportunities to change these policies to increase services to persons with communication disorders.

Changes in marketplace opportunities and demands or vigorous and creative approaches by competitors can erode the referral base of the passive practitioner. Those who want a growing business should view their practice as a dynamic process and actively pursue positive changes.

Personal Obligations

Personal responsibilities should be reviewed carefully in determining whether one is ready to assume the risks and commitments required for establishing and maintaining a private practice. Financial assets and obligations, as well as demands on time and energy made from outside the professional practice, influence the probability of success and contentment. (See Chapter 5 for additional information on financial commitments required by the practice.)

Can you meet your financial needs and obligations during the development of your private practice? The financial demands of establishing and maintaining a practice are discussed in detail in Chapter 9. Potential private practitioners need to look at both startup and ongoing costs and the anticipated time that will be required to build a practice that provides the desired or necessary personal income. Without a thorough evaluation of financial commitments that accompany ownership of a private practice, the practitioner is likely to experience financial distress quickly.

Do you have family commitments that will restrict the time and energy you can devote to your practice? As previously mentioned, private practitioners need to respond to the marketplace demands in scheduling patients and to be available to market the practice whenever opportunities arise. This requires not only flexibility in time schedules but also often demands that the practitioner work during hours that usually are devoted to family activities. Private practitioners need to assess the extent to which family responsibilities may restrict their availability to practice and, equally important, to determine whether the demands of the practice will have an undesirable effect on family relationships. Most successful private practitioners who have a family emphasize the necessity of the entire family's commitment to the practice and their willingness to adapt to the time and energy investment that the practitioner often devotes to the practice rather than to the family.

SUMMARY

Before initiating a private practice, individuals should examine their attitudes toward their professional practice and their personal characteristics and obligations in light of the demands that they will experience as a business owner, manager, and clinician. Plunging into private practice as an escape from an undesirable work situation or with visions of independence and sudden wealth can result in personal and professional disappointment or failure. Because most speech-language pathologists and audiologists have little experience or training in business management and have been taught to consider their work as a service they give, the business aspects of owning and managing a private practice often come as a shock. Many are either unwilling or unable to deal with their professional services as a product they must sell for a profit.

The personal and financial demands that accompany ownership of a private practice force the practitioner to devote substantial resources to the practice, thus reducing other investments of time, energy, and money. Individuals should look at their family obligations, both financial and personal, to determine whether they can allocate the majority of their resources to building and maintaining a private practice. It should be understood clearly that for the first year or more, beginning practitioners will have to devote most of their time and energy to building a practice and may derive little or no personal income from the practice. Persons who cannot live under these demands and conditions should seek employment other than as owner of a private practice.

REFERENCE

Macfarlane, W.N. (1977). *Principles of small business management*. New York: McGraw-Hill.

SUGGESTED READINGS

American Speech-Language-Hearing Association. (1985). Planning and initiating a private practice in audiology and speech-language pathology. Rockville, MD: Author.

Steinhoff, D. (1978). *Small business management fundamentals*. New York: McGraw-Hill.

Steps to starting a business. *Small Business Reporter*, Bank of America. (Available at any Bank of America or by writing to Small Business Reporter, Bank of America, Department 3401, PO Box 37000, San Francisco, CA 94137.)

Chapter 2

Part-Time Private Practice in Speech-Language Pathology and Audiology

Deena K. Bernstein, Ph.D.

In recent years, increasing numbers of speech-language pathologists and audiologists have turned to private practice. Some have opted for full-time private practice, whereas others have chosen to deliver clinical services in part-time private practice.

For 1982 the American Speech-Language-Hearing Association (ASHA, 1983-1984) reported that 1,583 members were engaged in private practice activities 30 hours or more a week, satisfying the ASHA's definition of full-time private practice, and another 6,397 members were engaged in part-time private practice (less than 30 hours a week). In 1984 the ASHA membership survey revealed that, although the number of full-time private practitioners rose to 2,955, part-time private practice still predominated (6,376).

Although the majority of those engaged in private practice activities do so on a part-time basis, only full-time private practitioners are listed in the *Guide to Professional Services*. In the foreword to the 1983–84 *Guide,* Spahr explains why part-time private practitioners are not included.

> Consideration was given to the inclusion of certified individuals in part-time private practice in the 1983-84 *Guide*; however, data from the surveys of the ASHA members who indicate that they are in private practice revealed that 82.3% of these individuals spend *fewer than 30 hours* per week serving the public. Since the *Guide* serves as a reference source for many consumers, it was felt that only those individuals available for service to the public through the day and on a full-time, regular basis should be included in this list. (p. iii)

To the part-time practitioner this rationale may seem inadequate because the effect of such an exclusion from the professional guide places the part-time private practitioner at a disadvantage. Part-time private practitioners must rely on their own resources, such as advertising and marketing, to inform potential clients of their availability to deliver clinical services.

This chapter presents a current profile of part-time private practice and introduces some technical issues related to the establishment and maintenance of a part-time private practice.

A PROFILE OF PART-TIME PRIVATE PRACTICE

In a most comprehensive survey completed in 1984, the ASHA queried its membership to determine the scope of both part-time and full-time private practice in speech-language pathology and audiology. Data from the survey were analyzed in order to determine the highest degree and certification status of part-time private practitioners, their primary and secondary employment settings, and their primary and secondary professional activities.

According to the survey, 88 percent of all part-time private practitioners have a Master's degree as their highest degree. Eighty-six percent of those engaged in part-time private practice are certified in speech-language pathology, and 11 percent are certified in audiology.

Of the total membership with the Certificate of Clinical Competence (CCC) in speech-language pathology, 26 percent are engaged in private practice activities; of these, 20 percent are in part-time private practice, and 6 percent are in full-time private practice. Of the total membership with the CCC in audiology, 32 percent are in private practice, with 19 percent in full-time private practice and 13 percent in part-time private practice. A greater percentage of private practice audiologists are in full-time private practice, whereas a greater percentage of private practice speech-language pathologists are in part-time private practice.

Analysis of the data also revealed that the typical part-time private practitioner engages in clinical activities *in addition to* other professional employment. Part-time private practitioners are primarily employed in schools (29 percent) and hospitals (13 percent). Others are employed in colleges and universities (10 percent), special schools (11 percent), and nonhospital rehabilitation centers (7 percent). In sum, the majority of part-time private practitioners (91 percent) are professionally employed outside of private practice and engage in part-time private practice in a supplemental fashion but probably in no less an effective capacity.

The data regarding the secondary work settings of part-time private practitioners are difficult to interpret. Although 24 percent of the respondents claimed an office as their secondary work setting, 23 percent claimed "none." "None" indicates that these part-time private practitioners neither rent offices nor work in physicians' offices, nursing homes, and/or health agencies (other possible answers on the questionnaire). It would seem that they deliver clinical services in their homes (not considered an office) or in the homes of respective clients. Included among these practitioners are those with other professional commitments, as well as retired individuals and professionals on temporary (or permanent) leaves. The home context may provide the part-time private practitioner with an inexpensive setting for a professional practice.

In the secondary work setting the part-time private practitioner primarily provides clinical and consultative services, 74 percent and 17 percent respectively. Clinical services include all diagnostic and rehabilitative activities.

Thus, as of 1984, the majority of part-time private practitioners are speech-language pathologists who are primarily employed in a school setting. As part-time private practitioners they deliver services in an office and, perhaps equally probably, in their home or in a client's home. Lastly, their services primarily involve the assessment and remediation of speech and language disorders. In contrast, a greater proportion of audiologists are engaged in private practice, but they tend to deliver clinical services on a full-time basis. A smaller percentage are part-time private practitioners. Such part-time practitioners seem to engage in service delivery either in a rented or residential office or in a physician's office.

Given this emerging profile, three areas of concern to the part-time private practitioner are addressed: (1) the professional requirements necessary for establishing a part-time private practice, (2) the various locational and organizational arrangements for the part-time private practice of speech-language pathology and/or audiology, and (3) the initiation and maintenance of a part-time private practice, including financial considerations, time management, fee structure and referrals. These three topics are relevant for both full- and part-time private practice and are outlined in this chapter because they are too often overlooked by professionals contemplating private practice on a part-time basis. Furthermore, many of the issues introduced in this chapter are elaborated on in following chapters.

PROFESSIONAL CREDENTIALS NECESSARY FOR ENGAGING IN PRIVATE PRACTICE ACTIVITIES

Professional Certification

An individual engaged in the practice of speech-language pathology and/or audiology in the private sector, either on a full-time or part-time basis, must possess the appropriate Certificate(s) of Clinical Competence (CCC) granted by the ASHA. Minimum requirements for the CCC include a Master's degree or its equivalent with major emphasis in speech-language pathology, audiology, or speech, language, and hearing sciences; satisfactory completion of a general education, academic clinical practicum, and the clinical fellowship year; and passing scores on the National Examination in Speech-Language Pathology and/or Audiology. Appendix 2-A describes the detailed criteria for certification.

Application for the CCC should be made after the completion of the educational and clinical practice requirements and before or shortly after the clinical fellowship year has begun. Appendix 2-B details the procedures for obtaining the CCC.

The CCC provides evidence to the public that the practitioner is professionally capable of delivering independent clinical services to the communicatively impaired. Thus, to practice in the private sector, whether on a full-time or part-time basis, it is imperative that all the requirements for the CCC be met. Individuals with a B.A. or B.S. degree in speech-language pathology and/or audiology or degrees in other related fields without the CCC are, with few exceptions, ineligible to engage even in part-time private practice.

State Licensure

Although state licensure in the fields of speech-language pathology and audiology is relatively new, 36 states already require a license for the practice of speech-language pathology and/or audiology, and the number of states with licensing requirements is likely to grow. Those states in which a license is now mandatory are listed in Appendix 2-C. Although the specific criteria and procedures for licensing speech-language pathologists and audiologists vary from state to state, licensing standards substantially resemble ASHA's requirements for the CCC. An individual wishing to engage in private practice on either a part-time or full-time basis and living in any of the states listed in Appendix 2-C may consult Appendix 2-D for that state's licensing requirements. For example, in some states, it is *mandatory* for an individual to possess the appropriate license for the practice of speech-language pathology and audiology, *regardless* of the setting in which he or she works. In those states *all* professional settings—schools, hospitals, clinics, rehabilitation centers, universities, agencies, private practice, etc.—are included under the licensure laws. In other states, some work settings are *exempt* from only employing individuals who possess the professional license. For example, speech-language pathologists or audiologists may work in a school setting without a license; *but* should they wish to provide clinical services in the private sector, they must obtain their state's professional license.

Because state regulations change from time to time, professionals seeking to engage in private practice should familiarize themselves with their states' licensure requirements prior to establishing the practice. Local and state speech-language and hearing associations are well informed about their respective states' licensure and state education teacher certification requirements and are an invaluable resource to the speech-language pathologist and/or audiologist wishing to obtain licensing and/or credential information. Alternatively, professionals may consult their state's licensing agency (see Appendix 2-D).

THE ORGANIZATION AND LOCATION OF A PART-TIME PRIVATE PRACTICE

Two of the first decisions that the part-time private practitioner must make concern how to organize and where to locate the practice. The following questions are frequently asked: Is an individual practice more desirable than a group practice? Is a residential office preferable to one in a professional building? Should one deliver services *only* in one's office? Should one make home visits? There is no one correct answer to these questions as the organization and location of one's practice are a function of individual preference, which in turn depends on many factors: the type and scope of the practice being contemplated, the availability of financial resources, and the number of hours per day and the time slots within the day available for service delivery. The speech-language pathologist and/or audiologist contemplating a part-time private practice may want to consider some of the alternative arrangements discussed below, as well as referring to Chapter 7, Selecting the Location and Site for a Private Practice.

The Residential Office

Many doctors, dentists, and other health-related professionals practice from offices in their residences. Today other professionals, such as lawyers, computer programmers, engineers, architects, and businessmen, are emulating the health-related specialists. For the professional practicing at home there are the following advantages:

(a) the proximity of the office to one's family, (b) the ease of switching from one set of responsibilities to another, (c) the convenience of not having to commute between office and home, (d) the tax benefits, and (e) the savings accrued by not having to pay monthly rent.

To ensure an effective residential practice, the physical workspace in the home must be suited to the delivery of clinical services. One must separate the flow of family activities from the office, maintain it free from the distraction of pets and family members, and ensure that the lifestyle and privacy of the clinician are maintained while at the same time protecting the privacy of the client. Within the separate work area, space must be allocated for a waiting room and toilet facilities. Other clients—both children and adults—are accompanied to the office by family members or caretakers who must wait for them during their sessions. Providing adequate facilities for clients, family members, and/or caretakers ensures their comfort and creates a more conducive work setting. In sum, a professional environment should be maintained.

To complete the residential office, a sign that identifies the professional and directs clients to the office is advisable. If the residential area has zoning laws regulating the location of offices in residences, the permission of the local zoning or planning board may be required. One might need to seek permission for locating a sign outside the residence, satisfy various building regulations, and/or make parking space arrangements for prospective clients.

The cost of establishing a residential office varies from individual to individual and depends on many factors, including the degree of renovation required, the size of the space in need of renovation, and the elaborateness of the furnishings to be purchased for the office. (For further discussion on possible professional liability in using a home office, see Chapter 4 on the liability risks inherent in home office settings.)

The Professional Office

Another option that the speech-language pathologist or audiologist may want to consider is locating the practice in a professional building. Before doing so, however, the professional must take into account the costs inherent in such a site. Overhead expenses, such as rent, heat, telephone, and electricity, must be carefully estimated. These costs are fixed and are not dependent on the number of clients for whom the professional provides services. A discussion with one's accountant will quickly reveal the breakeven point at which costs can be covered and when one might expect to derive a profit from the practice. Should the decision be made to rent a professional office, consideration must be given to how one will maintain adequate financial resources and reserves. It is estimated that the part-time private practitioner should set aside at least sufficient resources to cover expenses for 1½ years. In addition, during the initial startup period, aggressive marketing should be pursued in order to make the practice profitable. (For a more complete discussion of the marketing of a private practice see Chapter 14.)

Because office rentals in professional buildings are usually costly, often speech-language pathologists and/or audiologists sublet office space from other professionals such as physicians, psychologists, social workers, and educational testing and remediation groups. Under such a sublet arrangement, the communication specialist can either use space that is not used by the primary lessees at any various times during the working day or use the space utilized by the primary lessees when they are not using it, e.g., evenings.

To help defray the high cost of office rentals some communication specialists establish a team or group practice. In this model, two or more speech-language pathologists and/or audiologists may decide to band together and rent office space. Such an arrangement may be particularly helpful if the two or more professionals use the same space during different hours of the day. For example, a speech-language pathologist who teaches late afternoon and/or evening courses in a university may decide to set up a private practice with a speech-language pathologist who works in the public schools. Because the schedule of the primary work setting of each professional differs, the workspace may be used during the late afternoon and evening hours by the public school clinician and during morning and early afternoon hours by the university professional. The greater the flexibility of the individuals in terms of the times of day they can devote to private practice, the easier it is to make such an arrangement work. If a joint or group practice is being contemplated or a space-sharing arrangement is being considered, it is wise to consult a lawyer in order to work out the details legally and formally regarding office space and financial responsibility. The legal aspects pertaining to a private practice are discussed more fully in Chapter 3. See also Chapter 7 on the pros and cons of shared space.

Renting office space entails a financial commitment. The part-time private practitioner must understand the scope and consequences of this commitment and effectively plan for it. Moreover, he or she must actively market the practice so that adequate revenues are generated to meet these monthly expenses.

The Physician's Office

Approximately 1.4 percent of speech-language pathologists in part-time private practice provide services in a physician's office. In contrast, 16.4 percent of part-time private practice audiologists deliver services in a physician's office, the second most frequent setting for their practice (ASHA, 1983-1984). Although it is not possible to determine from the survey the specialty of the physician in whose office the audiologist located the practice, it is reasonable to assume that the physician is an otologist. The decision by an audiologist to locate a part-time practice in a physician's office is probably related to the high startup costs for a part-time endeavor.

Although there are a number of possible working arrangements for the audiologist who delivers services in a physician's office, most frequently the audiological booth and equipment are purchased by the physician and the fees for all services are paid to the physician. The audiologist in turn receives either (a) a set fee for services or (b) a percentage of the fees charged by the physician. Thus the audiologist avoids the financial burden of startup costs and the need to generate referrals. The audiologist must realize, however, that only a portion of what is collected for audiological services will be received. This amount is significantly lower than what the audiologist would receive if he or she worked independently.

The Client's Home

Often speech-language pathologists in part-time private practice provide clinical services in the home of their clients. Such an arrangement allows (1) the clinician to use the client's environment as a natural therapeutic context, (2) the clinician to observe the client's behavior with caretakers and significant others, (3) caretakers and significant others to observe the therapeutic process, and (4) the clinician to model appropriate therapeutic procedures and techniques for the parents and significant others to undertake as partners in the intervention process. Much has been written about the use of parents and significant others in the diagnostic and intervention process and the benefits to a client when a clinician chooses to provide services in the client's home.

Many private practitioners compute the fee for home visits by adding to a base fee the additional cost of travel. Care should be taken, however, that the fee for home visits should be neither too high nor too low. The clinician who provides clinical service in the client's home often does not realize that what is 40 minutes in an office (and is so charged) turns out to be 60 minutes in a client's home (but charged at a 40-minute rate). This may be due to the informality of the home setting. Thus, the clinician is undercharging for services rendered. There is also the problem of overcharging for home visits, which often occurs when the clinician anticipates insurance reimbursement. This issue is discussed in the section on insurance.

Consulting

The second most frequent professional activity engaged in by part-time private practitioners is consultation. Such activities are primarily carried out in schools, hospitals, agencies, and senior citizen centers. In the consulting mode, the speech-language pathologist or audiologist either provides services to clients or supervises service delivery.

Payment for consulting services may be either on a fixed sum basis or on a client-by-client basis. The source of the funds for payment to the consultant may come either from special grants (for short periods of time) or from an agency's operating budget.

Consultantships are generally obtained as a result of one's academic reputation, professional visibility, and/or personal recommendations. However, it is possible to expand a consulting practice through effective marketing, networking, and/or public service.

Contracting and Subcontracting

The term "contracting" is used in the profession to denote the assumption of responsibility for the provision of clinical services in a particular setting in return for a fixed payment or sum. Although the services of an employee differ little from those of an independent contractor, there are significant financial differences for institutions and contractors employing them. Such institutions as hospitals, nursing homes, and school districts are required by law to withhold income tax and make payments toward Social Security taxes and retirement funds for employees, but are exempt from doing so for independent contractors. Therefore, independent contractors are significantly less expensive than employees. Contractors, in turn, are self-employed. It is their responsibility to pay their own taxes and to build their own retirement fund, and to assume all financial responsibility for their future. Nevertheless, they have the tax benefits of operating a small business. (See also Chapter 9 on financial planning.)

When caseload demands are particularly heavy, a contractor may be compelled to hire other professionals to deliver the level of services agreed to in the contract. This practice is called "subcontracting." Earning a profit from subcontracting is in large measure a function of good planning and efficient business management.

Contracting has generated some controversy in our profession, especially in contracting to schools. Proponents of contracting believe that contractors deliver the same professional level of services to clients, but at a reduced cost. Those arguing against contracting claim that when the provision of services becomes dependent on a contracted sum, rather than on clients' needs, the quality of service diminishes and accountability is impaired. Before deciding to contract or subcontract, the speech-language pathologist or audiologist should carefully consider the commitment to quality service delivery held by the institution or contractor seeking services.

INITIATING AND MAINTAINING A PART-TIME PRIVATE PRACTICE

The financial rewards that accrue to an individual in part-time private practice are based on sound financial planning and management. Good fiscal management requires the balancing of the initial capital outlay necessary for initiating the practice, the income derived from the practice, and the costs of operating the practice. Each of these factors is briefly outlined in the sections that follow and all are discussed in greater detail in Chapters 5, 7, 8, and 9.

Financial Considerations: Initial Capital Outlay

The initial capital requirements for part-time private practice vary. As a general rule, however, audiology practices require a greater financial investment than that for speech-language pathology due to equipment needs. (See Chapter 8 for further details.) Obviously, a part-time practice may require somewhat less time, energy, effort, and funds than would a full-time practice.

In addition to general office costs, audiologists must invest in costlier basic equipment: an audiometric booth, a pure-tone audiometer, an impedance bridge, and other diagnostic equipment. The cost of this basic diagnostic equipment ranges from $15,000 to $30,000, depending on the range of equipment purchased at the outset and whether the equipment purchased is new or used. Other optional equipment that the audiologist may wish to purchase (perhaps at a later time) includes ENG and brain-stem equipment. Purchasing this optional equipment necessitates a larger facility and additional funds. (Alternatively, lease arrangements may prove more appealing. See Chapter 8 for details.)

If the audiologist obtains a license for dispensing hearing aids or lives in a state that allows the dispensing of hearing aids under the general audiology license (see Appendix 2-E), a variety of hearing aid models, hearing aid supplies, and assistive devices must be purchased. The number of hearing aid models and the materials necessary for adequately servicing hearing-impaired clients vary. To simplify the investment decision, Loavenbruck and Madell (1981) outline three approaches to the dispensing of hearing aids by audiologists. The capital outlay is a function of which approach is chosen. For a complete discussion of the business aspects of hearing aid dispensing, the reader is referred to Loavenbruck and Madell (1981) and Chapters 8 and 12 in this book.

In contrast to the audiologist, the initial capital outlay for the speech-language pathologist is smaller because there is less need to make a large investment for diagnostic equipment. The speech-language pathologist still *must* buy basic assessment materials, including one or more tape recorders and tests of articulation, language, voice, and fluency. Although these materials vary greatly in price and the number and type of assessment materials to be purchased depends on the projected caseload, $1,000 appears to be a reasonable amount to budget for the purchase of diagnostic materials by speech-language pathologists in part-time private practice.

Speech-language pathologists must also invest in materials to be used in remediation. Although money can be saved by constructing one's own intervention materials, the time spent in making these materials makes them less cost effective. Prepackaged materials and programs thus seem to be the norm. When selecting remediation materials, emphasis should be on flexibility for therapeutic programming. Toys, games, picture books, reading materials, and pictures are the most common materials and can be used both for language and articulation therapy. Although the purchase of crayons, blocks, dolls, trucks, balls, and Fisher-Price toys may serve the needs of younger children, older children may require games, reading material, and pictures. The speech-language pathologist considering a part-time private practice should set aside at least $500 for the purchase of materials to be used in remediation. In total, a minimum of $1,500 should be budgeted for diagnostic and therapeutic materials.

Sources of Capital

Although some speech-language pathologists and audiologists possess the initial capital necessary to launch their private practice, many must seek financing for their venture from external sources. Personal loans from banks, family, and friends are often sought. When external financing is used to initate the practice, interest on loans must be considered as an operating cost. More detailed information concerning the financing of a private practice is available from ASHA's 1982 Private Practice Workshop on audiocassette (Committee on Private Practice, 1982), as well as in Chapters 5, 7, 8, and 9 in this volume.

Fees

The success of a private practice is in part judged by the income it generates from fees charged. A question frequently asked by those contemplating private practice is "How much should I charge for services?" The Code of Ethics of ASHA (ASHA, 1982) has been interpreted as:

1. Individuals must not charge for services not rendered.
2. Fees established for professional services must be independent of whether a product is dispensed.
3. Individual fees must be commensurate with services rendered.
4. Price information about professional services rendered and products dispensed must be disclosed by providing or posting for persons served a complete schedule of fees and charges in advance of rendering services with schedules differentiated between fees for services and charge for products.

Although neither ASHA nor state speech-language-hearing associations publish a schedule of fees for services and products, it is important that part-time private practitioners establish their own fee schedule based on the general fee structure of other service providers in their area. If the part-time private practitioner has less experience or lower overhead costs than other service providers, then charging fees at the lower end of a fee scale may be considered. However, fees (1) should *not* depend on whether an individual is in part-time or full-time private practice, (2) should be reasonable for the services rendered, and (3) should be within the general fee scale of other private practice speech-language pathologists and/or audiologists in the same geographic area.

Because of the public nature of the setting in which most speech-language pathologists and/or audiologists work, they often have not had either the experience or the need to discuss money and fees for services rendered directly with clients. Learning to discuss fees openly with prospective clients or their caretakers is an essential part of the professional management of a private practice.

Insurance

Speech-language pathologists and audiologists in private practice are often asked about insurance coverage for their services. Because the type and scope of insurance reimbursement for the delivery of services to the communicatively impaired client differ from policy to policy, it is important for the speech-language pathologist and audiologist to become knowledgeable about insurance reimbursement practices. Flower (1984) provides an excellent overview of both private and governmental third party payment programs. Various types of private health insurance are described, and the coverage of speech-language pathology and audiology services under various insurance plans are outlined. In addition, ASHA's Division of Reimbursement Policy publishes up-to-date literature regarding insurance issues, particularly about Medicare reimbursement. Many regional, state, and local speech-language-hearing associations also publish guidelines about insurance reimbursement and present workshops to aid speech-language pathologists and audiologists "work their way" through the insurance maze.

Although some private practice speech-language pathologists and audiologists accept insurance assignments in lieu of their fees, others do not. Those who do not accept insurance assignment believe that payment arrangements should be made between clients and the clinician, not between the clinician and the insurance company. Although they help their clients file insurance claims, they believe that it is the clients' responsibility to know their eligibility for benefits and the nature of their coverage. The decision to accept third party payments ultimately rests with the individual private practitioner.

A third party payment condition especially relevant to the part-time private practitioner concerns the charges for clinical services delivered in clients' homes. Because fees for home visits are higher than the fees for office visits they may not be acceptable to the clients' insurance companies. Rejection of the provider's claims for these fees may come many months after the service has been rendered, resulting in a significant cash loss. Therefore, those clinicians who provide services in clients' homes and who wish to accept insurance reimbursement should double check with the clients' insurance carriers to ascertain whether their fees will be covered.

The communication specialist initiating a part-time private practice must be especially sensitive to the management of time as it is key to the practice's profitability and effective delivery of services. Three issues are crucial: (1) the *total* amount of time available for service delivery, (2) the *time slots* within which to deliver clinical services, and (3) the time necessary for performing other professional duties, including record keeping, report writing, and consultation with other professionals.

Time Management

The total time the part-time private practitioner can devote to private practice depends on the number of hours that are free from the responsibilities of his or her primary employment. Most speech-language pathologists and audiologists working full-time in hospitals, clinics, and agencies have a nine-to-five, 5-day-a-week schedule, leaving evenings and weekends free for private practice. Those who work part-time in the above settings or who teach in schools and universities have a more flexible schedule, permitting not only a greater number of hours per day but also a greater variety of time slots available for service delivery. Clinical services can be provided during mornings, afternoons, evenings, weekends, and full days in the summer, depending on the practitioner's specific work schedule.

Clinicians should realize that service delivery to some clinical populations may be limited by the clinician's availability to deliver services and the client's convenience or suitability to receive services. Matching these factors is an essential part of planning. For example, a speech-language pathologist or audiologist with a nine-to-five schedule cannot anticipate preschoolers as prospective clients. School-age children, adolescents, and adults might be the target clients instead. For the speech-language pathologist working in the schools, midafternoon hours might be suitable for school-age children and older preschoolers. Late afternoon and evening hours may be reserved for adolescent and adult clients. Because of the time flexibility of school-based professionals, it is no surprise that they predominate in part-time private practice.

An additional time consideration is the limitation by universities and other public institutions on the number of hours or days their employees may work outside their primary work settings. Although this is a concern for all part-time private practitioners, it is of crucial importance to audiologists. Their larger equipment investment necessitates that the equipment be used regularly if it is to be effectively amortized. The regularity envisioned by the audiologist may simply be in conflict with the "multiple positions" limitations of the primary employer. Therefore, before initiating a part-time private practice, speech-language pathologists and audiologists should check with their primary employers to determine the number of hours or days they may be employed outside their primary work setting.

Effective service delivery by the communication specialist requires that sufficient time be set aside for other professional tasks. They include the maintenance of good clinical and financial records, the writing of diagnostic and progress reports, the planning of therapeutic sessions, and consultation with other professionals. Too often, potential part-time private practitioners fail to anticipate the amount of time it takes to engage in these activities. Moreover, they often overlook the fact that time spent in the above activities reduces the time available for service delivery and hence the generation of income. In planning a part-time private practice, it is important to consider both the service delivery time and time required for other professional activities in determining the profitability of such a practice. Experience has shown that most private practitioners spend 1 hour performing other professional tasks, such as record keeping and report writing, for every 3 hours spent in service delivery.

One additional time-consuming factor deserving special attention involves establishing a referral base. This is discussed in the next section.

Referrals

The success of any private practice depends on the number of clients and referrals that a professional receives. The referral of communicatively handicapped clients to the speech-language pathologist or audiologist may come from a number of sources: pediatricians, neurologists, ear, nose, and throat (ENT) specialists, psychologists, social workers, educators (both special and regular), family and friends, health agencies, and community and consumer groups.

Referrals must be actively sought through various strategies that are available to establish referral contacts: advertising, sending letters or cards of introduction, personally meeting health care and other professionals, attending professional meetings and health fairs, lecturing to community groups, and providing free screenings for day-care centers, nursery schools, and senior citizen centers. It is also advantageous if a professional can obtain referrals from organized medical plans, consumer groups, and labor unions. Taking the time to establish these contacts in the beginning and to nurture them as time goes on is generally time well spent and rewarding from a business perspective. (Further suggestions on seeking referrals are found in Chapters 11 and 12.) Often the part-time private practitioner does not devote enough time to these activities because of compelling responsibilities of the primary work setting. This tends to constrain the growth of the private practice.

Referrals of communicatively impaired clients to part-time private practice may further be constrained by the rule of some hospitals, clinics, and school districts prohibiting professionals on their staff from providing services on a private basis to clients already being serviced at their facility. Speech-language pathologists and/or audiologists working in such primary work settings should consult their employers before accepting referrals and/or privately providing services to clients already on their caseloads or on the caseloads of their colleagues. Some settings may even require their employees to sign a noncompeting agreement, thus excluding private practice as a secondary employment opportunity.

In addition to the aforementioned potential conflict of interest, the part-time private practice audiologist is additionally constrained by the need for an adequate flow of referrals. Whereas the delivery of speech-language services usually occurs over a number of weeks or months, depending on the type of disorder and its severity, audiological services are usually dispensed over a shorter time span. Therefore, the audiologist requires a significantly greater number of referrals. To compensate for this difficulty, the part-time private practice audiologist must be especially sensitive to professional networking, advertising, and aggressive marketing for referrals. Such strategies may help ensure a continuous and adequate flow of referrals that would increase the profitability of the practice.

It is undoubtedly unwise to open a private practice precipitously. Before finally doing so a number of professionals should be consulted. An accountant should provide the clinician with input regarding bookkeeping practices, tax payments, financial record keeping, and the tax advantages that might accrue should the location of a private practice be in a residence. Should a practitioner decide to locate a practice in a residential office, an insurance broker should also be consulted to arrange for adequate accident and liability insurance. Professionals should also consider purchasing professional liability insurance available to all members of ASHA. Interested parties should contact the Professional Practices Division of ASHA for specific information regarding such policies. (For a detailed discussion regarding professional malpractice and liability, see Chapter 4.)

Seeking Professional Advice

Although there are many other reasons for entering a part-time private practice, a primary rationale may be the desire for additional income, and improved financial status. This chapter has described the necessary prerequisites for establishing such a practice.

SUMMARY

The basic assumption underlying this discussion is that speech-language pathologists and audiologists who wish to enter private practice, whether on a part-time or full-time basis, are experienced clinicians who have a thorough and complete knowledge of their respective fields. In addition, they must also master other business-related skills to plan and market their practices effectively. Accounting, business law, and marketing are some business skills needed. This knowledge may be acquired from adult education classes, ASHA's continuing education programs, and state and national workshops for private practitioners. Additional knowledge to be sought from courses or independent reading or consultation might include steps for establishing a practice, mechanisms for promoting a practice, and strategies for increasing third party payments.

The ASHA national office also provides taped and printed information for the private practitioner. Topics on taped cassettes include (a) fiscal planning and management, (b) financing a private practice, (c) marketing strategies and objectives, (d) equipping the private practice (speech-language pathology and audiology), (e) choosing an organizational structure, (f) managing payments, and (g) collections and contracting. Individual cassettes on these topics are available from ASHA's Professional Practices Division. This division also publishes information and references that assist the professional who is considering establishing and developing a private practice.

Lastly, ASHA's Division for Reimbursement Policy publishes comprehensive literature about reimbursement issues. Their free publication, *Guidelines for Speech and Hearing Facilities that Wish to Provide Outpatient Speech Pathology Services for Medicare Beneficiaries,* is particularly helpful. This division also answers questions about reimbursement policies and provides the professional with updated material regarding reimbursement for Medicare beneficiaries.

The maturity of a profession is often judged by the number of individuals who can function independently and profitably. This chapter has attempted to inform potential part-time private practitioners of the requirements and implications for maintaining a responsible part-time private practice in which service can be delivered with confidence. Those who enter private practice forearmed with this knowledge should find it a rewarding and challenging experience.

REFERENCES

American Speech-Language-Hearing Association. (1983-1984). *Guide to professional services*. Rockville, MD: Author.

Committee on Private Practice (1982). Questions and answers on private practice. Rockville, MD: American Speech-Language-Hearing Association.

Flower, R. (1984). *Delivery of speech-language-pathology and audiology services*. Baltimore: Williams & Wilkins.

Loavenbruck, A. & Madell, J. (1981). *Hearing aid dispensing for audiologists: A guide for clinical services*. New York: Grune and Stratton.

SUGGESTED READINGS

Battin, R., & Fox, D. (Eds.) (1978). *Private practice in audiology and speech pathology*. New York: Grune and Stratton.

Lehroff, I., & Koroshec, S. (1981). *Speech and language procedure manual*. Beverly Hills, CA: Irwin Lehroff, Ph.D. and Associates.

Lord, P. J., & Johnson, B.E. (1982). *Your private practice: Volume II, Planning and organization*. Lake City, FL: Healthcare Services Division.

Appendix 2-A

Requirements for the Certificates of Clinical Competence
(Revised, January 1, 1981)

The individual who is awarded either or both of the Certificates of Clinical Competence must hold a master's degree or equivalent with major emphasis in speech-language pathology, audiology, or speech-language and hearing science. The individual must also meet the following qualifications:

I. Standards

Equivalent is defined as holding a bachelor's degree from an accredited college or university, and at least 42 post baccalaureate semester hours acceptable toward a master's degree, of which at least 30 semester hours must be in the areas of speech-language pathology, audiology, or speech-language and hearing science. At least 21 of these 42 semester hours must be obtained from a single college or university. None may have been completed more than 10 years prior to the date of application and no more than six semester hours may be credit offered for clinical practicum.

   A. General Background Education. As stipulated below, applicants for a certificate should have completed specialized academic training and preparatory professional experience that provides an in-depth knowledge of normal communication processes, development and disorders thereof, evaluation procedures to assess the bases of such disorders, and clinical techniques that have been shown to improve or eradicate them. It is expected that the applicant will have obtained a broad general education to serve

   Appendix 2–A (Requirements for the Certificates of Clinical Competence, Revised, January 1, 1981) and Appendix 2–B (Procedures for Obtaining the Certificates) are currently undergoing revision. The reader should be aware that the Council on Professional Standards in Speech-Language Pathology and Audiology is in the process of reviewing certification requirements. One set of proposed revisions is published in Asha, July, 1985. In order to obtain information regarding current requirements for the Certificate(s) of Clinical Competence, individuals should contact the Certification Section of the American Speech-Language-Hearing Association, 10801 Rockville Pike, Rockville, MD, 20852.

27

as a background prior to such study and experience. The specific content of this general background education is left to the discretion of the applicant and to the training program attended. However, it is highly desirable that it include study in the areas of human psychology, sociology, psychological and physical development, the physical sciences (especially those that pertain to acoustic and biological phenomena) and human anatomy and physiology, including neuroanatomy and neurophysiology.

B. Required Education. In evaluation of credits, one quarter hour will be considered the equivalent of two-thirds of a semester hour. Transcripts that do not report credit in terms of semester or quarter hours should be submitted for special evaluation. A total of 60 semester hours of academic credit must have been accumulated from accredited colleges or universities that demonstrate that the applicant has obtained a well-integrated program of course study dealing with the normal aspects of human communication, development thereof, disorders thereof, and clinical techniques for evaluation and management of such disorders.

Twelve of these 60 semester hours must be obtained in courses that provide information that pertains to normal development and use of speech, language and hearing.

Thirty of these 60 semester hours must be in courses that provide 1) information relative to communication disorders, and 2) information about and training in evaluation and management of speech, language and hearing disorders. At least 24 of these 30 semester hours must be in courses in the professional area (speech-language pathology or audiology) for which the certificate is requested, and no less than six semester hours may be in audiology for the certificate in speech-language pathology or in speech-language pathology for the certificate in audiology. Moreover, no more than six semester hours may be in courses that provide credit for clinical practice obtained during academic training.

Credit for study of information pertaining to related fields that augment the work of the clinical practitioner of speech-language pathology and/or audiology may also apply toward the total 60 semester hours.

Thirty of the total 60 semester hours that are required for the certificate must be in courses that are acceptable toward a graduate degree by the college or university in which they are taken. Moreover, 21 of those 30 semester hours must be within the 24 semester hours required in the professional area (speech-language pathology or audiology) for which the certificate is requested or within the six semester hours required in the other area. This requirement may be met by courses completed as an undergraduate providing the college or university in which they are taken specifies that these courses would be acceptable toward a graduate degree if they were taken at the graduate level.

C. Academic Clinical Practicum. The applicant must have completed a minimum of 300 clock hours of supervised clinical experience with individuals who present a variety of communication disorders, and this experience must have been obtained within the training institution or in one of its cooperating programs.

D. The Clinical Fellowship Year. The applicant must have obtained the equivalent of nine months of full-time professional experience (the Clinical Fellowship Year) in which bona fide clinical work has been accomplished in the major professional area (speech-language pathology or audiology) in which the certificate is being sought. The Clinical Fellowship Year must have begun after completion of the academic and clinical practicum experiences specified in Standards A, B and C, above.

E. The National Examinations in Speech-Language Pathology and Audiology. The applicant must have passed one of the National Examinations in Speech-Language-Pathology and Audiology, either the National Examination in Speech-Language-Pathology or the National Examination in Audiology.

Appendix 2-B

Procedures for Obtaining the Certificates

The applicant must submit to the Clinical Certification Board a description of professional education and academic clinical practicum on forms provided for that purpose. The applicant should recognize that it is highly desirable to list upon this application form the entire professional education and academic clinical practicum training.

No credit may be allowed for courses listed on the application unless satisfactory completion is verified by an official transcript. *Satisfactory completion* is defined as the applicant's having received academic credit (i.e., semester hours, quarter hours, or other unit of credit) with a passing grade as defined by the training institution. If the majority of an applicant's professional training is received at a program accredited by the Education and Training Board (ETB) of the American Speech-Language-Hearing Association (ASHA), approval of educational and academic clinical practicum requirements will be automatic.

The applicant must request that the director of the training program where the majority of graduate training was obtained sign the application. In the case where that training program is not accredited by the ETB of ASHA, that director, by signature 1) certifies that the application is correct, and 2) recommends that the applicant receive the certificate upon completion of all the requirements. In the case where the training program is accredited by the ETB or ASHA, that director 1) certifies that the applicant has met the educational and clinical practicum requirements, and 2) recommends that the applicant receive the certificate upon completion of all the requirements.

In the event that the applicant cannot obtain the recommendation of the director of the training program, the applicant should send with the application a letter giving in detail the reasons for the inability to do so. In such an instance letters of recommendation from other faculty members may be submitted.

Application for approval of educational requirements and academic clinical practicum experiences should be made 1) as soon as possible after completion of these experiences, and 2) either before or shortly after the Clinical Fellowship Year is begun.

Upon completion of educational and academic clinical practicum training, the applicant should proceed to obtain professional employment and a supervisor for the Clinical Fellowship Year. Although the filing of a CFY Plan is not required, applicants may submit such a plan to the Clinical Certification Board (CCB) if they wish prior approval of the planned professional experience. Within one month following completion of the Clinical Fellowship Year, the CF and the CFY supervisor must submit a CFY Report to the Clinical Certification Board.

Upon notification by the Clinical Certification Board of approval of the academic course work and clinical practicum requirements the applicant will be sent registration material for the National Examinations in Speech-Language-Pathology and Audiology. Upon approval of the Clinical Fellowship Year, achieving a passing score on the National Examination and payment of all fees, the applicant will become certified.

Additional information as well as application materials for certification, including a schedule of fees, may be obtained by writing to Information Services Section, American Speech-Language-Hearing Association, 10801 Rockville Pike, Rockville, Maryland 20852.

States with Speech-Language Pathology/ Audiology Licensing Laws

Enactment sequence in parentheses, enactment date follows

Alabama (26) 12/75	Nebraska (30) 3/78
Arkansas (20) 2/75	Nevada (31) 7/79
California (6) 12/72	New Jersey (35) 1/84
Connecticut (11) 6/73	New Mexico (32) 4/81
Delaware (15) 7/73	New York (18) 6/74
Florida (1) 4/69	North Carolina (27) 7/75
Georgia (16) 3/74	North Dakota (22) 3/75
Hawaii (17) 5/74	Ohio (25) 6/75
Indiana (7) 4/73	Oklahoma (9) 5/73
Iowa (28) 2/76	Oregon (13) 7/73
Kentucky (3) 4/72	Pennsylvania (36) 12/84
Louisiana (5) 7/72	Rhode Island (10) 5/73
Maine (29) 4/76	South Carolina (12) 6/73
Maryland (4) 5/72	Tennessee (8) 4/73
Massachusetts (33) 1/83	Texas (34) 6/83
Mississippi (23) 4/75	Utah (21) 3/75
Missouri (14) 7/73	Virginia (2) 3/72
Montana (24) 5/75	Wyoming (19) 2/75

Source: Governmental Affairs Department of American Speech-Language-Hearing Association (ASHA), 1984.

Appendix 2-D

Licensure Requirements

STATE AND DATE EFFECTIVE	FEES	ELIGIBILITY/ RENEWAL REQUIREMENTS	INTERIM PRACTICE	RECIPROCITY	LICENSING AGENCY	SUPERVISING AUTHORITY	BOARD COMPOSITION	EXCLUSIONS OR EXEMPTIONS
Alabama 1975	Application $50 Initial license $50 (dual license for single fee) Exam $25 Reexam $50 Renewal $50 Inactive $50 (2 yr. max.) Annual renewal	Compatible with CCC No continuing ed. requirement	If ASHA certified or licensed in another state, territory, or D.C., may practice while application is pending. Persons beginning supervised professional experience must register with the Board.	Will waive exam if ASHA certified.	Alabama Board of Examiners for Speech Pathology and Audiology, P.O. Box 20833, Montgomery 36120-0833 205/834-8900	None	7 Members: 3 SLP 3 AUD 1 Public Member or Allied Professional	Physicians and supervisees; hearing aid dealers; those credentialed by Department of Education; federal employees; students and trainees and those acquiring clinical experience; persons within scope of another profession or occupation
Arkansas 1975	Application for exam —up to $50 Initial license $40 Renewal $25 Late renewal: monthly penalty $10 Annual renewal	Compatible with CCC License renewal may depend on continuing education requirements	If ASHA certified or licensed in another state, territory, or D.C., may practice while application is pending. Persons beginning required prof. exp. must submit an application to the Board.	May waive exam if have license from state with equivalent standards or ASHA CCC.	Board of Examiners for Speech Pathology and Audiology, P.O. Box 5198, Little Rock 72225 501/227-7407	None	8 Members: 2 SLP 1 SLP/AUD 2 AUD 2 Consumer 1 Public Rep. 1 member over age of 40	Physicians; hearing aid dealers; persons credentialed by Dept. of Education; state or federal employees; students/interns/ trainees and persons completing prof. experience requirement; persons within scope of another state-licensed profession
California 1974	Application $85 Professional Corp. $100 Renewal Fee $50 Delinquency Fee $10 Aide registration $10	Compatible with CCC; must have taken exam within 5 years preceding making application	May practice for 90 days if currently licensed by another state or if ASHA certified.	None	Speech Pathology and Audiology Examining Committee, Board of Medical Quality Assurance, 1430	Division of Allied Health Professions, Board of Quality Assurance, Department of Consumer Affairs	9 Members: 3 SLP 3 AUD 3 Public Members (1 ENT 2 Nonmedical persons)	Physicians and supervisees; hearing aid dispensers; persons credentialed by Commission for

Appendix 2-D Continued

STATE AND DATE EFFECTIVE	FEES	ELIGIBILITY/ RENEWAL REQUIREMENTS	INTERIM PRACTICE	RECIPROCITY	LICENSING AGENCY	SUPERVISING AUTHORITY	BOARD COMPOSITION	EXCLUSIONS OR EXEMPTIONS
California cont.	Biennial renewal	No continuing ed. requirement	Persons beginning required prof. experience must secure Board approval of plan.		Howe Avenue, Sacramento 95825 916/920-6388			Teacher Preparation; federal employees; students and trainees; those acquiring clinical experience; school audiometrists; persons within scope of other licensed profession
Connecticut 1974	Exam and reexam $25; Initial license $25; Temporary license $25; Dual license $50; Renewal (1 mo. before exp.) $15; Renewal $20; Annual renewal	Compatible with CCC; No continuing ed. requirement	No provision	May waive exam if ASHA certified or licensed by state with equivalent standards.	Speech Path. & Audiology Licensing; Dept. of Health Services; Div. of Medical Quality Assurance; 150 Washington St., Hartford, CT 06106 203/566-1039	None	None	Students/interns/ trainees and persons fulfilling prof. exp. requirement; hearing aid dealers; nurses and audiometrists under supervision of physician or audiologist; persons who consult/disseminate research findings/ offer lectures
Delaware 1973	Not to exceed Application—$25; Exam $25; Renewal $10; Delinquency $5; Replacement $5; Annual renewal	Compatible with CCC; No continuing ed. requirement	Persons holding ASHA certificate or equivalent, or a state license may practice pending approval of application.	Will waive exam if licensed in state with equivalent standards or if ASHA certified.	Board of Audiologists, Speech Pathologists and Hearing Aid Dealers, O'Neill Bldg., P.O. Box 1401, Dover 19903 302/736-4796	None	7 Members: 2 SLP 2 AUD 2 Hearing Aid Dealers 1 Consumer	Physicians and supervisees; those credentialed by Dept. of Public Instruction; students, interns, trainees or persons fulfilling prof. experience requirement; persons within scope of state licensed profession or occupation
Florida* 1969	State Board of Education sets fees.	Compatible with CCC; Continuing ed.	Persons who have not fulfilled prof. experience or exam requirements must	May waive exam and ed. requirements if ASHA certified or if licensed in state	Florida State Advisory Council of Speech-Lang. Path. & Aud.,	Dept. of Education	7 Members: 5 SLP/AUD 2 Public Members	Physicians; nurses; clinical psychologists; hearing aid fitters;

	Fees	Continuing Education	Temporary/Provisional	Reciprocity	Administering Dept.	Board / Address	Board Composition	Exemptions
(continued)	Annual renewal	requirement: 10 hours every year	apply for provisional registration.	with equivalent standards.		Dept. of Ed., Teacher Cert. Section, Room 452, Knots Bldg., Tallahassee 32301 904/488-2317		students/interns/ trainees; laryngectomees rendering guidance or instruction while supervised
Georgia 1974	Set by board: Application $30 License $40 Renewal $40 Inactive status $15 Reinstatement $100 Biennial renewal	Compatible with CCC Continuing ed. requirement: 40 hours in 2 years	Temporary, nonrenewable one year license must be obtained if meet all requirements except passing the exam.	May waive exam if ASHA certified or currently licensed in state or country with equivalent standards.	State Examining Boards of Georgia, Secretary of State	Georgia Board of Examiners for Speech Pathology and Audiology, 166 Pryor St., S.W., Atlanta 30303 404/656-6719	7 Members: 2 SLP 2 AUD 1 ENT 1 Public Member 1 Unspecified	Speech-language pathologists and audiologists certified by State Dept. of Ed. if employed by a chartered educational institution; students/interns and persons fulfilling prof. experience requirement; hearing aid dispensers; others certified under state law
Hawaii 1975	Determined by Dept. of Commerce and Consumer Affairs: License $25 Application $10 Biennial renewal	Compatible with CCC No continuing ed. provision	If ASHA certified or licensed in another state or D.C., may practice for 90 days after applying.	May waive exam if licensed in state or D.C. with equivalent standards.	Dept. of Commerce and Consumer Affairs	Bd. of Speech Pathology and Audiology, Dept. of Commerce & Consumer Affairs, 1010 Richards St., Honolulu 96813 808/548-4100	7 Members: 2 SLP 2 AUD 1 ENT 2 Public Members	Physicians; licensed hearing aid dealers (fitting and selling only); students/ interns/trainees and persons fulfilling prof. experience requirement; persons within scope of state licensed professions
Indiana 1977	Established by Board for exam application, initial license, renewal, and late renewal Biennial renewal	Compatible with CCC Continuing ed. requirement: 36 clock hours in 2 years	No provision Persons beginning required prof. experience must register with the Board.	May waive exam if ASHA certified or licensed in state or D.C. with equivalent standards.	None	Bd. of Examiners on Speech Pathology & Audiology, 964 Pennsylvania St., Indianapolis 46204 317/232-2960	6 Members: 2 SLP 2 AUD 1 SLP/AUD 1 Public Memb. 1 ENT Nonvoting advisor	Physicians and supervisees if not called audiologists; hearing aid dealers; persons credentialed by Supt. of Public Instruction; federal employees; students/interns/ trainees; and persons fulfilling prof. experience req.; persons within scope of state licensed professions

Appendix 2-D Continued

STATE AND DATE EFFECTIVE	FEES	ELIGIBILITY/ RENEWAL REQUIREMENTS	INTERIM PRACTICE	RECIPROCITY	LICENSING AGENCY	SUPERVISING AUTHORITY	BOARD COMPOSITION	EXCLUSIONS OR EXEMPTIONS
Iowa 1977	Board sets fees: Application $25 Perm. License $80 Temp. License $40 Late Fee $40 Perm. License Renewal $80 Temp. License Renewal $40 Reinstatement $25 Replacement $10 Verification $10 Biennial renewal	Master's degree or equivalent (course work not specified); 300 clinical practicum hours; Verification of 9 mo. full-time clinical exp. under supervision of state licensed SLP/ AUD; NTE score. Cont. ed. requirement: 30 hours every 2 years	No provision Temporary clinical license required for those lacking only clinical experience and for 3 months of practice by qualified nonresidents.	May waive exam if ASHA certified or licensed by state with equivalent standards.	Board of Speech Path. and Aud. Examiners, State Dept. of Health, Lucas State Office Bldg., Des Moines 50319 515/281-4401	State Dept. of Health	7 Members: 3 SLP 2 AUD 2 Public Members	Physicians; osteopaths and their supervisees; hearing aid fitters; industrial audiometric testers; students; persons employed in public schools within scope of employment
Kentucky 1972	Application $25 Exam $25 Initial license $50 Renewal $25 Late fee $10 Inactive license $5 Annual renewal	M.A. required but course work content not specified; 275 practicum clock hours No continuing ed. requirement	If ASHA certified or licensed in another state, may practice pending disposition of application.	May waive exam if ASHA certified or licensed by state with equivalent standards.	Bd. of Examiners of Speech Pathologists and Audiologists, P.O. Box 456, Frankfort 40602 501/564-3296	None	5 Members: 1 SLP 1 AUD 1 ENT 1 Public Member 1 Unspecified	Audiometrists supervised by physician; persons credentialed by the Dept. of Ed.; hearing aid dispensers; government employees; students/interns/ trainees; persons within scope of another state licensed profession
Louisiana 1979	Established by the Board Annual renewal	Compatible with CCC Board may provide for continuing ed.	No provision Interns/trainees beginning required professional experience must have a restricted license.	May waive exam if ASHA certified or licensed in a state with equivalent standards.	Louisiana Bd. of Examiners for Sp. Pathology & Audiology, P.O. Box 355, Prairieville 70769 504/673-3139	Dept. of Health and Human Resources	6 Members: 2 SLP 1 State Certified Teacher, Speech, Hearing, and Language Specialist 2 AUD 1 Physician	Employees of federal agencies; physicians and their employees who test hearing; licensed hearing aid dealers; aides; students/trainees/ Type C Teaching Certificate holders who must have a restricted license that must be reviewed on an annual basis

State/Year	Fees	Continuing Education/Renewal	Temporary/Provision	Waive Exam/Reciprocity	Board of Examiners	Department	Board Members	Exempt Persons
Maine 1976	Board sets fees: Application $25, Initial license $40, Temporary license $40, Renewal $80, Late fee $10, Biennial renewal	Compatible with CCC except 275 clinical hours required. Cont. ed. req. for renewal: 65 hrs. every 2 yrs. for single license. 80 hrs. required for dual license	If ASHA certified or licensed in U.S. jurisdiction with equiv. standards, may practice no more than 60 days in one calendar yr. Persons beginning req. prof. exp. need temp. license	May waive exam if licensed in another U.S. jurisdiction with equivalent standards.	Board of Examiners on Sp. Path. & Aud., Div. of Licensing and Enforcement, State House Station 35, Augusta 04333 207/289-3671	Dept. of Business, Occupational and Professional Regulation	7 Members: 2 SLP, 2 AUD, 1 ENT, 2 Public Members	Physicians and osteopaths; hearing aid dealers or trainees/students/interns; federal employees; those holding clinical credentials from Dept. of Ed. and Cultural Services
Maryland 1972	Board sets fees: Application and license $20, Application and lim. license $20, Renewal $10, Late fee $10, Reinstatement $25, Annual renewal	Compatible with CCC. Renewal of license contingent upon continuing education requirements: 10 hours every year; 15 hours if hold dual license	New residents may practice if authorized to practice in previous residence. Limited license required for those who have fulfilled all requirements except professional experience	May waive qualifications if ASHA certified. May waive exam if licensed in another state or jurisdiction with equivalent standards	Boards of Examiners for Speech Pathologists and Audiologists, 201 W. Preston, Baltimore 21201 301/225-5862	State Dept. of Health & Mental Hygiene	Speech Path. Board: 6 Members: 3 SLP, 1 AUD, 1 ENT, 1 Consumer; Audiology Bd.: 3 AUD, 1 SLP, 1 ENT, 1 Consumer	Employees of federal agencies, State Dept. of Education, state approved private schools for handicapped or chartered educational institutions; physician students; hearing aid dealers; volunteers in free screening; persons within scope of licensed profession
Massachusetts 1983	Set by Secretary of Administration and Finance. Biennial renewal	Compatible with CCC. May require reexamination for renewal or completion of continuing education requirements as determined by the Board.	No provision. Persons beginning supervised professional practice must be on file with the Board.	May waive exam for licensees from another state or territory of U.S., D.C. or Puerto Rico if meet state requirements.	Board of Registration for Speech-Language Pathology & Aud., 100 Cambridge St., 15th Floor, Boston 02202 617/727-1747	State Div. of Registration, Executive Office of Consumer Affairs	5 Members: 2 SLP, 2 AUD, 1 Public Member	Physicians and supervisees; hearing aid dealers; other professional license holders; teachers of esophageal speech; certified industrial audiometric technicians; students and trainees
Mississippi 1975	Exam $25, Initial license $25, Renewal $25, Late renewal $2/mo., Temporary license $25, Temporary license renewal $25, Aide registration $10, Annual renewal	Compatible with CCC. Continuing education requirements for renewal: 10 hours every year	May practice with ASHA certification license from another U.S. jurisdiction. Temporary license necessary for persons beginning the required professional experience requirement.	Will waive exam if ASHA certified. May waive exam if licensed from a U.S. jurisdiction with equivalent standards.	Mississippi Council of Advisors in Speech Path. & Aud., State Dept. of Health, Child Care & Special Licensure, P.O. Box 1700, Jackson 39205 601/354-6505	State Dept. of Health	5 Members: 2 SLP, 2 AUD, 1 ENT	Physicians and supervisees testing hearing; hearing aid dispensers; federal employees; students; industrial hearing testers; persons within scope of other licensed profession; public and private school employees

Appendix 2-D Continued

STATE AND DATE EFFECTIVE	FEES	ELIGIBILITY/ RENEWAL REQUIREMENTS	INTERIM PRACTICE	RECIPROCITY	LICENSING AGENCY	SUPERVISING AUTHORITY	BOARD COMPOSITION	EXCLUSIONS OR EXEMPTIONS
Missouri 1973	Initial license $50 Renewal $25 Dual licensure for single fee Reinstatement $50 Annual renewal	Compatible with CCC except 275 clinical practicum hours required No provision for continuing ed.	No provision	Will waive exam for person certified by ASHA or licensed in state with equivalent standards	State Board of Registration for the Healing Arts, P.O. Box 4, Jefferson City 65102 314/751-2334	State Board of Registration for the Healing Arts	Administered by State agency; no provision for advisory committee of speech, language, hearing professionals	Employees of government agencies or of chartered educational institutions; certified teachers of the deaf; physicians; students/interns/ trainees, and those completing prof. exp. requirement; persons within scope of licensed professions
Montana 1981	Board sets fees: Application $40 License $25 Dual licensure $25 Temporary $10 Probationary $25 Inactive $10 Replacement $10 Aide registration $20 Annual renewal	Compatible with CCC Continuing education requirement: 40 hours every 2 years	If ASHA certified or licensed by another state, may practice pending disposition of appl. Qualified non-residents must apply for temp. license to practice 30 days max. in calendar year. Persons beginning req. prof. exp. will be issued a probationary lic.	Will waive exam for persons certified by ASHA or licensed in state with equivalent standards.	Board of Speech Pathologists & Aud., Dept. of Professional and Occupational Licensing, 1424 Ninth Ave., Helena 59620-0407 406/444-3737	Dept. of Prof. & Occupational Licensing, Dept. of Commerce	5 Members: 2 SLP 2 AUD 1 Consumer	Federal employees; students/interns/ trainees; persons within scope of other licensed profession; hearing aid dealers, class A certificate holders from Conference of Executives of American Schools for the Deaf
Nebraska 1978	Initial license $75 Renewal $25 Certified Statement of Licensure $2 Late renewal $1 Biennial renewal	Compatible with CCC Continuing education requirement: 20 hours every 2 years	Temporary license issued to persons who meet all requirements except taking the exam; expires at time of next exam. Persons beginning the req. prof. exp. must register with the Board.	May waive exam for those with state licensure or those certified by national prof. accrediting org., if req. are equiv. to Nebraska.	Bd. of Exam. in Aud. & Speech-Lang. Path., Bureau of Examining Bds., Dept. of Health, P.O. Box 95007, Lincoln 68509 404/471-4925	Dept. of Health	4 Members: 2 SLP 2 AUD 1 Layperson	Federal employees; hearing aid dealers; those credentialed by State Department of Education; physicians and supervisees; students/trainees; persons completing the professional experience requirement
Nevada 1979	Initial application $50 Renewal Maximum $25 Reinstatement Maximum $25	Not compatible with CCC: M.A. in AUD or SLP or equiv. training & experience; 300	Temporary license issued to those licensed in another state who meet Nevada	May waive exam for persons certified by ASHA or licensed by state with equivalent	Board of Examiners for Audiology and Speech Path., U. of Nevada School of Medicine, Reno,	None	5 Members: 2 SLP 1 AUD 1 Physician certified in	Physicians and supervisees; hearing aid specialists; federal employees;

	Annual renewal	Continuing education / experience	requirements	standards	Address	Administering agency	Board composition	Exemptions
(continued)	Annual renewal	clinical exp. clock hours; passing score on exam; no prof. experience (CFY) req. Cont. ed. req.: 15 hrs every yr.	requirements except passing the exam.	standards.	89557 702/784-6001		-ENT - Neurology - Pediatrics 1 Public Member	employees of Dept. of Human Resources; graduate students; school nurses; those credentialed by State Dept. of Education
New Jersey 1983	$110—Includes $10 nonrefundable application fee and $100 two-year license fee that is refundable if application is denied.	Compatible with CCC. Continuing education may be required for license renewal.	Renewable one year temporary license may be issued to an applicant who has become a NJ resident and who was licensed by the state of his/her former residence.	Exam may be waived if hold a current license in state with equivalent standards.	Audiology and Speech-Language Pathology Advisory Committee, 1100 Raymond Blvd., Room 513, Newark 07102. 201/648-4033	Director of the Division of Consumer Affairs of the Department of Law and Public Safety	9 Members: 4 SLP or AUD (3 maximum from any 1 area) 2 ENT 2 Public Mbrs. 1 State Representative	Physicians, surgeons, and persons under the direct supervision of physicians; federal employees; students/fellows/ trainees; hearing aid dealers; persons within scope of other licensed professions; persons certified as speech correctionists
New Mexico 1981	Initial license up to $50 Renewal up to $50 Dual license $50 Late fee $25 Annual renewal	Compatible with CCC plus evidence of completed experience. Continuing ed. requirement for renewal: 20 hrs. every 2 yrs.	May practice for 90 days while application is pending if licensed from another state and if supervised by a licensee.	Will waive education and experience requirements if hold current license in state with equivalent standards.	Speech-Lang. Path. & Aud., Advisory Board; Health Serv. Div.; Dept. of Health & Environment: P.O. Box 968, Santa Fe 87504 505/827-7971	Secretary of Health and Environment Dept.	5 Members: 2 SLP 2 AUD 1 Public Member not in the profession	Employees of State Bd. of Education; physicians and dentists; certified teachers of the deaf; hearing aid dealers and fitters; students/trainees/ interns or persons fulfilling prof. experience requirement
New York 1976	Exam and initial license $125 Triennium fee $90 Triennial renewal	Academic, clin. practicum, & exam req. are compatible with CCC. Different experience year (CFY) supervision standards. Requirements are set by regulations of the Commissioner of Ed. No continuing ed. provision	No provision	No provision	Speech-Lang. Pathology & Audiology Unit, State Ed. Dept, Div. of Licensing Services, Cultural Ed. Center, Room 3041, Albany 12230 518/474-3832	New York Board of Regents	11 Members: 6 SLP 4 AUD 1 Public Member	Licensees of the other registered professions; persons acquiring clinical or academic experience; government employees; employees of public or non-public elementary, secondary, and post-secondary educational institutions; hearing aid dealers

Appendix 2-D Continued

STATE AND DATE EFFECTIVE	FEES	ELIGIBILITY/ RENEWAL REQUIREMENTS	INTERIM PRACTICE	RECIPROCITY	LICENSING AGENCY	SUPERVISING AUTHORITY	BOARD COMPOSITION	EXCLUSIONS OR EXEMPTIONS
North Carolina 1975	Application $25 Exam $25 Initial license $25 Renewal $25 Temporary $25 Late fee $10 Annual renewal	Compatible with CCC except for variations in req. for supervision of persons completing prof. exp., and in nonacceptance of aud. screening clock hours approved by SLP supervisors. No CE requirement	Non-renewable temporary license necessary for persons who have not fulfilled professional experience or exam requirements as long as practice is under supervision of a licensee.	Will waive written exam if ASHA certified. May waive requirements for persons licensed in states with equivalent standards.	Board of Examiners for Speech and Language Pathologists and Audiologists, P.O. Box 5545, Greensboro 27403 919/272-1828	None	7 Members: 2 SLP 2 AUD 1 Physician 2 Public Members	Federal agency employees; students and trainees; credentialed employees of public schools or state schools for the deaf & blind; physicians and their supervisees; counselors or instructors of laryngectomees; hearing aid dealers; indus. audiometrists
North Dakota 1975	Set by Board: total not to exceed $50 annually Annual renewal	No explicit mention of prof. experience requirement; requirements prescribed by Board based on appropriate national standards. Continuing ed. requirement: 6 hours every year	May practice under temporary one year permit if show evidence of qualifications.	May waive exam if licensed in state with equivalent professional standards	State Bd. of Examiners on Aud. & Speech-Lang. Path., Medcenter One, Box 640, Bismarck 58502-0640 701/224-6176	None	7 Members: 2 SLP 2 AUD 1 ENT 1 Hearing Aid Specialist 1 Consumer	Physicians; hearing aid dealers; licensed profes.; those credentialed by Dept. of Public Instruction; federal employees; students/trainees/ and interns; teachers of hearing impaired credentialed by Council on Ed. of the Deaf; audiometric technicians under direct supervision of licensed audiologist
Ohio 1975	Set by Board: Exam fee $50 max. Initial license (single or dual) $100 maximum Renewal $50 maximum	Ed. standards are compatible with CCC. Variations in clin. practicum & prof. exp. (CFY) req. Exam must be taken within 5 yrs. preceding	If ASHA certified or licensed in another state, may practice pending disposition of application Persons completing prof. exp.	Reciprocity decided on individual basis. Will waive ed. & exam req. if licensed in state with equivalent standards; however, Ohio	Bd. of Speech Pathology & Audiology, 65 S. Front St., Room #214, Columbus 43215 614/466-3145	None	5 Members: 2 SLP 2 AUD 1 Public Rep.	Federal agency employees; students/trainees/ interns and people fulfilling prof. exp. requirement; physicians, osteopaths, and

State/Year	Fees	CCC / Continuing Ed.	Reciprocity / Provisions	Exam Waiver	Board Address	Administering Agency	Board Composition	Exemptions
	Annual renewal	application. Cont. ed. req. if hold Ohio "grandfathered" license	requirement must register with the Board.	standards differ from most states.			5 Members: 3 SLP and/or AUD (both disciplines must be represented) 1 ENT	nurses; those certified by State Dept of Ed., supervisees of audiologists doing hearing testing
Oklahoma 1973	Set by Board: Application $50 Renewal $25 max. Replacement $10 Inactive $10 Intern license $20 Annual renewal	Compatible with CCC No continuing ed. requirement	No provision Interns/trainees beginning required prof. experience must apply for special license.	Will waive exam if ASHA certified. May waive exam if licensed in state with equivalent standards.	Board of Examiners for Speech Pathology & Audiology, P.O. Box 53592, State Capital Station, Oklahoma City 73152 405/722-6266	None		Public employees; persons licensed under other state laws; students; physicians & their supervisees; hearing aid dealers; certified teachers of the deaf & hard of hearing; persons involved in hearing screening programs.
Oregon 1973	Application $25 Exam $25 License $25 Renewal $25 Inactive license $10 Delinquency fee $10 Annual renewal	Compatible with CCC No continuing ed. provision	If ASHA certified or licensed in another state, may practice pending disposition of application Qualified nonresidents may practice for 30 days max. under a temp. license Persons completing prof. exp. requirement must register with the Board.	Will waive exam if ASHA certified or licensed in state with equivalent standards.	State Bd. of Examiners for Speech Path. & Aud., P.O. Box 231, Portland 97207 503/229-7861	Dept. of Human Resources	7 Members: 2 SLP 2 AUD 1 ENT 2 Public Members	Professional licenses of other state laws; school personnel credentialed by State Bd. of Ed.; federal agency employees; employees of accredited colleges or universities; hearing aid dealers; persons with Class A certificates from Conf. of Exec. of American Schools for the Deaf; nonresidents with temp. license or in cooperation with a licensee; students/interns/trainees
Pennsylvania 1984	Fees established by the Board Biennial renewal	Master's degree in speech-language pathology or audiology or education of the hearing impaired plus one year of supervised professional experience	No provision	May waive exam and ed. requirements if licensed by a state with equivalent standards, or if ASHA certified, or if have a current certificate from the Council on Education of the Deaf and 10	State Board of Examiners in Speech-Language and Hearing Board members have not been appointed	Bureau of Professional and Occupational Affairs of the Department of State	10 members: Commissioner of the Bureau of Prof. & Occupational Affairs 1 SLP 1 AUD 1 Teacher of the hearing impaired 2 Members at Large from the 3 licensed	Persons within scope of other licensed professions including physicians and surgeons, and trained individuals under the direction of licensed physicians from doing hearing

Appendix 2-D Continued

STATE AND DATE EFFECTIVE	FEES	ELIGIBILITY/ RENEWAL REQUIREMENTS	INTERIM PRACTICE	RECIPROCITY	LICENSING AGENCY	SUPERVISING AUTHORITY	BOARD COMPOSITION	EXCLUSIONS OR EXEMPTIONS
Pennsylvania cont.		No explicit mention of clin. practicum requirement Board may establish standards for license renewal.		additional graduate credits.			areas but no area can be represented by more than 2 Board mbrs. 2 Physicians, including 1 ENT 2 Public Members	testing; hearing aid fitters and dealers; persons holding a valid credential from the Dept. of Ed. and employees of the state or federal government; students and trainees; persons licensed by other states or who meet equivalent standards as long as practice does not exceed 5 days in a calendar year; agencies employing persons licensed under this law.
Rhode Island 1973	Application $25 License $5 Renewal $5 Annual renewal	Coursework and clinical practicum req. are compatible with CCC. Specific requirements for supervision of prof. experience. Special licenses granted to nonqualified persons having expertise in treatment of laryngectomies & in treatment of laryngeal impairment. No continuing ed. requirement	No provision	Will waive exam if ASHA certified or if licensed in state with equivalent standards	State Bd. of Examiners for Speech Path. & Aud., Dept. of Professional Regulation, Cannon Bldg., 75 Davis St., Providence 02908 401/277-2827	Department of Health	5 Members: 2 SLP 1 AUD 1 ENT 1 Consumer	Federal employees; school personnel credentialed by State Department of Education; hearing aid fitters and sellers; others licensed under state law

State / Year	Fees	Continuing Education	Temporary / Reciprocity	Waiver of Exam	Licensing Board	Agency	Board Composition	Exemptions
South Carolina 1974	Application $35, License $35, Renewal $35, Delinquent Fee $35, Inactive $10, Replacement $10, Annual renewal	Compatible with CCC. No continuing ed. requirement	Persons licensed in another state may practice pending disposition of application. Provisional license necessary for persons fulfilling prof. experience requirement.	May waive exam and educ. requirement if ASHA certified or if licensed in another state with equivalent standards.	State Bd. of Examiners in Speech Pathology & Audiology P.O. Box 11876, Columbia 29211 803/772-9554	None	7 Members: 2 SLP, 2 AUD, 1 ENT, 1 Hearing Aid Dealer and The Exec. Dir. of Health & Environmental Control or designee.	Other qualified licensed persons if engaged in a practice as defined by state law; state & federal employees; students & trainees; hearing aid dealers; teachers of deaf certified by Conf. of Exec. of American Schools for the Deaf; trained audiometric industrial screening technicians if supervised by physicians, otological consultant or licensed audiologist
Tennessee 1973	Maximum limits: Application $50, Exam $25, Initial License $100, Renewal $100, Delinquent Fee $100, Annual renewal	Compatible with CCC. No continuing ed. requirement	If ASHA certified or licensed in another state, may practice pending disposition of application.	Will waive exam if licensed in another state with equivalent standards	St. Bd. of Examiners for Speech Path. & Aud., Dept. of Public Health, 283 Plus Park Blvd. Nashville 37219 615/361-6705	None	6 Members: 2 SLP, 2 AUD, 1 AUD or SLP, 1 ENT	Professionals licensed under another law; persons credentialed by State Dept. of Ed.; students/interns/ trainees and those completing CFY; audiometric testers supervised by physicians; hearing aid dispensers; federal employees
Texas 1983	Set by Committee May not exceed: Application $75, Examination $50, Initial License $75, Renewal $75, Delinquency $50, Temporary $25, Duplicate license $10, Annual Renewal	Compatible with CCC. Continuing ed. requirement: 10 clock hours per year for single license; 15 clock hours per year for dual licensure	No provision. Persons who have completed all qualifications except the exam must apply for temporary certificate of registration.	Will waive exam for persons licensed in states that have equivalent standards and for persons who hold ASHA certification.	Texas State Committee of Examiners for Speech-Language Pathology and Audiology, 1100 West 49th, Austin, 78756-3183 512/458-7531	Texas Department of Health	9 Members: 3 SLP, 3 AUD, 1 Licensed Physician certified in otolaryngology or pediatrics, 2 Public Mbrs.	Persons within scope of other licensed professions; persons certified in speech and hearing therapy by the Central Education Agency; persons completing the prof. exp. req. (interns); qualified nonlicensed, nonresidents if

Appendix 2-D Continued

STATE AND DATE EFFECTIVE	FEES	ELIGIBILITY/ RENEWAL REQUIREMENTS	INTERIM PRACTICE	RECIPROCITY	LICENSING AGENCY	SUPERVISING AUTHORITY	BOARD COMPOSITION	EXCLUSIONS OR EXEMPTIONS
Texas cont.								practice does not exceed 5 days in a calendar yr; university/colleges teachers not engaging in practice or supervision; physicians and surgeons; persons employed by TX Dept. of Health in hearing or speech services programs; persons trained by the TX Dept. of Health in hearing screening training programs; persons in industrial settings and licensed registered nurses from doing hearing testing; psychologists
Utah 1981	Set by Dept. of Business Regulation & the Div. of Occupational & Professional Licensing Biennial renewal	Not compatible with CCC; variations in course work & clinical experience; practical exam required Cont. ed.: 3 credit hours or 30 clock hours in instruction of grad. level prof. training every 5 years	No provision	No provision	Speech Path. & Audiology Adv. Comm.; Div. of Occupational & Prof. Licensing; 160 E. 300 South, P.O. Box 45802, Salt Lake City 84145 801/530-6625	Div. of Occupational & Prof. Licensing	5 Members: 4 SLP & Aud - 1 Private Practice 1 Non-school clinic setting 1 Elem. or secondary school 1 university or college training program 1 lay member	Physicians; hearing aid dealers; persons credentialed by State Dept. of Public instruction; government employees; university employees; persons licensed under another law; students and persons fulfilling prof. experience req.; audiometric testers supervised by physicians

State/Year	Fees	Continuing Ed.	Continuing Ed. Req.	Experience	Exam Waiver	Board	Dept. of Commerce	Members	Exemptions
Virginia 1972	Application $70 Renewal $40 Delinquent renewal $60 $80 (renewal and penalty) Biennial renewal	Compatible with CCC	No cont. ed. provision	No provision	May waive exam if ASHA certified	Virginia Bd. of Examiners for Aud. & Speech Path., Dept. of Commerce; 3600 W. Broad St., Richmond 23230 804/257-8508		7 Members: 2 SLP 2 AUD 1 ENT 2 Citizen Members	Persons licensed in another profession; employees of federal, state, county, and municipal agencies or chartered educational institutions; students/interns/ trainees
Wyoming 1975	Application $25 License $50 ($100 for dual license) Renewal $25 ($50 for dual license) Delinquent renewal fee $5/mo. or $20 maximum Inactive renewal $10 Reciprocal license $25 Annual renewal	Compatible with CCC	No continuing ed. requirement	No provision Persons completing prof. experience requirement should be registered with the board.	May waive exam for persons licensed in state with equivalent standards or persons certified by a nationally recognized speech and hearing association	Board of Examiners for Speech Pathology and Audiology, P.O. Box 3311, University Station, Laramie 82071 307/766-6426	None	5 Members: 2 SLP 1 AUD 1 Consumer 1 Physician or Dentist	Physicians & supervisees conducting hearing testing; hearing aid dealers or certified hearing aid audiologists; personnel certified by State Dept. of Ed. working in public schools or dev. dis. programs funded by Dept. of Health and Soc. Services; students/ interns/trainees and persons fulfilling paid clin. experience requirement

*Information is based on available National Office data. Information for other states is based on current information submitted by state licensure boards.

Source: Governmental Affairs Department of American Speech-Language-Hearing Association (ASHA), September 1985.

Appendix 2-E

States That Allow Audiologists to Dispense Hearing Aids Under Provisions of Audiology Licensing Acts

*Alabama
*Oklahoma
*Utah
 New York

*Based on Attorney General's Opinion

Source: Governmental Affairs Department, State Regulatory Policy Division of American Speech-Language-Hearing Association (ASHA), 1985.

For information regarding those states in which audiologists are exempt from the hearing aid dealer's (HAD) examination and/or a hearing aid dealer apprenticeship, contact the state's licensing agency.

Chapter 3

Legal Issues for Private Practitioners in Speech-Language Pathology and Audiology

Robert Henley Woody, Ph.D., Sc.D., J.D.

Private practice in speech-language pathology and audiology has firm roots in some of the most traditional sources. In citing possible employment options for speech-language pathologists, Van Riper (1978) acknowledges that private practice is appropriate (if prefaced by clinical certification from the American Speech-Language-Hearing Association (ASHA), but with his usual sagacity, he cautions: "There are many problems that arise in private practice that should be seriously considered . . . it is no bed of roses" (pp. 445–446). Since that time, there have been even more thorns plaguing those who would seek to harvest the fruits of private practice. Notably, there has been an increase in legally based expectations of society, which have been manifested through malpractice suits particularly.

A substantial body of law has developed for the practice of human services, including speech-language pathology and audiology, along with such other disciplines as psychology, social work, and counseling (Woody, 1984). Although much of this body of law is not drawn from speech-language pathology and audiology per se, the legal system generalizes the same principles to virtually all of the health-related professions. In this chapter, the primary legal issues relevant to private practice in speech-language pathology and audiology are explored. Specific guidelines that provide for the best interests of the patients while simultaneously creating legal safeguards for the practitioner are also described.

As an "outsider," the author has always viewed speech-language pathologists and audiologists as holding a strong allegiance to the ASHA. To be sure, having a professional identity firmly connected to one's principal professional organization is beneficial to society; however, from a legal point of view, even the honorific professional organization must place enhancement of the profession in a position secondary to promoting societal objectives.

ISSUE NUMBER ONE: DETERMINATION OF PROFESSIONAL PRACTICES

Some professional organizations have endorsed practices that yield payoffs to the profession and/or practitioner, but afford scant help to the public. For example, *Goldfarb v. Virginia State Bar* (1975) involved a mandatory fee schedule imposed by a local bar association on its members. The U.S. Supreme Court held that public policy did not exempt professionals, even or perhaps especially attorneys, from antitrust scrutiny. The conclusion was that public policies must regulate professional actions, particularly those that could lead to a monopoly.

Private practitioners in speech-language pathology and audiology must accept that public policy is their primary source of control. Thus, when certain expectations are cast on the private practitioner in the form of legal liabilities, it is a contradiction of professionalism to attempt to deny their legitimacy:

> . . . professionalism is the child of society. It cannot exist without the endorsement of society. Public policy prescribes what will earn endorsement. Like it or not, the human services professional of today must function under a public policy that imposes many possible legal sanctions. . . . It is unprofessional to attempt to deny, consciously or unconsciously, that these public policy legal sanctions are justified. (Woody, 1984, p. 401)

Stated differently, the facets of professionalism are produced by society and they are maintained and monitored by the legal system. There is no inalienable right to professionalism—what society has created, society may terminate.

ISSUE NUMBER TWO: STANDARD OF CARE

Societal Issues

Perhaps nowhere does the possible difference between the interests of a profession and of society emerge in more pronounced fashion than in the shaping of the nature and quality of professional practices.

> As society recognizes a profession, it imposes upon that discipline a concomitant responsibility or duty—a set of expectations as to what should and should not occur in professional practice. In other words, the *quid pro quo* for societal recognition is professional accountability to society. When society judges professional practice to be substandard, it attaches legal liability. It is this interface between public policy and professionalism which creates the legal framework for malpractice. (Woody, 1985, pp. 509–510)

Society requires that all professional practices meet an acceptable standard of care.

Implications for the Standard of Care

The standard of care does not proscribe all errors, nor does it prescribe perfection. However, it does require that the practitioner possess and exercise the knowledge and skill of someone who is in good standing in the profession and that reasonable care prevail (Prosser, 1971). In general, the practitioner is expected to stay informed about scientific progress, such as new treatment procedures, to offer only those services that have a solid academic base and that are endorsed by a substantial number of practitioners, and to implement any feasible safeguards for the welfare of the patient. The standard of care emphasizes that the practitioner is a true professional, one who has academic-scientific training that will distinguish his or her judgments from those of the nonprofessional public. Society expects the professional to pass the technical-scientific advances on to the consumer in the form of quality services.

The concept of the standard of care receives strong endorsement from the Code of Ethics of the ASHA (1984). It states:

ASHA Code of Ethics

(1) "Individuals must not exploit persons in the delivery of professional services, including accepting persons for treatment when benefit cannot reasonably be expected or continuing treatment unnecessarily" (p. 1); (2) "Individuals shall maintain high standards of professional competence" (p. 1); (3) "Individuals shall continue their professional development throughout their careers" (p. 2); and (4) "Individuals must not misrepresent their training or competence" (p. 2).

Each of these ethical points has a legal counterpart.

In a legal analysis of the standard of care, the particular selection of an intervention must be predicated on a concept of normal functioning. In speech-language pathology and audiology, this concept of "normal" may be difficult to define, given the changes that occur at the various life-span stages. In this instance, the practitioner should seek a reference point in the professional literature, even if there is still a degree of ambiguity.

Legal Issues

Using a common-law concern for normality, Catlin (1984) reviews studies of normal hearing and concludes that available measurement procedures do not achieve the goal of standardizing everyday communication, as witnessed by self-appraisals having "variability in verbalizing phenomenal experience and differences in cultural climate" (p. 250) and the lack of a means for testing a patient's veracity. He also notes the ambiguity created by the fact that "two individuals with identical amounts of hearing loss may report widely discrepant degrees of experienced difficulty" (p. 250). Notwithstanding these uncertainties about normal hearing, the practitioner who is acquainted with the sort of research reviewed by Catlin and who incorporates these notions into his or her services will have gained protection against societal criticism.

The preceding example of the ambiguous definition of normal hearing should not be misinterpreted as meaning that society will tolerate faulty conceptualizations. When society's needs and expectations are translated by the courts, such as in malpractice actions, there is a willingness to accept the "state of the art" or, more appropriately, the "state of the science." On the other hand, it is well established in tort law that an entire profession can be guilty by omission, not just by commission (Prosser, 1971).

If a professional attempts to defend current practices by the explanation that no other private practitioner of speech-language pathology and audiology provides that

Duty to Warn or to Protect

service, it may or may not be an acceptable legal defense. If a procedure is not now, nor has ever been part of the established practice of speech-language pathology and audiology, society is still free to decide that certain procedures or systems are incumbent on a discipline. In effect, society might say, ''Since we are willing to endorse professionalism, with all of the concomitant benefits, such as good income and high status, for private practitioners of speech-language pathology and audiology and since they have highly intimate and confidential relationships with their patients, we believe that it would be in our best interests to have them, as well as psychologists and psychiatrists, hold the duty to report any threats of dangerousness to self or others that are accessible during their treatments, even if it means breaching the perimeter of confidentiality that surrounds their services.''

The foregoing is not a hypothetical expectation. Indeed, the duty to warn has become clear-cut (Knapp and Vandecreek, 1982), and there is no logical reason to believe that, under certain circumstances, it would not be imposed on practitioners of speech-language pathology and audiology. Through the courts, society has in fact asserted that safeguards against dangerousness are more important than confidentiality, privileged communication, or the tenets of therapeutic interventions (Woody, 1984).

The issue of duty to warn or duty to protect has been of concern to psychotherapists for some time. As reported in the American Psychological Association's (APA) *Health and Services Support Network* (November 11, 1985), ''in several courts psychologists, psychiatrists, and treating institutions have been held liable for patients' violent acts, even though research has consistently shown that violent behavior cannot be accurately predicted on an individual basis and that no diagnosis or treatment for dangerousness exists in psychology and psychiatry'' (p. 10). The APA has proposed a model law that it hopes will be adopted by state legislatures. For example, a new California law that became effective as of January 1, 1986 states that there shall be no monetary liability on the part of, and no cause of action shall arise against, any person who is a psychotherapist if that individual should fail to warn of and protect from a patient's threatened violent behavior except where the patient has communicated to the psychotherapist a serious threat of physical violence against a reasonably identifiable victim or victims. The law further specifies that should there be a duty to warn and protect under the limited circumstances noted above, that duty is discharged when the psychotherapist makes reasonable efforts to communicate the threat to the victim or victims and to a law enforcement agency (American Psychological Association, 1985).

As of 1986, the issue of duty to warn has been addressed in one state. However, the reader should note that this law deals only with psychotherapists, although such laws might possibly encompass other helping professions at some time in the future. Meanwhile, speech-language pathologists and audiologists are well advised to be sensitive to the legal constraints placed on psychotherapists and to recognize that such constraints may be placed on other professions.

Theory-Based Practice

The standard of care necessitates reliance on a solid academic model for practice. In the theoretical sphere, this means basing techniques on a theory or model that is endorsed by a substantial number of practitioners.

Does the preceding discussion imply that society discourages experimentation or the seeking of new, improved procedures? No, it means that (1) experimentation must be predicated on an academic rationale and the techniques derived therefrom must have been cultivated by tried-and-true developmental methods; (2) review from professional peers would endorse the appropriateness or readiness of the techniques for application; and (3) in the end, there is a scholarly framework for practice.

In practical terms, the challenge is for the practitioner to take the time to think through what he or she is doing or plans to do with patients and to formulate, sometimes in writing and sometimes only in the mind, the academic justification for those actions. For example, having an organizational framework for assessing communicative abilities can facilitate the evaluative procedures and the formulation of intervention strategies, such as the guidelines for cultivating pragmatic abilities in children posited by Roth and Spekman (1984a, b). Having *any* theoretical-technical framework for a specific procedure, as long as it is from an authoritative source, can provide effective protection from legal allegations.

The standard of care for the practice of speech-language pathology and audiology advocates for (1) an academic-scientific stance, as opposed to artistic verve or apostolic zeal; (2) an ongoing professional education in order to stay abreast of research advances; and (3) a broad spectrum of informational sources. On the third point, there seems no doubt that speech-language pathology and audiology must function within an interdisciplinary framework. As Butler and Wallach (1984) state, "Although a surge of optimism has swept through a number of professional fields regarding the expanding knowledge base and its eventual application to practice, all too frequently disciplinary boundaries fragment information and interaction between and among researchers" (p. 362). The legal mandate for quality in professional practices will not tolerate disciplinary isolationism.

Disciplinary Concerns

Despite the need to function within an interdisciplinary framework, the practitioner should not stray into unfamiliar territory. Some speech-language pathologists and audiologists are prone to fancy their becoming psychodiagnosticians and/or psychotherapists. Although some state statutes may proscribe performing certain functions without holding licensing or certification, often a properly credentialed professional in one discipline has considerable latitude for drawing from the functions of another discipline. In the case of psychodiagnostics or psychotherapy, there are certainly speech-language pathologists and audiologists who have acquired training and skills consonant with those functions, yet lack the legitimizing authority of licensure or certification in, say, clinical psychology.

Regarding psychodiagnostics, professionals in speech-language pathology and audiology sometimes have made long-time use of psychometric tests, yet often without adequate training in their usage. For example, Demorest and Walden (1984) point out that there is an increase in the practice of using questionnaires or self-report inventories as supplements to traditional audiometric measures for assessing communication problems, and they assert that psychometric principles for selection, interpretation, and evaluation of self-assessment inventories must be honored. The practitioner who attempts to use such tests without adequate training in the psychometric principles is courting legal sanctions.

An important legal principle is the following: When a professional holds himself or herself out as a specialist (or the patient has a reasonable basis for believing that he or she is a specialist, even though the professional has not expressly said so), the service will likely have to fulfill the standards of specialists on a national level. There are, of course, some differences among states on this matter, but the trend is definitely toward nationwide specialty standards, and some states have even codified this principle into statutory law.

To illustrate this legal principle, *if* a practitioner of speech-language pathology or audiology made use of a personality test—say, the Minnesota Multiphasic Personality Inventory—and failed to detect a propensity for dangerousness, which then resulted in the personal injury or death of another, any lawsuit against the practitioner for failing to warn an intended victim would be difficult to defend against on the basis of "I'm no clinical psychologist." When one seeks the benefits, such as charging a patient for administering a personality test, one must be prepared to meet the liability, i.e., having the skills for administration, scoring, and interpretation of the personality tests that would be held by the reasonable, prudent user of the same test, essentially without regard for disciplinary identity. (The foregoing comments are not intended to endorse or prohibit a speech-language pathologist's or audiologist's use of a particular type of psychological test. Such authority remains with state licensure/certification laws and with the professional-ethical requirements of having established competency through training and usage.)

ISSUE NUMBER THREE: THE PRACTITIONER-PATIENT RELATIONSHIP

Entering the world of private practice places a significant degree of responsibility for the life of another person on the professional. This topic has, of course, been the subject of many treatises. Thus, the focus here is specifically on the legal liability associated with the relationship that is formed between the practitioner of speech-language pathology and audiology and his or her patients.

Legal Liability

Without a laborious itemization, suffice it to say that a professional code of ethics has the practitioner-patient relationship as its primary dimension. In other words, ethics proscribe and prescribe the tenets of the relationship. Some professions have become very specific about that relationship in their ethics codes, such as declaring that any sexual contact between a professional and patient is an ethical violation. In the Code of Ethics for the ASHA (1984), it is stated, "Individuals must not participate in activities that constitute a conflict of professional interest" (p. 2). For a practitioner to socialize or enter into financial dealings with a patient can potentially create a conflict of professional interest.

Probably most violations of the professional-patient relationship occur because of faulty handling of transference or countertransference.* As might be surmised from earlier comments about the theoretical framework for practice, any extratherapeutic relationship between the professional and the patient will be difficult, or more likely impossible, to justify by a theory of intervention. Nontraditional notions about treatment are likely to be evaluated legally by a comparison to traditional notions, some of which may have only tenuous relevance to the nontraditional ideas (Glenn, 1974), and any attempt to justify a deviation from the traditional professional-patient relationship, such as a sexual involvement, will find little or no legal recognition (Woody, 1983b).

The training received by practitioners of speech-language pathology and audiology may create a problem in this regard. A student's supervisory relationship would logically be an ideal laboratory for developing skills for handling transference and countertransference. Although not necessarily reflective of the training done in most institutions, Pickering's (1984) sampling of interpersonal communication in speech-language pathology supervisory conferences revealed that there were few in-depth analyses of issues associated with interpersonal concerns involving patients, i.e., the focus was solution-oriented. Of more general concern, the legal framework for the practitioner-patient framework is uncompromising in the requirement that the patient's welfare is primary. Consequently, no training is complete until a sense of *definition* for and a *control* of the practitioner-patient relationship have been inculcated.

Ethical Issues

Although an ethical dictate should not be confused with a legal dictate, in point of fact there is a distinct connection between the two. If a profession maintains an ethical premise for the benefit of the public, the court would surely view the premise as a part of the standard of care that should apply to the practitioner. Some state statutes have incorporated, by reference, a disciplinary code of ethics. An ethical principle that is phrased as a general intent would not likely be a behavioral prescription per se, but one that delineates proscriptions would likely be deemed to constitute a standard to be fulfilled.

ISSUE NUMBER FOUR: INVOLVEMENT WITH OTHER PRACTITIONERS

A commonly held concern among private practitioners, regardless of discipline, is that there is little contact with other professionals. That is, a schedule filled with one-to-one appointments—hour after hour, day after day, week after week, and so on—often leaves the practitioner feeling alone and isolated from professional peers. This problem may be remedied by becoming a member of a group practice.

---

*Transference refers to a client's unconsciously motivated reaction to the therapist in a manner inappropriate to the current reality; countertransference refers to the same sort of conditions but as relevant to the therapist's reaction to the client (see Cherney, M.S. (1985). Countertransference revisited. *Journal of Counseling and Development, 63,* 362–364).

Group Practice: Pros and Cons

Group practice does, in fact, offer many advantages over solo practice. As noted in the preceding chapter, its benefits are often fiscal, such as being able to share and thereby reduce overhead costs for office rental, secretarial services, etc., and being able to make mutual referrals, i.e., to broaden the scope of services for the group practice and, in the process, promote a larger clientele. There are also such professional benefits as having consultation about difficult cases readily available. And, of course, there is the benefit of having a colleague with whom the trials and tribulations of everyday practice may be shared over a cup of coffee.

So much for the benefits. What about the disadvantages? Unfortunately, today's litigious era creates numerous legal liabilities for professionals in group practices. Moreover, the legal liabilities extend beyond the formal group practice into some rather casual professional relationships.

Vicarious Liability

The basic legal principle of concern is *vicarious liability*. That is, one receives liability through a relationship with another source (Kionka, 1977). Traditionally, there has been a "master-servant" liability, whereby an employer is held liable for the actions of his or her employee. This is a relationship from which one person, the employer, benefits—read: financially benefits—from the actions of another, the employee. Consequently, when the employee is negligent and damages occur to a third party, there is negligence imputed to the employer. Indeed, this principle goes beyond negligence and is really an application of liability to all who are parties to, among other things, a joint venture or enterprise.

The model for vicarious liability is drawn from medical malpractice (King, 1977), but it is applicable to speech-language pathologists and audiologists in group practice. For example, although there may be innocence as to personal fault, if there is a relationship between practitioner one and practitioner two, and the faulted practitioner (number one) was within the contemplated scope of that relationship (within a group practice) when damage is incurred by his or her patient, the faultless practitioner (number two) can be held liable for the liability-producing acts of the other practitioner. To illustrate, if practitioners one and two were members of a group practice, and if there was mutual consultation about cases, albeit perhaps informally, and especially if there were mutual financial benefits from the association, either practitioner would likely be held liable for the actions of the other practitioner.

Vicarious liability extends to the functioning and conduct of nonprofessional support personnel, such as secretaries, technicians, and students, who are associated with the professional. Given the direct and indirect financial benefits presumed to come from having support personnel, any act by a support person is considered legally to be under the auspices of the professional. Even if the act was not known to the professional, the legal principle holds that the professional should maintain reasonable safeguards, such as monitoring *all* acts with *all* patients. Failure to do so could result in liability because the professional *should have known* about the support person's contact with the patient.

In the concept of vicarious liability there is a strong legal message for the private practitioner of speech-language pathology and audiology. The first dictum is: Do not get involved with any other practitioner, including support personnel, without a thorough knowledge of his or her competencies and personal/professional values. The second dictum is: Do not continue with any other practitioner without adequate qualitative treatment safeguards for the welfare of any and all patients.

Many private practitioners affiliate after only becoming minimally familiar with each other, often simply to save money, such as overhead expenses. In the long term, however, the monetary risk may be high and the liability unreasonable to accept. Casual affiliations should be avoided.

When an affiliation is based on mutual professional respect, there should always be a case-monitoring system, which should be applied to *all* cases of *every* professional. To allow a professional to self-select the cases that will be reviewed or supervised by colleagues is to court disaster. If a colleague is, in fact, guilty of negligent behavior and knows it—for example having a sexual contact with a patient—it is certainly unlikely that this behavior will be voluntarily shared with colleagues, even though they potentially hold liability for his or her actions.

There should also be a standardized diagnostic system applied to all patients. Given the duty to warn, it seems particularly important to have some method for inquiring about signs of dangerousness to self or others. If the practitioner lacks the skills for this function, such as not being competent in clinical-diagnostic interviewing about depression and acting out or not being able to interpret personality test data, the required solution may be to hire a consultant, e.g., a clinical psychologist or psychiatrist. This is one of the expenses necessary for being in business, notwithstanding all pretensions of professionalism, private practice is a business!

One potential problem area involves students. To be connected to a university training program is enticing, especially for private practitioners who have experienced the previously discussed professional isolationism. Such a training function can, indeed, spice up an otherwise routine practice and contribute to the development of the discipline. **Supervision Issues**

Before considering the legal aspects of supervising a student, the ethical consideration should be noted. The Code of Ethics of the ASHA (1984) is clear-cut on this matter, stating, "Individuals must not offer clinical services by supportive personnel for whom they do not provide appropriate supervision and assume full responsibility" (p. 2).

Legally, the private practitioner is liable for a student's actions, just as he or she is liable for any other associates, such as a paraprofessional aide or other support personnel. Consequently, it is best to select carefully the types of cases and kinds of services with which the student or aide/support person will deal and allow that individual to be involved with the patient only under supervision. If the supervisory time is too costly—after all, it does take the practitioner away from what would otherwise be income-generating services—then this is a proscription against accepting the responsibility of being a trainer. Experience reveals that students seldom, if ever, bring in enough fees to cover the supervisory time. Thus, it should be recognized that the payoff for accepting the students will certainly be other than financial.

ISSUE NUMBER FIVE: A LEGAL-PRAGMATIC FRAMEWORK FOR PRIVATE PRACTICE

By this point, Van Riper's (1978) statement about private practice being "no bed of roses" should have acquired a special legal meaning. Although the private practice of speech-language pathology and audiology affords a viable employment alternative, one that can be personally and professionally stimulating and rewarding, today's world of private practice regardless of discipline or specialty carries a degree of legal liability that is basically unequalled in other employment realms. This should not, however, dissuade entry into the private practice of speech-language pathology and audiology. What the contemporary focus on legal liability does mean, however, is that there must be prudence and pragmatism, as opposed to zeal and greed. The following worthwhile guidelines should allow one to circumvent unnecessary legal liability.

Private practice should be conducted with a commitment to a high standard of quality care, as might be expected of an ordinary, reasonable, and prudent professional. There should be no false pretenses of competency, and care should be taken to ensure that patients have a clear understanding of the private practitioner's qualifications and a realistic expectation of treatment risks and benefits.

Diagnostic and treatment interventions should be carefully planned and be based on a solid academic rationale. Detailed records are in the best interest of both the patients and the private practitioner. (See also Chapters 4, 9, and 10 on record keeping.) Limits of confidentiality or privileged communications should be specified, including an orientation to the power of a subpoena, the duty to warn of dangerousness, the right of a health insurance carrier to obtain otherwise confidential information, and, in some instances, an employer's potential access to the information transmitted to the health insurance carrier. Remember that the foregoing is also referred to in the ASHA's (1984) Code of Ethics, that states, "Individuals must not reveal to unauthorized persons any professional or personal information obtained from the person served professionally, unless required by law or unless necessary to protect the welfare of the person or the community" (p. 1). Any innovative or experimental procedure should be reviewed and approved by professional peers. There should be strict adherence to a doctor-patient model for the relationship with *every* patient; the private practitioner is particularly vulnerable to criticism and/or legal action if he or she enters into a nonprofessional relationship with a patient.

Recognize that private practice is a "business." Do not let a patient accrue a deficit in payment. Many a practitioner has allowed a patient to build up a sizable debt for services. Although this may consciously be done for the convenience of the patient or in the name of altruism and nurturance, in point of fact this practice is often connected to financial gain. Consciously or unconsciously, the private practitioner may be considering the risk of not getting paid to be secondary to the prospect of losing payment by referring the patient elsewhere, such as to a public tax-supported clinic where the client would not have to pay. This faulty judgment may reflect poor (unethical?) business practice and clinical malfeasance. Wright (1981a) found that 12.3 percent of complaints against psychologists were in response to an attempt to collect a fee due for services. He further asserts, "Be aware that in allowing a substantial unpaid balance to build up, the practitioner may, by that action, negatively affect the therapeutic relationship or, in unstructured circumstances, court a malpractice action when the effort is ultimately made to collect the bill'' (Wright, 1981b, p. 1541). There is every reason to believe that these findings apply equally to the private practitioner of speech-language pathology and audiology.

Another business reality is to accept that the private practice of speech-language pathology and audiology requires certain expenses. For example, arranging for a clinical supervisor, learning to rely on an attorney, and carrying malpractice insurance that covers both damages *and* the cost of legal representation are each important. Also, one should accept the notion that when a legal question is raised, it is best to set aside any thought of having a "therapeutic encounter" with the patient in favor of having an attorney deal with the matter. The decision to deal personally with a disgruntled patient, rather than paying an attorney to do so in a legally proper fashion, may be another vestige of greed. An attempt to save on legal fees, which are, in fact, a tax-deductible business expense, and to try to salvage the patient for future business is faulty in concept.

The majority of legal claims by patients probably classify as nuisance suits (Wright, 1981b). Nonetheless, one bad legal case can destroy a private practice, even if the practitioner is innocent of any wrongdoing. Chapter 4 discusses professional liability in further detail.

SUMMARY

Speech-language pathology and audiology has matured into a well-defined, publicly endorsed profession. The caveat offered is that one of the accoutrements of professionalism is liability. One must set aside the "Ivory Tower" notions on which training is commonly predicated and adopt an unabashed business orientation. In other words, just as a businessperson does not incur unnecessary risks, so the practitioner has a large investment and must safeguard against any loss of potential benefits. Many of the author's legal clients from the human service professions still sound apologetic when they speak of their earnings from their services. Such reticence is, in fact, unprofessional and jeopardizes the quality of service to the patient and our society, as well as exacerbating the legal vulnerability of the practitioner. Stated differently, it is essential to recognize that human service is more than healing; it is an industry that is subject to societal regulations and sanctions. The law protects only those practitioners who maintain allegiance to a contemporary service delivery model.

REFERENCES

American Psychological Association. (1985). California passes duty-to-protect bill. *Health and Services Support Network*.

American Speech-Language-Hearing Association. (1984). Code of ethics (revised January 1, 1979). Rockville, MD: Author.

Butler, K.G., & Wallach, G.P. (1984). The final word: From theory to therapy. In G.P. Wallach and K.G. Butler (Eds)., *Language learning disabilities in school age children* (pp. 360–364). Baltimore: Williams & Wilkins.

Catlin, F.I. (1984). Studies of normal hearing. *Audiology, 23*, 241–252.

Demorest, M.E., & Walden, B.E. (1984). Psychometric principles in the selection, interpretation, and evaluation of communication self-assessment inventories. *Journal of Speech and Hearing Disorders, 49*, 226–240.

Glenn, R.D. (1974). Standard of care in administering non-traditional psychotherapy. *University of California, Davis Law Review, 7*, 56–83.

Goldfarb v. Virginia State Bar. (1975). 421 U.S. 733.

King, J.H., Jr. (1977). *The law of medical malpractice in a nutshell.* St. Paul, MN: West Publishing Co.

Kionka, E.J. (1977). *Torts in a nutshell: Injuries to persons and property.* St. Paul, MN: West Publishing Co.

Knapp, S., & Vandecreek, L. (1982). Tarasoff: Five years later. *Professional Psychology, 13*, 511–516.

Pickering, M. (1984). Interpersonal communication in speech-language pathology supervisory conferences: A qualitative study. *Journal of Speech and Hearing Disorders, 49*, 189–195.

Prosser, W.L. (1971). *Handbook of the law of torts* (4th ed.). St. Paul, MN: West Publishing Co.

Roth, F., & Spekman, N.J. (1984). Assessing the pragmatic abilities of children: Part 1. Organizational framework and assessment parameters. *Journal of Speech and Hearing Disorders, 49*, 2–11. (a)

Roth, F., & Spekman, N.J. (1984). Assessing the pragmatic abilities of children: Part 2. Guidelines, considerations, and specific evaluation procedures. *Journal of Speech and Hearing Disorders, 49*, 12–17. (b)

Van Riper, C. (1978). *Speech correction: Principles and methods* (6th ed.). Englewood Cliffs, NJ: Prentice-Hall.

Woody, R.H. (1983). Avoiding malpractice in psychotherapy. In P.A. Keller & L.B. Ritt (Eds.), *Innovations in clinical practice: A sourcebook. Volume II* (pp. 205–216). Sarasota, FL: Professional Resource Exchange. (a)

Woody, R.H. (1983). Ethical and legal aspects of sexual issues. In J.D. Woody & R.H. Woody (Eds.), *Sexual issues in family therapy* (pp. 153–167). Rockville, MD: Aspen Systems. (b)

Woody, R.H., & Associates. (1984). *The law and the practice of human services.* San Francisco, CA: Jossey-Bass.

Woody, R.H. (1985). Public policy, malpractice law, and the mental health professional: Some legal and clinical guidelines. In C.P. Ewing (Ed.), *Psychology, psychiatry, and the law* (pp. 509–525). Sarasota, FL: Professional Resource Exchange.

Wright, R.H. (1981). Psychologists and professional liability (malpractice) insurance: A retrospective review. *American Psychologist, 36*, 1485–1493. (a)

Wright, R.H. (1981). What to do until the malpractice lawyer comes: A survivor's manual. *American Psychologist, 36*, 1535–1541. (b)

Chapter 4

Professional Liability: Management and Prevention

Rebecca Kooper, J.D. and Carol A. Sullivan, M.S.

GLOSSARY

ANSWER: A pleading by which the defendant sets forth the grounds of his defense.

CIVIL LAW: Laws concerned with civil or private rights and remedies, as contrasted with criminal laws.

COMMON LAW: A body of principles which derives its authority from judgments of the courts.

COMPLAINT: The original or initial pleading by which an action is commenced.

DEFENDANT: The person against whom relief or recovery is sought in an action.

DEPOSITION: A form of discovery by addressing questions orally to a person.

INTERROGATORIES: A series of written questions drawn up for the purpose of being propounded to a party, witness or other person having information in the case.

NEGLIGENCE: The omission to do something which a reasonable man guided by ordinary considerations, which ordinarily regulate human affairs, would do, or the doing of something which a reasonable and prudent man would not do.

PLAINTIFF: A person who brings an action; the party who complains or sues in a civil action and so named on the record.

PROCESS SERVER: A person authorized by law to serve process papers on the defendant.

STATUTORY LAW: The body of law created by acts of the legislature in contrast to law generated by judicial opinions.

SUBPOENA DUCES TECUM: A process by which the court, at the instance of a party, commands a witness who has at his possession or control some document or papers that is pertinent to the issues of a pending controversy, to produce it at trial.

SUMMONS: An instrument used to commence a civil action.

TORT: A private or civil wrong or injury, other than a breach of contract, for which the court will provide a remedy in the form of an action for damages.

Source: Black's Law Dictionary by H. Black, 1979, St. Paul, MN: West Publishing Company. Copyright 1979 by West Publishing Company.

In addressing the needs of speech-language pathologists and audiologists in private practice, it is increasingly apparent that practitioners must continue to stay informed of current and future legal issues. It is well known that medical malpractice actions have been increasing in recent years. Americans are filing more than three times as many medical malpractice claims as they did 10 years ago and are winning record settlements, as reported by the American Medical Association (AMA Report, 1984). This trend is also reflected in the increased numbers of cases filed against professionals in the field of speech-language pathology and audiology as noted by the current provider of professional liability insurance for members of the American Speech-Language-Hearing Association (ASHA). A 10 percent increase of claims filed for the years 1980 through 1985 has been reported (Wohlers, personal communication, 1985).

This chapter provides a general overview of pending and litigated cases in the medical malpractice field and filed claims in speech-language and audiology. Specific recommendations derived from this analysis for the prudent management of private practice are suggested. The goal of this chapter is to give readers a legal and professional framework for maintaining an appropriate standard of care by providing information based on recent pending litigation that may permit the prevention of liability claims.

Due to the confidential nature of much of the material reviewed, it is not possible to cite specific information, dates, or places on a number of occasions. Such reticence permits the authors to analyze substantive legal issues emerging within the profession and, equally important, provides protection for all parties involved in litigation. Due to the unresolved nature of these cases the authors are unable to provide specific citations of cases when discussing issues pending litigation.

PROFES-SIONAL LIABILITY

Speech-language pathologists and audiologists must be fully aware of the personal and professional consequences of ignoring the possibility that one's professional competence may be called into question. It is well known that our society is becoming increasingly litigious. This may be due to a number of factors, including increased public awareness of the legal process, increased understanding of the potential for recovery of costs when an injury is deemed to be serious, a perceived deterioration of patient-professional relationships in the health field, and media publicity of medical malpractice awards. Each of these factors is examined in turn.

Increased Public Awareness of the Legal Process

Historically, use of the judicial system has been limited largely to the upper class. However, "justice for all" has been a goal of modern-day legislatures and judiciaries. The creation of small claims courts and legal clinics has opened the legal arena to those to whom it had previously been closed. In addition, many people have become more familiar with the legal system through such procedures as filing for divorce or attempting to resolve a work-related problem through union-initiated court procedures. This familiarity may encourage future use of the judicial power to resolve disputes if and when a situation ever arises in which a person feels unjustly injured, either monetarily or physically.

Degree of Injury

Legal action is tedious, time consuming, and expensive, thereby requiring considerable perseverance on the part of the individual who brings an action. Why then do individuals persevere? It appears that those who believe themselves to be significantly injured are more likely to persevere. There is a direct relationship between the degree of injury as measured in terms of duration and the extent of the liability for a disabling condition. For example, the failure to diagnose properly a profound hearing loss in a preschool child results in obvious long-term communicative impairments. At times, it may seem incomprehensible when individuals with minimal injuries initiate a legal action. However, understanding the reasoning that made this injury *appear* significant to the plaintiff will aid us in comprehending the factors that encourage an individual to initiate an action against a professional.

Deterioration of Patient-Professional Relationships: A Lesson from the Medical Field

The quality of the relationship between the injured party and the one accused of causing the injury becomes surprisingly important in determining whether the injured party will go to court. A breakdown in the professional relationship between two parties is often the factor that may change the patient's perception of an injury from insignificant to significant and thereby encourage the injured party to seek judicially determined compensation. It has been speculated that the increase in medical malpractice actions might be due, in part, to a breakdown in the relationship between the public and the medical profession (Dempsey, 1980). Such actions may be a result of the public's growing frustration with the medical field and health care services.

The sources of these frustrations are numerous. With the advent of medical clinics and medical group practices, patients may rarely see the same physician during consecutive visits and may therefore fail to establish the necessary relationship needed to ensure trust and respect. The high cost of a routine health care office visit is staggering. The time spent waiting to see a physician can sometimes be excessively lengthy. The increased specialization of the medical professionals leaves patients seeking various specialists, hoping to find the correct medical person to treat their ailments. This search is also time consuming, frustrating, and, very likely, expensive. Professionals in the field of speech-language pathology and audiology need to be aware of such frustrations with the medical field in general because they may affect allied health care professionals as well.

Media Publicity of Medical Malpractice Awards

There are, of course, other factors that may be contributing to the increase in malpractice actions initiated in the last two decades. Media publicity surrounding the award of high medical malpractice claims must have an effect. The fact that these awards are a rarity and are thereby noteworthy of media coverage is often overlooked by the public. The general public is unaware that most claims are settled out of court or dismissed because it is the few cases receiving large monetary settlements that tend to receive wide publicity. The possibility of a large award for a malpractice claim may encourage the public to file legal actions.

Professional Liability: A Definition

Professional liability is defined as negligent conduct on the part of a professional acting in his or her professional capacity (Roady & Andersen, 1960). The legal basis undergirding professional liability lawsuits is founded in tort law. A *tort* is a civil wrong that has caused physical injury. Tort law concerns itself with the compensation of an individual(s) who has suffered injuries due to the results of the acts of another. Determining when this compensation should be awarded and the specific amount to be awarded is the responsibility of the courts. The law of torts is divided primarily into two areas: intentional torts and negligence. The following discussion focuses only on negligence because this concept is the basis of professional liability actions.

Negligence law is concerned with compensating individuals who have been accidentally injured due to the acts of another party. It is involved with the establishment of a minimum standard of care to which we professionals, as members of society, must adhere in order to ensure the safety of others. For example, if someone loses control of his or her car due to a mechanical breakdown that should have been previously detected, the party responsible for detecting that breakdown is liable for any injuries caused by the subsequent accident. In other words, negligence exists if one fails to use ordinary care to avoid injury to others. **Negligence and the Law**

How has this standard of care to which we all must conform been defined? The courts have dealt with this problem of developing a *uniform* standard of behavior by using the "reasonable person" standard. Individuals are liable for their own negligence if their acts caused injury to another, and it is found that they failed to act the way a person of ordinary intelligence exercising reasonable judgment would have acted in order to prevent the injury (Roady & Andersen, 1960). It is irrelevant if the failure to conform to this "reasonable person" standard is due to forgetfulness, carelessness, or even an honest mistake. Motive is not an element to be considered.

There are two primary sources of laws that define a negligent action; statutory law and common law. Statutory laws are created by legislative bodies acting according to their constitutional power. Statutory laws can be created by federal, state, or local legislative bodies. For example, a state law requiring an audiologist to obtain a license to practice in that state is a statutory law. **What Are the Sources of the Definitions of Negligent Actions?**

In contrast, common laws are created by the development of legal principles from previously decided cases. Usually, a decision of an appellate court establishes a precedent to be followed in that jurisdiction if a similar fact situation should arise. Therefore the common law is of judicial origin and is ever-changing and regional. An example of common law would be the well-known case, *Brown v. Board of Education* (347US483, 1954), in which racial integration in public schools was judicially mandated. In this case, judicial law established legal precedence.

Although simple negligence is concerned only with a minimum standard of care to which one must conform, there are circumstances when higher standards are required. Professionals, when acting in a professional capacity, are expected to conform to a standard consistent with their professional expertise. As professionals in the field of speech-language pathology and audiology, we are expected to conform to a higher than "ordinary care" standard. However, because there is a lack of case law in our field, there has been no definitive standard developed through the common law. Therefore, as health-related professionals, we can only evaluate the standards that **What Are the Elements of a Professional Liability Action?**

have developed over time in other professional fields, especially in medicine. It would seem to be wise to anticipate what standards we could be required to follow.

Medical Malpractice and Professional Negligence

Medical malpractice is a form of professional negligence. The standard of care that has developed for physicians to follow is elevated to a level of skill that other members of the profession commonly possess and exercise. A failure to cure a patient is not in itself a sufficient basis for a medical malpractice action. There are essential elements that must be proved for a patient to prevail in an action, including the following:

- that there existed a relationship between the professional and the client
- that the professional breached some duty owed to the client
- that the breach was the proximate cause of an injury (Cramer, C., Cramer, D., 1983)

Standard of Care for Speech-Language Pathologists and Audiologists

The national association, ASHA, has established regulations requiring its members to obtain a Certificate of Clinical Competence (CCC) in either speech-language pathology or audiology if they are to engage in the delivery of clinical services. Practicing without appropriate certification would be considered to be a deviation from a standard of care because the professional association has set national standards for professional conduct.

In addition to ASHA certification, 36 states require speech-language pathologists and audiologists to be licensed by their own state licensing board in order to practice within their own state borders (ASHA, 1985). (See Appendix 2–C in Chapter 2 for a list of states that require licenses.) Practicing in those states without the requisite license would be equivalent to practicing below the acceptable standard established in those states.

Although the standard of care may have been thus established in those states requiring licensure, a more difficult standard to define is the standard that decides which professional decisions concerning clinical performance fall within our profession's reasonable standard of care. Decisions establishing the proper standard are reached only after the conclusions of trials where a ruling is based on expert testimony. In each case, expert witnesses are usually other certified speech-language pathologists or audiologists from the local area who would be most familiar with the facilities providing services in that jurisdiction. Such witnesses usually indicate their own ability to practice in the field by stating those professional certificates and/or licenses they possess and their professional experience and affiliations. They might be asked to describe the types of duties and responsibilities they encountered in their practices, as well as to give a description of the type of population with whom they work. In other words, their credibility as experts in the field must first be established. Then the witnesses are given the facts in the case and asked if, in their opinion, the treatment being questioned falls within the acceptable standard of care. The witnesses do not have to agree with the treatment that was given, but only must give an opinion regarding the acceptability of the treatment in their professional judgment. Likewise, the speech-language pathologists or audiologists whose treatment is being challenged need not prove that their treatment was the best treatment. They need only show that the treatment rendered is within the standard that most other professionals in the area would find to be acceptable or reasonable.

Guidelines for developing a professional standard of care in speech-language pathology and audiology are suggested below. Obviously, these suggestions are for the reader's consideration only and represent an attempt to stimulate thinking about determining how standards may be established that will best protect the consumers and the profession.

SUGGESTED GUIDELINES FOR ESTAB-LISHING A STANDARD OF CARE

It might appear to be an oversimplification to state that speech-language pathologists or audiologists are practicing within an acceptable standard of care as long as they perform the duties that they are professionally prepared to render. However, there are high-risk populations that are inherently problematic. For example, when evaluating the extent of an infant's hearing or attempting to establish the functional language age of a multihandicapped child, there are greater chances for error due to the possible limitations of such children's responsiveness. This example leads to the first suggested guideline for establishing a standard of care, proper evaluation.

Speech-language pathologists and audiologists have a duty to evaluate their clients properly. As an example, within the practice of audiology, certain safeguards are necessary in order to best serve the patient and the professional. When audiologists perform evaluations on infants, it is best to utilize some of the objective tests available today (BSER and impedance audiometry) as a supplement to standard behavioral testing. Having another professional independently confirm your diagnosis may also serve as an excellent safeguard against future legal action.

A Duty to Evaluate Prop-erly

One must also exercise caution when reporting to parents that their infant child appears to be hearing within the norms established for his or her age group. For instance, behavioral audiological testing of an infant does not indicate if the child has hearing within 20dB HL, the established level for normal hearing, but only gives normative data for the child's responses according to developmentally established norms for a specific age group. Therefore, parents need to be advised about the limitations of the testing procedure and of the need to return for further testing at specific intervals until it can be shown that a child responds at 20dB. In another case, speech-language pathologists should advise parents of the limitations of the diagnostic instruments used for evaluating their child. Indeed, in both cases, the fact that the parents are so advised should be carefully documented by professionals in their records and filed for ready access.

Other problems may also arise when informing parents that their child's hearing appears to be within normal limits. For example, if there is a history of genetically caused deafness that has been determined either through genetic counseling or through a carefully taken history of hearing loss in other family members, the parents must be advised that there is a possibility that the child's hearing may deteriorate within the first few years of life. Arrangements should be made for periodic evaluations as well. Again, the dissemination of this advice should be carefully entered into the child's record.

In the area of speech-language pathology, other sensitive situations may occur. A common example is the placement and participation of speech-language pathologists on evaluation teams or committees for the handicapped in schools, hospitals, and rehabilitation centers. At times the speech-language pathologist may disagree with the conclusions reached by the team. Although in the minority concerning the outcomes of the evaluation or recommended treatment of a client, it is important that the clinician's opinion be noted for the record. As a member of a team, it is recommended that the speech-language pathologist make his or her position known through a written statement. In this statement, the clinician's conclusions and recommendations should be clearly stated and should include the reasons supporting this minority opinion. This statement should be placed in the patient's records or in the client's file.

A Duty to Provide Competent Treatment and Counsel with Informed Consent

The goal of therapy, even when it is delivered by a competent clinician, cannot always be a "cured patient." The *limitations* of any therapeutic process must be carefully explained to patients or to their parents when therapy is initiated. At that time, the results of any assessments and a plan of treatment should be discussed. Progress should be reviewed after an evaluation period, and decisions to continue treatment must be made *with*, not *for*, the patient.

Many of the same concerns hold true in audiological practice. The audiologist also has a responsibility to provide proper counsel and treatment, particularly when recommending a hearing aid. A recent case in the U.S. District Court addressed itself to the issue of product design of hearing aids and professional responsibility when injuries occur due to the pediatric ingestion of hearing aid batteries. In this case, the parent of a hearing-impaired child brought a legal action against the hearing aid manufacturer after the child ingested a hearing aid battery. The battery was surgically removed with subsequent complications and injury to the child. The legal action against the manufacturer claimed faulty product design for failure to provide a child-proof battery compartment. Subsequently, the manufacturer sued the audiologist who dispensed the hearing aid, claiming failure to properly counsel the parent regarding inherent dangers of batteries to children. The case went to a jury trial and it was concluded that the manufacturer was guilty of product-design failure and failure to provide adequate warning in their literature to the dispenser. The parent was found guilty of negligence to the extent of 15%. Charges against the audiologist were dismissed as the audiologist had counseled the parent both verbally and in written material regarding the cautious handling of hearing aid batteries and their insertion. (*Piersa v. Oticon*, 1986). At the time of publication, this case is pending in the U.S. Court of Appeals.

The benefits and limitations of hearing aid use should be carefully explained to adults as well. Patients need to understand that a hearing aid does not restore hearing to normal. Also, medical clearance for the fitting of a hearing aid is required by Food and Drug Administration (FDA) regulations. Although adults may waive this requirement, the audiologist may bear full responsibility for any medical complications that arise from a fitting based on a waiver of medical clearance. It is recommended that this clearance be obtained for each client, rather than accepting a waiver.

With the advent of impedance audiometry, audiologists can obtain much information about the function of the outer or middle ear. If tympanometric testing reveals a problem in either area, the patient should be sent for an otological evaluation to determine the nature of the problem, because such a diagnosis falls within the domain of medicine.

The importance of genetic hearing loss has already been discussed. A recent California Supreme Court ruling reinforced the importance of recommending that parents seek genetic counseling if there is any possibility that the cause of their child's hearing loss may be genetic. Again, this recommendation should be recorded and entered into the child's file (*Turpin v. Sortini*, Cal, 643, P 2d 954).

Another issue that arises soon after the confirmation of a child's hearing loss is the type of program the child should enter for language, speech, and auditory training. It is the clinician's role to provide information to the parents regarding available educational programs. It is wise to explain carefully the difference between total communication and oral schools of thought, as well as the differences between oral-aural programs and oral-visual programs. Parents should be encouraged to visit different sites. Because the child is the primary responsibility of the parents, the selection of educational philosophy rests with the parents. Although professionals may have certain biases in this area, this is not the time to impose such educational biases on the parents. Rather, it is imperative that parents understand all alternatives before they make this important decision.

A Duty to Refer

Speech-language pathologists often become specialists in specific subareas of expertise within the larger field. Although national certification in speech-language pathology may attest to the professional's competence across areas of the field, many professionals believe that the extent of information currently available is so great as to preclude one person from gaining expertise in all areas. Thus, accepting a client who needs highly specialized services that are not within the clinician's greatest areas of expertise should be done only if sufficient professional supervision can be obtained.

Specialization problems may present themselves in audiological practice as well. Some audiologists see a great number of infants and become quite proficient in infant audiological evaluations, whereas others may rarely see an infant in their offices. Prudence dictates that the professionals who have any doubt about their ability to evaluate a certain class of patient should refer such patients to another audiologist.

DISPUTE RESOLUTION: LEGAL PROCESSES

States that license speech-language pathologists and audiologists have set standards that govern the profession, and they have the power to enforce those standards by monitoring professional conduct. Specific state agencies usually have the power to impose penalties for professional misconduct, which may include censure, fine, or license suspension or revocation. Professionals should consult their state's licensing board to determine which agency handles complaints from the public concerning professional malpractice or misconduct and to learn what powers this agency possesses.

Where Are Complaints against Professionals Likely to Be Filed?

The public may also file complaints with the ASHA Ethical Practice Board. Its role is to determine if a speech-language pathologist or audiologist has violated any provision in the ASHA Code of Ethics. After an investigation, if a violation is found, this board has the power to (1) censure, (2) issue a cease-and-desist order, (3) withhold or revoke membership, (4) withhold, suspend, or revoke the CCC, or (5) take other measures it deems appropriate. However, it should be noted that financial compensation for an injury can *only* be awarded by the judicial system. The professional becomes part of this adversarial system the moment he or she is handed a summons by the process server that orders a court appearance or to answer a complaint by a specific time. The summons names the parties to the action; that is, it may name the client as the "plaintiff" and the professional as the "defendant." A complaint that outlines the grounds for the action may either be served with the summons or may follow soon thereafter. In the complaint, the elements necessary to prove a professional liability action must be supported by a statement of the facts that led to an injury for which the plaintiff seeks compensation.

Responding to a Complaint or Summons

On receipt of this summons and/or complaint, it is highly recommended that you contact your attorney and your insurance representative immediately. Do not talk to anyone else about the case until you have sought legal counsel. Act promptly because you are now operating under certain legal time constraints. Your attorney must respond to the complaint promptly with an answer. This document either admits, denies, or claims ignorance of each of the plaintiff's allegations. When meeting with your attorney before he or she writes your answer, be prepared to tell all the facts pertinent to the case. Do not withhold information that you feel may be damaging. Your attorney is able to best judge which facts will be helpful in developing a proper defense. Remember to bring all the records that you have kept concerning this patient. The more the attorney knows, the better able he or she will be to prepare an answer that contains all the defenses that are vital to the protection of your rights and provide evidence that answers your patient's claims. Remember, too, that whatever you say to your attorney is confidential, and this confidence is protected by law.

Once the complaint and the answer have changed hands, certain pretrial discovery procedures may be initiated that enable each party to obtain information about the adversary's case. Evidence is acquired either through deposition or interrogations or by issuing a subpoena duces tecum. *Subpoena duces tecum* is a subpoena requiring one party to bring certain papers or documents to the court for the other party to examine. A *deposition* is a party's statement made under oath in response to an oral question by the litigant's counsel. Answers are then recorded and typed for use at the trial. *Interrogatories* are written questions devised by one party and served on the adversary who supplies written answers under oath.

Most cases are settled during this stage of the proceedings. When this occurs, there is *no* determination of liability. This is a compromise achieved by the opposing parties, which eliminates the need for judicial resolution of the controversy by the opposing parties. When deciding when to accept a settlement, carefully consider the advice of your attorney.

There are many definitions of insurance, but a key underlying concept is the anticipation of losses through prediction and the transferring of the financial burden of the losses (Huebner, Black, & Cline, 1968). The insurer estimates potential loss based on prior experience and potential future claims. The rate per unit of exposure is then established. The insured party elects to transfer the risk to an insurance company on acceptance of terms set forth, and the company provides coverage for an established rate.

There are numerous types of insurance that are appropriate for consideration in private practice, some of which have been discussed in other chapters. Property and general liability insurance are primary categories for coverage. It is *general liability insurance* that provides the speech-language pathologist and audiologist with financial protection from personal and corporate liability should patients physically injure themselves on business or personal property. It is *professional liability insurance* that provides financial protection for legal representation for claims of a professional nature and, if faced with a judgment against you, provides financial compensation to the limit of your policy.

INSURANCE

As can be seen, private practice is a small business that is vulnerable to a variety of problems that may result in a loss of assets. There are three principal areas of loss that are vital to the survival and success of a business enterprise. The first is the cost of loss or damage to tangible and intangible property; the second is the cost of indemnification of others due to the conduct of business resulting in legal liability; and the third is the cost of loss of productivity due to the death or disability of those individuals who are involved in the operation of the business (Castle, Cushman, Kensicki, 1981). In addition, in private practice consideration must be given to the provision of health, disability, homeowner's, automobile, and employee insurance benefit plans. Such plans are discussed in Chapters 5 and 8. This chapter addresses primarily the topics of general liability insurance and professional liability insurance. Unlike other types of insurance, *liability insurance* only compensates third parties for injuries. The current trend of the increased numbers of liability claims filed and the publicized large settlements identified earlier should serve as an inducement for all private practitioners to acquire appropriate and sufficient liability coverage.

Types of Insurance for Private Practice

The alternative to insurance is to assume personal financial responsibility for any injuries that may occur on your property or for any potential professional liability claims. You may determine that your risk is minimal, and hence the possibilities of a claim being filed against you are negligible. Should you determine that you prefer to be self-insured, you need to be financially prepared to hire attorneys to represent you whether you consider the case to be valid or not. If a judgment is made against you, you will need to provide funds for the court-determined settlement cost. Considering these obligations, most professionals prefer to limit their personal loss through the purchase of insurance.

What Is the Alternative to Insurance?

Who Can Be Insured?

The ASHA group insurance plan provides professional liability insurance to the speech-language pathologist or audiologist who is a member of ASHA and who holds the CCC or who is in the process of obtaining it. In addition, professional liability insurance is available for student members of the National Student Speech-Language-Hearing Association (NSSLHA).

The availability of insurance outside the professional organizational domain is more problematic. Recent increased exposure for medical and health care providers in the area of malpractice has significantly reduced the availability of coverage and agencies who write policies. Because malpractice suits have the potential for high settlement claims and cases have a "long tail"—that is, a relatively long period of time between the incident and the final disposition—higher litigation costs result. When seeking to obtain professional liability insurance other than through ASHA, insurance agents must be contacted and inquiries made about potential underwriters who can provide a specific policy.

In What Work Settings Will Your Insurance Provide Coverage?

There are two types of professional liability policies. One type covers an individual who works as an employee and does not engage in private practice. The definition of an employee is one who works for another party whereby the company deducts payroll taxes from wages earned. The second type provides insurance to the self-employed individual who may work in a private practice as an individual whose federal income and Social Security taxes are not deducted from the wages. The self-employed person may be practicing as an individual with or without a trade name, may be a member of a legal partnership, or may be incorporated, owning all or part of the stock, although listed as an employee of the corporation (Wohlers, personal communication, 1985).

Professional contracts that extend a private practice to hospitals, nursing homes, or agencies require additional coverage to extend liability insurance coverage for those work settings. Clinicians whose primary work setting is in the public school, hospital, or agency and who provide clinical services to part-time private practices should obtain additional coverage for their private practice. Failure to provide proper coverage places a clinician in a position of high risk.

Who Is Responsible for Employee Liability?

If your private practice has employees, you, as the employer, are liable for their professional acts of negligence. Liability suits that are filed will be against *you*; as an employer you need to provide coverage for yourself against acts of negligence by an employee. Coverage is available through the ASHA insurance plan entitled "Contingent liability of employer for acts of employee." This coverage is required for *each* employee in your employment.

Variables That May Determine Degrees of Exposure

The degree of exposure to litigation may vary according to geographic area. Such states as New York, California, Illinois, and Florida have the highest incidence of medical malpractice claims. In addition, suburban areas have a higher rate of claims than rural areas.

The type of clinical services performed also varies in the degree of risk involved. A review of the cases filed through the ASHA professional liability insurer indicated that the failure to diagnose hearing disorders was a more prevalent area of litigation than failure to diagnose a speech-language disorder (Wohlers, personal communication, 1985). Thus far, audiology has a greater exposure to potentially high-risk situations. For example, audiological procedures that include the making of earmolds and clinical tests, such as ENG with caloric stimulation, provide greater risk as they are invasive procedures. In a 1981 survey of private practitioners in 48 states, it was noted that 56 percent of all clinical service was for hearing-impaired patients (Chapey, Chwat, Gurland, & Pieras, 1981). The need to acquire and to provide professional liability insurance in private practice settings where audiological services are given becomes apparent by virtue of the statistical risk measures alone.

In speech-language pathology, cases that have an underlying organic basis requiring medical or surgical intervention prior to speech therapy also pose greater risk. For example, failure to refer cases in which symptoms can be observed for medical evaluation and treatment is crucial. Underlying organicity that, if untreated, would impede the efficacy of speech therapy or endanger the patient's health may result in questions regarding standards of care. Clients with voice disorders should be examined by a referring physician. Patients who have symptoms of velopharyngeal insufficiency, neurological impairment, cleft palate, or possible hearing loss should be medically examined before treatment. A letter or report from the physician should be obtained *prior* to treatment. It is advisable that therapy for these patients be provided by a speech-language pathologist or audiologist who is experienced and knowledgeable in the specific disorder.

Age of the Clients as a Risk Factor

The age of the population served is an important variable. As reported previously, the audiological diagnosis of infants and preschool children represents a potential liability because the results may be contingent on subjective clinical observations and history taking from parents.

Age as a factor, when paired with a multihandicapping condition, tends to increase the risk factor exponentially due to the lessening of the potential accuracy of the patient's responses. Evaluations of patients, who by virtue of age or disability are unable to respond, require that data be collected from a family member. This information is as accurate as the perceptions of the informant and interpretative ability of the clinician allow. Thus, the accuracy of the data is contingent on the informant/ clinician dyad, and this must be noted in the written report. Evaluations that are subjective by nature of age provide higher risk.

In the area of general liability, elderly patients represent a high-risk population due to the higher incidence of falls, which increases the potential for personal injury on the practitioner's property.

How Much Coverage Is Needed?

When determining the amount of insurance coverage to obtain, the variables listed previously, including geographic location, type of clinical services rendered, and the age of the clinical population, are important factors. The number of employees that the policy covers is an additional consideration. The risk is increased as the number of employees is increased. In addition, the risk is higher if the employees are performing their professional duties at locations where direct supervision is not provided. Hiring policies need to include the ascertainment of professional credentials not only to verify qualifications but also to establish whether or not direct supervision may be necessary.

The amount of coverage currently available through the ASHA-approved professional liability insurance varies in the two plans offered. Plan 1 offers $1 million for each claim and $1 million for each year. Plan 2 offers $1 million for each claim and $3 million for each year. In selecting the plan that would be most suitable for your practice, consider the applicability of the variables noted above to your practice.

Where Can Professional Liability Insurance Be Obtained?

Insurance can be obtained by writing to the following address:

ASHA Group Insurance Plans
1500 Higgins Road
Park Ridge, Illinois 60068

What Types of Insurance Coverage Are Available Through the ASHA Insurance Plans?

The following types of coverage were available as of 1986.

- business ownership
- contingent liability of employer for acts of an employee
- employee coverage
- additional insured coverage
- comprehensive general, including product liability

If comprehensive general insurance is purchased, then the practitioner may select any or all of the following: (1) nonowned automobile liability, (2) personal injury liability, and (3) fire-legal liability.

What Are the Liability Risks of an Office in a Home Setting?

As indicated in Chapter 2, there are specific potential liability considerations when establishing a private practice in a home setting, whether it is full- or part-time. Office space that is located as an integral part of living space is difficult to arrange in order to meet the needs of both patients and family. In terms of personal liability, exposure to family dogs may lead to an unexpected occurrence of dog bites and subsequent injury. If young children reside within the home, toys or other objects in traffic pathways may be a safety hazard.

In addition, a private practice in a home environment may necessitate both external and interior modifications. For example, safe parking must be provided, as well as safe sidewalks. Paths or sidewalks to the home area must be well lit and free of snow or ice during winter months. If patients with physical handicaps are seen, there must be a provision of special railings or ramps for at least one entryway.

Planning for unexpected emergencies that may arise during the loss of electrical power or in hazardous weather conditions must be undertaken in order to prevent possible injuries. For example, specific provisions need to be considered for emergency lighting if there is a power outage. In addition, exits need to be marked in order to meet local fire codes. Fire alarm systems should be installed to provide maximum safety for occupants in the home.

As noted in Chapter 5, when leasing space in a commercial building, an inquiry must be made before signing a lease agreement about the insurance coverage on the building and the terms or conditions of the insurance contract. Private practices located in commercial buildings typically provide their own liability insurance that covers their immediate office. They must be certain to name the building owner as an additional insured party to the policy. The building owner carries a liability policy in addition to the office tenant's policy. This additional policy covers any potential accidents that could occur in the building hallways, stairs, parking lots, or elevators.

What Kind of Liability Insurance Is Needed in Commercial Buildings?

When planning a private practice, current trends in the numbers and frequency of professional liability and personal liability claims necessitate being well informed, as well as protected from any unforeseen event, however improbable it may seem at the time the practice is established. Obtaining appropriate insurance is one means of reducing risk. In the insurance industry, risk is thought of as the raw material of insurance. The term "risk" is defined as "uncertainty as to financial loss" (Huebner, Black, & Cline, 1982). Private practitioners, unlike speech-language pathologists or audiologists who work in institutional settings, must provide the necessary protection to retain personal and business assets. Once this protection is secured for a private practice, considerations must be given to the prevention of litigious occurrences.

PREVENTING LITIGATION

The most effective time to analyze potential professional liability is before a legal action is brought against you. A proactive approach that includes becoming informed about current litigation in the field and knowledgeable about the standard of care as it evolves through litigation presents the opportunity to implement procedures or actions to avoid similar litigious occurrences or recurrences.

Proactive Concepts

Although the number of cases that have been filed for legal action remains relatively small in number, it is growing each year. As noted earlier in this chapter, the standard of care for reasonable practice is established in the courts through the processing of legal actions. Where the standard of care is unclear so that a jury would have difficulty determining whether a doctor, speech-language pathologist, or audiologist had complied with it, it behooves professionals to do more than is technically required by the professional norm as they perceive it (Leiberman, 1981). To apply this concept to speech-language pathology and audiology, it is advisable not only to be fully knowledgeable of the Code of Ethics of ASHA but also to keep abreast of current literature and practice in the field and to apply these principles to the highest standard of patient care.

Patient-professional relationships are established both through interpersonal dynamics and through the organization of the office facility, business process, and selection of personnel. The relationship with a patient begins with the referral source and continues through such steps as the making of appointments, locating the private

The Patient-Professional Relationship

practice office, involvement in the therapeutic process, the paying of bills, the filing of insurance claims, and the termination of therapy. Throughout this process, the patient and the professional share responsibility in the relationship. The patient's responsibility is primarily to one's self in seeking professional care. The degree to which a patient chooses to facilitate the process is an individual decision. However, the basic framework for the therapeutic process is typically established by the professional, as noted by Woody (1984). The professional has a responsibility to provide a standard of care to the patient that "preserves the highest standards of integrity and ethical principles vital to the successful discharge of responsibilities of all Members and Associates" (ASHA Code of Ethics, 1983).

By assuming responsibility for providing the highest standard of care, the professional undoubtedly lessens the possibilities for litigation. The fundamentals for the standard of care may be found in the most recent revision of the Code of Ethics of the ASHA (see Appendix A). These standards provide an excellent guide for professional conduct, because the underlying intent of the Code of Ethics is to provide consumer protection. The ASHA Code of Ethics has broadened over recent years as the scope of professional practice has become more clearly identified. As part of maintaining a standard of care, it is advisable to stay apprised of revisions of the Code of Ethics.

Office Procedures: Another Basis for Prevention

Communication Considerations

The patient-professional relationship typically begins with a telephone call and the making of an appointment. The opportunity to establish rapport and to initiate the organization and maintenance of records of contact with the client is provided by the telephone call. If you are in a private practice, there must be public access to your office telephone number. It can be published in the *Yellow Pages* of the telephone directory under a professional heading, or if you prefer and are known by name, it can be listed in the White Pages of the directory. Additional listings may be available in professional service guides. If you are receiving referrals from other professionals, make up business cards available with your telephone number to be given to patients at the time of referral.

When the patient telephones the business number there should be either a responsible adult or a message-answering unit to receive the call. In establishing accountability for all telephone calls, the phone-O-gram message books, with NCR paper for immediate copies, provide an excellent record of patient contact. These books can be used for future documentation of patient contact if needed for court. When a home telephone is used for business purposes, difficulties can arise. Children may answer and fail to take messages, serving as a potential source of frustration and anger for patients.

Although the provision of appropriate telephone answering procedures may not seem important, the prompt returning of patients calls is essential in maintaining a healthy relationship. In reviewing medical court cases, one common complaint given to attorneys in the history-taking process of a case was, "I called and called to explain my problem but no one returned my calls." Unreturned phone calls convey to the patient the feeling of being ignored. If several attempts have been made unsuccessfully to reach a patient, it is wise to write a note informing the patient of your attempts to call and giving times and dates when you are available for phone contact. Be sure to maintain copies of this correspondence in the patient's file.

When telephone contact is made, an established procedure for making appointments is needed. It is helpful to set up an appointment book with specified times and dates prior to the patient contact. (See Chapters 10 and 13 on computer software for scheduling of appointments.) At the time the initial appointment is made, the patient needs to be informed fully of the appointment time, individual fee for service, and time of payment and must be able to ask questions regarding the professional services. This telephone conversation provides an opportunity to inform the patient fully of the nature of the clinical service. Directions to the office can be given over the telephone or, perhaps more efficiently, mailed to the patient before the time of the appointment. Doing so enables the patient to plan his or her time or the time of relatives and friends who provide transportation and increases the likelihood that the patient will be available at the appointed time.

Policies must be established about assigning appointment times for various procedures. Variables that may determine the length of the appointment include (1) age of the patient, (2) type of problem, (3) procedure to be performed, and (4) whether it is a first appointment. In addition, it is important to obtain the telephone number, address, and referral source when making the first appointment. This information is useful if there are unpredicted scheduling changes that necessitate contacting the patient. Facilitating this process lessens patient annoyance about unexpected changes and may serve to solidify a positive patient-professional relationship. An important aspect of setting the stage for such a positive relationship is the provision of information regarding patient fees.

Fees and Billing Considerations

Policies regarding fees for services and time of payment need to be established before seeing the patient. These policies should be written and available to all personnel who are in direct contact with the patient. The fees can be discussed with the patient at the time of the appointment or at the time the service is rendered.

If the practitioner is dispensing products, it should be noted that some states have consumer protection laws that require giving the consumer a written estimate of, say, hearing aid repairs. Whether consumer protection laws include hearing aids is interpreted on a state-by-state basis. When dispensing hearing aids, however, it is always helpful to the consumer if a contract stating costs and payment dates is available. This contract reduces the possibility for misunderstanding and potential conflict.

When consumers have a question regarding fees, they should be given straightforward answers. Individual fees should be established to reflect the average fees in the geographic area and should be commensurate with services rendered. Other considerations when establishing fees may be the fee schedules of other allied professionals, e.g., physical therapists, occupational therapists, psychologists, etc. (See Chapter 5 for suggested fee-setting formulas.)

Written Reports and Their Legal Implications

All requests for the release of information to a third party must be obtained in writing from the patient. Verbal permission to send a report, which is given either in person or over the telephone, is nonverifiable. Requests for patient information that are received from attorneys must include a release form signed by the patient. The only exception to this policy occurs in situations where the practitioner has been advised in writing that the parent of a child does not have authority under state law concerning matters of guardianship due to separation or divorce.

Maintenance of Written Records

The establishment of a patient record for appointments, fees and payments, insurance transactions, hearing aids dispensed, hearing aid repairs, battery sales, and hearing aid insurance is essential. This record may be kept by hand, typewritten, or placed on the computer. Initially, most records are kept manually. Appointments records can be maintained in the general appointment book. Notes should be made in the appointment book when a patient cancels an appointment or fails to come for the appointment. This information may serve as possible evidence for malpractice defense. The patient may be found responsible for contributory negligence for failing to keep appointments or obtain follow-up care.

A general ledger system maintains information for billing and signals the late payment of a fee. The late payment for services may alert the clinician that the patient is dissatisfied. Daily records that track fees, payments, and the filing of insurance forms can provide patients with accurate information and prompt service. (See Chapter 13 for suggestions on computer software to assist in this effort.) These records provide the clinician with specific information needed to monitor transactions and assist in maintaining good public relations with patients. The subject of financial transactions is one of the most sensitive topics for patients, particularly when there are limited resources. Respecting this sensitivity through the accurate keeping of records lessens the possibility for misunderstanding.

Audiologists, in particular, need to maintain records about the sales of batteries, hearing aid repairs, telephone calls, and hearing aid insurance. These provide important information for testimony if lawsuits are filed involving hearing aid usage. In addition, notes need to be made if there was a trial usage period and if the patient accepted or rejected the aid at the end of that period of time. This denotes in writing a respect for the consumer's rights by the practitioner in the process of dispensing.

Patient-Professional Interaction

A cornerstone for the prevention of litigation and the provision of the highest standard of patient care is the therapeutic relationship. The professional may facilitate the relationship through warmth, the provision of structure, nonjudgmental clinical understanding, and professional knowledge. These qualities can be communicated in addition to whatever counseling techniques are used. For example, the professional should carry a caseload schedule that is realistic and allows patients to be seen with reasonable punctuality at the appointed time. Doing so conveys respect for the patient. In addition, setting a policy that no telephone calls will be received during a therapy session communicates a sense of importance to that client and to that therapy time. Maintaining a separate professional relationship, uncomplicated by socialization with patients who are currently in your care, is essential, as stated in Chapter 3.

Doing so gives the therapist the freedom to deal with issues of resistance, anger, loneliness, or other intense feelings without the complications of social relationship.

Speech-language pathology and audiology is a profession whose members interact with physicians, dentists, psychologists, physical therapists, occupational therapists, teachers, and administrators, among others. Information is often communicated through reports, telephone calls, and patient reports. However, there are three potential areas of difficulty in such relationships: (1) a lack of personal and professional communication; (2) failure to demonstrate a unique base of skills and knowledge related to diagnosis and treatment of a mutual patient, and (3) failure to recognize the professional boundaries, as well as perceived or real threats to professional territories (McFarlane, Fujiki, & Brinton, 1984).

Professional-Professional Relationships

These areas of difficulty can be resolved by first, structuring your caseload to include only the types of clinical cases about which you feel knowledgeable, and second, by pursuing a continuing education plan that may include attending conferences, taking additional graduate courses at a local university, reading professional journals and books, and/or discussing cases with colleagues who are professionally knowledgeable.

When working mutually with other professionals on a case, not only keep open lines of communication through letters or phone calls but also limit the boundaries of your judgments to your professional area of expertise. Be very cautious about criticizing other professionals to patients, as there are often a variety of theoretical approaches and solutions to a problem. Such caution is warranted because this is the kind of dialogue often repeated in a courtroom setting. Patients have been known to relay information in the manner in which they perceived it, rather than as the professional intended it. Frequently there is clinical or behavioral information that would lend a more objective perspective to the case management, but may not be available unless excellent case records have been kept.

When diagnosing a serious communication disorder, such as a profound hearing loss in an infant or young child, recommend that the patient seek a second opinion. Give the patient several referral sources whom you respect professionally. Additional medical validation for the diagnosis must be sought. The area of failure to diagnose is a particularly sensitive one, with an increased possibility for injury in the field of audiology. However, there may be risks in the areas of speech and language disorders as well, and all practitioners, especially private practitioners, should recommend that second opinions be obtained as warranted.

Obtaining Second Opinions

Primary responsibility for a hearing-impaired child's safety rests with responsible parents. Present technology facilitates the fitting of virtually all hearing-impaired infants and children with ear-level hearing aids. Recent statistics indicate an emerging problem with pediatric ingestion of button cells. As no hearing aid currently exists on the market that guarantees the safety of an infant or young child who may remove the battery and swallow it, the parents should be instructed not to change the battery in

SOME SPECIAL CONCERNS

Hearing Aid Ingestion

the child's view. In addition, parents should be alerted to the significance of the child's removing and playing with the hearing aid. If this behavior does occur, the parent should be instructed to secure the battery compartment with strong tape. Warnings to the parents that battery compartments are not childproof and may provide a hazard to the child must be given both verbally and in writing.

If a child ingests a hearing aid battery, the parent should immediately be instructed to contact the child's pediatrician. A new hotline has been established at the National Capital Poison Center, which has a 24-hour National Button Battery Ingestion Hotline at (202) 625-3333 or (TTY 202-625-6070). When calling, the battery identification number from the package or from a matching battery must be provided. The child's physician may call the National Capital Poison Control Center collect for advice when a battery has been swallowed. Personnel are on duty 24 hours a day, 7 days a week.

Button batteries may also cause injury when they are placed in the nose or in the ears. Young children and the elderly have been particularly involved in this kind of accident. Symptoms to watch for are pain or a discharge from the nose or ears. The clinician and the parents are advised not to use nose or ear drops to facilitate the removal. The person must be examined by a physician, as these fluids can cause additional injury should a battery be involved (National Poison Center Network, 1981).

Dislodging of Ventilating Tubes

When taking earmold impressions, it is advisable to obtain a physician's written clearance to make the earmolds *prior* to the procedure. Before making an earmold impression, the audiologist must examine the ear with an otoscope to determine the status of the ventilating tubes, if present. Extreme care must be taken while taking earmold impressions. Whenever possible, they should be made prior to the insertion of the tubes. If a tube becomes dislodged, the otolaryngologist or attending physician should be contacted immediately for medical intervention.

The Presence of Substances in the Ear Canal

If a cotton block or impression material remains in the ear canal following an earmold impression and cannot be easily removed, the patient should be referred to the physician immediately for removal. The presence of foreign substances should never be ignored.

Electronystag-mography (ENG) Problems

With ENG, which should only be performed on written authorization by a physician, certain potential problems may be encountered. It is conceivable that the tympanic membrane, if thinly scarred, can be perforated by a high-velocity water irrigation. The membrane may be also inadvertently perforated if the irrigating tube is placed too deeply in the external auditory canal or if the patient startles at the onset of caloric irrigation, thus causing a perforation. Thus, it is critical that the referring physician should certify that the patient is able to be tested with water caloric irrigation, i.e., the ear is perforation-free prior to the procedures. If it is not, a finger cot in the ear canal, a GRAMS closed loop system, or an air caloric system should be used.

The clinician should determine if any orthopedic problems may limit the patient when testing for positional nystagmus or performing a hallpike maneuver. Patients with a history of cardiac disease or syncope should be considered at higher risk for this procedure.

It may be advisable to have the ENG patient accompanied by someone else who can drive him or her home after the procedure. Smelling salts should be available in case of fainting, and adequate time should be allowed for the patient to recover from the subjective effects of caloric stimulation before leaving the office. In case of untoward reactions, contact the referring physician immediately (Sullivan, personal communication 1985). In addition to clinical situations where injury could remotely occur, there are other potential risks for patient injury on the premises.

Patient Injury on the Premises

If an injury occurs on your property, assist the patient by first contacting the appropriate medical emergency agencies. If the injury is minor, refer the patient to his or her physician for medical evaluation. Do not administer medication, even over-the-counter drugs. Do not discuss liability with the patient. Call your insurance agent and report the accident; your insurance agent will advise you regarding further procedures. Insurance policies that are designed to provide coverage for a home and for office space within the home should be offered by the same insurance company. This prevents legal debate between the clinician's insurance companies as to which company provides coverage on the claim.

Emergency Numbers

It is important to display clearly police, fire department and other emergency numbers on the telephone that is available for the use of employees or other persons lending assistance. Instant access to such information could be a critical matter.

SUMMARY

Professional liability claims are rising steadily, commensurate with current trends in medicine and as a result of increased publicity and large settlements. As one columnist stated, the American dream is to suffer a nondebilitating injury on which one can retire. Despite this apparent humor that recognizes that legal actions are being filed at unprecedented rates, some malpractice suits do represent professional errors in judgment that resulted in patient injury. In the private sector, clinicians must provide their own liability insurance because they have no access to larger institutions, such as schools, universities, and hospitals, that might share in the expense of litigation.

It is imperative that the private practitioner become fully informed about the current Code of Ethics of the ASHA and current practices within the field in order to implement the highest standard of care. Consideration should be given to the *prevention* of litigious situations, which may in turn, reduce the incidence of litigation.

The field of speech-language pathology and audiology must continue its vigorous efforts in self-regulation. Failure to regulate the profession at the national level may result in a higher incidence of malpractice suits. The process of regulation from within requires the cooperation of all members. Litigation is an economically and emotionally costly process. It affects all members by potentially increasing professional liability costs. Finally, the mere possibility of litigation can threaten the fundamental relationship of trust between the patient and practitioner. Professionals must do their best to reduce that threat through such preventive measures as holding to the highest standard of practice, upholding the ethics of the profession, and providing the patient with well-designed consumer protection procedures.

REFERENCES

American Medical Association Committee on Professional Liability. (1984). Report to the Board of Trustees.

American Speech-Language-Hearing Association. (1985). Code of Ethics of the ASHA. *ASHA* 27:67–68.

Black, H. (1979). *Black's law dictionary*, 5th ed. St. Paul, MN: West Publishing Co.

Castle, G., Cushman, R.F., & Kensicki, P.R. (Eds.). (1981). *The business insurance handbook.* Homewood, IL: Dow Jones-Irwin.

Chapey, R., Chwat, S., Gurland, G., & Pieras, G. (1981). Perspectives in private practice: A nationwide analysis. *ASHA* 23:335–339.

Cramer, C., & Cramer, D. (1983). *Medical malpractice,* 5th edition. New York, NY: Practicing Law Institute, p. 235.

Dempsey, D. (1980). Medical malpractice in perspective: Nebraska Hospital Liability Act. *Nebraska Law Review*, 59:363–424.

Huebner, S.S., Black, K., Jr., & Cline, R.S. (1982). *Property and liability insurance*. Englewood Cliffs, NJ: Prentice-Hall, Inc.

Kramer, M., & Armbruster, J. (1982 or 1983). *Forensic audiology*. Baltimore: University Park Press.

Leiberman, J.K. (1981). *The litigious society*. New York: Basic Books.

McFarlane, S., Fujiki, M., & Brinton, R. (1984). *Coping with communicative handicaps*. San Diego, CA: College-Hill Press.

National Poison Center Network Computer System for Documenting Data on Poison Exposures. Pittsburgh, 1981.

Roady, T., & Andersen, W. (1960). *Professional negligence*. Nashville, TN: Vanderbilt University Press.

Sullivan, R. (1985), personal communication.

Wohlers, A.H., & Co. (1985), personal communication.

Woody, R.H. (1984). *The law and the practice of human services*. San Francisco: Jossey-Bass Publishing Co.

SUGGESTED READINGS

Flaster, R. (1983). *Malpractice*. New York: Charles Scribners and Sons.

Keeton, W.P. (1984). *Prosser and Keeton on the law of torts*. St. Paul, MN: West Publishing Co.

Chapter 5

Constraints and Commitments: An Introduction to the Financial Aspects of Private Practice

Robbin Parish, M.A.

Speech-language pathologists and audiologists considering a private practice must first review their own attitudes about business in general and the type of business inherent in private clinical practice. Many times our perceptions of ourselves as professionals and as business people are in conflict, e.g., our ability to assist speech-, language-, and hearing-impaired persons and our ability to receive appropriate monetary rewards for that assistance appear to be incongruent.

Since its beginning, the image of the profession has been one of "giving our services away," although the costs have actually always been borne by some entity, i.e., a hospital, agency, or university. Although this image has changed greatly, there continue to be programs that charge nothing to the consumer for services rendered. Clinicians employed in these settings and clients receiving the services may incorrectly assume that the program is "giving" the services away. They may not understand that someone, somewhere, is subsidizing those services and thus "paying" at least part of the price. Because of this misconception, students-in-training, clinicians in nonprofit centers, and clients of these professionals may believe that services should be rendered without charge and that we should in fact, give them away. Moreover, it seems that a segment of our profession still continues to believe that it is unfair to charge for our time, expertise, and education. We even fail to consider the fact that other professionals who provide services such as attorneys, physicians, and accountants, are helping others while making a profit.

All human service businesses are labor-intensive. Time is a critical factor as there are only a finite number of hours available to the practitioner. Every single decision, whether it is the purchase of a computer, hiring an associate, locating an office, or seeing a patient, must be prefaced with thoughtful consideration of the impact of that decision on the practitioner's time. Attorneys, physicians, and accountants have long realized this fact. It is time that speech-language pathologists and audiologists also recognize it.

Chapters 1 and 2 asked that you examine your own perceptions about the profit motive. You may now realize that you can help communicatively handicapped individuals and earn a living by doing so. If the two words *sell* and *profit* are not offensive to you, then you are probably ready to entertain more seriously the idea of going into business.

However, even before considering the financial aspects of any business, a plan must be formulated. After all, business is planning! It is axiomatic that, in order for any business to get off the ground, a basic business plan is necessary. Contrary to popular opinion, there is probably no definitive single text on how to be a "good" businessperson, and in fact, there are hundreds of books on the subject. In addition, many schools of business provide courses in management, finance, accounting, and so forth and award degrees in such areas as the Master's of Business Administration. Although there is no lack of information about business skills, the person who "makes it" in the business world must know first and foremost *how* to plan.

BUSINESS PLANNING

Planning for a private practice in speech-language pathology and audiology is very similar to planning for a new patient. Consider the following similarities:

TREATMENT PLAN	BUSINESS PLAN
Diagnosis	Statement of purpose
Statement of the problem	Business concept
Long-range goals	Long-range financial goals
Objectives	Objectives and time
Procedures	Financial aspects

The basic business plan, like the treatment plan, is used by the businessperson as a guide. It is like a road map designed to reach identified financial and personal goals. Needless to say, this plan should be written and should include the practitioner's best judgment on *when* things will happen, *how* they will happen, *how* much money will be needed, and eventually—the bottom line—how much business profit is anticipated or desired.

Statement of Purpose

After completing Section I of this book, you may want to write a simple description of your intended private practice as its statement of purpose. It should specify not only your goals but also the population to be served. Consider the variations inherent in the following statements:

- The ABC Speech Clinic is established to provide diagnosis and treatment to children and adults with communication disorders in the West Houston area.
- The ABC Speech and Hearing Clinic is established to provide diagnosis and treatment to the communicatively impaired in the greater Houston area.
- The ABC Audiology Clinic is established to provide testing of human hearing and hearing aid services and sales to the citizens of Harris County and surrounding areas.

- Betsy Smith & Associates is established to provide diagnosis and treatment of voice disorders in the adult population in South Houston.
- The ABC Clinic is established to provide afterschool speech-language pathology services in the Spring Branch School District.

It can be easily seen that each of the above statements reflects a different scope of practice, whether it be geographic or addressed to specific or general large treatment populations.

Concept Statement

The statement of purpose should be followed by a concept statement, which should reflect exactly how the business is to be operated. Will patients be seen in an office, one's private home, or in hospitals, nursing homes, or other facilities? Will consulting services be offered? Will services be contracted? Will the practice be itinerant—that is, travel from place to place—or will it be located in a single site? These questions must be considered because the financial plan depends on the answers, as well as on your capabilities and your business concept.

Consider how the following business concepts may assist in determining possible private practice financial goals:

- Diagnosis and treatment of communication disorders will be conducted in a small office by certified and licensed, if appropriate, speech-language pathologists.
- Diagnosis and treatment of communication disorders will be provided at any agency requesting services and with which an employee/employer contract may be arranged. Speech-language pathologists will be provided to the company as needed.
- Diagnosis and treatment of communication disorders will be provided both in the office and by contract arrangement to the hospitals, nursing homes, and schools in the greater Houston area.
- Diagnosis and treatment of communication disorders will be conducted by speech-language pathologists and audiologists by contract with agencies in the Houston area.

Short- and Long-Range Goals

As one's business concept evolves, a more realistic identification of a long-range financial goal emerges—be it just breaking even or the more unlikely goal of "making a million." The long-range financial goal is the cumulative result of all business activities. In order to reach that goal, certain objectives must be established to keep you on-track and constantly moving forward. In order to provide a realistic projection of the time and finances needed to open and operate the business, these short-term objectives should answer the questions of who, what, when, and how. They should involve the following activities, as well as others that will be identified as one's financial awareness increases:

- projecting expenses
- projecting income

- interviewing professional consultants
- selecting a business form
- securing funding

**Time
Commitment**

By identifying one's short-term objectives the time commitment required to achieve them will be clarified. As others have painfully learned, there is no such thing as a "nine to five job" when you own your own business. As planning proceeds, you will come to realize that your business may consume all of your life. You will find that even your dreams are filled with plans for your day-to-day business affairs. In assessing the amount of time required by your business you must determine how to manage that time most effectively. The old saying that "time is money" becomes a startling reality in private practice where all you have to "sell" is time. Thus, to estimate your involvement, begin by noting the following:

- Estimate how many hours you expect to be involved in your venture. Be generous with your time. Understand that the amount of time you spend in the beginning will accrue future benefits.
- Estimate the number of patients that you plan to see on a daily basis.
- Estimate the maximum number of patients that can be seen daily, weekly, and monthly.
- Estimate the number of hours that can be devoted to the management of the business.
- Estimate the amount of time you intend to spend with your family, your spouse, or on other aspects of your personal life. Many entrepreneurs forget that time is finite and that initiating a private practice is a major commitment. Almost everyone who has begun a business of any kind reports that there never seems to be enough time to go around. Even when the practice becomes well established, time commitments are likely to continue to be intensive because there are always new challenges and opportunities. (See Chapter 11 on increasing the practice.)

After estimating the total number of hours to be committed, it is now important to look at revenue-producing hours. How many contact hours in the day will be revenue-producing, i.e. patient contact hours? How many hours will actually be paid hours? (Many speech-language pathologists and audiologists forget to identify separately the revenue-generating hours or to specify these hours in their financial plan.) How many hours will be revenue generating as opposed to nonrevenue-generating hours? For example, how many hours will be spent bringing potential consumers to your service? In addition, do not forget professional time—the time committed to colleagues, professional association activities, and community endeavors. Without such involvement, the professional will tend to feel as if he or she were alone on an island. Indeed, professional commitments enhance your reputation and can create the camaraderie needed for continued professional and personal support and encouragement. It is a good idea, particularly at first, to seek professional involvement through associations and not through employees.

Finally, be practical in assessing potential time commitments. A colleague recently disclosed that, when she opened her private practice, she and her partner hired two full-time speech-language pathologists and a full-time secretary! When the doors opened, she had five people on the payroll and no patients! An ambitious venture, to be sure, but one that clearly revealed a need for further analysis of both time and personnel commitments.

Where and how do you begin to set up a private practice? Many speech-language pathologists and audiologists fear opening a practice of their own because of their lack of knowledge in finances. The language used by the banker, the accountant, or the venture capitalist may seem foreign to them. Speech-language pathologists and audiologists, as well as others in the health care professions, frequently spend most of their educational and professional hours caring for the patients they serve. Because of the time and energy it takes to care for others and to learn the skills to provide such services, they have given little attention to developing expertise in setting financial goals and in handling money. However, as you begin to look realistically at your business plan and to use actual figures that reflect your time and energy commitments, you will soon become very savvy in dealing with money. Although there are consultants available, you, the novice, must learn at least the basic ''lingo'' of the business world if success is to be yours. The consultants may help refine and expand the basic business and financial plans, but the private practitioner must be in charge.

Because your consultants—your attorney and accountant—will be important to your business success and may develop a close and enduring friendship with you, it is imperative that you interview each and every prospective consultant to determine his or her interest, attitude, and understanding of you and your business. These consultants of course charge for their services, and they may well seem expensive to the novice. Remember, however, that they are in a service business just as you are and that their advice is meant to save you from making serious financial mistakes. Your consultants should more than ''pay for themselves.''

FINANCIAL CONSULTING RESOURCES

The time to meet and become acquainted with the banker, loan officers, and even presidents of banks is when you begin to prepare your business and financial plans. Meet as many bankers as you can. Ask friends, relatives, and colleagues for the names of their bankers. Request introductions. As you interview each one, determine whether the banker understands the unique aspects of your business and your ultimate goals. Spend time interviewing each banker, and understand that your banker may become your ''best friend'' in the business world. The chemistry between you and the banker and your business must be right. The right kind of banker can mean the difference between success and failure in any business. Choose carefully!

After you have interviewed several bankers, spend more time with the ones that you liked. Take them to lunch; educate them regarding the profession and the communicatively handicapped client. Mail brochures, pertinent statistics, and articles relevant to the profession to them. Make sure the banker knows you *and* your profession before asking for money. By the time you are ready to ask for money the banker may be willing to offer a reasonable commitment of funds.

The Banker

A colleague who did not follow this advice went to a bank near her home, requested information on obtaining a loan for her practice, and met the loan officer with whom she would be working. She informed the officer that she would like to borrow money to start her practice in speech-language pathology, but failed to ask pertinent questions about the intricacies of a bank loan or to realize that the then-current prime interest rate was 21%. The banker was more than happy to arrange the loan for her—at two points above the prime rate, making the total loan commitment a great deal higher than she was capable of paying. Naively, she accepted the numbers and signed her name on the dotted line. She was thus committed for 2 years at an exorbitant interest rate. Had she interviewed bankers, asked searching questions, and explored a number of "best offers," it is likely that she might have saved money and developed a close working relationship with a trusted business consultant.

The Attorney

A lawyer can help you plow through the myriad problems associated with starting a business—from understanding a lease agreement, selecting a form of business, drawing up contracts for employees, and developing contracts with agencies; the attorney will represent you in lawsuits as well. (See also Chapters 3, 4, and 16.) Remember that many attorneys specialize in different areas of law. There are tax attorneys, real estate attorneys, attorneys who are also certified public accountants, and so forth.

Your attorney should be able to help you with the specifics of your business or refer you to someone who can. When interviewing each, make sure that the attorney or another lawyer in the firm can handle your specific problems. Remember also that attorney fees vary and that they typically charge by the hour. Therefore, plan ahead and know what you want the attorney to do *before* you make the appointment. Also, make sure that the attorney understands your intent so you will not be charged for the time it takes to discover your purpose. Attorneys charge for their time, overhead, and profit, just as other professionals do.

For example, a colleague asked his attorney to apply for nonprofit status for the community agency he was starting. The colleague had thoroughly researched the application and had specific questions regarding the application. The attorney could not answer the questions, but assured him that, given time, he would have all the answers and would be able to file the application. Many dollars later, my colleague realized that he was paying the attorney to do the research that he himself had already done! He dismissed the attorney and then asked other nonprofit organizations for names of attorneys who had helped them obtain nonprofit status. He quickly found an attorney who specialized in expeditious handling of applications for nonprofit status. Although this new attorney was expensive, this colleague saved many thousands of dollars by going to the expert.

The Accountant

An accountant can be of considerable help in analyzing business and financial plans and in helping project future business. Many people feel that an accountant simply prepares tax returns. That is not so. An accountant who knows and understands your business can be a valuable resource. Record keeping, financial advice, and business projections are just a few of the services an accountant can offer. It is imperative, however, that you become conversant, at least to some degree, with accounting terms and that you question unfamiliar concepts the accountant uses. It is critical that you understand the accountant's explanations, either spoken or written. Do not be afraid to ask questions!

Insurance Broker

Another important professional on your team is the person who can assist you in determining the amount of needed insurance coverage: not too much and not too little. This person should not only sell you the insurance but should also be someone who will look out for your best interest. Again, it is important that you interview several insurance brokers and look carefully at all policies.

Commercial Real Estate Broker

A real estate broker who specializes in office leases can be of extraordinary help, not only in negotiating lease agreements but also in securing exactly what is wanted in lease terms. (See Chapter 16 on dissolving a practice for further information about the services of a broker.) The broker and your attorney can protect you by making sure that you are well apprised of the arrangements for which you are about to contract. Remember, however, that it is your name on the lease. Ask questions as necessary.

Real estate brokers receive a fee from the lease that has been negotiated. Usually, their fee is reasonable compensation for the headaches that you would have to endure if the broker were not helping you. You may wish to have your attorney also check the contract. (See Chapters 7 and 16 for further suggestions and caveats on lease arrangements.)

Consider the following example. Two speech-language pathologists in Houston were expanding their practice and needed more space. After spending numerous hours looking at office space, they finally decided on a space that was twice as big as the original office. Although their practice was growing, the income that they were making was insufficient to cover the rent payments of the new space; their current office was not large enough to handle the number of patients needed to generate the revenue necessary to pay for the new space. They were in a quandary. A colleague suggested that they contact a real estate broker. The broker was able to negotiate a long-term lease with the office building, including 6 months free rent and an office space that they could design and have built to their specifications at no extra charge. The lease also included options to renew the lease for two 3-year periods and the right of first refusal on all contiguous space. These two clauses were added by the broker and the attorney after determining that the practice was growing and that the women did not wish to leave the new location for at least 10 years.

FORMS OF BUSINESS: AN OVERVIEW

Before you can decide how and when you are going to start your business, you must decide on its organizational form. Although your own accountant and attorney can help you make this decision, you should be familiar with the major organizational forms of business: sole proprietorship, partnership, and corporation.

Sole Proprietorship

This form of business is probably the easiest to initiate, sell, or dissolve. You, as the owner, form a company and transact a business. The owner is taxed on business profits that are considered personal income. The owner is also personally liable for the debts. If the owner is sued, all personal assets can be taken to pay off those debts. In addition, there may be local rules regarding forms of business that are not corporations. If you decide to use a trade name, such as Speech Pathology Associates, you will have to register the name and your own name and address at City Hall or some other governmental agency. This procedure is called filing a dba (doing business as). You, the owner (or partner) are "doing business as" Speech Pathology Associates.

Partnership

This form of business is similar to a sole proprietorship except that two or more people enter into business together, sharing the costs and the profits. Each partner is liable, and each partner is taxed personally. Partnerships are similar to a marriage: Partners must get along well personally and complement one another's abilities.

Although partnerships offer beneficial tax breaks, there are many problems inherent in this form of business. Because personalities are so important in a partnership, it is critical to consider all aspects of the potential partner(s). Many times business owners form a partnership simply because the partner can supply the necessary capital to finance the practice. Anyone "will do"—as long as he or she has money! Although some individuals can survive such a business marriage, life may become very difficult over the years. Before taking a partner, investigate all aspects of his or her character, including personality, financial status, and professional expertise. After gathering information from friends, banking references, previous employers, and business associates, enter into a partnership agreement with a written agreement, preferably drawn up by your attorney. This agreement should describe the practice in detail, including, but not limited to, the following:

- *Control of business:* Risks in partnerships can be lessened by one person (preferably you) having control of the business. When you own at least 51 percent of the partnership, all final decisions regarding the partnership must be made by you. Many first-time business owners make the mistake of splitting the partnership equally among the partners. As a result, arguments may not be settled except by a distasteful compromise or by defeat. Deadlocks result when equal partners stop speaking to each other, and the business begins to decline. Even the day-to-day routine becomes a crisis. The "marriage" begins to fall apart.

  Although there is no divorce court in the business world, a business relationship can be dissolved through a buy-sell agreement. This agreement, signed by all partners at the beginning of their venture, allows one partner either to buy out the others or to sell his or her share of the business to the other partners or to someone else. Your attorney can draw up a buy-sell agreement that is tailored to the needs of the partners.

- *Key-man insurance:* This is life insurance taken out by each partner that names the other partners as the beneficiaries. If a partner dies, the partnership is usually dissolved unless an advance written agreement has been made that the surviving partners will buy the dead partner's share from the estate. Key-man life insurance ensures the partners that the business has enough money to buy out the interest. Your attorney and your insurance broker can assist you in purchasing this important form of insurance.

- *Consideration of time, functions, and duties of each partner:* Indicate how much time each partner will devote to the practice, including the number of patient contact hours and the administrative duties. Decide who will sign the checks and be responsible for clerical personnel, professional employees, and clinical affairs.

- *Division of profits and loss:* Indicate how the profits are to be divided among the partners. Will each partner take money at the end of the month, quarter, or year? Will partners be able to borrow against unearned income? Will salaries be paid immediately, or will partners wait until profits exceed losses? In the event of a loss, who is responsible and how will the loss be accounted for? Always consider a "best case" and a "worse case" scenario when considering the division of profits and loss. Remember that each partner represents the others when signing a check, contract, or any business transaction. All partners are liable for the actions of each one.

Corporation

This entity is probably the most complex form of business organization. It usually requires an attorney to design the "Articles of Incorporation." The corporation is considered a legal entity, meaning that it has a separate identity from the owner. If, as owner, you incorporate a company, you become an employee of that corporation. The profit earned by the corporation is taxed separately from the owner's income as an employee.

The major drawback of a corporation is that income tax is paid on corporate profits, as well as profits on dividends paid to the stockholders. There may be additional drawbacks or strengths depending on proposed changes in the national tax structure. However, no matter what changes may occur in the tax structure, it will probably be years before the tax dust settles. Frequent contact with your accountant and your attorney is required for the foreseeable future!

More detailed information on these forms of business is found in Chapter 9.

FINANCIAL PLAN

The financial plan requires your best judgment in projecting the expenses and income of your business. Budgeting projected income and expenses becomes the single most important aspect of a successful business. In order to budget successfully, the costs of everything must be determined. At first, the budget will be a series of assumptions regarding the costs of beginning the practice. Later, projected costs will be replaced by the actual (or historical) costs, and future costs can be projected with greater ease. Researching expenses projected in the business plan and estimating your time involvement enable you to make a realistic budget. See also Chapter 13 on computer applications for advanced planning strategies.

Expenses

There are three major types of expenses: fixed, variable, and capital. Initially, a "guesstimate" of the probable amount of expenses to be incurred is necessary. At first, such guesstimates serve as a financial projection or budget to be used daily, to determine if you are on budget; later they serve as a comparison of actual to budgeted costs.

Most new business owners tend to underestimate their expenses and overestimate their income. Try to be as reasonable and realistic as possible in your projections. When determining expenses, project at least for the first 2 years. It is always a good idea to project expenses and income on the assumption that you will not see a single patient for at least the first 6 months of the practice and you will not break even for at least a year. Obviously, income will vary over that period.

In addition to business expenses, you should also look at your personal and family expenses. However, never, include *both* personal and professional expenses in your financial plan. Instead, make a separate financial plan for your personal financial needs.

It is essential to analyze the following components of a professional financial plan.

Fixed Expenses   These expenses must be paid on a routine basis and include the following:

- *Rent:* Rents vary according to a particular lease. (As indicated earlier, seek help in securing a lease.) Try not to accept the original rental fee; instead, negotiate for space and dollar amounts. Ask other tenants what they are paying or, more appropriately, contact a commercial real estate broker. Remember that for some time you will be paying this rate or more, if there are escalation clauses which are also negotiable.

- *Interest on loans:* Try to negotiate with the lender for a reasonable interest rate loan for a period of time, and arrange a regular pay-back system in which payment consists of the same number of dollars.

- *Insurance:* Insurance needs include, but are not limited to, fire, casualty, liability, burglary, professional liability, health insurance, and workman's compensation for employees. Interview insurance brokers and read different policies. Look for and ask about hidden costs and fixed premiums, and then select the best policy.

- *Maintenance:* Most leases include building maintenance costs. Make sure that you know what is included in the lease and if maintenance costs are permitted to increase. Read escalation clauses carefully. Determine when you are billed by the lessor and budget accordingly, or request in the lease agreement that you be billed quarterly for escalation costs.

- *Subscriptions:* Current periodicals are necessary for the waiting room. Remember, too, the need for professional journals for yourself and your employees.

- *Wages:* Salaries paid to the professional(s) or to other employees are called wages, regardless of the number of patient contact hours. A good rule of thumb to follow for determining professional wages and maintaining a business profit margin is to make certain that, for the services of a speech-language pathologist on full salary, the client be charged at least three times the speech-language pathologist's salary. If, for example, you pay the speech-language pathologist a salary of $1,000.00 a month, that person should bill at least $3,000.00 a month in order for the employer to make a profit. Many well-run businesses try to hold total personnel costs at 40 percent of gross income. Initially, an owner may find that a full-time, salaried professional employee is not affordable. In that case, part-time contractual professionals can be employed and paid on a percentage basis for hourly service. The part-time professional is paid a fee based on a mutually agreed-on percentage of what was charged *or* collected. The employer supplies the facility, the materials, and the secretarial work. Professional fees are listed under variable expenses.

- *Professional dues:* Although these costs are usually fixed for at least a year, inflationary increases should be anticipated.

- *Taxes:* Federal withholding and Social Security taxes must be deducted from employees' gross paychecks each time they are paid. The employer must pay a tax deposit to a tax deposit account, which is the amount withheld from each check, in addition to the employer's contribution to Social Security. (Employers must match the Social Security taxes deducted from each employee's paycheck.) Obtain recent withholding tables from the Internal Revenue Service to determine specific amounts of taxes to be withheld. In addition to payroll taxes, you must include property taxes, school taxes, and city, county, and state taxes as expenses.

This category includes expenses that fluctuate with business volume or that are unknown. Some examples are listed below.

Variable Expenses

- *Telephone:* Investigate a lease/purchase option for telephone systems and compare long-distance services before choosing a system. Plan for the future; ensure that it is possible to add onto the telephone system, but beware of buying too much initially. In these days of deregulation, it may even pay to change systems or companies. Overall, again the cost trend is likely to be upward.

- *Utilities:* The cost of utilities varies according to use and size of your office. Ask other tenants in the building with the same amount of space to give you an estimate of their yearly utility costs.

- *Travel and entertainment (T&E):* Be careful with the use of credit cards. T&E expenses can build up quickly, and the IRS is not always in agreement as to the appropriateness of reported T&E expenses!

- *Repairs:* Check your lease agreement. If repairs are not included as part of the lessor's responsibility, try to negotiate an agreement to include these expenses.

- *Unemployment taxes:* Check with the IRS and your state agency or your accountant regarding these taxes.

- *Printing and postage:* Even if you live in a large metropolitan area, investigate respectable, out-of-town stationery firms for the purchase of business cards, letterheads, and the like. Companies dealing in large volumes in specialty items may be less expensive than the "home-town" printer. Initially, expect to use more postage than usual, at least during the first 6 months as you will be marketing your services, as well as ordering supplies.

- *Professional services:* As mentioned above, service fees are paid to professionals for hourly service to your practice. Remember that this compensation for professional services does not require the employer to pay Social Security, unemployment, or withholding taxes. However, an IRS 1099 Form must be issued to these professionals at yearend. Check with your accountant regarding this method of paying professionals.

- *Legal and accounting fees:* These expenses vary unless the attorney or the accountant is on retainer. Again, determine how you want to use each of these consultants and discuss expenses with them. Initially, you may find it less expensive to contract with or pay a retainer to each one, but later you may only need their advice for special problems. Consider enlarging your budget so that you will not be intimidated by legal and accounting fees from utilizing these valuable experts.

Capital Expenses

These are frequently, although not always, one-time-only expenses and should be included in your startup costs. These include the following:

- *Deposits:* The first and last month's rent deposit is usually required; telephone, utility, and leased furniture and equipment deposits are also usually required.

- *Furniture and equipment:* Major purchases can deplete one's finances very quickly. Consider leasing furniture or equipment with an option to buy if you are cash poor. (Check with your accountant concerning depreciation deductions versus deductions for lease payments.)

- *Testing materials and supplies:* Investigate educational supply houses for treatment materials and national business supply houses for office materials. Select testing materials carefully. As is indicated in Chapter 2, it is not necessary to buy every test on the market.

- *Building permits:* When building or remodeling your premises, these permits are required. Check with the city or county government for rules and regulations regarding permits.

- *Architect-contractor fees:* Again, if you are building or remodeling your office space, you may incur these fees. Learn to negotiate! Remember in projecting expenses that "almost everything" in life is negotiable. Try to receive at least three bids for everything you are buying, whether it is a piece of equipment or a consultant's expertise. Requesting bids takes time and energy, but will result in significant savings.

INSURING YOUR PRIVATE PRACTICE

One of the shocks encountered by any new business owner is the amount and cost of insuring the practice. However, only insurance can protect you and your investment. What kind of insurance do you need? Your insurance broker will be able to advise you on the insurance needed to cover you and your practice.

Present your agent with detailed information about the equipment, particularly portable equipment, furniture, materials, and supplies that will be in your office, or car, or on your premises. Place a value on every item, either based on the receipts for purchase of these items or on an estimate as to the value of each. Remember to request insurance that will reimburse you for the *replaceable* cost of the item. If the insurance premiums for replaceable costs are too high, remember to contact your insurance broker on a yearly basis to increase the coverage so that, in the event of a loss, you are not financially overwhelmed.

Fire and Theft Insurance

For example, one colleague thought she was well covered because her insurance covered the original costs of the items. She was burglarized 6 years after starting her practice. Because she had not requested insurance for the replaceable cost of the items, she received $3,000 less than the replacement costs of the audiometer, typewriter, computer, and other needed equipment. The insurance company paid for the original costs, less the deductible.

This policy insures you and your business for any accidents that occur in your place of business or on your property. It is NOT professional liability insurance. For example, general liability insurance protects you from lawsuits regarding a patient falling and breaking an arm in your office. (For an interesting discussion of specific general liability concerns, see Chapter 4.)

General Liability Insurance

This policy protects your professional career, including your diagnostic and treatment decisions. For a more complete discussion of professional liability and the outcome of court decisions, the reader is referred to Chapters 3 and 4.

Professional Liability Insurance

This kind of coverage varies by state but usually is required for all businesses. Check with your state insurance board to determine what coverage you need for your employees.

Workman's Compensation

This policy protects you from any event that would cause your business to be interrupted so that you could not conduct your day-to-day transactions, i.e., fire, serious illness, or other misfortune that might require you to close down for a period of time.

Business Interruption Insurance

An important consideration for the owner of any business, this insurance covers a disability that would prevent you from conducting your business. Read these policies carefully, as some policies do not cover you if you are unable to work at all, i.e., at ANY trade or occupation, not necessarily the occupation in which you were engaged prior to the disability. Some disability policies only cover specific disabilities, such as a "loss of one limb," or "one eye." Others do not appear to consider loss of speech, a stroke, or other communicative impairment as a disability.

Disability Insurance

Group health insurance for small companies—less than three people—is expensive and is sometimes difficult to obtain. Many companies also require that life insurance

Health and Life Insurance

be included in the health policy. Make sure that the insurance company selected has a good rating by talking to other small business owners who have a similar policy with the same company. Inquire about rate changes in the last year, and ensure that your policy covers payment for diagnosis and treatment of speech, hearing, and language disorders.

INCOME

Factors Affecting Fee Setting

Placing a price on your service depends on several factors. Assuming you are going into business in order to make a living and perhaps even a good living, you must consider the following three factors:

1. the costs of providing the service, including time and all concurrent expenses
2. the current fees that the competition is charging
3. the ability and willingness of clients to pay

How does one determine the costs of services? Your projected budgeted expenses should provide a good start. What is your time worth? Although most businesses consider 22 working days a month and 40 hours a week to be a full-time effort, a clinical practice is not the same as clerking in a store.

Fee-Setting Formulas

If you are opening a full-time practice, you might assume that you have 176 possible hours of patient contact, revenue-producing hours per month. However, of those 176 hours, you must take time for planning, attending conferences, writing reports, managing the business, and doing public relations and marketing. Therefore not all 176 hours will be direct revenue producing! Assume that patients will be seen for 20 hours a week (4 hours a day) for a month (22 days) and that expenses are $4,000 a month. Then use the following formula to determine the breakeven point:

$$\text{Breakeven} = \frac{\text{expenses}}{\text{hours to be charged}}$$

$$\text{Breakeven} = \frac{\$4,000}{88 \text{ hours}} = \$45.45 \text{ an hour}$$

If you have considered a healthy salary for yourself in your budgeted expense projections, you can assume that charging $45.45 an hour will cover both your salary and the overhead costs. But where is the profit? Where is the reimbursement for your time and extra effort in getting the business off the ground? Where are the profits to cushion the practice in the event you cannot or choose not to schedule 88 hours of patient visits a month?

A colleague in private practice recently revealed that, although she used this formula, she forgot to account for school holidays, illnesses, make-ups, no shows, or emergencies. In addition she was not routinely seeing 88 hours of patients a month. As a matter of fact, in 6 years of practice she had never consistently seen this number of people in a 1-month period. This was partially because the clients who made up the caseload were inconsistent in their day-to-day attendance. She finally devised a make-up schedule that allowed the patient to make-up missed appointments; however, if the patient were unable to do so *and* had not cancelled the appointment 24 hours in advance, this patient was charged for the visit. The practitioner adhered to this policy. She prepared for school holidays by allowing patients to extend their appointment time and to come on other days. However, she still lost money and there was no cushion. Once again, she reevaluated her time and expenses, averaged the number of charged patient contact hours scheduled per month, and revised her budget projections. In addition, she added 100 percent of the revised cost per hour to the total and reduced her anxiety commensurately. Her revised formula for making a 50 percent profit on the practice became:

$$\text{Profit} = \frac{\text{expenses}}{\text{average hours charged}} + 100\%$$

$$\text{Profit} = \frac{\$4,000}{80 \text{ hours}} \qquad \$50.00 + \$50.00 = \$100/\text{hour}$$

However, if the going rate in the community had been considerably lower than this revised fee estimate, then *expenses* must be reduced or charges for "patient involvement" hours instituted. Conferences, report writing, preparing insurance reports, telephone conversations, and various other patient involvement activities reduce the number of revenue-producing hours. Thus, one should consider charging for these services based on the number of hours the professional is involved with the patient file. This practice is in accord with the fee structures of other professions; attorneys, accountants, and physicians charge for their time, as well as their client/patient contact hours. These hours are important to the client/patient and must be included in your fee structure either as physicians charge (indirectly) or directly as accountants and attorneys charge.

PERSONAL FINANCIAL STATEMENT

The accountant can prepare a financial statement that indicates your assets (what you own) and liabilities (what you owe) on a given day and provide you with a balance sheet; it is a reflection of your personal worth (Table 5-1). A personal financial statement is required by bankers or others who may serve as sources of funding (Table 5-2).

Assets are typically listed on the left side of the paper and liabilities on the right or as shown in Table 5-1. Personal assets include those tangible items that are in your name. In some states, if you are married and share all possessions, then your assets are one-half of everything that you and your spouse own together. In addition to the market value of your home, your assets include your life insurance, car, personal effects (jewelry, clothing,) stocks and bonds, land, investments, savings accounts, retirement accounts, and any monies owed to you both. Your liabilities include your mortgage and any debt service, including car payments, rent, or the like. The bottom line, or your net worth, equals your assets minus your liabilities.

Table 5-1 ABC Speech-Language Hearing Clinic Balance Sheet for August 31, 1985

ASSETS	
Current Assets	
Cash in Bank	$ 900
Savings	50
Accounts Receivable—Patients	3,000
Deposits	1,100
Taxes on deposit	400
Property and Equipment	
Furniture & Equipment	2,000
Depreciation	(1,100)
Total Assets	$6,000
LIABILITIES	
Current	
Notes Payable	$3,000
Taxes Payable	400
Total Payroll Payable	400
Total Current Liability	$3,800
Equity (Owner's)	$2,200
Total Liability & Equity	$6,000

This particular exercise can both surprise and frighten you. However, after pulling this information together, you should have an excellent picture of your worth and the risk you are undertaking. As the business matures, you will be expected to produce a business balance sheet. (See Chapter 13 for information on how to use computer hardware and software in originating and updating financial statements.)

BUSINESS FINANCIAL STATEMENT (PROFIT AND LOSS STATEMENT)

A profit and loss (P&L) statement indicates whether you are making or losing money. Usually, the accountant prepares your statement on a quarterly basis. However, if you would like to keep a monthly P&L for your own peace of mind, use Table 5-3 for a guideline.

Cash Flow Projection

Projecting cash flow in private practice is difficult. However, by averaging scheduled patient contact hours and other revenues, if any, it is not difficult to determine that some months can be leaner than others. If you are able to anticipate the less busy times, you can make up for lack of income by scheduling consulting opportunities, day-care screenings, or the like, or you may even be able to take a vacation.

Although specific months vary, depending perhaps on geographical and climatic conditions, colleagues report that December, January, June, and July are "down"

Table 5-2 Personal Financial Statement

Name:
Address:
Business:
Age:
Marital Status:

ASSETS:

Cash On Hand/	
Banks	$ 700
Stocks	2,000
Property	50,000
Automobile	5,000
Personal (Jewelry)	1,000
Total Assets	$58,700

LIABILITIES:

Mortgage	$32,000
School Loans	10,000
Credit Cards	1,000
Total Liabilities	$43,000

TOTAL NET WORTH: $15,700

months. Referrals decrease, patient interest wanes, and appointments are cancelled. Knowing the "down" months can also help you in suggesting vacation weeks for your contractual employees. Table 5-4 provides a 13-month projection of cash flow.

Computers or microprocessors using standard software packages can be profitably used to project cash flow. See Chapters 10 and 13 for further information.

FINANCING THE PRIVATE PRACTICE

Most businesses require capital in order to get underway. Even if you have drawn a salary while you were planning your venture, you will soon realize that more money is needed to open and operate your practice. Where can you go for the funds?

The Bank

If you have done your homework and cultivated the banker, opened a family checking account, and educated the officers, you are ready to present your case. Put your business plan, financial plan, personal financial statement, list of consultants, and time lines together in a packet. Make a formal appointment and be prepared to answer the following four questions:

1. How much money do you want?
2. How are you going to repay the loan?
3. What is your collateral?
4. What insurance do you have to protect the loan?

Table 5-3 ABC Speech-Language Hearing Clinic Income Statement for Month Ended August 31, 1985

REVENUES	
Services:	
Diagnosis	$2,000
Treatment	3,000
Total Revenues	$5,000
OPERATING EXPENSES	
Advertising	$ 60
Subscriptions	20
Legal/Accounting	100
Insurance	80
Telephone	130
Office Supplies	65
Treatment Supplies	100
Rent	1,000
Postage/Printing	50
Utilities	150
Travel/Entertainment	200
Salaries	1,750
Miscellaneous	300
Total Operating Expenses	$4,000
Net Operating Income	$1,000
Net Income Before Taxes	$1,000

Bankers approach such requests differently, but if you have developed a friendship with your banker and you both are comfortable with the relationship, your presentation and the banker's response may well be positive. However, in the event the first bank cannot or will not loan you money at the rate that you wish to pay, go to your next friendly banker. Continue until you receive the funding that you need at the price

Table 5-4 Cash Flow Projection Chart: Revenues & Expenses for August 1984 –August 1985

	AUG.	SEPT.	OCT.	NOV.	DEC.	JAN.	FEB.	MAR.	APR.	MAY	JUNE	JULY	AUG.
BEGINNING CASH AVAILABLE	3,000	4,000	4,000	4,000	2,000	(500)	(1,500)	(500)	1,500	3,500	7,500	6,500	5,000
+ REVENUES	5,000	4,000	4,000	2,500	1,500	2,000	4,000	5,000	6,000	8,000	3,000	2,500	5,000
− EXPENDITURES	4,000	4,000	4,000	4,500	4,000	3,000	3,000	3,000	4,000	4,000	4,000	4,000	4,000
= ENDING CASH BALANCE	4,000	4,000	4,000	2,000	(500)	(1,500)	(500)	1,500	3,500	7,500	6,500	5,000	6,000

(interest rate) that you can afford. Remember to obtain three bids. Many times, for a variety of reasons, loans are not made at the interest rate that you are willing to pay. In some cases, small banks specializing in funding women, minorities, or specialty businesses may be of help. In any case, other sources of funding may be available to you and should be explored. (See Chapter 9 for other potential sources of funding.)

The SBA is a source of help only after you have been turned down by a major private lender. Thus, if the bank turns you down, you may ask them to make the loan through the SBA. The SBA loan procedure is similar to the bank's procedure, but check with your local SBA office for more information.

Small Business Administration (SBA)

Venture capital firms are companies interested in investing in businesses with high-growth potential. They lend money, but in return want a part of your business, probably the controlling part if they feel it will be a rapidly growing business. Although some speech-language pathologists and audiologists succeed remarkably early in the life of their practice, this does not generally occur. Therefore, venture capital firms or individuals may be only marginally interested in you and your plans.

Venture Capital Firms

"Easy" sources of income may become a long-term problem. When borrowing from family members, *always* enter into a legal contract with the family member. Regardless of your primary lending source, you are committed to keeping good records, paying your loan on time, and keeping the lender involved or apprised of your business. These requirements may result in more family togetherness than is desirable.

Family Members

Many practices fail due to lack of good records; the business simply "gets away" from them. Patients and their progress are equally as important as, if not more important than, the business aspects, such as recording debits and credits. Your accountant can help devise a system to fit your practice. Again, it is imperative that you and your accountant understand the totality of your practice. A bookkeeping system should be adapted for each business; there are as many bookkeeping systems as there are businesses. Research each system before you purchase one to be sure that it meets your needs and the needs of the practice.

BOOK-KEEPING

Many private practices have moved into the computer age. Practitioners are using computers for every detail of business planning, financial planning, record keeping, patient charts, and even the delivery of clinical services. The computer can be very useful in an ongoing business; however, if you are just beginning a business and have not yet determined your specific needs, it may be wise to delay the acquisition of this important tool. (See Chapter 9, 10, and 13 for further details regarding computer applications for both the novice and the experienced private practitioner.)

Good business requires good planning. In order to understand the financial implications of a private practice, the professional must be able to plan ahead. The business plan includes the statement of purpose, a business concept, and long- and

SUMMARY

short-term objectives. The financial plan includes expenses, income, and projections. All good planning involves time and consultants' expertise and input. Financial success will come to those who plan carefully, offer quality services, and market those services well. The reward is not only in helping the communicatively handicapped client but also in making a good living while doing so.

SUGGESTED READINGS

Lowry, A.J. (1981). *How to become financially successful by owning your own business*. New York: Simon & Schuster.

Rausch, E.N. (1979). *Financial management for small business*. New York: AMACOM.

Walker, E.W., & Petty, J. (1978). *Financial management of the small firm*. Englewood Cliffs, NJ: Prentice-Hall.

Welsh, J.A., & White, J.F. (1983). *The entrepreneur's master planning guide—How to launch a successful business*. Englewood Cliffs, NJ: Prentice-Hall.

Chapter 6

Ethical Concerns in Private Practice

Richard M. Flower, Ph.D.

The mere inclusion of a chapter entitled "Ethical Concerns in Private Practice" in this book seems to imply that the delivery of speech-language pathology and audiology services through private practice entails unique ethical considerations. Our profession has the too-prevalent attitude that, when clients themselves or third parties pay fees for services, those services are automatically cast into an ethical twilight zone. For evidence to support this contention, one need only read the *Issues in Ethics* statements formulated a decade or more ago by the Ethical Practice Board of the American Speech-Language-Hearing Association (ASHA). An incomprehensible line of reasoning leads to the assumption that as long as a speech-language pathologist or audiologist draws a salary from an institution—usually a public institution—the rules are different: Clients with dubious prognoses may be admitted to and maintained endlessly in treatment programs, recommendations and referrals may be made with no regard for their economic consequences, and plans may be formulated and carried out without regard to the client's informed consent, because after all "it's not costing them anything."

Ethical considerations related to speech, language, and hearing services remain fundamentally the same regardless of the system within which those services are delivered. Having said that, we must also recognize that the character of those considerations—that is, the ethical quandaries encountered, the bases for decisions on ethical matters, and the consequences that may result from unethical practices— may be quite different depending on the setting. Institutional environments generally provide better insulation for limited professional competence than does private practice. Similarly, they shelter professionals from difficult ethical decisions and conceal and protect professionals engaged in ethically dubious practices in ways that are generally unavailable to private practitioners. For all of these reasons, then, a special discussion of ethical concerns is probably warranted in a text focused on private practice in speech-language pathology and audiology.

Someone once observed that many members of our profession have the peculiar notion that the profession of speech-language pathology and audiology and the ASHA are one and the same. This is an obviously naive and nonsensical belief. There are similarly prevalent misapprehensions that ASHA's Code of Ethics somehow offers the last word with reference to the ethical conduct of the members of this profession. The Code is an ever-evolving document prepared and revised by some of the most concerned and experienced members of the ASHA. It defines standards of acceptable conduct required for maintaining ASHA membership and certification. Furthermore, it provides a valuable guide to all members of the profession, regardless of the setting in which they provide clinical services. Yet, it is not now, nor will it ever be, the last word in resolving all ethical concerns in the practice of speech-language pathology and audiology.

With the advent of state licensure has come a new set of confusions about definitions of ethical practices. Even though some states do include allusions to ethical practices in their licensure laws, they usually consider only patently immoral conduct or obviously harmful professional practices. Limited competence, poor judgment, subtle misrepresentation, and similar matters are seldom, if ever, dealt with effectively by licensure.

More effective legal influence over unethical behaviors may be provided by the increasingly frequent threats of litigation. For example, a clinician's engagement in practices that violate ASHA's Code of Ethics might well be used in defining breaches in standards of care, i.e., what a reasonable practitioner would do under similar circumstances. Identifying such breaches is an essential step in malpractice litigation. Nevertheless, there will always remain—and properly so—a significant gulf between what is legal and what is ethical.

The search for adequate definitions of such terms as ethics and ethical soon leads one into lofty allusions to right and wrong, moral and immoral. As in every aspect of contemporary life, such binary distinctions are often elusive in the daily practice of a profession. Ethical practices can be defined as those practices that best contribute to the quality of care provided to a client. In an earlier work, I proposed five criteria for judging the quality of clinical services: efficacy, coordination, continuity, participation—that is, the informed participation of clients and families in all decisions—and economy. Ethical practices are characterized by the realization of these criteria.

Discussions of ethics have probably engaged more writers than virtually any other topic throughout the history of literature. This fact alone should relieve any author of the pretense of comprehensiveness. Being relieved of this responsibility, I offer no apologies for concentrating this discussion in the six areas that seem most likely to present ethical quandaries for private practitioners of speech-language pathology and audiology: (1) professional competence, (2) confidentiality and informed consent, (3) fees and other financial arrangements, (4) advertising and marketing, (5) inter- and intraprofessional relationships, and (6) recommending and dispensing products.

PROFESSIONAL COMPETENCE　　The obvious first ethical responsibility borne by any provider of human services is the acquisition and maintenance of requisite knowledge and skills. Even though this responsibility is no more nor less incumbent on private practitioners, it may have particular implications in this setting. Private practitioners seldom have the immediate support system available to institutional employees. Informal consultations from more expert colleagues are more likely to be available in institutional settings. Generally, then, private practitioners must be more self-reliant when they encounter problems in clinical management. Furthermore, well-defined expertise is generally more tolerable in an institutional setting, where clients may be directed to staff members with special interests.

Private practitioners may also be penalized when they decline referrals because of insufficient expertise. Referral sources seldom differentiate among communication disorders. Thus, if a private practitioner declines a particular referral because of insufficient expertise, future referrals from that source may be unlikely. Understandably, then, private practitioners can be tempted to define their competencies generously.

For a whole host of reasons, private practice probably imposes greater demands for broader expertise than does practice in most other settings. In fact, economic survival usually requires a higher level of clinical proficiency than is tolerable in most other settings.

Any discussion of private practice in our field must also consider the large number of individuals who see a few clients privately to supplement their salaries from institutions or to maintain minimal professional involvement during periods of primary commitments to homemaking and motherhood. These individuals can play a very important role in the total delivery system of speech, language, and hearing services. Yet, regrettably, in too many instances their immunity from the economic pressures of full-time practice leads them to be less scrupulous in appraising their competence to provide the services they offer. Ethical constraints related to professional competence are the same for the private practitioner who serves only one client as for the private practitioner who is fully engaged.

As with any "young" profession (I sometimes believe we are aptly covered by Oscar Wilde's conclusion about the United States, "Their youth is their oldest tradition"), we have undoubtedly focused almost exclusively on entry-level professional competence, with little formal recognition that entry-level competence is insufficient in most settings, particularly in private practice. The first ethical constraint to be imposed on any private practitioner is that he or she must have substantially surpassed entry-level competence before embarking on independent private practice.

The Practitioner's Competence

During their early years of practice at least, successful private practitioners must usually encourage referrals from the widest possible array of sources. Most private practitioners constantly face quandaries related to accepting referrals in areas of limited competence and the economic consequences of turning away referrals from potentially productive sources. As with other professional quandaries, there are no simple solutions. Again, the obvious first solution lies in the level of general expertise a private practitioner brings to that practice. Not only does success in private practice demand a higher level of competence than is required for survival in other settings, it also probably requires a wider diversity of competence. Practitioners whose competence is restricted to particular areas of diagnosis and treatment or whose interests fall within a limited range of practice are probably best advised to form partnerships with practitioners presenting different areas of expertise.

It is also important to remember that the acceptance of a referral does not necessarily imply that all services will be provided by the practitioner. Often, the nature of the communication disorder and the services the client requires can only be determined after he or she has been seen. At that point, it may be quite legitimate to effect, usually with the informed participation of the original referral source, further referral to another private practitioner or to an institution where the needed expertise and other required special resources are available. This is a professionally legitimate service when the referral is skillfully effected so that appropriate resources are identified, the needed service or services can be provided, the client is likely to be accepted for the service, and the client understands and accepts the likely financial consequences. (We too often neglect to recognize that skillful referral management may be as important a competency as those more directly involved in diagnosis and treatment.) Most professional referral sources understand and appreciate this kind of client management.

Such referral practices predicate the availability of suitable resources. Unfortunately, this assumption is invalid in many communities. In those instances when a private practitioner does not feel competent to serve a particular client and cannot achieve with dispatch whatever competence is necessary, good ethical practice would require declining the referral, even though it may entail loss of a referral source.

Signifying Professional Competence

At one time, ASHA openly acknowledged that entry-level competence was insufficient for the pursuit of all professional endeavors through the awarding of two levels of certification: basic and advanced. Although the idea had theoretical merit, it courted a host of practical problems and confused employers, other professionals, and the public at large. Nevertheless, its discontinuation eliminated the only official recognition of higher levels of competence.

The Ph.D. degree has achieved some significance as denoting superior professional qualifications. This is paradoxical because, typically, Ph.D.s are awarded for scholarly and research endeavors that often have no direct relationship to clinical competence. Most first-rank universities would, in fact, resist efforts to pervert this scholarly degree into a symbol of the attainment of a particular level of professional proficiency. Efforts toward "professionalizing" the Ph.D. have occasionally even led to the demise of Ph.D. programs in our field.

The creation of a "clinical doctorate" remains an ever-popular topic for discussion. Two or three universities have embarked on such programs with, as yet, limited success. Of greater concern are "nontraditional" doctoral programs at universities that have few if any of the resources usually associated with institutions offering graduate degrees. In a few instances these institutions may have honestly strived to offer professionally significant educational opportunities that both permit graduates to identify themselves as holders of doctoral degrees and to expand substantially their professional competencies. Others, however, bestow degrees more on the basis of the receipt of a substantial sum of money than on the basis of the completion of rigorous requirements.

From a marketing standpoint, the mere presence of "Ph.D." on professional cards, stationery, and in Yellow Page listings may offer substantial advantages to a private practitioner. Its value lies in the implication of higher levels of competence than are found among practitioners who do not hold that degree. Therefore, when that degree was obtained on the basis of academic activities little related to professional competence, in a field other than the field of professional practice, such as linguistics, elementary education, or clinical psychology, or from an institution that imposed substantially lower requirements than are imposed by most other universities, the use of a doctoral degree in connection with a professional practice is probably unethical.

The interests of many private practitioners in speech-language pathology and audiology would probably be served by the development of some means of formal specialty recognition such as is provided by most other health and human services professions. Usually some form of board certification is used to signify completion of additional education, clinical practicum, and examination requirements. Although that certification generally has no formal legal status—that is, any licensed practitioner can legally function throughout the entire scope of practice of the profession—it is widely recognized by referral sources, by the public at large, and, to some extent, by third party payers. Furthermore, in the instance of litigation, a professional is in a precarious position when he or she does not hold specialty certification in the area under scrutiny.

The profession of speech-language pathology and audiology has been reluctant to establish any formal system of specialty recognition. Although innumerable groups within the profession have endorsed the concept, every system proposed for implementation has been rejected. Proposals inevitably run aground when it becomes apparent that every system for recognizing special expertise also constitutes a system of recognizing that some members of the profession do not have that expertise. Thus far, private practitioners have been no more vigorous in their support of plans for effecting specialty recognition than has any other group of practitioners. I believe this to be regrettable because formal specialty recognition might well assist private practitioners toward acceptable practical solutions to many ethical dilemmas.

Continuing Professional Competence

Our profession's concentration on entry-level competence has not only overemphasized a minimal level of acceptable preparation at the time of beginning practice but it has also led to inadequate regard for continuing professional education. Rapidly changing technologies demand that ethical practitioners, and most especially ethical private practitioners, frequently update their information in those fields in which they are providing services. Once again, although continuing education may be particularly important for private practitioners, it may also be particularly problematic.

Major problems in obtaining further education relate to economics. Many institutions pay fees and expenses for their employees to avail themselves of continuing education, particularly because evidence of regular pursuit of continuing education is a common requirement for accreditation. Even parsimonious institutions virtually always offer short-term salaried leaves for such opportunities. However, private practitioners must not only cover the cost of continuing education but they also lose income and even continue to cover overhead expenses for the time spent pursuing this education. It is essential, nonetheless, to recognize that continuing education is an inevitable ingredient of ethical practice and must eventually be included in the overall financial planning of every private practitioner.

Honesty also demands recognition of the gulf that exists between university departments of speech-language pathology and audiology—where many continuing education programs are based—and the realities of the daily practice of the profession. Private practitioners are justifiably outraged when they make the investment required to participate in a continuing education program offered by academicians who have no real understanding of clinical practices or who are themselves obsolescent. One very healthy development is the increasing involvement of private practitioners as providers of continuing education, either actually serving as sponsors of such activities or participating as instructors in activities offered by other sponsors.

Employee Competence

Private practices, as they expand, often employ other speech-language pathologists or audiologists, adding new ethical considerations. Not only are professionals ethically accountable for their own conduct but they are also responsible for the ethical conduct of their employees. Prominent among these responsibilities is ensuring that employees have the competencies required to perform the duties they are assigned.

In many instances, clinicians employed by private practitioners are fully qualified professionals. Differences between these employees and the private practitioners themselves relate primarily to the way in which they derive their income, i.e., on the basis of a salary or shares of the fees collected, rather than from the profit margin of the practice. Here, ethical concerns regarding employees are no different from the concerns faced by the private practitioners themselves. However, special concerns arise with respect to the employment of junior-level clinicians with little experience—particularly clinicians completing the Clinical Fellowship Year required for ASHA certification—and to the employment of paraprofessionals or other support personnel.

Economically naive members of our profession have often expounded on the exploitation of clinical fellows and other neophytes by private practitioners and other service providers who are dependent on fees for services. Yet, in most instances, when these clinicians are supervised sufficiently to ensure quality of care, the actual costs are substantial and often differ very little from the employment of experienced professionals.

Ethical problems are most likely to arise when services are delivered in dispersed settings. Frequently, private practitioners provide contract services to clients in several different nursing homes or through home health agencies. In these settings clinicians are often scrutinized less closely by members of other professions, and the clients themselves may be less able to assess the quality of care they are receiving. To remain within the bounds of ethical practice, private practitioners must plan carefully to ensure adequate monitoring of new professionals when they are physically separated from the practitioner's primary worksite.

Quandaries may also surround the amount of information that should be provided to clients and to contracting facilities about the level of experience and the overall status of junior employees. Good practice may entail and, in fact, state laws may require countersignature by the supervisor of all reports and progress notes of clinical fellows. (It must always be clear, however, who actually provided the documented services.) In addition, an ethical employer must ensure that every employee is competent to provide assigned services in the circumstances in which they are delivered, including the type of services, the characteristics of the client population, and the amount and kind of supervision available. If employees meet such compe tency criteria, it is unnecessary to make an issue of their status as clinical fellows. If they do not meet those criteria, they should not be so assigned under any circumstances.

Our profession, for many different reasons, has been less successful in the use of paraprofessionals than have some other professions. Except in such areas of practice as industrial and school hearing-conservation programs, their use has been sporadic. When paraprofessionals are employed, the legal and ethical responsibilities for their activities unequivocally and exclusively rest with their employer. Unlike the situation of clinical fellows and other junior-level professionals where there is shared responsibility, paraprofessionals bear no direct ethical or legal responsibility for the services they provide.

A regrettable practice has emerged in some states that license speech-language pathologists and audiologists. Individuals who do not qualify for licensure but do meet other professional requirements—for example, who hold speech, language, and hearing specialists' credentials issued by state education agencies—are employed as paraprofessionals to circumvent licensure requirements. So long as they are restricted to support functions under the close supervision of a licensed professional, this situation may be acceptable, albeit undesirable. When their scope of responsibilities exceeds support services and approaches independent professional practice, however, the situation is not only ethically untenable, it is also patently illegal.

CONFIDENTIALITY AND INFORMED CONSENT

The increasing spectre of litigation in all health and human services fields has forcefully directed the attention of professionals to issues related to confidentiality and, to an even greater extent, to issues concerning informed consent. The legal and ethical concepts underlying confidentiality and informed consent are quite forthright. Two principles undergird practices related to confidentiality. First, except under certain overriding circumstances, information about a client should be released only with the specific permission of the subject of the information or of his or her legal agent. Second, the client or his or her legal agent also has the right to review clinical records to ascertain the contents of those records, to ensure their accuracy, and to correct any inaccuracies.

Two further principles underlie practices related to informed consent. First, every person, or whatever persons are assigned legal responsibilities for the welfare of that person, has the right to accept or reject whatever services are proposed. Second, that person must be given sufficient information to make reasoned choices among whatever options are proposed.

Responsibilities related to confidentiality and informed consent are essentially the same regardless of the setting in which speech-language pathologists and audiologists deliver services. Once again, however, problems may manifest themselves in different ways when a professional is engaged in private practice. Furthermore, the actual responsibilities are often less straightforward than the delineated principles imply.

Confidentiality

Among the many services taken for granted by institutionally based professionals, particularly those based in large institutions, are records management departments. Too many professionals regard such departments as instruments of Satan, existing solely for the purpose of frustrating easy clinical service delivery. Records are unavailable when needed. Records librarians are constantly badgering professionals to update reports. Departments are held accountable for records transferred to other departments (incidentally, usually without any notification to the records department that such a transfer was effected). But clinicians also conveniently forget that they are relieved of most of the headaches related to records management, including many aspects of ensuring confidentiality. In private practice, however, the clinician must assume primary responsibility for all aspects of records management—perhaps with some clerical assistance—including the responsibilities related to maintaining confidentiality.

One ingredient of success for a private practitioner is the ability to keep overhead expenses within reasonable limits. The cost of records management constitutes one element of overhead expenses. Reasonable assurance of confidentiality must be accomplished, therefore, at the lowest possible cost.

Private practitioners may again encounter special problems when they are delivering services through a nursing home or a home health agency. Sometimes the responsibility for custody of records is ill defined so that private practitioners may be held responsible for breaches of confidentiality of which they were unaware and unable to control. Records management is another area that should be precisely defined in all contractual arrangements with nursing homes and home health agencies.

In certain other instances, private practitioners may be tempted to overlook practices related to confidentiality. Clinical reports may constitute one of the very best marketing devices available to private practitioners. When a professional receives a well-written, perceptive, and helpful report about a client, that professional is likely to remember the name of the author of the report in the future, should the occasion for referral for a similar service arise. In most instances, a client's consent is obtained for reporting to the referral source and to other individuals immediately concerned with his or her care. However, when other professionals become involved in the client's care, the clinician can seize the opportunity to send a report, even though specific permission has not been obtained. Although this might seem to be in the client's interest, it defies the ethical principle that every client has the right to determine whether information should be released to another party.

Presumably the income and even the continued employment of every speech-language pathologist or audiologist are to some degree related to the extent of services he or she provides. Unless a sufficient number of clients seek a clinician's services and avail themselves of whatever continuing services are recommended, it is unlikely that the clinician will maintain employment in virtually any setting. In no setting but private practice, however, is there usually such a direct relationship between productivity and income and survival. This would seem to place an additional premium on a client's acceptance of a clinician's recommendations. Although this situation may introduce some ethical hazards with respect to informed consent, no real incompatibility need exist. In fact, most experienced and successful private practitioners have long since learned that fully informed consent is in their best interest, that clients who do not understand what is entailed by whatever has been proposed are likely to eventually present problems that are difficult—and often expensive—to solve.

It is also assumed that private practitioners are more likely to introduce some degree of "salesmanship" in informing clients of their recommendations. So long as full and accurate information is provided, there is nothing unethical about being persuasive in making recommendations. Clients frequently complain that professionals are so passive in making recommendations that little guidance is provided about the advisability of following those recommendations. If we accept the notion that our primary responsibility as clinicians is to provide those health and human services that fall within our purview and that those services can benefit the people who need them, our recommendations should reflect some enthusiasm. If we do not accept that notion, we should probably be otherwise employed.

The previously cited principles concerning informed consent might imply that a program of services merely begins with a detailed discussion of recommendations, resulting in turn in the client's insightful selection among whatever service alternatives are proposed. Although this scenario can occur, some complications are likely. Speech-language pathology and audiology services may involve much more than the mutual agreement of the client and the clinician, at least if the client is to receive any assistance from whatever third party payer may be involved. In a growing number of instances, recommendations made by clinicians must be reconciled with restrictions imposed by payers. This can be extremely confusing to clients with communication disorders resulting from medically related conditions, i.e., conditions for which physician services and hospitalization have been covered. These clients may be confused and distressed when speech-language pathology and audiology services are not covered, or as is more likely, only a limited segment of the needed services are covered.

A compounding factor is the usual requirement of physician authorization for reimbursable services. If the attending physician does not support recommendations made by speech-language pathologists and audiologists, services are generally not reimbursable. Furthermore, physicians must recertify services; consequently, ongoing services may lose coverage if a physician refuses to recertify them. To make matters worse, even when such services are recommended, certified, or recertified by

Informed Consent

a physician, coverage can be denied by a payer, sometimes almost capriciously and even after extensive services have already been provided.

In view of the above, it is simplistic to propose merely that it is ethically incumbent on private practitioners to inform clients and to ensure that they understand all consequences of their recommendations. It may only be reasonable to expect a clinician to outline the procedure to be followed in determining the likelihood of reimbursement and, most importantly, to clarify the client's personal financial liability in the event claims are denied, deductibles have not been met, or, for any other reason, reimbursement falls short of total fees for services.

Further complications may arise with respect to informed consent when a client is served in a nursing home or in some other extended care facility. In this instance, the facility is the provider of services so far as most payers are concerned, and the contracting private practitioner becomes a supplier of services who has no direct contact with the payer. Therefore, whenever possible, information about financial liability should be given to clients and their families by the facility, rather than by the private practitioner. It may be wise to clarify this responsibility in the contract between the facility and the private practitioner.

The entire area of informed consent with respect to services provided to nursing home patients is obviously much broader than financial liability. A significant portion of these patients may not be able to participate independently in decisions related to their care, yet it may also be difficult to establish contact with families to enlist their "fully informed" participation in decisions. Even though a request for treatment from the attending physician or from the nursing staff scarcely qualifies as informed consent, in many instances it must suffice.

FEES AND OTHER FINANCIAL ARRANGE-MENTS

As noted earlier, no unique implications involve professionals who themselves collect fees for services instead of some institution collecting those fees. Nevertheless, private practitioners are concerned more directly in setting and collecting fees than are institution-based clinicians. This factor alone may involve professionals in private practice in more ethical dilemmas than face their colleagues in other settings.

Establishing Fees for Services

ASHA, as do most professional associations, refers to the establishment of fees in its Code of Ethics: "Individuals' fees shall be commensurate with services rendered." Although necessarily ambiguous, this statement represents a substantial improvement over the previous version of the Code, which enjoined, "He must not exploit persons he serves professionally . . . by charging exorbitant fees."

With respect to the current Code statement, good ethical practice is completely consistent with good business practice. A precise accounting of the costs of providing services, including a reasonable profit margin, is essential in ensuring that "fees are commensurate with services rendered." Furthermore, any private practitioner who fails to do precise cost accounting is not likely to succeed financially.

Our profession's failure to accrue good cost data is probably one reason for our undistinguished record in securing adequate third party coverage. Furthermore, lacking such data, payers establish reimbursement levels well below prevailing private fees in the name of cost containment. They often imply that these levels represent usual and customary rates, leading clients to conclude that practitioners are charging exorbitant fees. This implication of unethical behavior by the clinician is obviously untenable. The only safeguard is scrupulously accurate accounting of services costs.

Thorny dilemmas face all fees-supported services providers with respect to the disparities between levels of third party reimbursement and cost-based customary fees. I have already alluded to the problem of interpreting these disparities to clients in the discussion of informed consent. There are no easy answers to questions about the level of financial liability that should be assigned to clients when reimbursement falls short of customary fees. From an ethical standpoint, it is quite reasonable to assume that the client is personally liable for balances between billed fees and allowed reimbursement. In actual practice, however, it may be difficult, if not impossible, to pursue that liability in many instances.

Public third party payers, in particular Medicaid, may establish reimbursement rates that are significantly below customary fees, and beneficiaries of these programs often cannot be held personally responsible for the difference. Some private practitioners, understandably, refuse to provide services under these circumstances. An interesting dilemma arises, however, when a significant number of these clients are served. Whether in the form of bad debts or inadequate reimbursement, differences between fees and payments must be dealt with as a cost of delivering services. As all costs, they must be included in the accounting that leads to establishing fees. Put crudely, the fees paid by other clients must offset the deficits incurred by serving beneficiaries of public third party payers. However unfair this may seem to the economically naive, it is inevitable in today's health and human services system, a system that has created its own morality.

A somewhat related concern involves rendering services to anyone, either without charge or at greatly reduced fees. This can be a particularly sensitive situation when a private practitioner relies substantially on physician referrals. Physicians sometimes extend "courtesies" to a variety of people—to other physicians and their families, members of the clergy, relatives, friends, and the like—and request that these same people be exempt from fees when referred to speech-language pathologists and audiologists. Typically, however, physicians operate their offices on profit margins many times greater than those of private practitioners of our profession. Because these clients are usually well able to pay for their services or are adequately covered by private insurance, it is unfair, and perhaps even unethical, to absorb the cost of serving them, once again increasing the overall cost of providing services. On the other hand, if good relationships with important referral sources are fostered by serving some clients without charge, it is probably a legitimate cost of doing business. Nevertheless, it may require infinite tact and wisdom to keep such services within reasonable bounds.

Further dilemmas arise when a client can no longer afford to cover the fees entailed in the services they require, as in instances when their financial circumstances change, when a third party payer does not authorize continuing services, or when they have exceeded the limits of their insurance coverage. If clinicians make every effort to find alternative sources for needed services, they are well within the limits of ethical practice when they terminate services. When the situation is personified in an actual client, however, the decision to terminate may be difficult, particularly when suitable affordable services are unavailable.

Delinquent Accounts, Bad Debts, and Retroactive Denial of Claims

Although issues related to delinquent accounts, bad debts, and retroactive denial of claims have few direct ethical implications, they can lead to dilemmas for private practitioners who are dedicated to the delivery of human services. On the one hand, there is nothing unethical about clinicians expecting fair recompense for their services. On the other hand, there are widespread negative attitudes about health and human services providers who pursue delinquent accounts and bad debts too vigorously. Therefore, the course to be followed may be determined by professional propriety, rather than by actual ethical concerns. Clinicians may ultimately pay a high price for breaches of propriety with respect to these financial matters. Too vigorous pursuit of delinquent accounts may be viewed as improper and ultimately impair a practitioner's status in the community. The economic consequences of losses in reputation may ultimately be much greater than the losses from bad debts. Every private practitioner should become familiar with the prevailing customs of other professionals in the community before deciding on his or her approach to such matters.

Furthermore, it is important to remember that unpaid bills may denote serious dissatisfaction with services. Vigorous pursuit of delinquent accounts may encourage such counteractions by clients as malpractice suits. Whether justified or not, the cost of defense against litigation far exceeds the cost of writing off bad debts.

Issues concerning disparities between third party coverage and customary fees have already been discussed; nevertheless, the problem of retroactively denied claims deserves special mention. In reality, clinicians can only be confident that services are reimbursable when they, or their clients, actually receive checks from the third party payer. (Even that statement may not be entirely accurate in that Medicare, in particular, occasionally seeks refunds of previously allowed reimbursement.) Even though services are appropriately authorized, certified, recertified, or whatever, claims are often denied retroactively. In these instances a clinician may have already provided substantial services. The first proper course of action usually entails appealing the denial of the claim. Thereafter, the earlier-mentioned considerations related to the liability to be assigned to the client again obtain.

Contract Services

As already noted, in order to qualify for reimbursement under Medicare and under other insurance programs, speech-language pathologists frequently execute contracts with such institutional providers as nursing homes and home health agencies. Licensing and accrediting agencies may require that these institutions have speech-language pathology services available, at least "on call." On this basis, institutions may execute contracts with private practitioners, but seldom, if ever, call on them to see patients. Presumably, the ethics of institutions that are party to such practices could be called into question. Nevertheless, the speech-language pathologists are also culpable, because they are lending their names under circumstances that mislead licensing and accrediting agencies and, ultimately, consumers and potential consumers.

Ethical considerations, as well as sound business practices, are best served when these contracts specify regularly provided services, such as screening and staff orientation, to ensure the physical presence in the institution, at least occasionally, of the speech-language pathologist. Thus the clinician does not merely rely on the discretion of nursing staff and attending physicians to decide whether or not speech-language consultations are required.

ADVERTISING AND MARKETING

Advertising and other overt marketing efforts by professionals were once considered absolutely unacceptable. These efforts were usually banned in codes of ethics and often even made illegal in statutes enacted with the support of the professions themselves. Two main factors accounted for the changes in attitudes that have occurred recently. First, consumer activists held that bans on advertising were anticompetitive practices that resulted in the maintenance of high fees. Second, there have been steady increases in the numbers of practitioners of most professions so that professionals are turning to advertising and marketing in order to succeed in the increasingly competitive domain of the delivery of health and human services.

No longer, then, are advertising and marketing by professionals anathema. However, differences still exist between what is acceptable in the realm of professional services and what is acceptable in the world of commerce.

Advertising and marketing practices are probably unethical only when they actually misinform or mislead consumers and potential consumers. Most questions relate to the propriety of those practices. The public at large, as well as the members of other professions and indeed the members of our profession, still maintain different standards for the advertising and marketing practices of professionals. These differences may be subtle, but they are telling.

Paid Advertising

Traditionally, professionals were restricted to the use of discreetly worded "announcements of services" engraved on cards or published in telephone directory Yellow Pages. Today, however, even once-conservative health professionals and institutions employ newspaper and magazine advertising, radio and television commercials, signboards, and virtually every other medium to promote their services. These efforts have probably been most successful in urban communities where a major segment of the population has no established relationship with a primary health care provider and faces an open market when services are required. Because these expensive campaigns are proliferating despite the generally adverse economics of the health care industry, one must assume that they are successful.

Nevertheless, it is important to remember that acceptability to the community is a major determinant of propriety and effectiveness. A calendar distributed by a highly reputable and successful audiology practice in a southwestern city featured a photograph of the staff wearing comic cowboy gear and encouraged establishing contact with the center's "hole in the ear gang." Although other professionals and consumers in the community where the center is located might find this advertising approach acceptable and attractive, it would seem ridiculous and even offensive in other communities.

The increasing involvement of audiologists in hearing aid dispensing has encouraged their assumption of many of the advertising practices of commercial dispensers. This may be inconsistent with the notion that the increasing involvement of audiologists in hearing aid dispensing is "professionalizing" this delivery system, i.e., protecting it from some of the abuses once prevalent in the strictly commercial system. Presumably, advertising practices figured prominently among those abuses. Therefore, audiologists should weigh the propriety of their advertising and assess whether other professionals and the public will associate it with segments of the hearing care system they often distrust. Furthermore, there may be considerable reason to question the ultimate effectiveness of typical advertising in motivating potential purchasers of hearing aids. A recent major survey conducted by the Hearing Industries Association—the organization of manufacturers of hearing aids and related equipment—found advertising to be a minor factor in motivating hearing-impaired consumers to seek assistance.

Interprofessional Marketing

Increasingly, private practitioners, particularly audiology practitioners, are serving clients who come to them directly without referral from another professional. Most practices, however, still rely substantially on referrals. Therefore, the most important of all marketing efforts is directed at broadening the referral base. Once again, so long as the services that are provided and the practitioner's competence to provide those services are accurately presented in interprofessional marketing, no frankly ethical issues are likely to arise. On the other hand, questions about professional propriety are very likely to surface.

Traditional announcement cards, giving such basic information as the practitioner's name, highest degree, certification and licensure status, and a brief list of offered services, are accepted by professionals in all communities. More detailed brochures delineating services in greater detail may be acceptable to some communities and professionals but not to others. At issue here is the subtle, even ephemeral, differentiation between informing and soliciting. Few professionals resent being informed about potential referral resources, but they can be completely turned off by efforts that they perceive as solicitation.

Private practitioners sometimes make effective use of educational materials in interprofessional marketing. Some of these materials may be directed at the professionals, helping them recognize and appropriately manage clients with communication disorders, e.g., brochures offering suggestions to pediatricians to help them identify children with possible speech, language, and hearing problems or brochures for industrial physicians informing them about the recognition and prevention of noise-induced hearing loss. Other materials may be designed for distribution to the professional's clients or patients to offer them useful information about the prevention, identification, and management of communication disorders. These educational materials may be prepared by the speech-language pathologist or audiologist distributing them, or they may be commercially published materials that are purchased by the private practitioner and imprinted with his or her name and address.

Some private practitioners have made effective use of newsletters, mailed at regular intervals to referral sources. These newsletters offer brief discussions of recent trends in the management of communication disorders and of the services provided by the practitioner.

The use of all of these published materials is much more likely to be acceptable, and indeed more effective, when sent to professionals who have previously referred clients, even very occasionally. Professionals, particularly physicians, are deluged with all manner of announcements, newsletters, and brochures. Most are immediately consigned, unread, to the wastepaper basket unless the professional has some particular interest in the source or topic.

Unequivocally, the best and most universally acceptable interprofessional marketing tool is the skillful management of each referral. When a professional and the client he or she refers are well served, that professional is not only likely to refer other clients in the future but may also recommend that colleagues utilize that speech-language pathologist or audiologist as a referral source. Once a clinician has established this identity, brochures, newsletters, and other published materials may encourage further referrals. Without that identity, however, their effectiveness is usually limited, and their use may even be regarded as professionally improper.

Screening and Public Education

Although more widely used by institutions, some private practitioners use screening as a marketing tool. Few ethical dilemmas arise when screening programs are carried out in situations where practitioners are already providing diagnostic, treatment, and consultative services, such as in nursing homes, home health programs, and private schools; when they are specifically retained to provide such services as in industrial hearing conservation programs; or even when they are voluntarily providing screening services to demonstrate the needs for services in particular programs, e.g., in child care programs or senior centers. However, problems arise when screening services are offered indiscriminately to the general public. Although pursued in good faith by clinicians, these screening services are fraught with hazards. In particular, they may be considered as improper solicitation, even "ambulance chasing," by the more conservative professionals in a community and even by potential consumers.

Beyond ensuring that the techniques to be employed are appropriate and effective, the primary ethical issues in publicly offered screening programs relate to the understandings and expectations of clients and to the management of the individuals who are identified as requiring further services. These issues are compounded by the fact that such screening programs usually offer "free" services.

A significant portion of the people who present themselves for screening services are already aware that they have communication problems. They are seeking more than the information that they may have a problem and should seek further diagnostic services, which is the usual extent of conclusions reached from practical screening techniques. The situation is complicated when they are informed that the more extensive services they were seeking from the "free" program may entail substantial costs. This may appear to be the "bait and switch" approach used by unscrupulous salespeople. The general public may also be wary of free screening services in the field of communication disorders because of their widespread use by hearing aid dispensers with unsavory reputations.

Even when the purpose of a screening program is clear, problems may occur in identifying the sources of further services. From a legal standpoint, solicitation is usually differentiated from public education efforts on the basis of the intention to induce potential consumers to avail themselves of a specific provider's products or services. Therefore, when a screening program leads to informing clients of various available resources of required services, no solicitation is involved. When, however, only a single resource is proposed, this clearly represents solicitation, a practice many professionals consider improper. Yet, the only conceivable reason for private practitioners to offer screening services to the general public is to secure clients for diagnostic and rehabilitative services. Therefore, if it is improper to limit referrals from those screening programs, the programs become a dubious marketing effort. Furthermore, from a purely practical standpoint, many, if not most, people who present themselves to free public screening programs are unable or unwilling to pay for private care. This may cast further doubt on the wisdom of public screening as a marketing tool.

As with all practitioners of our profession, it is ethically incumbent on private practitioners to inform the public about communication disorders and about resources for assistance with those disorders. So long as such efforts are general, few questions about ethics or propriety arise, although some physicians have registered strenuous objections to public education efforts that do not specify medical consultations as the first step in seeking assistance. Questions more frequently arise when public education efforts become publicity, i.e., newspaper or magazine items or radio or television coverage that identifies a particular professional or product. Such publicity may appear spontaneously, but more often it is sought by a professional or by a public information specialist on the professional's behalf.

Publicity can be a valuable marketing tool. It is, however, an extremely hazardous tool, both from the viewpoint of ethics and from the viewpoint of effectiveness. In most instances, the professional is at the mercy of the reporter or other interviewer, the rewrite desk, the editor, and every other person and procedure intervening between the professional's intentions and whatever reaches the eyes and ears of the public. If the professional appears to be naive, eccentric, or duplicitous to the public or to other professionals, publicity can be quite damaging. Therefore, wise practitioners should carefully appraise opportunities to be featured in such efforts.

INTER- AND INTRAPRO-FESSIONAL RELATION-SHIPS

The growing competition between and among the professions concerned with the delivery of health and human services has substantially altered concerns and standards regarding professional ethics and propriety. At one time, any overt effort by a professional to gain a competitive edge was considered to be grossly improper, if not outright unethical. The general acceptance of the concept of professions as closed secret societies in which one practitioner would seldom speak out against another practitioner was closely related. There was also a unilateral tradition in health-related fields that permitted physicians to criticize and disparage the members of other professions with complete freedom; but any member of those professions who, in turn, spoke out against one or more physicians might well be denied physician referrals from that day forward.

Although by no means dead, these traditions have changed and the changes have been generally salutary, particularly with respect to consumer welfare. Contrary to the objectives of consumer groups, increased free competition between and among health and human services has not effected notable reductions in costs. Nevertheless, it has probably effected some general improvements in the quality of care. When professionals are constantly closely scrutinized by competitors, they are probably more meticulous, and the grossly inept are likely to be weeded out. Furthermore, there are added incentives to maintain professional currency and to be more considerate of client convenience and economics.

Relating to Members of Other Professions

Major ethical quandaries may attend the virtually universal requirement of medical authorization for reimbursement under public and private health insurance plans. For quite proper reasons, our profession has emerged as independent from medical prescription. It is even widely accepted that acceding to the provision of services by prescription from members of other professions represents unethical conduct. However, the distinguishing characteristics of prescriptions have never been entirely clear. The differences between accepting referrals and accepting prescriptions probably represent a continuum, rather than a binary distinction. A referral seeks the opinion of another professional or asks that professional to participate in another manner in a client's care. A prescription specifies the precise manner in which diagnostic and treatment services are to be carried out. Thus, when a physician enters "evaluation and treatment" as an order in a record or even on a prescription form, it is not really a prescription. In contrast, when a physician "refers" someone for speech-language pathology and audiology services and specifies the tests to be conducted or the rehabilitation approaches to be followed, it becomes more of a prescription than a referral.

The essential ethical issue is not merely a matter of professional territory or pride; rather it is an issue of consumer welfare. Speech-language pathologists and audiologists are more expert within the scope of practice of their profession than are other professionals. (If they are not, they should not be practicing and, most especially, not practicing privately.) Although suggestions from other professionals with respect to diagnosis and treatment may be invaluable, the final decisions about the approaches to be employed must always rest with the speech-language pathologist or audiologist.

Although ethical quandaries may arise when highly competent and well-informed professionals are concerned, those quandaries are compounded when professionals are functioning beyond the limits of their competence or are using obsolescent practices. It is neither proper nor ethical to protect these practitioners. Doing so is, in fact, a violation of consumer welfare. Wise clinicians, however, focus clients' attention on differing professional opinions, rather than pointing out limitations in professional competence. They present the best available information as clearly as possible and delineate the recommendations that emerge from that information. They can openly recognize disparities between their recommendations and those made previously by other professionals and speculate about the basis of those disparities, including the possibility that the other professionals may not be familiar with recent information. They may even suggest that a client seek a second opinion from another member of the profession. Undeniably, clients often accept inaccurate information from certain professionals, particularly physicians, more readily than they accept recommendations from members of less prestigious professions. Furthermore, speech-language pathologists and audiologists may lose referral sources when inter-professional disagreements about client management occur. Nevertheless, the ultimate ethical responsibility of any professional is the delivery of the best possible services to every client. Preserving interprofessional cordiality at the expense of quality of care clearly violates that responsibility.

There are some further popular misconceptions about referrals made by speech-language pathologists and audiologists to other professionals. Some institutions require that, in making referrals to professionals who are not affiliated with that institution, at least three different names must be offered. Although this practice may preserve harmony with professionals in the community, it is by no means based on ethical concerns. Most professionals have long since identified other professionals who provide the best services in particular instances. When they specify only those professionals in making referrals, they usually serve a client's best interests. Further-more, successful practitioners of all professions tend to develop close and cordial working relationships with a limited circle of other professionals who, in turn, refer clients to them. So long as all of the professionals involved are competent in the areas of needed services, this situation is quite proper and, because of the previously established level of cooperation and communication, probably leads to the best client care. Nonetheless, too close restriction in a private practitioner's circle of referral sources and resources can be precarious.

The growing competition among professions, particularly the competition that has resulted from overcrowding in some human services professions, has led more and more members of those professions, such as neuropsychologists, clinical linguists, occupational therapists, and otolaryngologists, to offer services previously assigned to speech-language pathologists and audiologists. Some members of our profession have looked to licensure to protect them from this competition. However, except in medicine where the unlicensed practice of medicine can lead to serious conse-quences, licensure has not dealt with scope-of-practice infringement effectively. Clearly, however, it is quite proper to identify scope-of-practice infringements to administrators, to consumers, and to the offending professionals themselves. It is also extremely important to preserve reimbursement restrictions so that only speech-language pathologists and audiologists—and, regrettably, usually physicians—can qualify for reimbursement within the scope of practice of our profession. In the final analysis, nonetheless, as in every other segment of our competitive society, the right to provide services will ultimately be won by those professionals who can convince administrators, bureaucrats, consumers, payers, and other professionals that they can provide the best services with the greatest economy.

It is incumbent on all speech-language pathologists and audiologists to promote the welfare and prestige of the entire profession. Such promotion, however, cannot be ethically accomplished at the expense of consumers. Therefore, the same standards of conduct apply in intraprofessional relationships as in interprofessional relationships: When intraprofessional disagreements occur with respect to client management, any differences in conclusions, recommendations, and management approaches should be clearly identified to clients, and sufficient information should be provided, insofar as possible, to permit them to reach informed decisions. This standard obtains whether the other concerned professionals are private practitioners or are employed by a medical center, a school district, a university, or by some other institution.

One problem faced by our profession, but long since solved by other professions, is the number of presumed clinicians who do not meet accepted standards for entering practice. Several states do not offer licenses; consequently, no legal controls exist to define the members of our profession. The majority of licensed states exempt individuals employed in certain settings, most notably in the schools. In those states many, even most, clients may be served by clinicians who do not meet acceptable professional standards. Therefore, in instances where clinicians do not meet acceptable standards, it is quite proper to include this information in accounting for differing opinions. Similar comments regarding qualifications may also be appropriate when services have been provided primarily by students in university clinics. So long as a clinician presents acceptable credentials, such as state licensure or ASHA certification, differing conclusions and recommendations are probably better dealt with as differing professional opinions, rather than as manifestations of differing competence.

Public Law 94-142, which mandates "a free, appropriate education" for all handicapped children, has introduced an additional set of concerns to all speech-language pathologists and audiologists who serve children outside a school setting, perhaps particularly to private practitioners. Sometimes, local education agencies can be required to pay for services provided privately when "appropriate" services are unavailable within the school setting. In these instances, private practitioners may seem self-serving when they conclude that a child's school program is inadequate. Nevertheless, those practitioners would be ethically derelict if they neglected to communicate those conclusions to the child's family. First efforts should probably be devoted to arranging a suitable school-based program. If that is not possible, however, the focus should shift to arranging appropriate out-of-school services. Propriety may be served when a private practitioner in these circumstances mentions all appropriate private resources in making recommendations, but it is certainly acceptable for the private practitioner to include his or her name among those resources.

A further ethics-related issue in intraprofessional relationships primarily concerns the ways in which institution-based practitioners relate to private practitioners, rather than the reverse. One obvious reality of private practice is that clients must be able to pay for their services or have some other available source of payment. Often, therefore, private practitioners must refer clients to institutions, either after initial evaluations or following a period of treatment, when financial resources are

Relating to Other Speech-Language Pathologists and Audiologists

exhausted. Such situations are inevitable in our nation's human services delivery system. When institution-based clinicians criticize private practitioners for effecting referrals under these circumstances, they are violating acceptable ethical practices with respect to intraprofessional relationships.

RECOM- MENDING AND DISPENSING PRODUCTS

Major changes have also occurred in recent years in the roles of the professional in dispensing products. Proscriptions against direct participation in dispensing were based on beliefs that financial gain might interfere with professional judgment. These attitudes among speech-language pathologists and audiologists were further extensions of the belief that their services should somehow be divorced from economic considerations. Because virtually every clinician's income bears some relationship to his or her productivity, this attitude is nonsensical. Albeit sometimes very indirectly, productivity, and hence income, is ultimately influenced by the recommendations the clinician makes. Situations in which recommendations involve the purchase of products dispensed by the professional are only differences in degree, rather than in kind.

As did many professions, speech-language pathology and audiology once held direct involvement in the sale of professionally related products to be unethical conduct. The attitudes expressed in that proscription have fortunately changed substantially in recent years. Nevertheless, some unique ethical quandaries and questions of propriety may arise when clinicians venture into product dispensing. Because hearing aids are the products most likely to be dispensed by our profession, the major part of this discussion focuses on those devices.

Selection and Trial of Devices

From a professional standpoint, the hearing aid selection process may seem forthright. A particular client's needs for amplification are estimated, and likely instruments are preselected; then the "best" instrument is chosen on the basis of performance on a test battery. The obvious first flaw in this procedure is that every hearing-aid-selection test battery yet devised fails to withstand objective scrutiny. Beyond this, however, the assumptions that a wide array of instruments is available and that all dispensing decisions are strictly impartial may also be questionable.

Prevalent practices in the hearing aid industry can result in economic inducements that can substantially influence a dispenser's recommendations. In the first place, there are significant differences among the arrangements made by manufacturers' representatives with respect to supplying instruments for use in selection procedures. These obviously influence the array of available instruments. Furthermore, there are substantial financial advantages when a dispenser purchases multiple instruments from the same manufacturer. Consequently, it can be very tempting to deal with only two or three manufacturers, again restricting the range of available instruments, although a relatively limited array may meet the needs of a large majority of clients. Finally, when dispensers maintain an inventory—in contrast to ordering each instrument individually from the manufacturer after an aid has been finally selected—the longevity of an instrument in the inventory can easily sway a dispenser toward recommending that aid.

Again, these are dilemmas with no easy answers. As in every area of service, audiologists in private practice must obviously be aware of these economic factors or they will not survive. On the other hand, when such factors exert major influences on professional decisions, serious ethical concerns arise.

As already noted, there are no absolutely valid approaches to objective hearing aid selection. Consequently, virtually all audiologist-dispensers permit clients a trial period with the instrument, usually 30 days or so. Because this practice offsets some inadequacies in conventional selection procedures, it is probably an important aspect of good client care. Fortunately, most hearing aid manufacturers have adopted generous instrument return policies, so that dispensers do not suffer substantial losses when a client ultimately rejects a particular instrument. Nevertheless, the dispenser must usually absorb some added costs in these instances. It is quite legitimate to recoup some of these costs by charging rental fees or in some other way asking clients to pay for the use of the instrument during the trial period. Beyond this, however, dispensers should avoid overly aggressive efforts to dissuade clients from returning aids they find unsatisfactory.

"Bundling" Versus "Unbundling" of Professional Fees and Instrument Costs

Although many professions have come to accept their practitioners' participation in dispensing products, they may still hold that the actual cost of the product should be clearly differentiated from the professional fees associated with selecting and dispensing that product. Occasionally, the few public third party payers who provide coverage for the purchase of hearing aids have attempted, usually unsuccessfully, to write such requirements into their regulations. The lumping of product costs with all associated costs is commonly called "bundling," and the reverse is "unbundling."

Particularly in the instance of hearing aids, tradition has been on the side of bundling. When clients go directly to a commercial dispenser, their hearing is tested and their needs for amplification are appraised without charge. Furthermore, after a hearing aid is purchased, all follow-up services are provided without charge. Typically, however, when audiologists dispense aids, fees are charged for initial diagnostic studies and for the appraisal of amplification requirements that lead to recommendation of the aid to be dispensed. Furthermore, particularly when they are extensive, fees may also be levied for follow-up visits. Under these circumstances, the actual purchase price of the instrument is probably lower than when costs are bundled. Nevertheless, clients who are familiar with the usual commercial dispensing system may be confused, and often resentful, when billed for these fees.

Although good professional practice may ultimately be on the side of unbundling, some temporizing is probably in order. Certainly all costs directly related to supplying the hearing aid are legitimately included within the price of the instrument. This may even include costs relating to time spent in providing selection and follow-up services. The distinguishing feature may be that bundled costs consist of those virtually always entailed in supplying an instrument, i.e., where liability is legitimately shared by all clients receiving the service. On the other hand, certain clients may require more extensive diagnostic, selection, orientation, and follow-up services than is typical. These individuals may well be expected to pay additional fees for services. Even in the instance of more typical clients, however, it may be wise to show some apportionment of charges to clients to help them understand how those charges are derived. Furthermore, at least those studies that can be considered essential to diagnosing the type and extent of the hearing impairment may be reimbursable by many health insurance programs, as may some follow-up rehabilitation procedures. In these instances, apportionment of charges is essential.

Maintenance and Other Continuing Responsibilities

Further unique considerations entailed with product dispensing, particularly hearing aid dispensing, relate to the continuing services that must be available to clients purchasing those products. New batteries are required continuously, and from time to time, new earmolds must be made. In addition, as with any moderately delicate appliance, repairs are sometimes necessary. Although it may be less important to a battery supplier, hearing aid dispensers, professional or commercial, must assume some continuing responsibility for the maintenance of the aids they provide to clients. Those responsibilities may be cursory, including initial "trouble shooting," sending defective instruments to manufacturers for repairs, supplying loan instruments for use during the interval required for repairs, and the like. Nonetheless, however cursory, these services are essential.

Professional dispensers have often acted unfairly to their clients and to commercial dispensers by discouraging return visits for maintenance services. Presumably, the essential reason for audiologist participation in hearing aid dispensing is "professionalizing" this aspect of the hearing care system. If, after a hearing aid has been dispensed, consumers are discouraged from seeking continuing services from audiologists, they will immediately turn to commercial dispensers for the assistance they require. When this occurs, all further services, including the selection and fitting of future aids and all rehabilitation counseling, will probably be provided by the commercial dispenser.

Unfortunately, in recent years the practice of audiology has focused primarily on diagnostic services. In appropriate instances, diagnostic services may terminate with hearing aid selection and dispensing. Thus, dispensing of a satisfactory instrument is the final step in the diagnostic process. If, however, audiology is also devoted to rehabilitation, services must be viewed as ongoing, accommodating changes in a client's disabilities and daily needs, as well as considering new technological developments that may improve a client's communicative effectiveness. Discouraging clients from maintaining continuing contacts with the audiologists who dispense their hearing aids seriously restricts the scope of audiologic practice.

It would be very naive, nonetheless, to assume that these issues are as straightforward as have been presented here. Continuing services can be expensive. Again, consumers who are familiar with the commercial dispensing system do not expect to pay for charges other than repair costs. The mere existence of fees for these services may encourage them to leave the professional dispensing system. Presumably, the only answer lies in factoring typical requirements for follow-up care into the cost analyses that lead to establishing fees and costs associated with initial acquisition of the hearing aid. Under these circumstances, then, some continuing services can be provided without levying further fees.

In the future there may be more extensive involvement of speech-language pathologists and audiologists in dispensing products other than hearing aids. Some audiologists who provide services in industry are also involved in supplying various noise-protection appliances. Thus far the sale of assistive listening devices other than hearing aids has been limited throughout the entire hearing care system, but it seems likely that as more become available and their use more general, audiologists may increasingly participate in dispensing these devices.

Speech-language pathologists are also becoming more and more involved in the recommendation of prostheses: augmentative communication systems, electrolarynxes and other electrical and mechanical devices used by alaryngeal speakers, and speech prostheses used by tracheoesophageal speakers. In some instances, as with tracheoesophageal prostheses, it may be essential for the clinician to dispense the device if he or she is to serve these clients, thus making product dispensing inseparable from the service. Other assistive listening and augmentative communication devices may as well be purchased from a manufacturer or another vendor. Among other reasons, such devices are recommended by most practitioners only occasionally, and it may not be economically feasible to be directly involved in their sale. With the possible exception of augmentative communication devices, services and products are usually clearly separable. Therefore, bundling/unbundling concerns are less likely to arise, as are other significant ethical quandaries.

Occasionally, clinicians develop materials they employ in treatment programs that may be published either privately or commercially. Increasingly these materials are in the form of computer software. Sometimes, ethical concerns, or at least concerns about professional propriety, are raised about requiring clients to purchase such materials. There are clearly hazards in terms of potential conflicts of interest. On the other hand, a clinician might legitimately prefer to use materials he or she has prepared in carrying out treatment programs because they usually best represent approaches the clinician prefers. If these materials are central to the services the client requires and if the client appears to benefit from the approaches taken, their use seems quite legitimate. Nevertheless, it is probably best, wherever possible, to add the cost of such materials in computing fees for services because they are inherent to the treatment program. If additional charges are levied, they are best limited to the actual cost of the materials, excluding royalties or other profit to the clinician.

Other Treatment-Related Equipment and Materials

SUMMARY

Recent years have seen substantial changes in the ways all health and human services professionals deliver services. These changes have led to re-evaluation of traditional standards of ethical conduct and professional propriety. Within the profession of speech-language pathology and audiology there has been a similar re-evaluation, which applies to all settings in which services are delivered. Nevertheless, different quandaries may arise in different settings. Therefore, although the same essential standards apply to private practitioners of speech-language pathology and audiology as to other clinicians, different problems may be manifest and different decisions may be required in private practice. In the final analysis, however, in all settings, the overriding determinants of ethical and proper conduct are the factors that also determine the quality of the services provided.

Part II

Establishing a Private Practice in Speech-Language Pathology and Audiology: The Realities

Chapter 7

Selecting the Location and Site for a Private Practice

Patricia R. Cole, Ph.D.

The private practitioner should consider several issues in choosing the city or region and the specific site for a practice. The general economy, population characteristics, community attitudes, and health and education services should be evaluated in light of the nature of the practice to be established. Once a city or region is chosen, the particular site selected should be accessible, safe, financially affordable, and suitable for the type of professional practice being established.

LOCATION OF THE PRACTICE

Location refers to the region or city being considered for establishing a practice. The practitioner should evaluate a potential location relative to the opportunities and demands for services rather than simply deciding whether it is a desirable place to live. Surveys conducted by the American Speech-Language-Hearing Association (ASHA) provide information on factors to consider in selecting a location for a practice (ASHA, 1983a,b). The annually published *Editor and Publisher Market Guide*, available in most public libraries, provides information about each United States and Canadian city that has a daily newspaper. This publication gives a concise review of population estimates, personal disposable income, total retail and food sales, banking industries, and other information that can be useful in evaluating a potential location for a private practice.

General Economy

From a business perspective, the key consideration for any location is whether the community needs and can support a private practice. The general economy of the region should be evaluated. Is the business climate expanding, declining, or static? Are businesses well established and prosperous, new and expanding, faltering, or unusually speculative? What are the primary industries in the area, and what is the projected future for such industries? Is there a decline or growth in the real estate market? What is the unemployment rate? Information of this nature may be available through the local Chamber of Commerce office, local newspapers, and selected publications found in local libraries.

Communities with well-established and expanding businesses and with a steady record of low unemployment are likely to support a private practice on an ongoing basis. Those with faltering or extremely speculative businesses pose a higher risk for poor economic conditions. A realistic appraisal of the current and projected economic status of the region is important in determining whether a new business in speech-language pathology or audiology is likely to thrive.

Population Characteristics

The population characteristics of the city or region should be assessed. What is the age of the majority of the population, and does the predominant age group fit with the kind of practice to be established? What is the marital status of the majority of the population? What occupations are most prevalent? What is the average income? Is the population stable, or is it a highly transient community? Do most people own or rent their living space? Do most residents work in the city or area, or do they commute to other parts of the region to work?

The nature of the population has a significant effect on setting up and maintaining a private practice. Obviously, if the majority of residents are retired or single, the likelihood of a growing demand for services for young children is small. If the average income places most families in lower-income brackets, many will not be able to pay for private services. If the population is transient, a practice will not have the benefit of long-term care and, more importantly, will not have the benefit of former patients as a referral source.

Information about population characteristics is available in census reports, which can be found in public libraries. County government offices have census tract information, showing population density and distribution within the county. Some county offices have information from the current and previous years to reflect patterns and rates of growth.

Community Attitudes

Community attitudes toward health, education, and rehabilitation programs assist in determining how receptive the residents will be toward a private practice. What is the education level of adults in the community? What percentage of high school graduates attend college? Is there an institution of higher education located in the community? What kinds of volunteer or community organizations are active in addressing education, health care, and social services? What kinds of health care facilities are available? What rehabilitation services, either public or private, are well established?

The presence of education-oriented families and of active consumer or citizen support groups in health, education, and rehabilitation suggests that the community is attuned to the importance of services such as those to be offered by the private practitioner. The presence of a college or university often encourages a community focus on educational pursuits and is accompanied by an increased demand for services that enhance educational achievement. The absence of such conditions may mean that, although services are needed, it will be more difficult to establish a private practice because of a lower level of awareness of need by persons in the community.

When choosing a location, competition for patients should be considered. Given the size and nature of the population, is the need for speech-language pathology and audiology services greater than the availability of those services? Are the existing facilities considered to be effective, convenient, and well known? Is there sufficient growth potential to signal a need for additional services of the type to be offered? Are the existing services delivered through public or private agencies? Are other rehabilitation services being delivered successfully in a private practice arrangement?

Competition

The presence of other sources for the types of services one plans to provide should not preclude setting up a practice, but careful analysis should be done to determine whether there are sufficient gaps in services to warrant additional practices. It is possible that the existence of other successful practices signals that the community is aware of and receptive to the types of services you will provide and therefore that people will avail themselves of the services quickly. However, one should attempt to determine whether existing services are sufficient to meet the current and projected needs of the community before opening a new private practice.

The private practitioner's status in the community can be a positive factor in building a business. Individuals who have a favorable professional reputation in the community, who have worked with agencies or individuals likely to refer patients, and who are familiar with the programs in a community have an advantage over those who do not have established community contacts.

Professional Status

A region or city that is stable or growing economically, supportive of health and education programs, inhabited by an active and growing population, and not saturated with services for persons with communication disorders should provide a reasonable opportunity for success for persons establishing a private practice. Once a city or region has been selected, the practitioner needs to determine the specific place within the city to locate the practice.

The specific site for a practice deserves careful consideration. Accessibility, safety, convenience, and physical appearance are important to prospective patients. To the practitioner, cost and convenience also are important.

SITE SELECTION

In choosing the site for a practice, the practitioner first should consider the perspective of the patients. Can it be reached easily from major thoroughfares that extend throughout the general area to be served? Is it reasonably accessible to those who will rely on public transportation? Is it in a safe part of the city, and can it be reached without requiring patients to travel through high-crime areas? As they approach the site, will patients recognize the appropriateness of having a professional office there?

Accessibility and Safety

Most practices will serve some patients whose mobility is restricted. Are parking lots, entrances, hallways, restrooms, and water fountains accessible to persons in wheelchairs? Is the building accessible in wet or icy conditions? Can doors be opened and elevators used by persons in wheelchairs? Can a parent reach the office with reasonable ease when accompanied by the child receiving therapy and by his or her siblings?

The accessibility and safety factors that are important to patients also are important to the practitioners working in a facility. Appointments at irregular hours may require both patients and practitioners to travel through the area at times other than regular business hours, making safety and accessibility very important.

Parking

The availability of adequate parking is important to patients. In choosing a location, the practitioner should determine the amount of parking space available to everyone who uses the building, the number of people who use the parking facilities, and whether parking has been a problem for others who work or receive services in the building. For some office buildings, a specific number of parking spaces are allocated for each office, whereas in others, parking is available on a first-come-first-served basis. Some parking facilities charge a parking fee, which may be paid either by the patient or by the practitioner who sees the patient. Because inconvenience in parking may cause patients to seek services in another facility, private practitioners should pay attention to the availability of convenient parking when selecting a site for an office. It usually is wise to discuss the parking situation with other occupants of the building, as well as with the leasing agent.

Shared or Private Space

As discussed by a number of authors in this book, private practitioners may have the opportunity to share office space with persons in related professions, such as psychologists or physicians. The advantages and disadvantages to sharing office space are reviewed in Chapters 2 and 3.

For many practitioners, the most attractive aspect of sharing office space is the potential for reduced overhead costs. By having a common waiting area and storage space and by sharing certain office equipment and perhaps receptionist/secretarial staff, several practitioners can divide some overhead costs. A second possible advantage is the potential for patient referrals among those sharing an office. For example, a speech-language pathologist or audiologist and an otolaryngologist or pediatrician may see patients who need both medical services and evaluation or treatment services for a communication disorder, thereby finding it natural to refer to one another. A third possible advantage is the ease and convenience of consultation among persons from different professions who share common office space. For example, a speech-language pathologist who works primarily with multihandicapped or learning disabled children may benefit from frequent consultations with an occupational therapist whose expertise includes these types of conditions.

There are several potential disadvantages to sharing office space with persons outside one's own practice. By locating in the same space with persons from other professions, the practitioner may in effect eliminate referrals from others who practice the profession of those with whom space is shared. Speech-language pathologists and audiologists have found that, by housing their practice in the office of an otolaryngologist, they eliminated referrals from other physicians in the community. Despite the fact that the business affairs of the practices were completely separate, other physicians seemed to perceive a business relationship between the professionals and did not refer to the speech-language pathologist or audiologist. Similar effects on referrals have been reported when office space has been shared with psychologists, educational tutors, or others in allied health disciplines. It has been reported that in some states it may be illegal for different professions to form a group practice that is also a private corporation (PC). Therefore, it would be well to investigate this matter because even a group practice in speech-language pathology and audiology might fall into this category.

A second important consideration in deciding whether to share space is the patient population served by all those professionals who will have common waiting or treatment areas. The preferences of patients, the necessary furnishings and equipment, and the extent to which patients are embarrassed or distressed about others knowing that they are receiving a particular service are all important factors. For example, the furnishings and decor of a waiting room set up for small children may be inappropriate for adult patients. Older patients may find the presence of small children to be distracting or unnerving. For these reasons, those contemplating the sharing of office space should consider the patient population to be served by each professional who will utilize the space.

A third potential disadvantage of sharing office space is the chance for disagreement about each person's fair contribution to the overhead costs. The number of patients each sees, the amount of secretarial support required, and the wear-and-tear on furnishings and equipment caused by patients in different practices are important considerations in determining each practitioner's appropriate contribution to office costs. Shared costs for such minor items as coffee, paper cups, or magazines for the waiting room also should be considered. What may appear as a simple and straightforward arrangement in the beginning can become a major conflict as the different practices grow and as the need for replacing or repairing shared items arises. If office space is to be shared, there should be a detailed written agreement stating clearly what financial arrangements will be followed about all shared furnishings, personnel, equipment, and supplies.

A fourth important consideration in deciding whether to share space with persons outside one's own business relates to the professional competence, reputation, and habits of those with whom the office will be shared. All professionals who practice in a common office facility may find that referral sources judge their competence on the basis of their experiences with others practicing in that office. This can have either a positive or negative effect, depending on the professional reputation of officemates. Beginning practitioners may benefit from sharing space with an established, well-respected professional, but are likely to be affected adversely by sharing an office with someone with a questionable reputation. (See Chapter 3 for the legal implications inherent in the shared space arrangement.)

A fifth area for consideration in an office-sharing arrangement is the extent of liability each practice will have for the actions of the other or for events that may occur on the premises. For example, if someone is injured in the waiting room and the injury is attributed to negligence on the part of property holders, is everyone who shares the office space liable? If a patient sues a practitioner because the secretary released information without proper authorization, is everyone who uses that secretary's services held accountable, or is liability limited to the individual practitioner who serves the patient? Although these events may seem unlikely, they can occur with damaging effects on the financial status and professional reputation of a practitioner. (See also Chapters 5 and 9 for a discussion on professional liability.)

Size and Physical Arrangement

In selecting office space, the size and physical arrangements will be determined by the population to be served, the potential growth of the practice, staff size, and cost. If a substantial part of the patient load will be young children accompanied to the office by adults and siblings, the waiting room area will need to be larger than if patients are likely to come alone. The size of therapy rooms will be determined by the age of patients and whether they are seen in groups or individually. If the clinician's office is also to serve as a treatment room, the size and arrangement will need to be such that the materials and documents on or in the clinician's desk remain confidential.

Space for the receptionist/secretary and for storing business documents and patient records must be designed to ensure confidentiality. Space away from the area in which patients are served should be provided for that purpose. If the receptionist/secretary uses the telephone in any manner that would disrupt complete confidentiality of patients or of business transactions, he or she must have separate space for conducting business. Additionally, patients are more likely to interrupt the secretary/receptionist for social visits if the patient waiting area and the receptionist's office are in the same room.

Conditions of a Lease

Once a site meets the criteria discussed above, the practitioner should examine the details of the lease before signing any agreement. It is important to remember that spoken agreements between landlord and tenant mean little or nothing. Only what is written in the lease agreement signed by both parties can be enforced. In considering a lease, several items are very important.

Is the rental price reasonable? The practitioner should be familiar with the cost of renting comparable space in the area in which the property is located in order to know whether the rental price is reasonable and fair. This information can be obtained by talking with commercial realtors familiar with the area or by checking rentals on similar property in the vicinity of the office being considered.

Who pays for alterations in the space? Frequently a landlord offers to alter the rental space to meet the tenant's needs. It is important to obtain in writing who will pay for which alterations and what the total cost will be. If the landlord offers to have the alterations made, it is wise to check with contractors to determine if the proposed cost is reasonable. The practitioner may find that he or she can save money by contracting independently for construction or renovation of the office space.

Who pays for which services? The lease agreement should spell out clearly who pays for utilities, janitorial services, pest control, and repairs to plumbing and electrical items. If cleaning services are paid for by the landlord, the practitioner should know exactly which services will be provided (superficial dusting, mopping floors, and so forth) and how frequently each type of service will occur (daily, weekly?).

When is the building open? Many office buildings, particularly in cities, are open only during specified hours and on certain days. In some buildings, tenants can enter the building at any time, but heating and air conditioning run only during regular business hours on weekdays. Obviously, such arrangements would preclude providing services during evening hours or on weekends. Because a speech-language pathologist or audiologist in private practice may see patients at irregular hours, it is especially important to have a written agreement about building use that ensures that services can be provided at all times that patients may be seen.

Does the lease contain escalation clauses? Leases that are longer than 1 year usually contain escalation clauses tied to such factors as cost of living increases, real estate tax increases, and maintenance costs. Such clauses allow the landlord to increase rent automatically at specified intervals. Practitioners should be especially careful that the lease agreement contains reasonable limitations on increases based on items, such as maintenance, over which the landlord has total control. It is sometimes possible to include in the lease arrangement a cap on the total increase that the escalation clause can bring in any year's rent. (See also Chapter 16 on the sale or dissolution of a private practice in regard to this and the following discussion on lease arrangements.)

Does the lease contain renewal options? The practitioner should read carefully the conditions stated for lease renewal. The option to renew should include some statement about a maximum increase in rent at the time of renewal. The practitioner also should read carefully the conditions for giving notice of intent to renew. It is desirable that a 1- or 2-month, rather than a 6-month advance written notice, be acceptable for exercising the option to renew the lease.

Does the lease include provisions for subletting? Because conditions may arise that cause the practitioner to need or want to sublet the space, the lease agreement should contain specific provisions for subletting part or all of the leasehold. These agreements are likely to contain some reasonable restrictions on who can occupy the space, but the practitioner should try to gain permission to sublet to acceptable tenants.

Until problems occur, most practitioners are not aware of the importance of having a clearly written lease agreement that covers the contingencies that may arise. It is important to remember that the lease agreement proposed by the landlord probably has been written by an attorney whose job it is to protect the landlord's interests. Practitioners should not be fooled when told, "This is a standard lease." Lease agreements are negotiable, and the practitioner should seek to include protections for his or her practice, just as landlords will insist on provisions to protect their interests. Many private practitioners have found that using the services of a commercial real estate specialist results in better negotiations for all aspects of a lease. Unless the practitioner is experienced in evaluating lease agreements, it is wise to have an attorney review the lease before it is signed.

SUMMARY

Careful selection of the site and location of a practice is an important part of planning the practice. Economic conditions, population characteristics, community attitudes, and competition should be analyzed carefully before deciding on a location.

Also, the practitioners will benefit from familiarity with the service agencies and providers who will serve as referral sources. In choosing a specific site for the practice, accessibility and safety, size and physical arrangements, and cost are important. The practitioner should be very cautious about sharing space with other professionals in an attempt to reduce overhead costs, because the disadvantages can outweigh the advantages of this type of arrangement. Leasehold agreements should be studied carefully to ensure that the interests of the practitioner are protected. It often is wise to seek the assistance of a real estate attorney or a commercial real estate specialist to review the lease before it is signed.

REFERENCES

The geographic distribution of speech-language-hearing professionals. (1983). *Asha, 5*: 31. (a)

Factors related to state service levels. (1983). *Asha, 7*: 31. (b)

1984 Editor and Publisher Market Guide. (1984). New York: Editor and Publisher Company, Inc.

Macfarlane, W.N. (1977). *Principles of small business management*, New York: McGraw-Hill.

SUGGESTED READINGS

American Speech-Language-Hearing Association. (1985). *Planning and initiating a private practice in audiology and speech-language pathology*. Rockville, MD: Author.

Chapter 8

Establishing and Equipping an Audiology Private Practice

Dennis Hampton, Ph.D.

The audiologist entering private practice has many options when determining the legal structure and the style of the practice. The audiologist's personality, experience, and clinical interests will affect his or her preference for solo or group, part-time or full-time, independent or affiliated, and/or any of the other variations of private practice. These variations and their advantages and disadvantages are reviewed in this chapter in the context of the three major legal structures and the five most common service delivery models in audiologic private practice. Equipment needs, equipment financing, and potential interactions with suppliers and manufacturers are also discussed because, obviously, the legal structure and style of the practice will affect equipment needs.

LEGAL STRUCTURES: A BRIEF REVIEW

Every business organization, whether a hospital or a candy store, a private office or an international corporation, has a legal structure. This legal structure determines both its legal and financial responsibilities, as well as the tax regulations and other state and federal laws and regulations that then apply to the organization. The three most common structures are sole proprietorship, partnership, and corporation. These structures have been discussed in some detail in Chapters 5 and 9 and are reviewed here within the audiologic framework.

The simplest and most common form of legal structure is the sole proprietorship, which made up slightly more than 70 percent of all business organizations in 1975. Of the more than 7 million sole proprietorships, almost half are service organizations. Most are small organizations. Although sole proprietorships comprise more than 70 percent of all business organizations, they account for only 8 percent of the total gross income (Glos et al., 1980). For a more lengthy discussion on various business structures, the reader is referred to Chapter 9 on financial planning.

Partnerships are the least common business structure, comprising less than 10 percent of all organizations. A partnership is made up of two or more people, usually in a general (unlimited) partnership. In most states, members may restrict their liability to the amount of their investment by becoming a limited partner, provided at least one member is a general partner with unlimited liability. Although a partnership may be formed without a written agreement, a formal agreement can help minimize disagreements and misunderstandings in the future, as discussed in Chapter 5. The agreement should clearly describe each partner's duties and responsibilities; vacation and disability policies; the distribution of salaries, benefits, profits, and losses; what steps are to be taken if a partner wishes to leave the partnership or dies; how a partnership interest is to be sold; how the agreement can be modified; and arbitration procedures. As noted in Chapter 9, legal assistance in the preparation of such a document is mandatory.

The third common legal structure is the corporation, along with such variations as the professional corporation and the Subchapter "S" corporation. Corporations make up about 20 percent of all business organizations, but account for nearly 90 percent of total business income (Glos et al., 1980). During the past 15 years, many lawyers, dentists, and physicians selected this structure, even when in solo practice, because of tax and pension plan benefits. Recent changes in tax and pension plan laws have eliminated most of these benefits, and speech-language pathologists and audiologists may no longer find a corporation structure to be as enticing as it once was. It should continue to be considered as an option, however.

Selecting a legal structure that is most suited to the needs and the style of the audiologist is a critical and complex decision, with many professional, financial, and personal implications (Olni, 1982). The help of an attorney and accountant familiar with the business and tax laws of the state is invaluable, but the practitioner will have to make the final decision based on his or her personal and professional needs. (The reader is referred to Appendix 8–A, which lists a number of publications available without charge from the Small Business Administration.)

SERVICE DELIVERY MODELS

Discussions of private practice often assume that there is a single private practice model, when actually there are a number of forms a practice may take. This discussion examines five different models: independent, hospital-affiliated, consultant, hearing aid office, and physician-affiliated. Although each is discussed separately, many practices are a blend of several of these service delivery models.

Independent Practice

In the independent or free-standing practice, the audiologist provides a range of diagnostic and rehabilitative services in an independent setting. There are no legal or financial relationships with professionals outside the field of speech and hearing. The advantages of the independent practice are flexibility and independence, direct and personal patient contact, high visibility, and diverse responsibilities.

Advantages of Independent Practice

Flexibility and Independence. Because there are no legal or bureaucratic relationships with anyone outside the audiology practice, the audiologist can provide professional services in the manner he or she chooses. Additional services, such as a new test or a new rehabilitation procedure, can be added simply by deciding to do so.

For example, the audiologist can add hearing aid dispensing or auditory brainstem evoked response testing without interacting with and perhaps needing to convince other people within the organization. Of course, these decisions must be based on a clear understanding of the needs of the patients and, if based on referral, the referring sources.

Direct and Personal Patient Contact. In a private office, the patient schedules an appointment to see a particular audiologist. A strong clinician/patient relationship usually develops because of this personal identification. For example, in the author's practice, some patients have been followed for nearly 10 years. Because the patient identifies with the individual audiologist, rather than with an office or an agency, these patients have almost always been seen by the same audiologist throughout those 10 years.

High Visibility. The independent practitioner is a very visible health care provider, without a larger agency to provide a buffer from the public view or from other health care providers. The audiologist personally receives the credit for the quality of the professional services, as well as the blame when there is dissatisfaction with those services. The private practice that becomes an established and successful practice does so in part based on the audiologist's clinical skills and personal style, resulting in a recognized professional reputation in the community. One of the rewards of private practice is the knowledge that, whether referred by a friend or a professional, an individual seeks your help because of your own professional reputation, rather than because of your affiliation with a larger organization.

Diverse Responsibilities. In the free-standing office, the audiologist must assume many nonclinical responsibilities. These include personnel issues (hiring and firing, salary and benefits policies, work schedules) and office management issues (space needs and costs, scheduling policies, professional fees, and billing procedures). Although some would argue that these nonclinical responsibilities are a burden, they also can be viewed as a way to control the provision of clinical services. For example, the secretaries are an integral part of the author's professional practice. It is the secretary who first meets (by telephone) the patient, schedules appointments, and obtains information about health insurance coverage. It is important to ensure that the secretaries understand and display an attitude and responsibility to the patient consistent with that of the owner.

The disadvantages of the independent practice include high overhead costs, a lack of guaranteed referral sources, a high degree of financial risk, and greater difficulties with third party programs.

Disadvantages of an Independent Practice

High Overhead Costs. Because the free-standing private office has no legal or financial support from a larger organization, it must bear all overhead expenses directly, including space, salaries, telephones, and all office and clinical equipment. Many of these are fixed expenses, whether the office is open 3 days or 6 days a week. Thus, the independent office is an expensive service delivery model and is very difficult to support on a less than full-time basis.

Lack of Guaranteed Referral Sources. In many settings, referrals are made to an audiology center because of its formal affiliation with a hospital, clinic, or physician. The free-standing office has no such affiliation and therefore has no guaranteed source of referrals. Instead, referrals are based on the informal professional relationships and the professional reputation of the audiologist. The referral sources are likely to be more broad based, but more subject to fluctuations than when a formal affiliation exists.

High Degree of Financial Risk. Although setup and operating costs can be estimated fairly closely, it is virtually impossible to predict in any meaningful way the number of patients who will be seen and who will be good referral sources. The combination of high overhead costs and lack of guaranteed referral sources makes the independent office the most risky of the service delivery models. The most effective tools to create a broad and dependable referral base are the audiologist's professional reputation, professional relationships, and knowledge of the unmet needs of the service delivery area.

Greater Difficulties with Third Party Programs. The independent practitioner faces greater difficulties with state, federal, and other third party payment programs. One of the great frustrations of the independent practitioner is that, regardless of his or her preparation, certification and, in most states, licensure, many third party programs require that audiology services be provided in association with a physician or a rehabilitation agency. Thus, a program, such as Medicaid, may cover an audiology service when provided in an agency setting, but may not cover the same service provided by the same person in his or her own office.

Hospital-Affiliated Practice

The hospital-affiliated private practice is based on a contractual arrangement between the service provider—audiologist—and a hospital. Usually the hospital provides space and billing services, and the audiologist, who provides professional services and equipment, bills the hospital on a fee-for-service basis.

Although this arrangement does not allow the freedom and flexibility of the fully independent office, hospital affiliation does minimize financial risk and greatly reduces such direct overhead expenses as secretarial salaries, office space rental, and telephones. It also provides strong referral relationships and more frequent contacts with other professionals. Finally, there is good coverage by third party programs because services are offered and billed through the hospital.

The hospital-affiliated practice is attractive to smaller hospitals or those that have not yet established an audiology program because it allows the hospital to provide a new service with virtually no capital expenses. Also, audiology services are primarily outpatient and can therefore be a new source of revenue for the hospital. In these days of cost containment and payment by diagnosis-related group (DRG), this contractual arrangement should become even more attractive as hospitals look for ways to minimize their in-house expenses and expand income-producing outpatient services outside the DRG system.

The consulting audiologist provides services to other organizations, usually on a long-term (annual retainer) or short-term (per diem) basis, rather than on a fee-for-service basis. Consulting arrangements are typically made with nursing homes, school systems, health agencies, and industrial companies. Although direct clinical services might be provided—for example, to patients of a nursing home—the consultant usually offers professional knowledge, experience, and judgment to design, supervise, or review hearing health care programs.

The consultant relationship usually provides a relatively steady flow of income without the ups-and-downs of a cash flow that is based on patient fees. Overhead expenses should be relatively low because there is less need for secretarial support and space. Also, services can be offered on a part-time basis without a commitment to keeping an office open and available full-time. The greatest disadvantages are the reduced patient contact and the loss of one of the chief benefits of private practice: freedom from the institutional setting.

Practice as a Consultant

In the hearing aid office, the audiologist specifically restricts services to the testing and fitting of hearing aids, with audiologic evaluations done only for the purpose of determining hearing aid needs. In this model, the audiologist is much like his or her counterpart in vision services, the optometrist.

Hearing Aid Office

The hearing aid office model has become more common in recent years as audiologists have bought out, or into, existing commercial hearing aid dealerships. Startup costs tend to be higher because of the buy-out expenses. However, these expenses can be spread out over several years and are offset by the advantages of an established caseload and an established referral system. Thus, in spite of greater startup costs, the financial risks are usually less than in the new independent office.

One disadvantage of the hearing aid office is the unnecessary limitation it places on the audiologic services provided. Because the office so heavily emphasizes and is so identified with the fitting of hearing aids, pediatric, diagnostic, and other nonhearing-aid-related services may be minimal or nonexistent. This represents both a loss of revenue and a probably unnecessary loss of professional involvement. Furthermore, this approach reinforces the perception of the prosthetic device as the solution to the problems of hearing loss and the cause of the hearing difficulties that almost always remain.

A more general effect of adopting the hearing aid office model is that all too frequently the practice of the professional audiologist becomes more similar to that of the commercial hearing aid dealership, rather than vice versa. We now see audiologists involved with telemarketing, free hearing tests, battery promotions, and other product-oriented marketing tactics that are only somewhat different from the door-to-door tactics that audiologists have criticized in the past. In the long run, these tactics are unnecessary and unproductive at best. At worst, they commercialize and trivialize a young and little recognized profession. There is no doubt that the audiologist faces a very difficult and long-term marketing task, but it is doubtful that the aggressive commercial sales approaches of the past are a long-term solution, especially because these approaches have been so unsuccessful.

To summarize, the purchase or joining of an existing hearing aid dealership offers the advantage of an established office, caseload, and referral routes. The chief disadvantage is the limited services offered unless the audiologist, for both business and professional reasons, expands into nonhearing aid audiologic services.

Physician-Affiliated Practice

In this model, the audiologist maintains a clear relationship with a physician or group of physicians, usually otolaryngologists, sometimes even sharing or using space provided by the physician. Typically, the relationship is not formalized by a written agreement. The audiologist provides evaluation services to the physician's patients, for which he or she bills indirectly, to the physician, or directly, to the patient. People who need nonmedical hearing health care are then seen independently by the audiologist. Rowland (1978) discusses the many different relationships possible within this model.

The advantages of this model are the built-in source of referrals and perhaps greatly reduced overhead costs, because the physician may pay all overhead costs, including rent and equipment costs. These advantages are critical to the financial success of the new practitioner, and so this model is attractive to someone establishing a new practice.

There are, however, disadvantages and even dangers in this approach to private practice. One disadvantage is the limitation on what the audiologist may do because of the close identification with the physician group. Also, other physicians may be unwilling to refer directly to the audiologist because of his or her identification with another physician group.

The danger of this approach lies in the dependence of the audiologist on the physician. The physician may own the office space and the clinical equipment and may determine which patients will be seen by the audiologist as well. Patients may view the audiologist as a technician or employee because of the close identification with the physician. Most worrisome is the possibility that the physician can decide at any time simply to replace the audiologist with someone more to his or her liking. Indeed, there are many stories of audiologists supposedly in private practice who found themselves "locked out." Without a signed agreement and without legal access and claim to space, equipment, and patients, the audiologist has no recourse. The best protection, in addition to a relationship based on mutual trust and respect, is a signed written agreement that has been reviewed beforehand by the audiologist's attorney.

Summary

Private practice comes in a wide variety of forms and structures and no two practices are exactly alike. Indeed, a practice may change its legal structure as it grows and evolves. For example, the practice might begin as a sole proprietorship, but change to a partnership or corporation when the need occurs. Conversely, a practice might begin as a general partnership and change to a sole proprietorship if all but one of the partners leave the practice.

The nature of a private practice is much more diverse than its legal structure. The most common service delivery models are the independent (or free-standing), the hospital-affiliated, the consultant, the hearing aid office, and the physician-affiliated models.

Although these models were discussed separately, many practices are a combination of several of the forms. For example, an audiologist might maintain an independent office where a major part of his or her clinical work is done. The audiologist may also do consulting work for several local nursing homes and small industrial companies, as well as maintain a hospital affiliation, providing in-hospital consultations and some outpatient services. The advantages of such a combination of service approaches include an increased and varied caseload, expanded sources of referrals, a more consistent and dependable cash flow, and opportunities for contacts with a variety of professionals.

Whatever the legal structure and service delivery model, the audiologist in private practice will find that the nature of the practice is always changing. This is probably one of the biggest attractions of private practice.

EQUIPPING AN AUDIOLOGY PRIVATE PRACTICE

The audiologist entering private practice faces a long list of important decisions, including office location, services to be offered, organizational structure, and financing. He or she must also make decisions about purchases of equipment, and this area often receives the greatest attention and concern. Actually, decisions about equipment are among the easiest and most straightforward of any to be made.

The specific items of equipment, the size and location of the sound-treated room, and the cost of equipping the practice are all important, of course. However the options are fairly limited, and equipment is a means, not an end. For those who need audiologic services, the audiologist's visibility, accessibility, clinical skills, and attitudes are each more important than the cost or extent of audiologic equipment.

Equipment needs, equipment financing, and equipment suppliers and manufacturers are discussed below, as well as hearing aids, although hearing aids could be considered consumer goods. Although the emphasis in this discussion is on clinical equipment, most of it also applies to office equipment, such as typewriters, telephones, photocopiers, and computers.

Equipment Needs

Equipment can be divided into two categories: *mandatory* equipment and *optional* equipment. Mandatory equipment is the equipment that is essential to carry out the functions of the office. For example, an audiology office obviously requires an audiometer (but not the latest two-channel digital version) and a sound-treated room (but not a two-room, double-walled suite). Optional equipment is that equipment that helps the clinician work more effectively or more efficiently (for example, an automatic X-Y plotter for an impedance audiometer) or allows the clinician to provide additional services (for example, a brainstem evoked response system).

Specific mandatory equipment items include a sound-treated room, clinical audiometer (one and one-half channel), tape recorder, soundfield system, impedance audiometer, portable audiometer, and hearing aids. Optional equipment includes electronystagmography, brainstem evoked response, and hearing aid electroacoustic analysis equipment, although some professionals would consider the latter to be mandatory. Table 8–1 analyzes the estimated cost of the equipment discussed above.

Table 8–1 Estimated Costs of Audiology Equipment

Item	Purchase Cost ($)	Annual Maintenance ($)
Clinical audiometer	2,500–4,000	150
Portable audiometer	500–1,000	75
Tape recorder	250–500	0
Soundfield system	1,000	0
Impedance audiometer	2,500–6,000	100
Sound booth	7,500	0
Brainstem evoked response	12,000–25,000	200
Electronystagmography	6,000–8,000	200
Hearing aid analyzer	4,000–6,000	100
Hearing aid supplies	1,000	200
Totals	$21,750–40,000	$1,025

Mandatory equipment often has optional features that should be evaluated carefully for their relative cost benefit. For example, a fully functional one- and one-half-channel audiometer can be obtained for $4,000 versus more than $10,000 for a dual channel "research" audiometer. Similarly, a single-wall sound-treated room is entirely adequate if properly located within the office. The author is doubtful that the private practitioner, who must recover equipment costs through direct patient fees, can justify the additional costs of the two-channel digital audiometer or the two-room, double-walled sound suite that frequently is available in graduate education programs in audiology.

Hearing aids can also be considered equipment, although in an accounting sense they would be considered "goods." The dispensing audiologist initially requires about a dozen hearing aids for testing, fitting, and loaning, along with hearing-aid-related supplies and equipment (Table 8–2).

Table 8–2 Basic Hearing Aid Equipment and Supplies

Tools	Earmold supplies	Hearing aid supplies
Bench or hand-held buffing equipment	Otoblocks	Batteries
Otoscope	Syringes	Tone hooks
Otolights	Impression materials	Receivers
Hearing aid stethoscope	Stock molds	Dehumidifier kits
Earmold reamer	Mold cleaners	Battery testers
Tubing expander	Earmold cement	
Tubing puller	Prebent tubing	
	Air (blower) bulbs	

The cost of related supplies and equipment is typically under $1,000. For a full discussion and listing of these items, see Loavenbruck and Madell (1981). In addition, assistive listening devices can provide important help to the hearing-impaired client. Information, demonstration displays, or the actual assistive listening devices should be available on-site in the practitioner's office.

Cost-Benefit Analysis

Cost-benefit analysis, which uses estimates of the total equipment costs and the projected income from use of the equipment, is used to estimate the fiscal effects of the purchase or lease of optional equipment. Such an analysis of mandatory equipment is less critical because this equipment is essential to the function of office and must be acquired regardless of the financial implications of doing so.

Direct costs include finance or leasing costs, maintenance, and calibration. Benefits include investment tax credits, other tax savings (including depreciation write-offs), and income from either specific fees charged (fee-for-service) or fees included within other charges to the patient, i.e., bundled fees. (See Chapter 9 for a further discussion of this issue.)

For example, suppose an audiologist is considering adding brainstem evoked response (BSER) audiometry as a clinical procedure. The equipment can be obtained on a lease basis at a cost of $400 per month for 48 months, with no tax credits or depreciation. Maintenance and supply costs for the BSER are estimated at $25 per month. Of course, the clinician's salary and other office expenses should be included as nonequipment-related expenses to determine the actual cost of providing the service.

Benefit (income) is determined by multiplying the projected number of procedures per month times the charge per procedure. In this way, the audiologist can determine how many procedures must be done in order to meet the direct expense of the equipment and thus whether obtaining the equipment is a sound financial decision. In this example, the audiologist projects four BSER evaluations monthly at a charge of $175 each, for a projected monthly income of $700, with no allowance for bad debts or limited third party payment. Thus, it can be seen that the projected caseload covers the direct equipment costs of $425 per month.

However, a more complete and realistic cost analysis would include the cost of the clinician's time and a relative portion of all office expenses, including secretarial salaries, telephone, and office space. When all is said and done, though, cost-benefit analysis is more often done to justify obtaining new equipment, rather than to decide whether the purchase would be a financially favorable decision. Certainly there are other important reasons for purchasing new equipment, such as broadening a referral base, providing a more comprehensive service, or simply developing an area of interest to the clinician. Regardless of the rationale for purchase, the cost-benefit analysis provides a picture of the financial effects of the equipment purchase.

Financing

Clinical and office equipment can be (1) purchased outright from existing funds, (2) purchased through loan financing, or (3) leased. Audiology equipment is relatively expensive, long lasting, maintenance free, and not quickly outdated. Equipment purchased today is likely to have a useful life of 7, 8, or more years. Although it may be tempting to purchase equipment outright or on short-term financing, either approach could severely jeopardize the financial health of the practice, incurring as startup expenses those costs that properly should be spread out over 5 or more years. Moreover, equipment loans are the easiest financing to obtain because there is a specific item to serve as both rationale and collateral for the financing.

Purchase versus Lease

As noted earlier, equipment can be purchased outright or leased. Purchasing the equipment has the advantages of ownership, depreciation write-offs, and tax investment credits, not deductions, of up to 10 percent of the purchase price in the year of purchase. In addition, the purchase can be financed, usually for a period of 3–5 years. The two chief disadvantages of equipment purchase are (1) equipment loans become financial liabilities of the practice, limiting the availability of nonequipment financing and (2) equipment loans are obligations of the borrower, regardless of the financial health or illness of the practice.

Leasing is somewhat more expensive than purchase, but carries less financial risk. If the practice should not survive or if the equipment becomes outdated or no longer useful for some reason, the lease can be cancelled ("walked away from"), although usually with a financial penalty. Also, by giving up actual ownership of the equipment or at least deferring ownership until the end of the leasing period, the leasing individual gains greater purchasing power. Although in the long run leasing costs are greater than purchasing costs, the initial down payment (security deposit) and monthly costs are lower than outright purchase and financing expenses. Thus, for the same amount of capital, more equipment or equipment with greater capabilities can be obtained through lease, rather than through direct purchase. This extra purchasing power, which is actually a way of deferring some of the costs of obtaining the equipment, may be especially important to someone with very limited financing.

Leasing can be arranged through the equipment manufacturer, banks, or leasing companies. Options may include keeping the tax investment credit of up to 10 percent and purchase of the equipment at the end of the lease.

New versus Used Equipment

It is probably apparent that new equipment may have more useful clinical applications, should be more reliable, and is more expensive than used equipment. It is also more easily financed, which is an important factor.

Used equipment can be very cost effective and clinically appropriate, provided there is some confidence in its reliability. Because the private practitioner frequently does not have time to shop around for "best buys" from unknown sellers, he or she should seek the advice of an equipment supplier. A dependable and reputable equipment supplier is also more likely to know about equipment availability, quality, and reliability.

Hearing Aids

Although in an accounting sense hearing aids are considered goods, rather than equipment, financing is still an important factor in their purchase. Hearing aids are either purchased directly from a manufacturer or from a distributor. Payment is expected on a short-term basis, usually within 30 days of the last day of the month in which the aid was ordered, with finance charges assessed for late payment.

If hearing aids are ordered and stocked carefully, the private practitioner incurs virtually no direct expense for specific aids. Hearing aids, whether for a specific user or not, can be ordered, dispensed, billed for, and payment collected within the 30- to 60-day period before payment to the supplier is expected. For example, a hearing aid is ordered on October 10, a bill statement is received from the manufacturer at the end of the month, and payment is expected by November 30. In the meantime, the hearing aid is fitted and the patient billed on October 20, and full payment by the patient is made well in advance of November 30, when the dispenser must pay the supplier.

This approach works easily and well, especially if the number of manufacturers and of specific hearing aid models and the total number of aids routinely available are strictly limited. These numbers vary with different clinicians and practices. One rule of thumb is that no hearing aid should remain in the office longer than 1 month. If it does, the practice, rather than the user, is paying for the hearing aid, and the actual cost of the hearing aid must now include the financing charges incurred while the hearing aid is in the office.

Bulk discounts are another advantage of restricting the number of hearing aid manufacturing companies that are used routinely. Hearing aids can cost up to 25 percent less than single unit price when ordered in groups of about ten. Manufacturer policies differ on whether discounts apply to all hearing aids ordered in a month (cumulative) or only to aids within a single order (noncumulative).

Choosing a Manufacturer

Clinical Equipment

There are dozens of equipment manufacturers, and there can be endless choices of specific pieces of equipment, manufacturers, and suppliers. Yet the basic considerations are unchanged regardless of the equipment purchased, and the basic factors remain the same: equipment capability, cost, reliability, service availability, and most of all, the equipment supplier.

Evaluating equipment capability, cost, and reliability is relatively straightforward. However, there is a tendency in audiology to incur unnecessary costs for equipment capabilities for which there are no clearly demonstrated needs. This may come from a history of having others finance audiological equipment, e.g. academic institutions or physicians. When the cost of purchasing unessential equipment capabilities must be passed on directly as patient fees, however, there should be a clear rationale for their purchase.

Service availability is a critical factor that is not always evaluated easily. It is usually better first to establish a working relationship with an equipment supplier and then choose the equipment. In other words, good service depends more on the equipment *supplier* than on the manufacturer.

Sometimes a specific equipment item is purchased directly from the manufacturer. Contact is then made with a designated service representative. Although this may be the only way to acquire a specific equipment item, there are potential hazards in this narrow relationship. As an illustration, after evaluating the capabilities, relative cost, and reputation for reliability, an audiologist chose a particular electroacoustic hearing aid analyzer system. However, the local equipment supplier did not represent this manufacturer, so the audiologist purchased it directly from the manufacturer and a service representative was assigned to him. Two years later that service representative closed up shop, and service could be obtained only by paying very high travel costs for a service representative located several hundred miles away or by shipping the equipment back to the manufacturer. Valuable time and instrument use was thus lost.

In more recent years, this more direct relationship between manufacturer and user has worked better using overnight delivery mail. However, the equipment user should first make certain that the manufacturer is prepared and committed to this kind of service so that equipment "down" time is kept to days, rather than weeks.

The equipment supplier is as important as the lawyer, accountant, loan officer, and equipment manufacturer. Ideally the audiologist will already have an established working relationship with the supplier and know the supplier's reputation for dependability and flexibility. The supplier can provide invaluable help in making equipment decisions, finding and evaluating used equipment, choosing specific models, and sometimes even obtaining financing. It is important to remember that, although new practitioners in particular are interested in keeping costs down, equipment suppliers are *not* discount houses. The audiologist/supplier relationship is ideally long-term; fairness and good service are more important than bargains.

As the reader may have inferred, the relationship between the dispensing audiologist and the hearing aid manufacturer is also usually a long-term, active relationship that is critical to both parties. The days are long past when some manufacturers chose not to have direct dealings with dispensing audiologists because of their desire to protect relationships with hearing aid dealers. There is an extensive range of hearing aid manufacturers, and the audiologist has a wide choice of those manufacturers who will best serve his or her needs.

Audiologists in traditional settings are accustomed to dealing with a large number of hearing aid manufacturers. Over the years, many manufacturers supplied clinics with free hearing aids for test purposes, and most clinics referred the patient to someone else for the actual fitting. However, it is difficult to maintain an active and cooperative relationship with a large number of manufacturers, and the dispenser should therefore limit active relationships to three or four manufacturers. The audiologist may have dealings with other manufacturers, either directly or through a hearing aid distributor, but they will not be primary suppliers.

Hearing aid manufacturers should be evaluated for the quality and reliability of their instruments, warranty and return policies, cooperativeness, prices, and, finally, hearing aid repair capabilities. Of these, probably the two most variable factors are hearing aid reliability and hearing aid repair capabilities. Information on repair capability (24-hour, 48-hour, or the like) is available directly from the manufacturer's manual or representative. Information on reliability is more difficult to obtain, although small unpublished studies have been done. The best sources are other dispensing audiologists who have dealt with a variety of manufacturers and know their track records.

Cooperation and assistance from the hearing aid manufacturer can be especially helpful to the new practitioner. For example, the representative can assist in arranging liberal terms for someone just establishing a dispensing practice, such as delaying the initial payment due date by several months. The representative can also provide advice about hearing-aid-related equipment and supplies needed, as can the earmold laboratory. Some manufacturers employ audiologists with dispensing experience who can also provide invaluable help.

The audiologist in private practice depends on reliable and effective equipment in order to provide comprehensive audiologic services. Fortunately, this equipment, although relatively expensive, is reliable, has a long and useful life, and requires minimal maintenance. A reputable equipment dealer is the best source for advice and guidance on specific equipment items that may then be obtained through lease or financed purchase. **Summary**

Planning is a prerequisite to the initiation of a successful audiology practice. Planning includes the selection of the appropriate legal structure and form of the practice, *followed by* the consideration of possible equipment needs and methods for the purchase of both clinical instrumentation and hearing aids, because tax considerations are at least partially affected by the structure and form of the practice.

Finally, additional information regarding the expansion and maintenance of a private practice may be found in Chapter 12, and marketing considerations in audiology are addressed in Chapter 14.

REFERENCES

Glos, R., Steade, R., & Lowry, J. (1980). *Business: Its nature and environment.* Cincinnati, OH: South-Western Publishing Company.

Loavenbruck, A., & Madell, J. (1981). *Hearing aid dispensing for audiologists.* New York: Grune & Stratton.

Olni, A. (1982). *Selecting the legal structure for your firm.* New York: Small Business Administration, Management Aid no 6.004.

Rowland, R. (1978). Clinical aspects of audiology. In R. Battin & D. Fox, (Eds.), *Private practice in audiology and speech pathology.* New York: Grune and Stratton, pp. 191–240.

SUGGESTED READINGS

Flower, R. (1984). *Delivery of speech-language pathology and audiology services.* Baltimore: Williams & Wilkins.

Loavenbruck, A., & Hampton, D. (1982). Private practice in audiology. *Audiology, 7*(2): 17–29.

Appendix 8–A

Publications Available from the U.S. Small Business Administration

Listed below are some of the brochures available without charge by writing to the U.S. Small Business Administration, 26 Federal Plaza, New York, New York 10278 or by calling (212) 264-9488.

MA 1.001	*The ABC's of Borrowing*
MA 1.010	*Accounting Services for Small Service Firms*
MA 1.015	*Budgeting in a Small Business Firm*
MA 1.016	*Sound Cash Management and Borrowing*
MA 1.020	*Profit Pricing and Costing for Services*
MA 2.004	*Problems in Managing a Family-Owned Business*
MA 2.010	*Planning and Goal Setting for Small Business*
MA 2.014	*Can You Lease or Buy Equipment?*
MA 2.016	*Check List for Going Into Business*
MA 2.018	*Computers for Small Business*
MA 2.025	*Thinking About Going Into Business?*
MA 6.003	*Incorporating a Small Business*
MA 6.004	*Selecting the Legal Structure for Your Business*
9	*Marketing Research Procedures*
87	*Financial Management*
89	*Marketing for Small Business*
115-A	*A List of Free Publications*
115-B	*A List of For-Sale Publications*

Chapter 9

Business and Management Aspects of Private Practice in Speech-Language Pathology and Audiology

Carol A. Sullivan, M.A.

The practice of speech-language pathology and audiology in the private sector has increased significantly in the past 5 years, partly due to the advent of hearing aid dispensing by audiologists, a relatively new dimension of audiological services. Most professionals in private practice, however, have received little or no training in the business and management aspects of private practice. Historically, graduate education programs in communication sciences and disorders have not provided information on the financial aspects of initiating or marketing a private practice. Rather, these programs have focused on the education and training of professionals for service delivery opportunities in schools, hospitals, and agency work setting.

In the past, the private practice sector was primarily comprised of experienced professionals who had either developed business acumen they could apply to the establishment of a practice or had sufficient funds to employ others to attend to fiscal matters. Now, however, the current interest in self-employment among both experienced and newly trained speech-language pathologists and audiologists requires a commensurate development of not only professional knowledge but also business knowledge and financial management skills.

As others have noted earlier in the text, the development of knowledge and skills in financial management is fundamental to providing professional service in an independent work setting. Possession of such knowledge and skills provides the opportunity to (1) establish economic independence, (2) apply professional knowledge in a self-directed manner, (3) engage in long-range financial planning, and (4) have flexibility in making financial decisions.

Financial management requires establishing financial records that document the transactions of business, both income and expenditures. It requires an understanding of the significance of the financial information necessary for making decisions

FINANCIAL MANAGEMENT IN A BROADER CONTEXT

149

regarding cash flow, personnel, expenditures, expansion, and investment. Documentation is one of the most powerful objective tools available for directing business and personal financial decisions. (See Chapter 15 for a more complete discussion of personal investment decision making.)

It is generally recognized that political decisions, world events, economic shifts, changes in federal or state laws, and even weather conditions all influence the financial world. To accommodate the economic flux produced by larger events, one needs a broad knowledge of the possibilities of managing one's finances. Management of an individual practice must be viewed within the larger context of state and national trends and events.

Three Staging Processes of Financial Management

The first process is the production of income. In the private practice, this process encompasses marketing, creating referral sources, establishing an office, and rendering a service. Financial management during this stage requires the establishment of an accounting system, preferably with the counsel of a professional accountant. (See also Chapters 5, 10, and 11.) This system translates the business transactions into statements that clearly state expenses and income, allowing one to determine the profitability of the practice. This knowledge can be used as a guide to making decisions in stages two and three.

The second stage of financial management entails becoming educated about legal tax procedures and instruments that are available to maximize the retention of income. Understanding how the tax system works, with the assistance of an accountant or financial planner, permits the preservation of income.

In the third stage of financial management, it is important to develop both short- and long-range investment goals through the development of a financial plan that disburses assets into investments that meet personal and business needs. (See also Chapters 5 and 15.)

FINANCIAL PLANNING

Using Financial Data for Decision Making

The recording of financial data provides the barometer for gauging the profitability of the private practice. The success of a practice is judged largely by its profitability; that is, the *net* income of the practice. The establishment of an accounting system is fundamental to furnishing a statement of financial position or a balance sheet that displays the assets, liabilities and owner's equity and provides necessary data for ascertaining an individual's or company's economic health. A simplified example of such a balance sheet may be found in Chapter 5.

Managerial Forecasting

The effective management of a practice necessitates planning that is based on financial information. For example, planning may include making decisions about the fiscal feasibility of establishing a part-time versus a full-time practice. Also included in planning are financial considerations that determine the type of facility, location, staff requirements, capital equipment, investment, and advertising.

In a larger sense, the use of managerial forecasting for predicting future directions for growth in the health care field is important in the development of long-range financial plans. Such factors as population growth, age of the population, governmental health agency trends, new instrumentation development, and social acceptance of prosthetic devices may assist in projecting the financial potential of a practice.

The potential growth of the practice is partially determined by evaluating past growth of income versus expenses over a specific period of time. When planning to expand a part-time practice to full-time, it is important to estimate income needs for a period of 2 years in the future and then ascertain potential income based on past performance growth patterns and current assets available to supplant income needs. Sufficient capitalization should be available to sustain income needs minimally over a 2-year period of time. (For other forecast predictions, see Chapters 2 and 5.)

Part-Time versus Full-Time Private Practice

Available capital may largely determine where the practice can be located. In determining location, it is essential to consider the average household income level of an area, the number of competitors, and the relative strengths or weaknesses of these competitors for the products and services to be offered. Reviewing the space needs for the practice, including room for expansion as the practice grows, is also important. Because an established location is a valuable asset and may be costly to change, it is fiscally prudent to obtain both a location and an adequate amount of space that will meet both short- and long-term goals. In planning space, consider the type of building, which may be a medical building, a shopping center store, or a home, and analyze the cost advantages of each location. Remember that restroom and parking facilities need to be easily accessible. Consider the financial aspects of insurance in each of the locations, as well as building maintenance fees. (For a more exhaustive discussion, see Chapter 7, Selecting the Location and Site for a Private Practice.)

Facility Selection

When planning employee staffing levels, the elements of both time and money must be considered. In a private practice it is the time spent in patient contact that produces revenue. Hence, time represents potential income. It is essential to plan one's use of time to maximize the financial growth of the practice.

Ascertaining the most efficient use of one's own professional training and the application of temporal resources is fundamental to financial success. First, examine your present goals for developing a practice. In the initial stage of development, the cost of an employee may be prohibitive. During this period, it may be advantageous to use such devices as telephone answering machines and to hire part-time personnel or use family members until the income level can support an employee.

Second, when office responsibilities have grown to exceed the current staff's capabilities on an ongoing basis, it may be advantageous to hire a new employee. However, before hiring new staff members, review the cost increases related to such an employee *and* that staff member's potential for increasing profitability through improving service or marketing. A new staff member's time can be partially allocated to responsibilities that, in fact, create new sources of income or reduce accounts receivable.

Third, when determining the need for additional employees, examine the current ongoing duties of present employees. Consider the amount of additional employee

Guidelines in Planning Staff Requirements

time needed and the specific tasks to be accomplished. Re-evaluate the anticipated employee's job description and the financial feasibility of the expenditure of the time.

Finally, there may be numerous solutions for increasing staffing that are less costly than hiring additional employees. Determine whether increasing overtime may be more economical. Other fiscally effective solutions may include the hiring of temporary or part-time help. In addition, it is efficient planning to train a part-time employee who can be knowledgeable about the office procedures and can cover for vacations and sick leave.

Capital Equipment

The acquisition of capital equipment requires considerable financial planning. Determining which clinical equipment is considered fundamental to the basic performance of services is a first step in establishing a practice, as discussed in Chapter 8. Such office equipment as computers, dedicated word processors, or electronic typewriters may enhance the speed with which reports, financial records, appointments, insurance claims, and inventory can be processed and can thus contribute to income.

Capital equipment can have a measurable effect on increasing revenue by increasing productivity, shortening collection time frames, improving inventory monitoring, and enabling regular patient follow-up.

Leasing or Buying Equipment

Generally, most equipment is available for either purchase or lease. Leasing equipment is similar to renting in that it incurs a monthly charge. The decision to rent or to buy is dependent on the financial needs of each business, as discussed in Chapter 8.

When deciding whether to lease or buy equipment one should consider three factors: (1) tax benefits that accrue through investment tax credits, (2) depreciation of the equipment, and (3) the interest that is paid on loans. The investment tax credit allows a credit against the business taxes of up to 10 percent of qualified investment in tangible property placed into business service during the year. Qualified investments include equipment that has a life of at least 3 years. The amount of the credit is predicated on the recovery period used for depreciation purposes (Schnepper, 1985). For example, instrumentation costing $10,000 and to be depreciated over 5 years would be given a 10 percent credit, thereby reducing its actual cost to $9,000. Additional considerations include cash flow benefits and the estimated termination value of the equipment.

Purchasing equipment gives you (the owner) the advantage of the tax benefits of deducting depreciation. For equipment purchased before 1981, there are three accepted methods of calculating depreciation of capital assets: straight line, double declining balance, and years-digits. The last two methods are accelerated methods of taking the deduction in which two-thirds of the cost of the equipment is taken in half the time of the estimated life of the asset. Property acquired after 1983 falls within the rules of the depreciation allowance that is based on the Accelerated Cost Recovery System (ACRS). The method by which the equipment is depreciated is determined by the useful life of the equipment, the resale value relative to the financial determination of the maximum tax benefit to the business. When purchasing an audiometer or other office equipment, the depreciation begins at the point of acquisition and ends when it is disposed of for tax purposes. The decrease in value is a business expense and is deducted from current income, thereby reducing current taxable income.

The two primary advantages of leasing equipment are (1) the monthly rental costs that provide tax benefits as a business deduction and (2) the deferral of outright purchase of the equipment. This deferral allows available income to be maintained for other expenses, as noted in Chapter 8.

Although leasing equipment may liberate cash, it is important to obtain a written contract. For example, it is preferable to negotiate a lease agreement with *no* security deposit, *no* unconditional guarantee of payments, *no* tie-in clauses forcing the private practitioner to buy supplies, service, or insurance from the lessor, and *no* separate agreement that the lease is void unless satisfactory equipment is delivered (Lowrey, 1981). Terms regarding servicing of the equipment need to be defined. Note also that service contracts can be limiting in that the practitioner is restricted to the service of one company.

Finally, it is important to negotiate the disposition of the equipment at the end of the lease agreement and to determine whether the lessor or the lessee receives the investment tax credit.

Advertising

Advertising serves the purposes of informing the public of a service or product and of creating a professional image. One can advertise through the Yellow Pages of the telephone directory, newspapers, direct mail, speaking presentations, or magazines. The financial goals of advertising include (a) increasing patient caseload, (b) establishing the business as a prime source for products and services, and (c) establishing a professional reputation in the financial community.

Decisions made about the types of advertising that yield financial profitability must consider the following issues:

- What are the media sources available to your patients?
- What forms of media are your potential patients most likely to receive?
- What is considered ethical practice within the boundaries of the Code of Ethics and standard practice of the American Speech-Language Hearing Association?
- What are the costs of the advertising relative to the amount of exposure, estimated population who receives the information, and potential response as measured in actual increased business?

Establishing a professional business image requires informing potential referral sources or patients of a new or established practice. In accomplishing this goal, it should be recognized that much of the advertising will not result in a direct financial return on a one-to-one basis of expenditure and income. However, it is possible to minimize the financial outlay and maximize the image-enhancing effect of advertising. Specific examples include the use of quality paper stock for business letterhead, envelopes and cards, the preparation of reports on a quality typewriter, and typesetting and printing of all promotional material. In selecting a business name, choose one that states the nature of the practice or your personal name if known in the professional community. Business courtesy, such as sending thank you letters to referral sources and prompt reports to professional referral sources, sets a professional image through the daily process of conducting business and is actually the least costly means of advertising a practice. Advertisements placed in newspapers, radio, or television are usually the most costly.

DETERMINING THE FINANCIAL ASPECTS OF THE ORGANIZATION OF A PRIVATE PRACTICE

As you know, your selection of one of the three basic forms of a business—sole proprietorship, partnership, and a corporation—is determined by weighing the financial and legal advantages of each structure and the form of ownership. This chapter discusses the financial aspects of each type of business structure.

Tax laws are rapidly changing, which has reduced significant financial advantages of incorporation. For example, the Tax Equity and Fiscal Responsibility Act (TEFRA) of 1982 eliminated the corporate benefit that allowed unlimited amounts of tax-free dollars to be put into retirement funds without distributing the profits into corporate dividends, hence avoiding taxes on profits. Today, there are limits on the amounts of dollars that can be placed in corporate retirement funds. However, there still remain differences, albeit smaller differences among the three business structures, that have legal and financial implications.

Financial Advantages and Disadvantages of Sole Proprietorship

The individual proprietorship of a practice allows the owner to take full responsibility for conducting a business and to reap the profits. In the sole proprietorship, the owner reports the taxable income or loss from the business, as well as income earned outside the business, on a single tax return. Therefore the gradient tax rate is applied to the total taxable income.

Any sole proprietor is fully responsible for all debts of the business. If the business incurs indebtedness in excess of the business assets, the sole proprietor's personal assets would be accessible to the creditors through the courts. The practice is completely dependent on the owner's abilities. If the owner becomes ill, the practice income may suffer substantially (Lowrey, 1981). This is the primary disadvantage to the sole ownership of a private practice. However, this risk can be minimized through careful financial management in the developmental stages of the practice.

Advantages and Disadvantages of a Partnership

As defined by the federal Uniform Partnership Act tax law, a partnership is an association of two or more persons, who as co-owners carry on a business for profit. A partnership is created by either an oral or, more commonly, a written contract. This contract is called a partnership agreement, or the articles of agreement. As noted in earlier chapters, in the partnership, each partner is individually liable for debts, as well as the division of income. The division of income is established in the partnership agreement. The partnership is particularly advantageous when the individual income falls within a low income tax bracket. However, if there are business losses, the partners are required to cover the losses through liquidation of personal property.

An advantage of a partnership is its ease and low cost of formation. In a partnership, the partner's mutual assets are bound together in a joint effort. Assets can be maximized and the liabilities and responsibilities shared, often enhancing the potential development of a practice. For example, a partnership of a speech-language pathologist and audiologist can provide interdisciplinary professional services that benefit the patient. The amount of capital to be provided for equipment in the formation of a practice can be divided proportionally among the partners.

In drawing up a partnership agreement, consideration should be given to the amount of monies to be contributed by each partner and the division of income earned from the practice. The conditions under which a partner can withdraw money and the payment of either partner's equity must be made clear. The division of assets and liabilities in the event of the death of the partner must also be established. The means of arbitration must also be predetermined in the event of a disagreement between partners. The agreement should also provide the means for dissolution of the partnership. (See also Chapters 5, 8, and 16 for a further discussion of this topic.)

An effective partnership gives the professionals an opportunity to exchange ideas, thus potentially strengthening the joint practice. The impact of debt, illness, or the lack of a specific ability in a particular area of business is reduced in a partnership.

Advantages and Disadvantages of a Corporation

In contrast to a partnership, a corporation is not a collective group of separate persons. Rather, a corporation's legal structure is that of a "legal person." The corporation can make contracts, incur indebtedness, own property, and perform business as if it were an individual. The officers of the corporation and stockholders are liable for the debts of the corporation to the limit of the assets held by the corporation. This limiting of liability protects the personal assets of an individual, as noted in earlier chapters. In an incorporated business, if there is a bankruptcy or if a product injures someone, the personal assets are protected except in instances of personal negligence.

A corporation has an unlimited life unless otherwise specified. Unlike a partnership or sole proprietorship, the existence of the corporation continues, even though stockholders may die. This continuity offers transferability of interest in the corporation through the selling of shares of stock.

When forming a corporation, a charter is obtained from the state. Obtaining this charter requires the professional assistance of an attorney whose fees may range from $500 to $1500. Fees vary according to geographical location and the complexity of the incorporation structure. The fee to establish a corporation must be weighed against its considerable tax advantages over a period of time.

A corporation in need of capital can obtain the financing by issuing stock. However, corporations often borrow from banks. In this instance most banks require that the owners personally guarantee repayment of the loan to the company.

Corporation taxes vary with the type of corporation established. There are two types of domestic operating corporations: the *S corporation* and the *C corporation*. They share common legal structures, but differ in the processing of taxes. In an S corporation, the profits and losses are considered a part of the stockholders' income and are taxed according to their individual tax brackets, much as in an unincorporated firm. In a C corporation, profits are considered separately from any salaries the shareholders might pay themselves, and corporate taxes are paid on these profits. If profits are paid to shareholders in the form of dividends, they can be taxed again as part of the shareholders' income (Button, 1985). In a small private practice the S corporation may be advantageous because it avoids double taxation. Income levels reaching $50,000 and over are in a position to benefit from a corporate structure.

Variations in state and local tax laws may apply to corporations that may differ from federal tax law. Consultation with an attorney and accountant is necessary to determine the structure that is most beneficial to each individual situation. There are no single or simple answers to the question of how one might best structure a private practice.

Professional Services Needed in Financial Planning

There are professionals with a variety of titles and types of professional education who can provide financial guidance. These include certified public accountants, tax accountants, bookkeepers, certified financial planners, and bankers.

When establishing a private practice, the counsel of a certified public accountant (CPA) is important. Accounting has been broadly defined as an economic information system that provides significant financial information about an organization. The role of an accountant is to offer professional services, including a financial accounting system, to monitor financial transactions. Some CPAs have chosen to specialize in tax law and its application to finance, and some are also attorneys.

A bookkeeper provides services that identify and record financial transactions for the preparation of financial statements. These statements are used for the purpose of managerial decisions, profit planning and cost control, taxes, and internal auditing.

To recommend investment strategies, the private practitioner may wish to engage the services of a certified financial planner who should be a member of the International Association for Financial Planning. This planner's role is to provide a general financial plan that includes short- and long-range goals to guide major financial decisions. The financial planner can recommend investments and insurance that will provide a level of income required to match the projected income needs of the investor taking into consideration current tax law. (For cautions and caveats about selecting such a planner, the reader is referred to the article, "Looking for Mr. Good Plan" (*Consumer Reports*, 1986). Also see Chapter 15, which is devoted to personal investment strategies).

Establishing an Accounting System for a Private Practice

The accounting system is needed to organize financial data for determining profits or losses, ascertaining taxes, regulating cash flow, and obtaining credit. The selection of an accounting system is made with the professional counsel of an accountant.

The process of the flow of business can be described in three stages. The first stage is the recording of all financial transactions that result in a change of assets or equities over a specific period of time. Assets can be both short or long term. A short-term asset consists of cash, fees owed to the practice, or inventory that can be converted to cash within approximately a 1-year period. Long-term assets consist of equipment, land, fixtures, furniture, or physical property that will be used daily while conducting business. Equities include current liabilities, which are debts owed or stock equity.

The difference between the amount of assets and liabilities is the owner's equity. At this first stage, the accounting system records the transactions, which include both income and expenses incurred in the process of conducting business.

In the second stage, the financial information collected in stage one is classified and summarized at the end of a period of time. This period is typically 30 days. For example, all hearing aid purchases from manufacturers are recorded on a daily basis as they occur during the period of a month. This information is recorded in stage one. In the second stage, the information recorded on a daily basis is classified according to either gross categorization or by manufacturer, and the amounts are summarized for the 30-day period of time.

In stage three, the data are presented in report form, and the results are interpreted. These periodic reports can then be used for making business decisions and ascertaining the profitability of the practice.

The stages of the accounting process document the transactions of daily business, summarize the data for a specific period of time, and translate the results into the periodic report. It is essential to understand the stages of the process and the documents that are used in each stage to record the data.

The field of accounting has specific terminology that is unique to the financial world. This terminology can be intimidating to the novice, dissuading him or her from using the financial reports for interpreting the fiscal status of the private practice. Specific financial reports that are commonly used by an accountant or bookkeeper in the normal course of conducting business are described below.

Understanding Financial Statements

Ledgers are specific forms kept in a looseleaf binder in which transactions can be recorded in chronological order. The entries name the category of the account in the ledger where it will eventually be recorded and state the amount of the transaction. This is the original entry source for data. If there is a high volume of transactions, they are first recorded in a journal.

Defining financial statements

Income statements report a summary of the flow of cash through the private practice, recording revenues and expenses for a specific period of time. When income has exceeded expenses, a profit is shown as *net income*. When expenses exceed income there is a *net loss*. An income statement is the transition document between the monthly balance sheets. One of the most important facts to remember when analyzing the income statement is that the net profit amount shown on the statement is not the equivalent of cash on hand because, in accrual accounting, the sale of a product or a service rendered is recorded at the time of the transaction, although the payment may not yet be received. In addition, some expenses may be prepaid, such as professional insurance at the beginning of a year, yet the cost is spread equally over each monthly income statement for an entire year (Coltman, 1984). If information is needed about the cash status of the practice, a cash budget needs to be prepared. Based on prior income and expenses, this cash budget can anticipate the amount of cash, credit, and expenses that will be available.

The *balance sheet* shows the assets and liabilities of the business on a specific date. When an asset is acquired, a *balanced entry* is one that also enters this asset as a liability. The balance sheet reflects the status of the business on any individual day.

ACCOUNTING PROCEDURES FOR PAYROLL

The accounting procedures for payroll must take into account gross earnings and the legal requirements for deductions on behalf of the employer and employee. It is essential to keep individual payroll records that denote hours worked, dates, cumulative totals of tax deductions, sick leave, personal days, and vacation time accumulated. Accurate records of employee payroll and related benefit information reduce the possibility of misunderstandings of earnings and benefits. The records should also include dates and amounts of salary increases. These records are used for both internal and external reports.

There are required deductions for retirement benefits, unemployment funds, supplementary benefits to spouses, and disability wages. The payroll records must account for these deductions. Reports must be filed quarterly or annually with the appropriate federal or state agencies that oversee the management of these funds. The following laws determine the amount of deductions to be taken by the employer and employee.

Federal Insurance Contributions Act (FICA)

The Social Security Act of 1935 requires that contributions to the retirement system be withheld by employers. Half of the deduction is taken from the employee's wages, and the remaining half is to be paid by the employer. Each employer is required to obtain an identification number from the Social Security Administration (SSA). This number is to be used on records that have the employee's name, address, total wages, amount subject to tax, and the period for this payment. Charts are available from your accountant or the SSA that indicate the amount of Social Security taxes to be paid in relation to each employee's wages.

Federal Unemployment Insurance Taxes

The Federal Unemployment Tax Act requires employers to pay unemployment compensation. These funds are paid to the federal government and are subsequently loaned to the states in the form of grants to provide income for the unemployed. This tax is to be paid by employers for those employees whose wages exceed $1500 in a quarter year or who work for 20 full days with each day in a different calendar week during the calendar year. An accountant who is used to establish an accounting system can provide the forms and procedures for paying this tax.

State Unemployment Compensation Taxes

This is a tax levied by the states that requires employers to file quarterly returns and to pay the tax at the end of a quarter. An employer must maintain records of employee wages, period of employment, and termination. Each state has different interpretations of the law; hence this information must be obtained from the state in which the practice is located.

Federal Income Tax Withholding

The amount of tax withheld is determined by the gross earnings of an employee. An employee is entitled to a personal exemption and an additional exemption if he or she is over 65 years of age or is blind. Each employer must file a quarterly combined return of FICA and federal income taxes. Each employer must give all employees a W-2 Form stating the amount withheld prior to January 31.

The financial goal for a private practice should be *to make a profit*. In attempting to reach this goal, there is no area of finance more stressful than having difficulties with the cash flow of a business. Maintaining a financial balance between expenditures and income is essential. Factors to consider include setting policies for fees, enhancing the timely payment of fees, and handling overdue accounts.

MANAGING CASH FLOW

Fundamental to this process is the setting of policies for fees and payment that bring income into the practice at the time the service is rendered. When setting fees, ascertain the average fee structure for a procedure in your geographical area. If your fees are more than 10 percent above the average in the area, they may be considered too high. When raising fees, consider more frequent, small, incremental increases, rather than fewer large increases. Be aware that delaying the receipt of income by accepting insurance assignment jeopardizes the cash flow status of a practice.

Setting Policies for Fees

Use diplomacy in stating the policy about fee payment at the time of the first appointment. Allow the patient the opportunity to accept or reject your fee for service. Discuss fees with the patient, answer questions, and, whenever possible, designate specific office staff, such as a secretary or bookkeeper who will handle routine payment and billing procedures with the patient. Itemize all bills, and whenever possible, obtain payment for service at the time of the appointment. If the patient is asked whether he or she would like to have a bill sent, the answer invariably is "yes."

Enhancing Timely Payment

When hearing aids are dispensed, set up contracts in advance that give the patient the total cost and a payment plan with established dates. Establish an accounts receivable file, keep it current, and send bills out once a month.

If an account is overdue, send a second notice that indicates on its face that the payment is overdue. A brief note from the bookkeeper that is mild in content can be included with the bill; it communicates the belief that the patient can be relied on to pay for the bill. Indicate that perhaps the office records might be incorrect and, if so, that the patient should please contact the office to resolve the difference.

Handling Overdue Accounts

An account still unpaid after the second notice should receive a notice stating that a serious overdue condition exists and that payment must be rendered in the next 10 days. If there is no response, then a letter should be sent from the clinician saying that the bill will be sent to a collection agency and that this action is likely to have a negative effect on the patient's credit rating.

Proper management of cash can enhance the cash flow position of the practice. Utilize an interest-bearing checking account whenever possible. If you have a

Maximizing Cash on Hand

business account that does not bear interest, place excess cash in a cash management account, which keeps cash accessible but pays interest on the surplus.

Arrange for 30- and 60-day interest-free credit from suppliers wherever possible. Use credit cards that have been established for business expenses, and pay before the 30-day period is completed. Prompt payment ensures free use of the money for the 30-day period of time. When paying routine bills, pay them on schedule, but avoid early payment.

One of the most effective ways to protect cash reserves is to control the level of fixed costs and cash-depleting expenses. Assessing current expenses and the degree to which these expenses are essential to the functioning of the practice gives information about where reductions in expenditures can be taken. For example, expenses for those personnel who earn revenues for the practice should be given a higher priority than expenses for personnel who perform nonrevenue-producing tasks. In effect, a cash flow budget predicts end-of-month expenses and allows planning for an account receivable intake to achieve a balanced cash flow. The data to predict monthly expenses can be derived from the balance sheet. The evaluation of expenditures and the resulting consequences of those expenses is fundamental to cost reduction planning.

Cash flow problems also can be reduced by planning for future capital expenditures. Assessing equipment needs, such as audiological instrumentation, office equipment, tape recording equipment, and computers, for estimated replacement costs and possible replacement dates is essential for the establishment of a capital equipment account. Predicting future costs allows for financial budgeting that lessens the probability of cash flow problems.

In long-term planning for capital equipment acquisition, money can be invested in a variety of ways to maximize interest and to achieve availability of funds in the planned time frames. Possible investments include time deposits, Jumbo certificates of deposit, corporate and municipal bonds, preferred stocks that pay dividends, U.S. Treasury notes, all of which have specific periods of time and specific rates of interest. An intermittent publication that briefly describes each of the stated investments is "Money Management for Dispensing Audiologists" (see Bebout, 1985).

HOW TO OBTAIN CREDIT

Establishing Credit to Obtain Credit

The initial phase of planning for credit begins with establishing a business relationship with a bank and developing sources of credit. Select a bank that provides service and with which you can develop a working relationship. (See also Chapter 4.) Make an appointment to meet a bank officer, discuss your business, and investigate possible resources for future loans. Avoid maligning a bank used previously, but rather intrigue the bank officer with your potential as a customer. When a bank has been selected, open a business checking account. If credit has not been established through prior loans, consider taking out a small loan. This loan should be taken with another bank or loan agency. As discussed in Chapter 4, banks are often hesitant to offer a first-time loan, particularly if the individual is self-employed. A first loan may require the signature of a co-signer. The timely repayment of a loan will give the loan officer evidence that you are a responsible borrower, and subsequent loans will be easier to obtain.

Experts stress the importance of a sufficient cash flow so that bills may be paid within the designated billing time frame. Paying bills to take the "cash discount" that hearing aid manufacturers offer establishes a favorable credit record for prompt payment and saves money. When a situation arises where the cash flow is inadequate to pay a bill on time, contact the creditors and suppliers. Communicate the fact that there will be a delay in payment and give an estimated date of payment.

Ignoring bills, paying late, and refusing to take calls from creditors can seriously damage a credit rating. Such negative information from creditors is reported to one of approximately five major national credit organizations, which have information fed into them from banks, retail stores, finance companies, and credit card companies. If payments on an account are 60 to 90 days late, credit agencies are notified. Credit agencies are required by federal law—The Fair Credit Reporting Act—to provide to consumers a copy of their credit report. This law gives the consumer the right to review the credit record and, if rejected for a loan to determine the reasons why. Before applying for a loan, request a copy of your personal and business credit report. Remember that information keyed into the system is not always correct, and you might have an opportunity to correct inaccurate data.

Sources of Credit

Selecting a source of credit depends on whether the practice's financing needs are short or long term. There are two main sources of financing: debt and equity. With debt, the lender does not have any equity relationship with the business. Banks are an example of a debt lender. Their return on the loan is the interest paid on the principal. In contrast, an equity investor has an active participation in the daily operation of the practice. An example of an equity loan is the borrowing of personal funds for a loan to the business. One of the primary variables that may determine where money will be borrowed is the strength of the borrower's credit history.

Personal Funds

The most common source of borrowing is personal funds from savings or short-term investments. Life insurance policies offer low interest rates, usually from 4.5 to 8 percent. However, the amount of the life insurance policy is reduced as the loan is subtracted from its face value. Borrowing money from friends or family who are willing to invest has the advantage of obtaining funds easily. However, disadvantages include the difficulties that may arise if the practice does not achieve a profitable status, thus making paying back of the loan difficult. Also, if a relative dies and the estate goes into probate, the entire amount of the loan may be demanded. All loans from family members should be covered by written agreements that include the rate of interest to be paid, date of final payback, and procedures all parties will follow if loans become delinquent.

Marketable stocks and bonds can be used for collateral on a loan. Loans can be obtained in an amount up to 75 percent of the market value of the stock. However, accounts in brokerage houses that are cash management accounts generally cannot be used as collateral. The inability to use this money as collateral is an important consideration when investing business capital.

Lending Institutions

Commercial banks or savings and loan associations are two sources of equity capital. The rate of interest offered depends on money market conditions, the specific business, its credit rating, size, and other factors. The smaller the private practice, the higher the rates because the risk frequently appears greater to the lender (Coltman, 1984). Long-term rates, in a changing interest market, tend to be higher than short-term rates.

In the current market there are a wide variety of types of loans with fixed interest rates or variable interest rates and with different percentages of points charged at the time of the loan. Because lending institutions are highly competitive, it pays to compare costs and to consult an accountant or attorney about the intricacies of the contracts.

Another source of capital is a line of credit given as an extension of a bank account. These credit lines specify an amount of overdraft allowed by the bank. The amount of the credit is determined by the bank's determination of the credit worthiness of the practice.

Factors to consider when selecting a bank. Banks market their services competitively to customers. When assessing a bank, it is important to consider its services and to compare the advantages offered among several banks in the community (Mahar, 1985). Some of the services available to the customer are:

- lowest annual percentage rate (APR) on loans
- low (or no) minimum required deposit in a non-interest-paying commercial account
- money-market accounts paying the highest rate of interest, compounded daily
- speedy crediting of deposits from out of town
- overdraft privileges
- low (or no) per-check charges for each check written or deposited
- sweep accounts, which automatically transfer money from a checking account into a money market account and return funds to checking
- night depository
- money transfer service
- financial planning service for small businesses

Federal Government Agencies

The Small Business Administration (SBA) makes loans to businesses at relatively low rates. These loans are intended to assist businesses in expanding, obtaining equipment and supplies, or acquiring capital. They can be obtained directly through the SBA or through the bank. There are three types of loans available: guaranteed loans, immediate participation loans, and direct loans. Each loan type differs in the conditions and the amount of interest rate charged. Further information is available by calling the SBA, which is listed in the telephone book under US Government.

There are a variety of indicators that signal an excessive amount of debt: when (1) payments on installment purchases become further apart and smaller in size, incurring interest charges (this may be the first clue that available cash is lessening); (2) the business is chronically in debt and the current month's bills are arriving before full payment of last month's bill, or debt is increasing; and (3) funds must be borrowed to pay current payroll or other current operating expenses, and debt is increasing. Another early signal is disorganization in the *management* of the practice. A general lack of interest in financial management with a primary focus on clinical work can endanger the fiscal viability of a practice. There needs to be a balanced effort in providing clinical service with sufficient time to monitor financial matters.

INDICATORS OF EXCESSIVE DEBT

Current tax law provides a myriad of deductions for the small business, such as a private practice, to reduce the taxes paid, *if* appropriate organization of financial data is present. Detailed record keeping, which includes receipts for all transactions, is imperative in order to justify deductions. For a small part-time practice, the documentation system can be as simple as an appointment book that justifies business activities and receipts in a file. However, a full-time active practice will need an accounting system, receipts filed by category or company, and a cross-reference system between the checkbook, journal, and receipts. Cancelled checks by themselves are considered inadequate evidence for documentation. It is the entire reliability of an accounting system and its ability to verify claimed deductions that satisfy an Internal Revenue Service (IRS) audit. If the practice has an accountant, it is advisable to be represented by the accountant, when it is audited.

GENERAL BUSINESS TAX STRATEGIES

Most business decisions, such as the structure of the business, the location of the practice, the purchase of capital equipment, the hiring of additional employees, increasing the inventory, the installation of computers, and the purchase of an automobile, have implications for tax benefits. Although the tax laws are complex, volumes of information have been written about maximizing the deductions, thereby decreasing real dollars paid in taxes. The application of tax law to the private practice can best be defined by an accountant or an attorney. However, it is to the benefit of the private practitioner to be very familiar with tax strategies in order to enhance the information given by a financial specialist. Knowledge of tax strategies is an area of financial management in which, if proper documentation is provided early in the fiscal year, the cumulative effort can save many earned dollars.

There are numerous books written on the topic of business tax law that list specific tax deductions, consider various business structures, and contain extensive information on preparing for an IRS audit. Two books that are pertinent to the topic of tax deductions and a small business are (1) J.A. Schnepper, *How to Pay Zero Taxes* and (2) W.M. Bradford, and G.B. Davis, *Business Tax Deduction Master Guide*.

Resources for Tax Advising in Small Business

Throughout this chapter, the importance of documentation has been stressed. Data management for both internal and external reports requires many hours of work. Either a bookkeeper or secretary may be needed to record daily transactions. In a

DATA COLLECTION AND COMPUTERS

small practice, this method of recording data may be satisfactory, but as the practice expands (with increases in accounts receivables and numbers of transactions in accounts payable), it may be cost effective to consider the use of computers. (See Chapters 10 and 13 for further elaboration on microcomputer use.) Software is available that has application to financial management, clinical services, and patient management. The multipurpose use of computers in the private practice can be clinically and financially beneficial.

An alternative might be the use of data processing services that handle financial data, compute and prepare paychecks, calculate income tax deposits and payroll tax reports, and provide patient mailing lists and labels. These companies charge relatively small fees to compute the data. When assessing the feasibility of buying a computer and accompanying software, consider services that can be obtained through existing computer firms.

SUMMARY: FINANCIAL KNOWLEDGE AND APPLICATION ENHANCE INCOME

From the moment a professional makes a decision to practice speech-language pathology or audiology in the private sector, he or she must learn how to manage the financial aspects of the practice. As indicated by a number of the authors of earlier chapters, professional time spent in planning is a profitable investment. The staging process of initiating a business takes time and includes the use of professional consultants, determining a location, selecting instrumentation and personnel, creating organizational forms, purchasing office equipment, and the like.

This commitment to self-employment must rest on a significant number of years of previous clinical experience. Only this experience can prepare the practitioner to provide and sustain the highest of patient care standards. However, in addition to the necessary background and experience in clinical practice, the professional needs to understand management strategies, finance, and the application of financial concepts to a private practice. It is the marriage of clinical and financial expertise that enhances the future growth of not only a single practice but also assists in strengthening the entire field of private practice in speech-language pathology and audiology. As the profession matures in the private sector, it is likely to develop along a number of new dimensions as yet unknown.

REFERENCES

Bebout, J.M. (1985). *Fixed Income Investments*. Intermittent periodical of Money Management for Dispensing Audiologists.

Bradford, W.M., & Davis, G.B. (1984). *Business tax deduction master guide*. Englewood Cliffs, NJ: Prentice-Hall.

Button, S. (1985). "Should You Incorporate?" *Home Office publication of Time Inc.*, 1(1), Spring.

Coltman, M.M. (1984). *A practical guide to financial management*. Toronto: International Self-Counsel Press, LTD.

Lowrey, A.J. (1981). *How to become financially successful by owning your own business*. New York: Simon and Schuster.

Looking for Mr. Good Plan. (1986). *Consumer Reports 1*, 39–44.

Mahar, M. (1985). When and where to borrow. *Home Office publication of Time, Inc.*, 1(1), Spring.

Schnepper, J.A. (1985). *How to pay zero taxes*. Reading, MA: Addison-Wesley.

Berry, J.F. (1985). Controlling your cash flow. *Home Office publication of Time, Inc.*, 1(1), Spring.

Cook, J.A., & Wool, R. (1985). *All you need to know about banks.* New York: Bantam Books.

Dreyfuss, J. (1985). Establishing credit. *Home Office publication of Time, Inc.*, 1(1), Spring.

Sellers, D. (1983). *Computerizing your medical practice.* NJ: Medical Economics Books Publishers.

Sullivan, D.J. (1979). *Practice made perfect.* FL: Medi-Publishing & Design Group.

Van Caspel, V. (1983). *The power of money dynamics.* Reston, VA: Reston Publishing Co., Inc.

Wortman, L.A. (1976). *Successful small business management.* New York: AMACOM Publishers.

SUGGESTED READINGS

Chapter 10

Computer Applications in Private Practice: Getting Started

Mariana Newton, Ph.D.

Over 1 million personal computers were sold in 1983, three times as many as in the previous year. Before the advent of the personal computer explosion, to most of us, computers were rooms full of mystical machinery—whirring disks, tape reels, electronic circuitry, and flashing lights—that were used by giant companies and the government. They swallowed punch cards that were unfolded, unmutilated, and unstapled and made mistakes that entangled transactions and piqued emotions. It is no wonder that smaller computers have been approached by administrative and office personnel in small businesses with hesitancy and even resistance. However, over time, the power of the microcomputer as a business tool has converted even the most recalcitrant.

WHY USE A COMPUTER IN A PRIVATE PRACTICE?

One factor markedly distinguishes the private practice of speech-language pathology and audiology from other clinical practice settings. That factor is competition. In salaried positions in schools, hospitals, community clinics, and universities, the administrative decisions that may affect survival and growth may be made far away from the clinician-patient relationship. The increase in recent years of the numbers of speech-language pathologists and audiologists in private practice will undoubtedly increase competition based on the value of their services to the public. The bottom line then will be that those who can provide services of value to the public at the lowest cost will flourish.

In order to provide services of worth at an affordable cost, the goal of the private practitioner as a businessperson must be to increase productivity. That is, the less time you, as a private practitioner, spend on work that does not maximally utilize your professional expertise, the more time you will have to generate income using those self-same professional talents. The computer is a valuable tool for increasing your personal productivity as a clinician, as well as increasing the fiscal productivity of your practice.

Not only will a computer free your practice time for income-generating activities but it will also relieve you of spending great amounts of time on boring tasks, either administrative or clinical. All of the work a computer does can be done by hand, but doing so takes a long time and is tedious. Moreover, a number of tasks that would assist financial stability of the private practice in the long run, such as public relations efforts and information management, including investment portfolios, simply do not get done because they take so much time away from activities that generate short-term gain. The computer is a superb tool for reducing the tedium and increasing the planning required for sustained growth, as noted in Chapter 8.

Only a few short years ago, the primary reason for *not* having a computer in the private practice was its cost. Not only were computers more expensive than they are now, but private practitioner's fees were just at, or even below, the actual costs of service delivery. Both factors have changed. The cost of hardware (the machine) and software (the programs) has steadily declined, and private practice fees have increased. An initial investment now can be recovered in less than a year's time, whereas the life of the equipment is at least 5 years. Even then, replacement probably will be dictated more by the practitioner's need or desire for more computer capability than by the computer's irreparable breakdown.

BASIC FACTS ABOUT COMPUTERS

Computers come in many sizes and shapes. Mainframe computers are big, expensive, and are designed with many terminals for multiple users. The terminals are connected to the computer by telephone line or direct cable. The computers used at the Houston space center and by big businesses are mainframes.

Minicomputers are smaller, less expensive, and can also do many jobs at one time, but they have a smaller storage capacity and can handle fewer users than mainframe computers. Minicomputers are typically used by medium-sized businesses or departments within a large business.

Microcomputers or personal computers are smaller than minicomputers. They are used for small businesses and are ideal for the private practice. They cost between $500 and $6,000, although costs are declining, and most do only one job at a time. They do not have as much storage space as larger computers, but their capacity/cost ratio is very favorable for the individual user.

A computer system includes both *hardware* (the memory, central processing unit, and peripherals, such as input and output devices, modems, and spoolers) and *software* (sets of electronic instructions to tell the computer what to do). There are two kinds of memory: *read-only memory* (ROM), which is permanent and built into the computer, and *random-access memory* (RAM), which temporarily stores data in the computer's internal memory bank for processing with the aid of a software program. The *central processing unit* (CPU) is the brain of the computer, consisting of the arithmetic unit, which does the calculations, and the control unit, which directs traffic through the processor. The speed of the CPU is largely determined by the number of bytes the processor can handle as a single unit. The Z80 central processing chip is a standard 8-bit chip, used by Apple, TRS 80 III and IV, and the Commodore 64. The 8088 chip is a 16-bit chip, used by the IBM-PC, and the 68000 chip is a very fast processor for Apple's MacIntosh. The larger the bit designation, the more addresses in memory the CPU can identify.

The computer is accessed with various input devices, the most common of which is the keyboard. Other input devices include touch pads, light pens, joysticks, optical readers, and the infamous "mouse." Output from the computer can be delivered on the screen or monitor, by a printer or plotter (for graphics), or by synthesized voice. Programs and data are stored on magnetic tape, floppy disks or diskettes of various sizes, or hard disks. Additional storage options are available for larger computers. Magnetic tape is relatively inexpensive, but is limited to sequential access only; hard disks are more expensive, but allow random access. A *spooler or buffer* is a temporary storage capability to hold data for output or transfer so that the memory of the computer can be cleared for other uses. A *modem* is a connection device allowing the computer to be linked by telephone line to other computers (see discussion of networking, bulletin boards, and remote data bases).

Programs are written in a variety of languages, such as BASIC, Fortran, COBOL, or Pascal, that the computer can understand. Each language is designed for a particular purpose. In addition, computers are controlled by other programs called operating systems. For microcomputers, the common term used is *disk operating system*, or DOS, e.g., TRSDOS, MS-DOS, NEWDOS, MultiDOS, DOSPLUS, CP/M, and UNIX.

Understanding the basics of computers is not essential to the use of the computer, just as understanding the intricacies of the inside of a sewing machine is not crucial to being a good tailor. Yet, understanding the speed and capacity of hardware is essential to deciding which kind of computer will be your initial choice or in understanding the computer that you own in relation to others that are available. For example, eight-bit machines are slower and have less memory than 16- or 32-bit machines, but they are less expensive. Likewise, a soft disk is less expensive, but also has a smaller capacity and may necessitate two disk drives, whereas a hard disk is probably sufficient with only one drive. The CPU chips and the operating systems largely determine what kind of software the computer will run. Hence, it is important first, to identify the needs of one's practice; second, the software that will meet those needs; and third, the choices in hardware relating to speed and capacity.

The discussion above is necessarily abbreviated. For further information, please read the selections listed under Suggested Readings at the end of this chapter.

WHAT ARE YOUR COMPUTER NEEDS?

The first step in identifying and understanding one's private practice needs for a computer is to analyze the size and scope of the practice. Such an analysis would include gathering data on the number of patients seen, the services required, the number of patient visits and the direct professional contact time per visit per patient, and the paperwork required for each patient *and* each procedure. Obviously, if the scope of the practice is small, certain tasks and procedures that are required only occasionally may be most efficiently done by hand. If the practice is larger and many similar tasks are done repeatedly for each patient, the computer may make the work more efficient and less tedious. Setting up a computerized billing system, for example, for ten patients is more trouble than it is worth. Yet, the time spent in setting up a computerized billing system for 500 patients is recovered very quickly. Careful analysis of the size and scope of every parameter of the practice will define the areas of need for computer assistance.

The second step in identifying need should be to analyze the efficiency of one's office. How quickly and accurately do things get done? Some procedures may get bogged down because of staff inefficiency, rather than the scope or size of the job. There may be too few steps in a procedure, causing frequent error and requiring considerable time for error correction. Or, too many steps may cause redundancy or unnecessary activity that clogs the system. Psychological factors that affect efficiency must also be considered. Those tasks that are the most tedious and the most boring are often the tasks that are put aside until later, not because they are hard to do but because they present no challenge to the personnel involved. These motivational factors are important and deserve considerable attention.

Motivation of personnel in an office is critical to productivity, both quantitatively and qualitatively. Hence, in analyzing computer needs, consider the opinions of people with whom you work—secretaries, technical support personnel, and professional colleagues. Very often, your identification of need based on an analysis of the size, scope, and efficiency of your practice matches their perceptions of need. (You are confirmed!) However, sometimes variances occur. Your personnel might identify needs based on factors that you may not have considered, e.g., their personal preferences, varying degrees of objectivity, and so forth. Although needs based on careful analysis may outweigh needs based on personal preference, the latter should not be ignored. Eventually, if and when a computer system is adopted, the full cooperation and enthusiasm of all staff members will be needed for implementation. Participation in the preparation for that move will yield big payoffs later when learning new ways of doing things can prove frustrating.

Almost every practice, private or otherwise, has needs for text management or word processing for correspondence, patient reports, running notes, research notes, and the like. Even expertly dictated material must eventually be put on paper as text. Once written as text, many first drafts require changes in content, style, or format.

Much of the reputation of a private practice depends on the written account of that practice. Physicians, educators, and agencies who refer to the practice rarely have the opportunity to observe directly the professional services rendered. Most often, they evaluate the professional services of the private practice on the basis of written reports of the services. Sometimes such evaluations are based on information presented; other times the evaluations are based on the style and format or the frequency and promptness of reports. Written communications emanating from a private practice, therefore, become a major public relations and marketing tool for the practice.

Not only do private practices have requirements for written output but they also have needs for information input. Many professionals depend on printed literature, such as business and professional journals and advertisements, to keep the practice current. Even with the best publications, the lag time between information availability and dissemination is quite long. Moreover, practitioners may have to wade through a considerable body of literature to find new information that directly pertains to their informational needs. Large computer data bases that catalog information about a large variety of subjects and that can be accessed from the office microcomputer via a telephone line provide fast, current information. Not only bibliographic and abstracted research information but also information on such topics as investments, financial planning, taxes and law is available from computerized data bases.

Every private practice in speech-language pathology or audiology has some financial management requirements. Patient billing, account management, payroll, third party reimbursements, and contractual arrangements are but a few examples. In order to keep track of financial obligations, orderly records of patients, providers, procedures, and services rendered are necessary. (See also Chapters 5 and 9.) In some practices of medium size, a combination of manual and computer-assisted management is best. This issue is discussed further in later sections.

Practices that include several professional associates and several support staff members require some way of keeping track of people, money, and projects. The more professional people in a practice and the more patients and projects, the more complex the effort required to manage data, to relate data sets to each other, to allocate resources, and to monitor and report activities. Personnel and patient records, scheduling, patient goals and objectives, patient progress data, income, direct and indirect expenses, taxes, budget, and equipment acquisition, maintenance, and use are all part of data management and represent common needs in a private practice for computer assistance.

SELECTING HARDWARE AND SOFTWARE TO MEET YOUR NEEDS

Only a few years ago, buying a computer was fairly easy. There were only two or three well-known computer manufacturers, 20–30 software packages, and a few stores to patronize. Now, dramatic growth and change in the computer industry have made selection more difficult. Hundreds of brands, thousands of software packages, and a store in every shopping center can confuse and mystify, rather than inform and edify. A process that may have taken a week or so now may take several months to a year.

The process of buying a computer is a series of consecutive steps. The first step, reviewed earlier, involves learning some general information about computers and identifying specific needs of your private practice. Subsequent steps are outlined below.

What Software Will You Need?

The needs you have identified in your private practice will determine the software to be selected. For general office use, standard software is available for almost all microprocessors. To clarify your specific needs, consider the following issues. First, identify which uses are the most important for your office and hence are first on your list. Focusing on a few specific applications with highest priority allows you to forget completely about irrelevant applications. Does the software require a minimum amount of memory or a specific operating system that will determine the components of the hardware? How much data can the program manage? How many records will be worked with at one time? How long are the documents that need to be written? What kind of calculations will be done? How fast must you have answers to questions? How fast will the software put information on paper? How much diskette storage is required? Ask yourself all the questions you can think of, and record the answers and some examples.

The answers to the questions may come from salespersons, written reviews of software, and documentation of software programs. Many computer stores have demonstration software available for the customer to try. A few hours with a demonstration program and a knowledgeable salesperson, using examples from your own practice, can be very enlightening. Other users of the software can be identified by a salesperson or by the manufacturer of the software. Consultation with users provides answers to questions about specific applications, user satisfaction, limitations and advantages of the program, and support from the program developer.

What Hardware Will You Need to Run the Software?

Based on your software specifications, determine how much memory your computer will need. Always allow for a little more memory than the amount specified by the biggest program selected to allow sufficient memory for the operating system. That is, if the program specifications indicate RAM requirements of 194K (194 thousand bytes of random access memory), you should plan to buy a computer with no less than 256K because some additional memory will be needed to manipulate data and run the program. How many disk drives are required for the software? What kind of print and how much printer speed are needed for the applications? Letter-quality printers are ideal for many office applications, but if graphics are needed, look at other kinds of printers or plotters. Are there other peripherals (input, storage, and output devices) that the software requires? In addition to manuals for software programs, several readily available computer publications (*Business Computer Systems, Business Software Review, Infoworld, Personal Computing*) review software, outline the hardware specifications, and provide information about running various software packages on specific hardware.

What about Compatibility?

Although many "look-alikes" and "clones" have come onto the market, particularly in regard to the IBM computers, there is rarely such a thing as complete compatibility. Compatibility claims for computers manufactured by the same company have the most validity. Computers manufactured by different companies have less compatibility. Software written for one kind of hardware may be used on other kinds of hardware, but there may be some features that do not run, cause read/write errors, or utilize different keystrokes for certain procedures.

The more important compatibility considerations for the private practitioner, however, concern whether there will be a need to exchange data stored on diskettes with other users. If so, compatibility of both software and hardware must be ensured. Offices that have more than one user and more than one computer will be much more flexible in computer utilization if there is compatibility between hardware, software, and disk operating systems.

Is the System Comfortable for You?

It is important to try various systems that may be under consideration. Consider the comfort of use, the "touch" of the keyboard, the appearance of the display screen, and even the sounds the computer makes. An example of an aspect of system comfort has to do with the physical relationship of the screen and the keyboard. Some computers house the screen, keyboard, CPU, and disk drives in a single case. On other machines, the keyboard can be separated from the screen by a cable. On still others, the keyboard, monitor, and disk drives are all separate units. Separate components make the computer much less portable. On the other hand, monitors separated from keyboards allow some adjustment in height and angle of the monitor. For users who wear bifocal eyeglasses, some adjustment of the height and angle of the screen reduces visual fatigue and adds considerably to user comfort. There are even those laid-back types who prefer to lean back in their chairs in the privacy of their offices with the keyboard on their lap. Or, two individuals may use the same unit if (1) the CRT screen can be rotated, (2) the keyboard unit can be placed on an adjacent desk, and (3) both operators are not required to utilize the system in an overlapping manner.

What Will Your Future Computer Needs Be?

Not only should software and hardware meet present needs, but you should consider the future as well. The rapid changes in both hardware and software make it almost impossible—cognitively or economically—to keep up with the latest developments. Nevertheless, do not buy too small so that within a short time you have outgrown the capabilities of your system. Rarely is a computer replaced because it wears out. More often, replacement is dictated by needs for increased capacity and capability. Plan for the future!

What Can You Afford?

Unlike the prices of most commodities, the price of microcomputers has steadily declined while their capabilities have increased. Computers that cost $3,000 in 1981 are now priced at $900. Moreover, there is some variation in price from vendor to vendor. So it pays to shop around . . . not only for price, but also for opinions. Avoid impulsiveness in making your purchase. Wait until consistent advice emerges about a system at the lowest possible cost, but do not wait "forever." Resign yourself to the fact that "something better" may emerge relatively soon after your purchase.

Popular computing magazines (*Byte, Micro 80, Compute, PC*) are filled with advertisements for mail-order sales of hardware and software. If you know exactly what you want and you do not need the advice of the salesperson, mail order may be an opportunity for increased savings. Check with the Better Business Bureau or a local user's group about the reputation of the mail-order firm.

WHERE DOES ONE GO FROM HERE?

Perhaps reading about how to use the computer in private practice has sparked your interest and enthusiasm and indeed has even convinced you that the computer can help increase productivity and decrease costs. Chapter 13 outlines the uses of the most common standard software programs in the private practice.

In addition, there are several sources of additional assistance that are free, user friendly, and fun. Most communities have computer users' groups. If you practice in a very small community, you may need to look to a larger town or city nearby. The users' groups are usually organized according to hardware brand or primary application. Consult computer stores that sell your kind of hardware, the Chamber of Commerce, or the nearest college computer department for information. These groups are glad to have users of all skill levels and are very helpful in teaching new applications, solving problems, and sharing information; many have their own bulletin boards. Join one!

The market is flooded with books about computers and computer applications. Many can be obtained from your community library or nearest college library. In addition, monthly computing magazines such as *Creative Computing, Business Computer Systems, PC, Byte, Micro 80,* and *Compute,* have useful articles, thousands of advertisements, software reviews, tutorials, and question-and-answer sections, as indicated previously.

Lastly, the American Speech-Language-Hearing Foundation sponsors an annual conference on the use of the computer as a professional tool. Although there is a fee for the conference, the presentations and exhibits are current and specific to the profession.

SUGGESTED READINGS

Ball, M.J., & Charp, S. (1977). *Be a computer literate.* Morristown, NJ: Creative Computing Press.

Barden, W., Jr. (1984). *What do you do after you plug it in?* Indianapolis, IN: Howard W. Sams Company, Inc.

Frenzel, L., Jr. (1983). *Crash course in microcomputers.* Indianapolis, IN: Howard W. Sams Company, Inc.

Green, H. (1984). High tech for small business. *New in Computing Magazine and Buyer's Guide,* 1(11), 31–33.

McGlynn, D.R. (1979). *Personal computing: Home, professional, and small business applications.* New York: Wiley.

Part III

Maintaining and Expanding a Private Practice in Speech-Language Pathology and Audiology

Chapter 11

Increasing the Practice: Focus on Speech-Language Pathology

Patricia R. Cole, Ph.D.

Private practitioners are responsible for building and maintaining a practice that is both productive financially and effective professionally. Doing so requires competence in financial planning and management, marketing, personnel management, and services to patients. Many tasks important in building a practice also are necessary components of maintaining or expanding a practice. This chapter addresses important considerations both for building a practice and for maintaining or expanding an established practice.

Perhaps the greatest challenge to the beginning private practitioner is establishing a consistent influx of referrals so that the number of patients seen at any time is sufficient to guarantee that revenue is greater than expenses. Those who have started a private practice are quick to acknowledge that the steady growth in referrals comes more slowly than they had hoped or anticipated. In the first year or more of a practice, the fluctuations in numbers of referrals from month to month are especially significant because the practice does not have a consistent base of patients on which it can depend for income.

The practitioner should take the initiative in locating a variety of sources for gaining new patients. Rarely will a single source provide a sufficient number of patients on an ongoing basis, even if it refers several patients in the first months of the practice. Gaining visibility and expanding awareness of the practice are essential to establishing a sustained increase in referrals. Once referral sources have been established, continuing communication with those sources is important to ensure their supplying ongoing referrals.

Increasing the visibility of the practice and the demand for services can be accomplished in different ways. The practitioner should consider the potential effectiveness of the several options; it may be helpful to talk with others who have built successful practices and with experts in the field of marketing of human service

BUILDING A PRACTICE

programs. The most obvious options are not always the most productive or cost-effective ones, and the practitioner should be prepared to invest time and energy in making the contacts and providing the services that will lead to an increased demand for services. (See Chapter 14 for information about marketing a private practice.)

Visibility

Obviously, referral sources must be aware of the existence of a practice before they will make referrals. Practitioners may attempt to heighten awareness of their services through public announcements, personal contacts, involvement in community projects and activities, and professional presentations.

Public Announcements

Public announcements may take the form of newspaper advertisements announcing the opening of a practice or the offering of some particular type of service. These announcements are more likely to be effective in small communities where newspapers are not filled with such items. If used in larger areas, it may be more effective to include newspaper announcements in the neighborhood sections or in sections that focus on health care or education. Practitioners should evaluate carefully the cost effectiveness of such announcements. The author and most of the colleagues to whom she has spoken have found that newspaper announcements have little, if any, lasting effect on referrals.

If print media are to be used, coverage of the practice in a newspaper feature story or on a radio or television "talk show" has greater potential for generating referrals. In these presentations, the practitioner has an opportunity to project a sense of himself or herself as a professional and of the significance of the services offered. Although the effects on referrals may not be long lasting, such coverage increases the general visibility of the practice.

Listings in the telephone directory and in community, professional, and consumer directories may be useful in increasing awareness of a practice. The practitioner can contact city government offices or the Chamber of Commerce to determine whether directories for human service providers are published. Professional and consumer advocacy organizations often publish provider directories or keep a file of providers for use when their members ask for sources of particular services. There usually is little or no cost for inclusion in such listings, and this provides an opportunity for contact with potential patients in specific populations.

Personal Contacts

The practitioner's direct contact with potential referral sources is likely to be more effective in generating referrals than are media announcements or presentations. Through these contacts the practitioner gains a personal identity with the referral source. Visits with other speech-language pathologists and audiologists, with members of related professions, with administrators and teachers in private schools and child care facilities, and with residential care personnel are important ways to inform likely referral sources of the services available through the practice. A business card and brief written description of the practice can be left with these persons, and it is always wise to follow the visit with a short letter expressing an interest in working with the individual or facility and the persons they serve.

Certain agencies in the community may contract regularly for speech-language pathology or audiology services, and personal visits to these agencies may be productive. All 50 states have vocational rehabilitation agencies that pay for evaluation and treatment services for certain persons with communication disorders. State agencies responsible for health care for children and adults, for indigent citizens, or for education services may contract with private speech-language pathologists and audiologists. Through visiting such agencies, the practitioner can gain information about referral policies, fee schedules, and evaluation and treatment contracts and at the same time provide an introduction to his or her own service program. A note of caution: Because many publicly funded agencies have set fees that may be significantly lower than the ordinary charges for private services, the practitioner may not be able to afford to sustain a practice in which the majority of patients' fees are paid by a public agency.

Although personal contacts with potential referral sources can be useful, they generally are not as productive as the practitioner had hoped. The practitioner needs to be sensitive to the varying degrees of receptiveness and interest demonstrated by the different persons and to follow up with visits or calls to those who showed the greatest interest. It is important to remember that these other service providers are more likely to refer patients on an ongoing basis if they realize that they, too, have something to gain by such referrals. Therefore the private practice owner should help them realize that their referrals will be viewed favorably by patients and families.

Many potential referral sources may have a limited understanding of communication disorders or of the speech-language and audiology profession. In working with such persons, the speech-language pathologist or audiologist should take the time to educate them about his or her services. This educational process may take repeated contacts over a period of several months, but in the long run the time and patience expended by the practitioner may result in many referrals for services.

Participation in community activities that are directly or indirectly related to one's professional practice can yield contacts with a broad range of referral sources. In most communities, there are advocacy organizations in the areas of education, rehabilitation, and health care. These may include organizations for families of retarded persons, children with learning disabilities, or autistic citizens; for families of persons with head injuries or of those who have had strokes; and for individuals who themselves have disabilities, such as mobility impairments, hearing loss, or learning disabilities. These groups hold regularly scheduled meetings and participate in a variety of projects that serve their own needs.

Community Involvement

Participating in family and consumer organizations can provide excellent opportunities for increasing awareness of a practice and the services it provides. Lending professional expertise and demonstrating a willingness to assist in a broad range of consumer-oriented activities can increase credibility and respect from persons throughout the community. This participation by professionals serves two purposes: It gives consumers a better understanding of the nature and importance of the services provided by persons in the profession, and it gives them an opportunity to know the practitioner as a professional and as a person.

Professional
Presentations

Workshops or seminars for health care and education professionals or for parent and family organizations provide excellent opportunities for public education and for making potential referral sources and patients aware of one's own practice. These workshops can be a part of an organization's regularly scheduled meetings, held as inservice programs, or offered independently.

Workshops or seminars can be held for the purpose of producing income in and of themselves, or they can be held as a means of generating future referrals. If the latter is the purpose, the practitioner may provide the workshop at little or no charge to participants. The author has held workshops for preschool teachers, ranging from 1–4 hours in length, charging a participant fee that only covered the cost of materials used. These workshops often resulted in screening contracts with the schools and in increased referrals from the participants.

Presentations to civic and service organizations are another avenue for increasing visibility in the community. These organizations often hold weekly or monthly meetings for which they seek speakers, and they welcome offers to provide information about a human service need. Although presentations to these groups may not be as productive as seminars for teachers or health care professionals, the general exposure gained can be useful.

**Professional
Credibility**

The most significant factor influencing the building and maintaining of a patient base is the professional credibility of the service provider and the practice. From the day a practice opens, the practitioner should work to establish and maintain an image as a competent and reliable professional. Several types of actions assist in establishing and maintaining professional credibility.

When a patient is referred by a professional who also serves that individual, the practitioner should provide the referral source with appropriate follow-up information. The information may be brief, and it should address the patient's condition and recommendations in a manner that is relevant to the referral source.

If other professionals or agencies are serving a patient being seen by the practitioner, a cooperative approach to patient management should be carried out. Regular contacts with others who work with the patient can both improve overall patient care and result in other referrals from those professionals or agencies.

When services are terminated, it is important to notify the other professionals or agencies working with the patient. The reason for termination should be explained briefly. These contacts may indicate the success of the services that have been provided, may be useful to the other person's involvement with the patient, and often are viewed as a professional courtesy. Additionally, they can serve as a reminder of the availability of the practitioner's services, sometimes overcoming the out-of-sight-out-of-mind situation that reduces referrals.

Referrals to other professionals can assist in building a patient base. These persons may reciprocate in hopes of gaining additional referrals. Additionally, they may be impressed with a practitioner's ability to recognize the need for other services or for a second opinion. Interprofessional and intraprofessional cooperation in patient management often is useful in gaining important professional contacts.

Participation in local, state, and national professional association activities can increase both visibility and credibility. Professional papers, committee work, and involvement in association public relations and public policy activities give one the opportunity to demonstrate knowledge and skills to colleagues, public officials, and the general public. From activities of this kind, the practitioner may receive direct referrals as well as positive recommendations to other referral sources.

In most private practices, current and former patients serve as a major and ongoing source of referrals. The favorable recommendation of those who have actually received services from a practitioner usually is given great credence by persons seeking services. For this reason, having patients who understand and value the services they receive is extremely important to building and maintaining a private practice.

Diversity of Services

Offering a diversity of services can be useful in building a patient base. Screening programs provided in schools or community health facilities can result in referrals of new patients, whether or not significant income is generated from the actual screening activity. Short-term or long-term consultant services can have a similar effect. Offering services at other-than-usual-business hours for the convenience of working families and flexibility in appointment schedules for shift workers can attract patients whose working conditions make scheduling a problem.

Contracting with home health agencies or nursing homes so that the practitioner goes to the patients may be useful in building a practice. Similarly, providing services at a school, rather than having patients travel to the practitioner's office, may make it possible for persons with transportation problems to receive services. However, in scheduling appointments that require the practitioner to travel, it is important to remember that time is money. The practitioner not only must consider the actual travel costs but also must avoid exchanging patient contact time for unreimbursed travel time.

Summary

To build a solid patient base, the private practitioner must become well known and well respected as a provider of services. Doing so requires constant efforts to gain visibility and credibility in the community. The practitioner must pursue new referrals actively through making personal contacts, cooperating with referral sources, and providing outstanding services to patients.

MAINTAINING AND EXPANDING THE PRACTICE

To maintain a profitable practice or to expand its size and scope requires planning and ongoing adjustments. The private practitioner must continue to promote the practice, to examine the efficiency and effectiveness of all activities, and to adjust policies and procedures in order to ensure the continuation of a healthy practice or expansion into a larger program.

Maintaining the Practice

Even when a practice has developed to the point where there seems to be a regular influx of new patients and therefore a stable patient base, the private practitioner needs to continue working to avoid a reduction in referrals, to keep employees productive and motivated, to ensure prompt payment for services, and to control costs. Nonproductive employees or a decline in referrals can drain the resources of the practice quickly. Cash flow problems caused by lax collection policies or by unplanned or unnecessary expenditures can bring about financial failure. Although Chapters 5 and 9 address the financial aspects of a practice in greater detail, a few of the important considerations are mentioned here because of their relevance to the successful maintenance of a practice.

Referrals

Practitioners must continue doing activities that ensure ongoing referrals of new patients, even when it appears that a constant base of patients has been established. The suggestions made earlier for building a patient base continue to be important for maintaining a healthy practice. Sustaining a cooperative working relationship with those who refer patients regularly, having periodic contact with sources that refer only occasionally, and making new referral contacts are important.

Adapting services to address unmet needs may be necessary. For example, if potential patients do not come into the practice because of problems in scheduling, setting up evening or weekend appointments may reach groups of new patients. If a reasonably large number of referral sources or patients are requesting services for homebound individuals, plans may be made to provide services for these persons. Practitioners should look carefully at what adjustments in service delivery can be made to ensure a constant number of patients to support the practice.

Fluctuations in Revenue

In most practices, there are predictable peak and slow periods that can be identified by charting new referrals and income on a monthly basis. For example, the author has found that January, August, and December usually are slow months for new referrals. In August and December there typically is an increase in cancellations of regularly scheduled appointments because of family vacations and holiday activities. Once these annual patterns have been identified, the practitioner can plan special kinds of services to keep income-producing hours at a reasonable level during predictably slow periods. For example, special screening programs, seminars, or visits to new referral sources can be scheduled for those times of the year when new referrals or regularly scheduled appointments usually are reduced. The slow periods also may be the best time for employees to take annual leave, because their absence during these times will have the least impact on income. By recognizing and making adjustments for predictably slow periods in the normal practice routine, adverse effects on income to the practice can be reduced. (See Table 5–4, Chapter 5, for a model forecast statement.)

Billing and Payments

Even when the practice seems to be financially stable, the owner should monitor monthly billings and payments to ensure that accounts are being paid on a regular basis. A secretary or bookkeeper may follow established procedures for billing and collections, but the owner of the practice is wise to keep a regular check on all accounts.

Cash flow can become a problem if accounts receivable grow too large, as noted in Chapter 9. It is important to have standard policies for billings and collections, for patients to be informed of these policies in advance of receiving services, and for the policies to be administered rigorously. For example, few health care professionals bill health insurance companies directly because payments from the companies often are delayed by 60 to 90 days from the date of billing. The practitioner may assist the patient in completing insurance forms and may provide necessary written statements to substantiate their claim, but most professionals require patients to pay for the service at the time of billing and to collect reimbursement from insurance companies themselves. Some prepaid health insurance programs require the service provider to bill the insurance company directly rather than collecting from patients. Under this condition, the practitioner, before delivering services, needs a written agreement that the insurance program will pay the charges billed for services as well as a statement of the length of time it will take for payment to be received. If payments are not received within the designated time period, the practitioner should contact the company to determine the cause for the delay and when payment can be expected.

The experience of most private practitioners is that the longer an account goes unpaid, the greater the likelihood that it will never be paid. To avoid losses due to failure to pay for services, practitioners should follow up immediately on overdue accounts. Although there are occasional legitimate reasons for failure to make payments, which may indicate that adjustments in collection procedures are needed, it is important for the private practitioner to establish and follow stringent payment and collection policies in order to avoid significant revenue loss. It does little good to have a full patient load if patients are not paying for services. A low collection rate can ruin even a well-established practice. (See Chapter 9 for information about billing and collection procedures.)

Control of Expenses

Controlling expenses requires the practitioner to stay informed of all of the costs associated with delivering services and maintaining the practice. It is necessary to keep a regular inventory of materials and equipment directly associated with delivering services and of supplies and equipment necessary for operation of the office. This procedure assists in determining where costs can be reduced and when expenditures will be necessary. Through planning, the expenditures can be made in such a way as to minimize cash flow problems.

Evaluating costs of insurance policies, making cost comparisons among several companies that provide supplies and equipment, and contracting for equipment maintenance services may assist in containing costs associated with operating the business, as noted in Chapter 5. Although a secretary or business assistant can gather this information, the practice owner should evaluate the information and make decisions about the best investment for the business.

Employee Productivity

In private practice, professional employees both produce and deliver the product being sold. The profit of the business depends largely on the appropriate utilization of their time, energy, and skills.

Flower defines productivity as "a euphemism commonly applied to describe a professional's primary responsibility, i.e., the activities that yield income to the professional or to the employer of the professional" (Flower, 1984, p. 211). In a private practice, professional staff members are employed because of the contributions they can make in delivering clinical services and the income they generate through service delivery. Their time should be devoted primarily to income-producing activities that enhance the growth and quality of the practice, not to tasks that can be handled by secretarial or other nonprofessional personnel. A study by Aleo and Pece (1977) reported that in community centers speech-language clinicians spent approximately 60 percent of their time in direct patient contact, whereas in hospitals they delivered direct services to patients about 64 percent of their work time. The remainder was devoted to activities other than working with patients. In a private practice, certainly no less and preferably a greater percentage of staff time will be spent in direct services for which fees are received.

The owner/director of the practice should examine his or her own activities and those of all professional staff members to decide whether time is being spent most productively. For all professional staff, an analysis of time utilization should be made at regular intervals with the goal of altering any policies or procedures that unnecessarily reduce productivity. This analysis should determine (a) the amount of time spent in income-producing activities, such as evaluations, remediation, and conferences regarding patients; (b) the time spent in nonbillable activities related to patient care, such as report writing, clinical record keeping, and planning; (c) the time spent in efforts to increase referrals, such as visits to schools or scheduling screening programs; and (d) the time spent in other activities, broken down into categories, such as answering the telephone for the practice, taking inventory or ordering supplies, working on professional association assignments, or attending to personal business.

The owner/director of the practice and the professional staff member(s) can analyze the time utilization reports and determine changes that need to be made to improve productivity. A reallocation of responsibilities may be needed to ensure that secretarial or clerical duties are assigned to a nonprofessional staff member. Changes in report writing or patient record keeping procedures may be necessary to reduce time required for these activities. Limitations on personal use of the telephone may be necessary. By examining time utilization on a regular basis, the private practitioner can adopt policies and procedures that are the most cost effective and the most productive for the business.

Employee Satisfaction

Employees are more likely to make a positive contribution to the practice if they feel that their professional and financial goals are being met. Opportunities for professional growth, for input in making policies about patient care, and for realizing financial gain are important to most professionals employed by the private practitioner.

Providing for continuing education opportunities for employees can benefit both the employee and the practice. Most productive employees feel that it is important to be up-to-date on new information about professional practices and issues. Regular participation in continuing education activities may encourage them to re-examine their practices and to adopt more beneficial and efficient approaches to patient care. These types of activities may reduce the likelihood of burnout or stagnation and improve the quality of patient care provided through the practice.

Active clinicians often have valuable suggestions for improving both patient care and the service delivery system. Regular opportunities for suggesting changes in patient care procedures, record keeping, or the type or manner of service delivery can keep clinicians feeling that they are a part of the practice and can result in improved attitudes and services. Although these opportunities may be available on an informal basis in many practices, it generally is wise to schedule a regular time for employees to meet with the owner/director of the practice to discuss policies, procedures, and services. Similar opportunities should be provided for nonprofessional staff, who may have suggestions for improving other aspects of the practice.

Professional employees always are interested in the financial gain they can expect from their work. In a private practice where revenue depends on billable hours produced by the professional staff, incentives to maintain or increase patient contact time can be a motivation to the clinician and productive for the practice. Many private practice owners pay clinicians on a commission basis so that their monthly pay is determined by the amount they billed or collected for patient services that month. Other practices provide a monthly base pay, with bonus pay for monthly or quarterly billings above a preset level. Some practice owners pay employees an additional amount for any new patients or contracts they acquire for the practice. Such policies often encourage the clinicians to maintain or increase billable hours and result in increasing the clinicians' motivation to take an active role in building and maintaining the practice.

Expanding the Practice

Once a practice is established so that there is a stable patient base and the business is realizing a consistent and reasonable profit, the practitioner needs to decide whether to expand or to maintain the practice at its current size. This decision should be made before significant numbers of patients have been turned away due to lack of time in the clinician's schedule to provide requested services.

In considering expansion, the practitioner should examine the following factors: (a) the present and potential demand for services; (b) the type of services to be increased; (c) the need for and implications of additional personnel; and (d) the costs and procedures for adding space, furnishings, and equipment that would be needed. Because the owner of the practice will take on additional administrative and possibly supervisory responsibilities with expansion, he or she should examine the long-range goals for the practice and determine whether the added responsibilities move him or her toward achieving these goals. Moreover, there are additional financial risks associated with expansion, because there is no guarantee if or when the investments required for expansion will be covered by the additional revenues that eventually should come with growth.

Demands for Services

Expansion of a practice generally is considered when either of two conditions arises: Either the practitioner has a full patient load and cannot schedule many of the new referrals being received, or favorable marketplace opportunities are available and the practitioner does not have the time or resources to take advantage of them. In other words, there is either a demand or an opportunity for services that the practitioner cannot meet in his or her present circumstance.

When the private practitioner becomes established through comprehensive marketing of the practice and demonstrated competence in service delivery, referrals may exceed his or her capacity to provide services. Before making a decision to expand on the basis of excessive referrals, the practitioner should look closely at the pattern and sources of referral over the past 6–12 months. This analysis should address whether the apparent excess is the result of a steady growth or of additional referral sources who are likely to continue sending new patients. A hasty decision to expand based on a sudden and unaccounted-for increase in referrals could leave the practitioner with added personnel and related expenses and, at the same time, a return to the previously normal number of referrals. An analysis of referrals can provide information necessary to make reliable predictions about the ongoing growth in the patient population and therefore about the advisability of expansion.

After working in a community long enough to become quite familiar with the population and the availability of services, a private practitioner may recognize unserved areas or populations. Identifying gaps in available services and recognizing ways to fill these gaps can lead the practitioner to plan sensibly for expanding services. Certain areas of the city or region may not have service facilities; particular age groups, such as infants or elderly persons, may not be served through existing practices; or appropriate programs for severely handicapped individuals may not be available. Conditions such as these may provide positive opportunities for expansion.

Professional Goals

Even when the marketplace is favorable, the private practitioner should examine his or her professional goals before expanding a practice. Persons in a solo practice are spared many problems that come with employing others to work in a practice and adding space, equipment, and administrative responsibilities and costs that are associated with a larger practice. The owner or director of the practice assumes additional responsibilities when a practice is expanded, and he or she must take time away from service delivery to address these duties. Therefore, it is important for the private practitioner to identify his or her long-range goals before making the decision to expand.

For those whose primary interest lies in working directly with patients, the distractions of administration may be undesirable. There is always the possibility of employing someone else to take on the additional administrative tasks, but such an arrangement is costly. In contrast, practitioners who would welcome a reduction in patient contact and who enjoy administrative work may find that employing others to see patients is a positive step toward achieving their professional goals.

Personnel

Adding professional personnel usually accompanies expansion of a practice. Before hiring additional personnel, the private practitioner should examine carefully the level of productivity of currently employed staff (see the previous discussion of employee productivity). The owner of the practice should determine the expected growth in patients before employing others to work in the practice. If slow but steady growth is anticipated, it may be advantageous to employ someone on a part-time basis with the understanding that he or she will see additional patients as referrals increase. In planning for expansion of the practice, the owner should evaluate carefully the costs of adding personnel and the likelihood of their generating revenue sufficient to cover these costs.

Professional personnel who work for a private practitioner may be employed on a contractual basis, or they may be part-time or full-time employees paid on a commission or salary basis. Those employed to provide contract services usually are paid a percentage of the amount that is billed or collected for the services they provide, and they are not restricted from working for other persons or agencies in addition to their work for the private practitioner. The private practitioner may provide space, materials, and equipment necessary for the services rendered but does not pay employee taxes or provide other fringe benefits. The full-time or part-time person hired on commission or salary generally is restricted from working for other agencies that are viewed as competition to the private practice. The owner/director pays employee taxes and usually provides some fringe benefits, such as professional liability insurance, health insurance, costs associated with some types of continuing education, or professional association dues.

When employing persons to work in a private practice, it is important that they be told of the necessity of their generating income on a consistent basis. Because professional personnel in many settings have little direct involvement with the cost of service delivery, they fail to realize that a high level of financial productivity is essential when working in a private practice. They must acknowledge and be comfortable with the fact that the money to pay both their salary and the costs associated with their delivery of services must come from the revenue they bring into the practice. They also must recognize that the owner/director of the practice intends to make a profit and that they are expected to contribute to that profit. To avoid misunderstandings and discontent after persons become employees, it is wise to explain the expectations the owner/director has for them before they sign a contract to work in the practice.

In selecting professional personnel for employment, the private practitioner should consider the person's interests and skills in light of the type of patients to be served. If the population of patients targeted in the expansion plans are infants, the clinician needs to have an interest and expertise in working with this age group. If the new employee is to be in charge of preschool and school screening programs, experience with this population, as well as the ability to contact, schedule, and interact with school personnel, is needed. To meet the needs of the practice and to accommodate the interests and skills of employees, the private practitioner should evaluate each applicant to determine whether that person is right for the responsibilities of the position he or she would fill.

Facilities and Support Services

Expansion of the practice usually requires an increase in office space and in materials for providing clinical services. The owner/manager of the practice should calculate the additional costs for office space and furnishings and for equipment and materials necessary for delivering services. At times existing space can be reallocated and materials and equipment shared so that cost increases are kept at a minimum as the practice is expanded. For example, if a therapy room is used only part-time by the practitioner, the new employee's schedule may be set up so that he or she sees patients at times when the room may be unused. Materials for evaluation of new patients can be shared if scheduling is done so that two clinicians do not need the same materials at the same times.

If expansion entails opening a separate office in a new location, some cost containment measures can be utilized. For example, secretarial assistance can be provided through the central or main office, either by computer communication or by having reports and records brought to the main office for typing. All billings, collections, and business telephone use can be done through the main office. Through planning, additional costs for establishing a second office can be contained.

Certain additional costs necessarily accompany expansion, and these should not be overlooked in planning. Additional liability insurance, an increase in the use of expendable supplies, additional furniture and equipment, and additional demands on secretaries or bookkeepers come with expansion. It is important to remember that certain expenditures are necessary in order to make productive use of additional employees and to avoid unnecessary disruptions in services. Efficiency and effectiveness are the important goals in planning for expansion, and costs should not be contained to the point where either of these suffers.

SUMMARY

The decision to expand should be made only after the private practitioner has analyzed his or her long-term professional goals and has determined that there is a reasonable probability of having a sufficient number of patients to support the expansion. Once the decision to expand has been made, careful planning can assist in containing costs without sacrificing effectiveness and efficiency.

REFERENCES

Aleo, E.L., & C.O. Pece. (1977). Review of time allocations and professional fees of speech-language pathologists and audiologists. *Asha*, 19, 755–758.

Flower, R.M. (1984). *Delivery of speech-language pathology and audiology services.* Baltimore: Williams & Wilkins.

SUGGESTED READINGS

Markin, R.J. (1971). *Retailing management.* New York: Macmillan Publishing Company.

Schultz, M.C., & Burkhart, M.C. (1978). Professional productivity: A case study. *Asha*, 20, 963–964.

Small Business Administration Publication: *Business basics (marketing strategy).* Publication 1009. *Selecting advertising media.* Publication 34. Washington, DC: U.S. Government Printing Office.

Chapter 12

Increasing the Practice: Focus on Audiology

Marlene A. Bevan, Ph.D.

Most practitioners entering private practice find they are motivated by two basic desires: a desire to earn more money and a desire to provide audiologic services in accordance with a personal belief about the most appropriate delivery system for these services. However, they soon find that maximizing income may not be as easy as it once appeared and that a private practice requires skill and business acumen not at all related to the audiology delivery system.

If the initiation of the practice requires additional funding from a lending institution, the professional is required to submit a business prospectus or plan. In this prospectus, the individual describes the nature of the business, the services that will provide the source of revenue for the business, the potential consumers of the services offered by the business, the costs associated with providing the service, and the resulting profit that can thereby be forecast for the business. This prospectus is an invaluable tool for judging the potential for success before investing in or beginning a new business. The reader is referred to Chapters 5 and 9 for further information on preparing a prospectus.

As the day-to-day realities of business materialize, some of the variables forecast in the initial plan may change; perhaps a competitor proves stronger than expected, or utility expenses are higher than anticipated due to inclement weather. The initial plan must be modified to reflect the current reality, and an adjusted plan begins to develop. Continuing evaluation of the plan and modification of the strategies to accomplish your initial goals provide the basis for the maintenance and expansion of an audiologic practice.

THE BUSINESS ENVIRONMENT FOR AUDIOLOGY PRACTICES

The private practitioner in audiology today establishes a business in a health care environment that has become increasingly competitive. Although previous analogies have described the participants in the hearing health care system as a "team," their interaction now seems to reflect more competition for the health care dollar than teamwork in the management of the hearing-impaired patient.

The hearing health care team is composed of three players: the physician, the audiologist, and the traditional hearing aid dispenser. Their identities and relationships are often a mystery to the consumer of hearing health care. A hearing-impaired consumer may enter the system through a visit to any player in the team, but a visit to one player will not guarantee a referral to any of the others. However, many patients will, over the course of time, visit one or all of the players on the hearing health care team. It is not unusual for a patient to receive many differing opinions about the best rehabilitative options for a hearing impairment from the separate members of the hearing health care "team." With so much confusion, it is not unlikely that the patient may begin to feel lost in the system. Because each player may offer different advice, the patient is often required to choose the managing professional and the source of continued care by themselves.

PROVIDING ONGOING MANAGEMENT OF HEARING REHABILITATION

The first protocol in the audiologic practice is to identify that practice as the primary provider of hearing health care and the ongoing manager of hearing rehabilitation. All service and delivery procedures are directed toward establishing a continuing relationship with the patient. Those of course include the appropriate referral procedures for services that are not within the scope of the audiologist such as the medical management of hearing pathologies. However, it is well within the best interests of both the patient and the audiologist to obtain as many services as possible within the same setting from the same professional. Therefore, audiology practices usually incorporate as many diagnostic and rehabilitative alternatives as are required to offer a full-service center for hearing health care needs. Audiology practices may include but are not necessarily limited to services for infant testing, toddler and school-age assessment, and adult evaluation. Rehabilitation services usually include the service and the product associated with that service. Every attempt is made to meet the needs of the patient within the scope of that practice; every attempt is made to provide the patient with one primary provider in the course of hearing health care rehabilitation.

Identifying yourself as a primary provider is the first step in maintaining an audiology practice. This process begins when you are able to demonstrate to the patient that you understand the problem as he or she is experiencing it and that you are capable of assisting the patient in finding acceptable solutions.

The initial intake interview is the basis for your relationship with the patient. Take time to listen to the patient's experience with the hearing handicap and to explore jointly the settings in which the problem becomes most evident. This opportunity to establish rapport and to share in the patient's viewpoint of the problem is the first step in building a continuing relationship with the patient. It provides the first opportunity to identify your capability to become the primary provider and to provide long-term rehabilitative management of the effects of the hearing impairment.

Hearing Aid Dispensing Within an Audiologic Practice

Within the audiologic practice, long-term management of the hearing-impaired patient is most appropriate when the patient demonstrates a hearing problem that may be considered permanent in nature. The most common solution to permanent hearing impairment is the utilization of amplification. The recommendation, selection, and adjustment services surrounding the utilization of amplification have become the cornerstone of the dispensing audiology practice.

Once a permanent hearing loss has been identified, the audiologist must begin to explore with the patient the possible benefits of amplification. The process of selecting a hearing aid can initially involve several types of amplification and can provide a structured environment in which the traditional comparison of possible aid benefits can be demonstrated for the patient. This procedure also affords the audiologist the opportunity to evaluate the effects of variations in circuitry, frequency response, and acoustic coupling on the aided performance of the hearing-impaired listener.

The final selection of the hearing aid manufacturer is not, however, directly related to the aided performance of the hearing-impaired listener. The potential for aided benefit, as defined in the hearing aid selection process, remains the standard for the final acceptable aided performance, but the choice of the specific manufacturer of the instrument is dependent on several other factors that can be best related to good practice management. It is of utmost importance to become thoroughly familiar with the product line of the selected manufacturer. The audiologist must recognize the variations available with each of the models, the modifications offered by the manufacturer, and the completeness of the product line. It is simply not possible to maintain an in-depth understanding of several product lines, as noted in Chapter 8; nor does the literature support the concept of clinical distinctiveness between hearing aid manufacturers. It is time consuming, at best, to maintain a large number of manufacturer suppliers within a single practice. Therefore, successful practices concentrate their recommendations within a few preselected manufacturers.

Selecting Hearing Aid Manufacturers

The manufacturers with whom you will be dealing should be selected on the basis of several factors. Utmost in good practice management is the provision of a quality product. If the repair rate for instruments provided through your practice begins to rise, you will be faced with unhappy patients, expensive repairs, and time-consuming paperwork. The availability of support personnel and services in dealing with patient complaints can also assist in solving a patient's problem rapidly and with the least expense to both the professional and the patient. Often a manufacturer may demonstrate a willingness to collaborate on those special cases for whom the standard stock aid or frequency response does not appear to meet the need. If asked, many manufacturers provide "rush" services with shortened turnaround time for patients leaving on vacation or with special circumstances. These special services can place the audiologist in a favorable light when compared to the competition. Lastly, the audiologist may qualify for pricing discounts based on quantity purchases by limiting his or her purchases to a select number of manufacturers. The preselection of a specific number of manufacturers makes good sense for the provision of increased services to the patient and for the economic health of the practice.

Facilitating the Patient's Adjustment to a Hearing Aid

Once the hearing aid has been selected, the audiologist, through an organized approach to hearing aid orientation, continues to build the ongoing relationship so necessary for good patient management. The initial utilization of amplification represents a totally unknown experience for the hearing-impaired listener. At this time, it is critical to provide the patient with a set of realistic expectations about the use of amplification. The patient needs to feel comfortable with the use of the hearing aid. The situations in which the instrument will function optimally can be identified, as well as more difficult listening situations. The patient must begin consistent use of the aid and evaluate his or her communication ability while wearing it. The audiologist can interpret the experience and help reassure the patient that his or her adjustment is progressing satisfactorily. Both written and verbal feedback is important during this phase of adjustment. Patients must learn to be comfortable with the use of amplification and must be encouraged to approach the audiologist for information and explanation of the results of amplification.

Providing Follow-Up Care

Good follow-up care cements the patient/professional relationship. It is important to check with the patient several days postfitting to ensure that the experience is going well. A short telephone call may leave a lasting impression that communicates the fact that the professional cares about the patient's experience with amplification. In-office follow-up during the initial adjustment period is necessary to ensure the patient and the audiologist that the instrument is being utilized appropriately and is being effectively maintained. Reassurance of the patient, whether child, parent, or grandparent, is always welcome and appreciated.

Throughout the first year of initial use the audiologist establishes the pattern of patient interaction and the basis for a continuing patient/audiologist relationship. If the relationship can be established the patient will look to the audiologist for the provision of additional services, related products, and continued information regarding the emergence of new hearing health products.

The Patient Index

Your most valuable practice asset is the patient who consults with you for all his or her communication needs, but establishing an ongoing relationship with your patients requires periodic and positive contact. Actively growing practices track their patients through the use of a patient index. It is a valued resource of the professional practice.

A patient index is a list of patients who have received some service through your practice. It allows you to identify these patients according to the services they received, the date on which they were received, or any other data about the services delivered to the patient. This information can be utilized to create a market plan for your patient population. Patients can be contacted on a regular basis through re-evaluation reminders that prompt them to contact the practice for necessary check-ups or hearing aid service. In addition, contact can be maintained through sending newsletters to hearing aid users to inform and educate them about the newest developments in hearing aids and realistic expectations for aided benefit. Newsletters can be used to stimulate questions and to create a desire to evaluate new options.

Battery programs that mail batteries to patients on a regular basis are often used in conjunction with patient indexing. In the mailing, many practices include a reminder to patients to have their instruments serviced on a regular basis.

Patient index programs can also be utilized to send out thoughtful greetings, such as birthday and anniversary wishes. These small gestures carry great weight when a patient is evaluating the quality of services received.

Not all patients may be appropriate for all types of patient indexing. However, with the use of computer technology, it is possible to code those patients with a specific diagnosis or personal profile and to match them with the desired services for indexing. Today's computer technology enables even the smallest private practice to maintain several different types of patient indexes simultaneously. It is possible to recall some patients for the battery program index while maintaining these patients on indexing for hearing re-evaluation or hearing aid rechecks.

The organization and implementation of recall services require time and planning. Although the professional must plan the services and designate the patients eligible for the service desired, professional time to execute the index may prove to be exorbitantly expensive. Technical or secretarial support provides a cost-effective method of delivering these services. However, practices relying on secretarial or technical support for administration of recall services need to communicate to their staff a disciplined policy of patient service and individual care. For maximum effectiveness, recall services must be delivered with the highest degree of personal attention. Whether the patient is recalled by clinician or technician, the emphasis must be placed on personal service. In today's highly technological society, warm and personal service is a benefit rated consistently high on the patient's shopping list for hearing health care providers.

Although recall services require an investment of time and energy on the part of the professional managing the practice, patient retention is to good practice management as interest is to savings. It is useless to attempt to build a patient caseload if you are not retaining the patients already served by your practice.

ANALYZING YOUR BUSINESS DEVELOPMENT

The practitioner must assess the health of the practice through several business indicators. Although the health of any practice is reflected in the profit/loss statement generated at the end of the fiscal year (see Chapter 5 for an example), it is necessary to collect information on a regular basis that will guide your day-to-day decisions. An accurate up-to-date analysis of the practice simplifies decisions regarding growth or maintenance and can be easily obtained through the use of small business office computers.

Management Information Systems

The emergence of affordable high technology places office computers within the reach of today's health care professional. The office computer can analyze your staff productivity and evaluate your cash flow position on a daily basis, as noted in Chapter 9. Computerized billing programs eliminate forgotten patient charges and simplify insurance billing procedures. New patient accounts can be recalled and traced to referral sources who will then automatically receive reports or acknowledgement of the referral. Delinquent accounts can be tracked, and if you desire, interest can be assessed. An analysis of all services provided, the percentage of revenue generated by each service, and the time required to perform the service enables the practitioner to make critical entrepreneurial decisions regarding practice management. Without this kind of information, the practitioner is unable to find simple solutions for daily management questions regarding profitability and expansion.

With appropriate business analysis, it is easier to make correct decisions regarding growth, directions, and alternatives for the practice. Your patient population can be statistically described and your percentage of the market share evaluated. Your potential for growth can then be determined from the general population statistics. The procedure for establishing a pricing strategy can also be obtained by computer-assisted cost analysis.

Although it is not within the scope of this chapter to guide the practitioner through an analysis of the hardware and software available to audiologic practices, it must be emphasized that the office computer is a basic tool in any audiology practice and should be considered as part of the initial equipment investment. (See Chapters 10 and 13 for detailed information on computer software.)

Pricing Strategies

Appropriate pricing strategies add to your ability to maintain and expand your audiology practice. However, no other aspect of practice appears to be quite so misunderstood. To determine how much you must charge to make a profit, you must be aware of the overall costs—both fixed and variable—to provide the service or the product. Chapters 5 and 9 provide an in-depth discussion of both types of costs.

Once the overall costs associated with the practice are calculated, divide them by the number of billable hours available to the practice to determine the cost per hour of services provided in the practice. Factor in the profit margin desired for the practice, and the result can be utilized to determine the minimal cost per billable hour for services provided by your practice. A review of the time allotted to each service multiplied by the charge per billable hour leads to the minimal base charge for that service as it is provided within your practice.

Consider pricing as a component of your market strategy. Some practices may decide to position their services to be comparable with other facilities in their area that provide similar services. This appears to be the most common strategy in the health care industry. There are two notable exceptions to this strategy, both of which appear to work extremely well. These are discount pricing and exclusive pricing strategies.

Discount Pricing Strategies

The popularity of *discount pricing strategies* can be seen in the increasing numbers of bargain factory outlet stores. There is a definite market segment that chooses its purchases based on the availability of a discount schedule; hence the popularity of advertising informing the consumer of "lowest prices" or bargain factory outlet stores. This approach can also be found in advertisements for the provision of optometric care, dental care, or legal advise at remarkably reduced prices. Inherent in this approach is the assumption that lowered pricing will increase market share and that the costs of service may be reduced by the elimination of personal service to the consumer or complex consultations. The consumer is offered a basic "one size fits all" approach to his or her needs. Therefore, the provider is able to reduce significantly the cost of providing the service while significantly increasing the number of services rendered.

Exclusive marketing recognizes that segment of the population who prefers a large amount of personal consideration. This market segment is willing to pay more to obtain a custom service and specialized care. For example, the existence and rapid proliferation of specialty products, such as designer eyeglasses, clothing, and accessories appeals to this population. Analyzing the socioeconomic status of your community will rapidly indicate whether this market is available to your practice.

Exclusive Marketing Strategies

Whatever pricing strategy your practice utilizes, it is imperative that you recognize the hidden costs involved in business transactions. When reviewing the overhead costs, both direct and indirect, there may be a cost you have not considered, i.e., the cost of paperwork required to collect your fees. Each time you prepare a billing statement or an insurance form or agree to delay the collection of fees for services or products rendered, you are incurring an expense. Although fees in your accounts receivable may be considered a business asset, the larger the percentage of your money that is tied into an accounts receivable fund, the poorer your cash flow situation and the less financially secure is your practice.

Accounts Receivable

There are three important rules for a successful practice. They are (1) get the money up front, (2) get the money up front, and (3) get the money up front. Waiting to collect payment for services already delivered may cause a cash flow crisis as you attempt to meet your current financial obligations, as was emphasized in Chapters 8 and 9. A simple written statement that payment is required at the time services are delivered informs patients that they are expected to pay at the end of the visit. Unfortunately, many patients may have received services from our colleagues for which no payment was required and therefore may not understand that your practice requires a fee for the same service. Explain your procedures and policies clearly so that there will be no misunderstandings that may sour an otherwise excellent patient relationship. You may display a sign that reminds patients of your financial policy. As the patient registers, he or she should receive a written copy of your financial policy that reinforces your intent to follow the policy. When you discuss future service or treatment plans, include an honest appraisal of the estimated costs involved. At the time of delivery of a product, a copy of the charges, in writing, also reduces the chance of a misunderstanding. As the time passes without reimbursement, your expenses to collect the initial billing increase. You must prepare additional billing statements, enter partial payment, refigure balances, and mail more billing statements. As your costs to collect increase, the absolute value of the payment decreases. To an extent, this same scenario is reflected in the third party reimbursement system.

On beginning a private practice, most audiologists eagerly seek to qualify for third party reimbursement systems. The patient can be reassured that services rendered are

Third Party Reimbursement Systems

completely or in part paid for, and the payment, once the patient's eligibility has been confirmed, is guaranteed. However, a closer examination of the procedures to obtain payment should instill a sense of caution.

Most provider participants are required to assess patient eligibility for coverage of the services or products delivered. Some insurance companies maintain "hotlines" to confirm patient eligibility; however, some require a written billing to begin the process of eligibility verification. If payment is for some reason denied, the patient is responsible for the bill and for the subsequent inquiries to the insurance company as to the reason for denial of coverage. While inquiries continue and correspondence mounts, the "costs" to collect increase. The excitement of being a provider in a prepaid plan system must be tempered by an examination of the payment history of that plan. Some private insurances have available hearing and hearing aid plans that guarantee fast and trouble-free reimbursement provided that the services are delivered to a bona fide eligible patient. State and federal reimbursement programs may be more complex and cumbersome.

Hearing services are usually available through the federally supported, state administered Medicaid programs. Audiologists should be aware that the requirements for participation in these systems vary markedly from state to state. Participation in these programs is easiest in states that legally recognize this profession through the auspices of licensing and regulation or through national certification offered by the American Speech-Language-Hearing Association.

Unfortunately the federal Medicare program recognizes no audiologist participants. Hearing tests, which may be a benefit if conducted for diagnostic purposes, are never reimbursable when performed for the purposes of prescribing amplification. Some diagnostic tests cannot be billed by an audiologist, but rather require a physician billing number or authorization code. The requirements for government program participation and service coverages vary from one state to another, so you must research the regulations that apply in the state in which you choose to practice.

Unfortunately, nothing can protect your practice from a cash flow crisis caused by massive delay in reimbursement due to bureaucratic red tape. If your money is delayed and you are forced to borrow to meet current obligations, the cost of the borrowed money increases your overall costs while the time delay for third party payment decreases the value of your billing. Eventually, if third party reimbursement comprises the majority of your billings, your business stability may be threatened and your economic survival brought into question. Many practices therefore limit the ratio of patients with third party or commercial reimbursement programs to private payers.

EXPANDING YOUR AUDIOLOGY PRACTICE

The underlying strategy for expanding your practice relies heavily on your ability to let your community know that you are capable of providing quality audiological services. You must immediately begin to establish your image in the community. Good public relations start with you.

Your Public Image

The manner in which the community views you as an audiologist affects community acceptance of your services. Your community interaction through service clubs and civic organizations helps you make a statement about what you believe and what kind of services you can provide.

Your behavior in public is also an indication to the public of your professional profile. All public activities and statements should be performed with this fact in mind. Even your dress affects the decisions your patients and the general public make about you. A professional demeanor and presentation assists in a positive perception of your public image. Your public image, dress, behavior, and community activities all serve as indicators of your personal beliefs and professional integrity. Active development of a public image and participation in community activities can have a positive impact on the acceptance of your practice and the expansion of your services. Time spent in community activities and projects develops your community clout and a valuable support base for your practice.

Expanding Medical/ Professional Referrals

Initially, it is well worth your time to contact the professionals in your community and to spend a few moments introducing yourself, offering your credentials, and describing the scope of your services. As new professionals join your community, this welcome gesture of personal contact is always appreciated. Brochures describing your practice and the indications for a meaningful referral can be helpful in establishing a satisfactory referral relationship.

Your professional report to the referral source is the best inducement to increased referrals. It must be delivered in a timely fashion if it is to be of assistance to the referring professional. You must discover when the patient will return to the referral source and deliver your report of services well in advance of that appointment. The report should be brief and clearly written so that the referring professional can easily understand your message. Reports written to general physicians may differ markedly from those written to specialists, such as otolaryngologists. If you are concerned about the clarity of the information you are trying to convey, a personal telephone call to discuss your findings, as well as the possible implications for medical and/or rehabilitative treatment options, is usually appreciated.

The professional report educates referral sources and, if successful, reinforces their decision to refer again. The referral source should receive information about the patient, which is either new or confirms a previous diagnosis. The report should inform the referral source and the patient about the latest up-to-date options for rehabilitative treatment.

Lastly, a good professional report reflects well on the referral source's management of the patient. If at all possible, the patient and the referral source should be convinced that the referral was worthwhile because of new information gained or because of suspicions that were confirmed. If, in fact, the patient appreciates the referral to you and expresses this appreciation to the referral source, that source will feel increased confidence in the positive outcome of future referrals to you.

Expanding Agency Referrals

Within most community structures, there exist agencies created by the local, state, or federal government to provide a service to specific populations. Such agencies are required to develop mission statements and provide an explanation of their goals and purposes. An initial review of those goals may suggest to the audiologist the need for audiologic services to enable the agency to accomplish its central purpose. This need may be readily apparent for agencies with educational goals directed toward young disadvantaged children, but it may be less apparent for the agency offering mental health counseling. As specialists in human communication, we may see a basic need for our services in all "people-centered" programs. However, it is often necessary to convince the agency of the appropriateness of our involvement and the need for our services.

Before approaching an agency, familiarize yourself with its goals and vocabulary. Often a matter of public record, this information can assist you in understanding the format of services provided and the population designated to benefit from them. Any proposal for audiologic services must be written to fit the overall goals of the agency and the vocabulary utilized by the agency to express those goals.

A proposal for services should identify the agency need and the relationship of that need to audiologic services; for example, early academic achievement depends on the existence of an adequate language base that in turn is dependent on adequate hearing ability. Therefore, programs seeking to improve early academic achievement must also be concerned with the status of the hearing of the children enrolled in these programs. The proposal should also direct itself toward the cost-benefit ratio of establishing audiologic services within the program, in addition to identifying the sources of outside funding that may be available and that may therefore reduce the total cost of the program.

No proposal should be considered complete without addressing the needs of the agency to educate its staff and personnel. In-service programs are a relatively inexpensive method to educate the agency and to reinforce, on an individual basis, the need for your services. Additional information updates should be continually offered to the agency. This attention to agency staff development reinforces your position as a known and interested resource in the area of concern for that agency.

Sometimes even the best proposal is rejected. This is frustrating if the services proposed were on target with the goals of the agency, and the costs appeared to be reasonable. A close examination of the political process associated with agencies may yield the reason for its rejection. Community boards, which are always associated with community agencies, may veto or reject a service proposal for many reasons. A less than positive personal image in the community may account for your rejection. Or the board may be more favorably impressed with your competitor for whatever reason. Finally, if the board is simply unfamiliar with you, they may be unwilling to commit their resources to your proposal and reject it.

If the proposal is vital to your continued development, then you must become familiar with the board's rationale and, over an appropriate interval work to remove objections to the proposal before resubmitting it. Participation on community boards will assist you in understanding the manner in which they identify problems and seek solutions. Membership on a community board identifies you as an individual who gives of his or her time to solve community problems. It is a credential that is easily recognized by other board members who may review your proposals, and it can be utilized as a basis of common interest and familiarity.

The self-referral is the best referral. This patient comes to your practice with a desire to be helped and a belief that you are the appropriate professional to offer that help. The patient's motivation is a tremendous asset to your ability to improve his or her communication skills.

Marketing is an assertive method to attract the self-referral. Initially you may find that you are marketing your services to the entire community. During the beginning stages of your practice, it may make little difference to you what type of consumer you attract. Over the long run, however, you will find that your time and resources are limited and that you cannot serve or please everyone. Therefore, you must consider the type of patient you wish to attract to your practice, and for the purposes of marketing, you must develop a target population.

A typical patient profile assists you in developing your target population. You must decide which type of patients you have the best opportunity to attract, their age group, their socioeconomic status, and the approach that will most satisfactorily attract them. For example, if you decide to market to the older adult with financial resources, you must identify which type of care appeals to them, what kinds of concerns they may have about hearing services, and how you can best attract their attention to your service.

One simple but effective marketing method is to tell your present patients that you appreciate their patronage. Encourage them to tell their friends about your services. When a new patient is referred by a previous patient, drop that patient a note thanking him or her for the confidence in your abilities. Inquire about the names of others who might benefit from your assistance. Offer to give your card to friends and relatives of satisfied patients within your target population.

Another method is to schedule promotional activities that give you an opportunity to meet the public and to discuss your philosophy about audiologic care. Public health fairs, senior citizen screening programs, newspaper articles, and radio or television talk shows are helpful in expanding your influence and informing people of your services. However, avoid those activities that utilize your time but do not permit you to identify your practice or suggest referral on identification of a problem.

Expanding the Self-Referral

Direct mail offers the opportunity to communicate a specific message to your target population. You have the attention of the reader and can design the content to reflect your desired message. You may educate your reader about your services and the method that they may use to schedule an appointment for those services. You may identify yourself as an alternative to an existing service or as the only provider of a specific service. Whatever the message, direct mail offers you the opportunity to communicate with the reader without competition from outside sources.

An effective piece of direct mail must offer an action step to the reader: "Call today for an appointment," or "Call today and let us send you our brochure on the latest help available for tinnitus sufferers." Offer an initial consultation at no cost or a trial option for 30 days. Consumers need to be reassured that their action will not necessarily result in a high-pressure sales effort.

Direct Mail Programs

Direct mail campaigns can be designed around your schedule, and the mail pieces can be chosen to fit your budget preferences. However, several negative responses may also arise from this type of effort. Because the piece is unrequested, it may be of no interest to the reader or may generate annoyance or, even worse, hostility. Many manufacturers offer professionally designed pieces of direct mail that advertise their product line and name. Unless you have reason to believe that the company name will evoke a positive response or recognition from the reader, it may not prove a worthwhile expenditure. The cost is high because the numbers required to generate a sufficient response are high. Estimates of response per thousand reflect a rate of one to two percent. In order to generate an adequate response of 50–100, you may need to consider a mailing of 5,000 to 7,000 pieces per direct mail campaign. In *general* business, of those new customers identified by direct mail, seven to eight will usually result in a sale. However, in the hearing aid industry, because customers have already identified the problem and the solution, and (as a result of direct mail) have identified you as the provider of that solution, estimates of sales based upon direct mail range as high as 50 to 75 percent (McGee et al., 1980).

Almost 70 percent of traditional hearing aid dispensers, whose referrals for hearing aid fittings are overwhelmingly self-referrals, use direct mail, according to a recent survey on fitting procedures (Cranmer, 1985). In contrast, only 40 percent of dispensing audiologists, whose referrals for fitting are still drawn primarily from professional referrals, use direct mail.

Open Houses

The basic goal of the open house is to attract new patients for the practice or to renew and strengthen ties with former patients. Announcements of open houses are often included in direct mail pieces. An open house gives the consumer the chance to "drop by" and visit the practice, providing a "look and see" opportunity. Attendance is increased if the practice offers a free gift of batteries or hearing aid cleaning and electroacoustic analysis. Attendance may also increase if you offer a drawing for a free dinner at a local restaurant or a battery program or hearing aid fitting. During the open house, the audiologist can meet potential new patients and discuss the services available at the practice. Hearing aid manufacturers are willing to offer support if their line of aids is specifically featured in some way or if you are willing to advertise the attendance of the factory representative. Patients ordering aids during the open house are offered a reduced price or more services for their immediate order.

Advertising

Although objections to professional advertising can be heard whenever this topic is raised, it is clear that, no matter what the objection, professional advertising is a reality. In a health care environment where too many service providers are chasing too few dollars, advertising offers the competitive edge to those providers who advertise. The provider may choose to advertise in the newspaper, radio, or television media or may attempt to cover all media. The decision of where to advertise can be based on the particular cost of the media in your area, the market penetration studies for the population you are attempting to reach, and the professional resources that you may afford. Here again, the hearing aid manufacturer may provide camera ready examples of print materials, which require only that your local newspaper insert your name, address, and telephone number. Some companies may share the costs of advertising if you mention their name in the ad.

Radio and television media may be more costly and difficult to use. Although some organizations, such as the Academy of Dispensing Audiologists and the Better Hearing Institute, sponsor public service announcements (PSAs) that offer local referrals on request for further information, it remains difficult to obtain field-tested or professionally developed video materials for audiologic practices. As the effectiveness of advertising in this media for health care advertising becomes better known, the effective use of this media by our profession will surely increase.

Contracting Your Services to Others

Contracting with another agency or professional to provide audiology services is an excellent method of expanding your business and controlling a steady source of referrals to your practice. Health maintenance organizations (HMOs) provide services to their enrollees by contracting with eligible service providers throughout their service area. Hospitals may contract with an individual if the services can be provided at less cost or with greater flexibility to their patients. Physicians may desire services within their offices if the provider can deliver the service more efficiently and economically than the physician.

However, the contracting facilities must always evaluate the service in relationship to the costs of providing that service within their own employment structure. As a rule of thumb, if you are successful and can provide the service with an adequate profit margin, you should expect the contract facility to begin to explore the feasibility of providing that same service without you. It is essential to understand that, if you are successful and profitable in the facility, you will probably be replaced at some future time by full-time services at lowered costs. As a result, it is therefore wise not to rely on any single source of referral for a significant percentage of your referrals. If all or most of your patients are generated by a single physician practice or contract facility, your practice base is most assuredly unstable and your future unsure.

In developing contractual relationships, it is imperative that you evaluate the potential these services have to detract from your practice. If at all possible you should avoid establishing service centers that will ultimately take patients from within your market and assist them in developing relationships with competing practices. However, with physician practice, if audiologic services will ultimately be provided within that practice, your participation in their development may offer the opportunity to build a basis for referral to your practice, should advanced or rehabilitative services be required in the future.

MAINTAINING OR EXPANDING: YOU MUST PLAN TO SUCCEED

The American folk tale of a rags to riches overnight success is a fantasy that appeals to us all. In reality, however, success is based on hard work and careful, continuing analysis of realistic goals. The method by which we actualize those goals is our strategic plan. The last time you may have developed a strategic plan may have been during the completion of the degree process in college. Certainly, the development of a strategic plan requires time and energy that is not always directly related to increased patient load and revenues.

For many business owners, planning, and the time it takes, are relegated to secondary importance. Because of the lack of a well-developed and continually updated strategic plan, many businesses fail within their first 5 years. Therefore, on a monthly basis, review your business financial data to obtain information about your profitability. Is your business profitable at this time? If not, what appear to be the main obstacles? Are your expenses too high, or is the volume of your business too low? The answers to these questions are directly related to the lifestyle you choose and the character of your work environment.

If the development of the practice is not proceeding along a satisfactory course, you must identify the problems and begin to alter its direction. Plan to do more of what you are good at and less of what you are not. Profitable services might be expanded and unprofitable ones dropped. Evaluate your resources and plan to utilize those that are readily available to you. Critically analyze the areas in which you lack expertise and find the means to overcome these deficiencies, if possible. Finally, develop a plan. Put it into action, evaluate the result, revise it, and try again. This ongoing process suggests discipline, and discipline is the building block of success.

The maintenance and expansion of an audiologic practice require a high level of energy and dedication. The rewards, reflected in self-fulfillment and satisfaction, justify the commitment.

REFERENCES

Cranmer, K. (1985). Hearing aid dispensing—1985. *Hearing Instruments*, 36:5, p. 6.

McGee, E.J., Govoni, N.A.P., & Eng, R.S. (1980). *Fundamentals of Direct Mail Marketing*. New York, New York: American Management Association, p. 130.

Chapter 13

Standard Computer Software Applications in Private Practice

Mariana Newton, Ph.D.

Many software programs—electronic instructions for the computer—are available that will meet the needs of private practice in speech-language pathology and audiology. Although some individualization of the programs may be necessary to fit particular circumstances, it is not necessary to "start from scratch" in developing programs for most office applications. This chapter provides an overview of common standard software programs, useful features, user suggestions, and various applications in the private practice.

WORD PROCESSING

Word processing is the most popular and widely used microcomputer application. No competent salesperson of personal computers would fail to mention word processing in his or her pitch. This application is the major reason that personal computers have found permanent places in homes, classrooms, and offices.

A word processor is a software program that allows one to use the computer much like a typewriter, with some important enhancements. Instead of seeing the printed letter immediately after striking the key, as in typewriting, the word processor stores your typing electronically, allows you to look at it on the screen, change it, add to and delete from it, rearrange it—all by pressing a few keys—and then, when you are satisfied, print it. The ability to perfect the text before committing it to paper is the feature that makes the word processor much more efficient than a typewriter.

Word processors consist of two parts: the text editor and the text formatter. *Text editors* are either screen-oriented or line-oriented. Most microcomputer text editors are screen-oriented. That is, one character on the screen represents one character in memory, and changes in the text are made instantly. Line-oriented word processors require the operator to locate the line on which a change is to be made and re-enter the entire line. The *text formatter* is the part of the program that sets the format of the words you have entered, such as margins, number of characters on a line, and number of lines on a page, and sends the information to the printer or plotter exactly as it will appear on the paper.

Each commercially available word processor program has a variety of features. Some features are considered standard because they are so essential; others are not essential, but are very useful. Still others are useful for some types of material and not for others.

For the private practitioner whose primary word processing needs are related to correspondence and patient reports, the following features are essential:

- *Word wraparound*: eliminates the need to use the <enter> or <return> key as a carriage return. The text continues to the next line when the right margin is reached, without keystrokes.
- *Insert and delete*: allows the user to edit by adding text between existing characters without retyping or to delete text and have the remaining text realigned to close the gaps
- *Block moves*: sometimes called *copy and move* or *cut and paste*; this feature copies or moves marked sections of text from one place to another within the text. An extension of the block move principle is the boilerplate or standard paragraph capability in some word processors. (The block move feature allows the creation of standard paragraphs and then the selection and arrangement of those paragraphs into a unique document, but the process takes longer.) Not only paragraphs but also notes, short articles, bibliographic references, running notes, and the like are contained in a computerized "index card file," to be called up and arranged to create a unique document. It is this feature that has been used in creating computer-assisted programs for writing patient goals and objectives.
- *Search and replace*: scans the text for all instances of a command or expression and replaces it with something else. Conditional replace requires the user to check each instance before replacing it. Global replace locates and changes all occurrences without confirmation of the command.
- *Automatic pagination*: determines page endings by the number of lines per page; eliminates the need to set all page breaks manually, although manual page breaks to avoid awkward breaks can be set also.
- *Headers and footers*: recognizes standard text lines that are to appear at the top or bottom of each page, e.g., patient's name and date of report at the top of second and succeeding pages, successive page numbers at the top right corner or at the bottom center of each page.
- *Screen/printing attributes*: commands to print boldface, underline, double underline, superscript, subscript, double-wide characters, italics, centering, and a variety of other options. The boldface, underline, and centering are the most useful commands for correspondence and reports. More advanced word processors use various fonts, or typestyles, done by a graphics generator. This capability may be useful in applications requiring automated printing of

phonetic symbols. For fun, the fonts can be used to generate notices, signs, and even a professional greeting card!

- *Directory*: allows user to leave the text and look at the directory of files on a disk and then return to the text without reloading the text in memory.

In addition to the essential features above, several additional features are highly useful for some aspects of the private practitioner's office operation:

- *Spelling checker*: scans document to identify words not found in the internal dictionary and calls them up in context for user determination of correct spelling. Some programs go one step further by suggesting alternative spellings. Most spelling checkers allow the user to add words to the internal dictionary; this is an important feature for a speech-language pathologist or audiologist because many words may be specific to the discipline and not usually found in a general dictionary.
- *Indentation*: sets a temporary left margin, which places a section of the text in a specified distance from the document margin. The feature is important for long quotations. Some word processors allow for reverse indentation, which is useful in preparing bibliographic material, in which the first line has a smaller left margin than subsequent lines of the entry.
- *Form letter merge*: allows the merging of, for example, names and addresses, with a form letter so that each letter will be personalized and originally typed. In more advanced word processors, the merge function includes the capability for merging unique data from an internal data base within the text of the document. This function is very useful in sending large mailings that need, for one reason or another, to be presented as unique, personal letters. If you are working with an integrated program, which contains word processing, data base management, spread sheet, and/or graphics capabilities in one program, you will have a more versatile merge capability. However, such programs have some disadvantages at the present time. (Read on for some comments on integrated programs.)
- *Macro keys*: programs keystroke sequences for recall with a single keystroke. For example, if you are writing a document in which the expression American Speech-Language-Hearing Association (44 keystrokes) occurs often, it will speed your work and reduce opportunity for error to have a single key programmed to enter this name.
- *Help file*: an "on screen" help file that can be accessed even while the user is working with a document on the word processor. This feature gives brief descriptions of the function keys and commands and instructions for accomplishing certain tasks. The information is available in the program manual, but the ready availability from the keyboard is very "user friendly."

Beyond the essential and "nice to have" features for the private practitioner, there are many other features of word processors that may be more useful for some professionals than for others. The usefulness of additional features will probably be determined most by the activities other than private practice in which the user is engaged. For example, if the private practitioner is engaged in extensive writing, programs that contain an internal thesaurus, such as *Einstein Writer, IBM,* or an indexing feature, such as *Ideaware, IBM,* may be desirable. For the research writer, variable tabular settings—for example, *Word, IBM*—for table preparation and graphics generators, such as *Ideaware, IBM,* are time-savers. For those working with colleagues in faraway places, the ability to send text via telephone lines, through *Zardax, Apple,* for example, is useful.

The uses of word processing in private practice have already been alluded to in describing various features of word processing programs. The extent of your imagination is your only limitation! A few comments about some specific applications may speed implementation of your ideas.

Correspondence

The word processor does not take the place of those small yellow memo papers lightly stuck to various papers. It is very helpful, however, in producing the routine and not-so-routine correspondence of the private practice. Standard paragraphs can be carefully selected and arranged, or routine letters can be produced quickly from boilerplates. Form letters can be merged with selected names and addresses as cover letters for clinical reports, appointment letters, or letters requesting payment. Consider sending a boilerplate welcome letter to new, potential referral sources, such as physicians or educators, in your community or a boilerplate letter to introduce yourself to agencies with which you may wish to contract for services.

Letter composition can be done easily on the word processor without the expressive stumbling caused by difficulties with the mechanics of the language . . . or of the typewriter! Revisions of all sorts can be accomplished before the letter is printed.

In an earlier chapter, various types of printers were briefly discussed. A letter-quality printer or a correspondence-quality dot matrix printer is best for correspondence. A letter-quality printer is slower, but produces print much like that from an IBM typewriter. The dot matrix printer is much faster, and newer models have exceptionally good print quality.

Correspondence is facilitated if the printer has both a tractor feed (holes on each side of the paper through which pins insert to advance the paper) and pinch feed (like a typewriter). For many single-page letters, as in form-merge letters, continuous tractor-fed letterhead is ideal. You can go off and eat lunch while the printer prints! For multiple page letters, the paper needs to be fed sheet by sheet, using a pinch feed. Some attachments are available now that feed single sheets into a pinch-feed mechanism; the cost may not be too high *if* you have a high volume of such correspondence.

Clinical Reports

Report writing is the bane of all professionals, including private practitioners. Most of our problems with paperwork are centered around the mechanics of its production. These problems cause delays in completion of reports. Yet, clinical reports that are written promptly after the patient is seen are more accurate, complete, vivid, and interesting than those written later.

The use of word processing offers the same advantages to report writing as to correspondence. Boilerplate paragraphs may be useful in combination with merge functions to speed the reporting of unique patient information in a standard paragraph context. In addition, composition of text that describes the uniqueness of a patient's communication and circumstances is facilitated by easy revision and formatting prior to printing. Patient data, which can be presented in tabular form, can be easily formatted so that it can be compared to subsequent data of similar character. Or, in some instances, a graphic display may be generated and data added on subsequent dates to present comparative information. The capability to manipulate information about patients with ease removes many barriers to effective, timely patient reports.

Contracts

More and more private practitioners are entering into contractual agreements with agencies for the delivery of services. Such contracts require careful legal review. The careful wording and review of model, or boilerplate, paragraphs by an attorney, prior to storage on diskette, will ready you to prepare a contract for an agency. Legal review of contracts prepared from already reviewed boilerplates would be accelerated, if even necessary at all. Moreover, the probability of error is greatly reduced, unless you inadvertently select the wrong boilerplate.

Patient Goals and Objectives

Highest professional standards require that written goals and objectives for each patient be prepared. Here again, there is some redundancy from patient to patient, as well as some unique material. The word processor helps overcome the mechanical production problems inherent when not only content but also sequence and conditional components are critical. Some commercially available programs address patient goals and objectives. Most are essentially boilerplated paragraphs related in a data base to descriptions of the patient's problem. Therefore, when selecting a software program, be careful to ascertain that you, as the user, can create new boilerplates and descriptions, e.g., add on to the program. A lack of flexibility in such a program reduces its usefulness if you have a wide variety of patients.

Running Notes

A running log of patient contact is an important part of the patient record. (See Chapter 4, Professional Liability, for confirmation of the importance of patient logs.) Some practitioners have found it useful to enter the log on the word processor, followed by the plan for the next action to be taken. Such notes can either be printed soon after they are entered or at the end of a day. If the log consists of many shorter entries, it may be more efficient for the running note to be written directly in the file. Whatever is most immediate and orderly will be the most accurate record.

Overlays

The most common application in the private practice for overlays is to facilitate the preparation of insurance forms. (Some practices request that patients do their own insurance filing, but there are advantages in doing it in your office. The use of correct terminology, disorder and service codes, and follow-up on denied claims makes a considerable difference in the claims review process.) It is helpful to obtain a standard insurance form on continuous feed paper in triplicate. A template of the information to be supplied can be constructed on the word processor, including indentations, line feeds (carriage returns), and other formatting information to fit the information on the form. Because the insurance forms will need to be inserted into the printer in place of other stock, it is efficient to set aside a time when all of the insurance forms for a period of time can be done together. The template can be loaded into the computer from a storage disk, the information inserted, and the forms printed.

There are a number of other applications of word processing, depending on the individual practitioner's activities and needs. For example, a curriculum vita may be an important document for some professionals. The various sections of the vita can be entered and stored, and then, as additional entries on the vita are appropriate, they can be inserted without having to retype the whole document. The preparation of research reports, public addresses, papers, and lectures lends itself to word processing. Material is easily organized on the computer screen, updates can be inserted without disturbing existing data, documents can be formatted and reformatted according to various style requirements, and written copy can then be produced.

DATA BASE MANAGEMENT

A data base management program is the computer software that puts bits and pieces of information into their proper place in an orderly fashion, so that the information can be retrieved, sorted, arranged, and compared—that is, managed. What the word processor is to the typewriter, the data base management program is to the filing cabinet. The language of data bases and their many uses may overwhelm the uninitiated, but they are really not that complex.

There are three widely used types of data base management systems in use today: file management systems, relational data bases, and network/hierarchical data management systems. The file management is the simplest program; the hierarchical system is the most complex.

File Management Systems

Like the simplest of filing systems, the file management program stores information in records, which are grouped together in files. Each record contains many bits and pieces of information that are categorized into fields. As with filing cabinets, the space available in a file management system is finite, limited in some cases by the number and size of records and fields accommodated by the program and, in other cases, by storage availability, e.g., disk size. In considering which file management system to use, careful attention should be given to limitations on the number of records and fields and the total number of spaces available for field labels and data.

The format of the file is determined by the user's instructions about the number of fields, how long each should be, in what order they should be, and whether the data are to be alphabetical or numerical. The information, once entered, can be retrieved in a variety of formats.

Consider your address book or desktop Rolodex file as a file management system. Each person constitutes a record. The fields might be surname, first name, street address, city, state, zip code, area code, telephone number, employer, and spouse's name. For example, if address labels are desired for all persons having the zip code 28603, the program scans all of the records to identify only those meeting such specifications and then sends the information to the printer with instructions to print vertically the fields designated, e.g., name and address.

The file management system is used also to merge data with other applications. For example, if one wishes to send "original" form letters to a variety of people (see the above discussion on word processing), the names and addresses in a file management system can be merged with the form letter on the word processor to obtain the desired result.

The relational data base management system is one step more advanced than the file management system. Both systems work with records and fields; however, the relational data base differs in some important ways.

Relational Data Bases

Relational data bases are so named because they organize the relationships in a data base into tabular form—rows and columns. In such a configuration, a relationship occurs when a row and column intersect. Because of these relationships, some mathematical rules can be applied to the data, and the date can be manipulated to reveal new, unforeseen relationships. Changes in records and fields can be made as needs are identified; all needs do not have to be anticipated before beginning the data base. The flexibility of a relational data base is one of its major advantages.

Many relational data base programs change the data in a field in every file with a single command. For example, in a data base in which one field is "price," the private practitioner may wish to change the data in each record by a percentage equal to the annual inflation rate. In a relational data base, the computer can be instructed to increase every figure in the field labeled "price" by 5 percent.

An appointment calendar is a good example of information that could be managed on a relational data base. The appointment calendar reflects a two-dimensional table: hours (or parts of hours) by days. When the office staff members make an appointment for the practitioner to see a patient, they identify an empty cell, an intersection of time and day. The patient's name is the data. Now suppose there are five associates in practice with the owner of the practice, and each has a data base. You may wish to combine the data bases. An appointment is needed at 3 P.M. on Monday. Instead of asking whether the private practice owner has an empty "cell" at that time, the user would ask whether the owner or any colleague has that "cell" open.

Let us take another example. There may be limited space in the office. There are five audiologists in practice together, but there are only two testing suites. Now, in addition to relating the five calendars together, the two testing suite schedules must be related with the five calendars. It is apparent that the number of variables to be considered changes the character of the data base considerably. A single practitioner's schedule is probably best handled by the traditional appointment calendar. But the schedules of many clinicians, in several rooms, with a large number of patients, is a more difficult data management problem and can be facilitated by using the computer and a data management program.

In a hierarchical data base, the basic unit of data is a set. It is structured much like a topical outline; it has various levels of data. The physical layout of the data is no longer important. Data must be described—with data description language, or DDS—and a particular data point may belong to some sets but not to others. Two or more similar data points may belong to completely different data sets. Data may be sorted within sets, but special programs must be written to retrieve the data because hierarchical data bases are not directly interactive.

Hierarchical Data Bases

A hierarchical data base might divide the private practice into departments—professional services, finance, and records. The department files might contain other levels of data on the services performed by each, inventories used by each, and so forth. The hierarchical data base is very powerful and requires careful analysis of a problem and advance attention to setting up the data base and the programs to access it. In addition, because of its complexity, it requires considerably more computer memory than many office microcomputers have or may cost more than you may want to pay. For private practice office purposes, the hierarchical data base is probably a more sophisticated application than is needed, unless the practice is very large.

Selecting a Data Base

As indicated earlier, any software does not run on all hardware. If data base management is to be one of the primary uses of the computer, software should be selected first, and *then* the hardware to run it should be chosen. In any event, compatibility of hardware and software, disk operating systems, and memory size is essential.

To begin the selection process, start at the end. Think about the design of the reports that the data base should generate. What information needs to be managed? For what purpose? What format should the reports take? For example, look at the titles, headings of rows and columns, and data contained in each cell. Are mathematical calculations necessary? Let your imagination run wild.

Next, make a list of all the data items needed to be entered into the data base in order to prepare the necessary reports. Identify independent and dependent fields. Are all the data needed available? Next, look through the list for redundancies. Then organize the data in a logical way for entry or analysis. From this point on, it is possible to estimate what the data storage capacity requirements will be (number of characters in one record times number of records).

With this information in hand, various available data bases can be compared. In addition to data storage capacity, several other features may be essential, desirable, or just nice to have.

- *Mathematical calculation*: Is there a need to calculate any of the data? Is it important to derive a column or row from combinations—percentages or averages—of existing columns or rows?
- *File size*: Are the files big enough for the needs of the practice? How many files will the data base accommodate? The data base must be big enough for needed applications, or it will not be efficient.
- *Data input flexibility*: The data on many data base programs are entered via the keyboard. For small files, this entry method is satisfactory. For larger files, however, other data entry mechanisms may be preferable. For example, data that can be written on a data card with a soft lead pencil can be quickly entered into the data base by an optical reader or light pen. Such devices reduce data entry time, data entry delay, and error.
- *Printed reports flexibility*: The reports a program generates are among the most important features of the program. The more flexible and powerful the report-

generating capabilities, the more useful the system will be. Flexibility in designing the formats of reports will permit use of special forms, such as standard insurance forms, and various data organizations.

- *Sorting*: This is one of the most important functions of data information management. Some programs sort only one field, such as alphabetizing a list of names or arranging a group of numbers in ascending or descending order. A multiple-level sort is much more powerful, but also requires more memory. As an example, a report that has patients' names in alphabetical order by order of birth needs to be generated. Consider not only how many levels of sort are available but also how much time it takes. The more levels of sorting to be done, the longer the time it takes.

- *Cross-tabulation*: Crosstabs, a very new and remarkable feature available on the Reflex data base program, are a much used tool of market researchers and statistical programs. The feature allows the creation of a table of relationships of two variables in the data base. For example, one variable may be the age of patients seen, and the second variable may be the distance they travel to the practitioner's office for therapy. Crosstabs provide a report of the relationship between age and miles traveled, showing these variables in an axis-abscissa relationship, with the data being the number of patients meeting the requirements of each cell.

- *Multiple users*: When a private practice has more than one person who needs to access a particular data base at a time, a multiple-user program must be employed. It is, of course, possible to set up several computer stations so that each user can access the data at any time. As is true with all software programs, careful, clear, and full written documentation of the program is critical to successful use. The ability to ''backup'' or make additional copies of the program for your own use is a safeguard against accidental damage or erasure.

Even the single private practitioner office will have many uses for data base management. Because such offices are usually minimally staffed, the staff time available for data manipulation and reporting is minimal. Data base management is therefore one of the most useful computer applications.

Is a data base appropriate for patient information? The answer to the question depends on what kind and how much of information is needed. Consider, as an example, the uses of the sample patient record shown in Figure 13–1.

The above information on each patient could be used in a variety of ways. When interfaced with an accounting sheet on a computer, of course, the statements can be printed by calling up the contact name and address, the patient's name and address, or the third party reimburser and joining it with the statement. If the record includes a file number, the linkage of name and statement is faster.

The practitioner may wish to recommend that some patients return for re-evaluation, as noted in Chapter 12. At the beginning of each month, the data base can be sorted by recall date, and those patients who have a recall date during the next month can be called up. The names and addresses are then merged from the data base with

Figure 13–1 Sample Patient Record

```
Surname:                        First Name:

Address:

City:                 State:          Zip Code:

Telephone:  Work:               Home:

Birthdate:            Sex:     ICD:

Third Party Reimburser:                 ID#:        Plan #:

Contact Surname:                First Name:

Relationship:

Address:

City:                 State:          Zip Code:

Telephone:  Work:               Home:

Recall Date:                    Service:

Notes:
```

the appropriate letter on the word processor, and original letters are printed and sent to each patient. When the patient responds to the letter by calling for an appointment, the appointment calendar data base is used to find the day, time, room, and clinician that are available.

As another example of data base usage, a list of all patients who are reimbursed through a particular source can be generated. The data base is merely sorted by third party reimburser, and any or all information about those patients is printed. Such a record would be useful for tracking the payment records of various third party reimbursers by ICD codes or by insurance plan numbers.

Some practitioners may consider putting diagnostic or therapy progress data on the data base for each patient. In some cases, doing so may be advantageous. However, it is important that consideration be given to the time needed for data entry, the amount of management the data requires, and the usefulness of relating the data to other information. Does the practice really need a computer record, or would a paper file record be more efficient? If the data management needs are few and the primary idea behind putting such data on the computer is simply to record the data, then it may not be a good idea.

On the other hand, the review of data on many similar patients across time periods may be desired. Comparisons of this kind, within a practice or among practitioners, are an important element of audit practices in patient care. From a research standpoint, computer assistance in the management of large quantities of clinical data may be helpful in transforming anecdotal evidence about the clinical process to empirical evidence that can be more clearly displayed and understood.

On-line data bases, or networks, have some important uses for the private practi- **NETWORKS**
tioner. These networks, such as The Source, Dow Jones News/Retrieval, or Com-
puServe, are large data bases that are accessed by connecting the computer to a
modem and the modem to a telephone. One then dials the telephone number of the
data base, "shakes hands" by giving a password and some preliminary information,
and a world of information becomes instantly available. Computer programs, news,
weather, sports, bibliographic information, home shopping, travel, education, and
club notices are but a few of the categories of information that are accessible. Of
particular interest to the private practitioner are a number of business and financial
topics: financial news and analysis, investment targeting, brokerage and banking,
personal finance, financial products, and computer programs for business. See also
Chapter 15, Planning for Personal Financial Success, for further information on
personal investment strategies. These information utilities all have a subscription fee,
and some have connect and time on-line fees as well. Beginning users of such
services take longer to find needed information, so costs are generally higher.
However, with experience, the practitioner will find that time on-line decreases, and
the subscription is less expensive and well worth the money.

Spread sheet programs, such as VisiCalc, Multiplan, or Lotus 1-2-3, provide **SPREAD**
another mechanism for data management that is particularly useful in the private **SHEETS**
practice. The spread sheet is a computer version of a big piece of paper that is divided
into rows and columns. Each column and row can be named (labels). Data (values) or
formulas are entered in the cells formed by intersections of rows and columns. A
spread sheet has certain enhancements over the paper version. Some are general in
nature; many are particularly useful in business applications.

Bigger is not always better. Spread sheets that are too big are awkward and time- **Size**
consuming to use. It is difficult to scroll up and down and from left to right (i.e., move
the cursor) over many cells to locate a particular one or to move about from one
section of the sheet to another. The user can easily become lost. In addition, it is
difficult to find mistakes in data, formula entry, and in logic. The solution is to create
several smaller spread sheets by "chunking" information into small units. When
each of the smaller tables has been proofread and corrected, the small tables can be
merged into a larger display.

The earliest versions of VisiCalc allowed the user to change column widths, but did **Variable**
not allow one column in a spread sheet to be a different width from all other columns. **Column Width**
The Advanced VisiCalc and other newer programs allow variation in width from
column to column. This capability makes labeling of the columns easier and fits the
spread sheet to the data, instead of the reverse. Further, the addition of a wider
column periodically, which may or may not be printed, for writing comments or notes
is helpful to an unfamiliar reader.

Macro keys in spread sheets operate under the same principles as macro keys in **Macro Keys**
word processing, as described earlier in this chapter. They permit the user to store a

long string of commands and call the whole command up with a few keystrokes. Frequently used, long formulas are a good application for macro keys.

Similar to macro keys are function keys on some computers that allow repetitive entries to be made with a single keystroke. This automation of the spread sheet saves entry time and reduces error.

Sorting/Report Generation Flexibility

A variety of options for sorting rows and columns and for printing reports is important here as it is in data bases. Flexibility allows the user to look at the data in different ways. For example, on a spread sheet of receipts and expenditures, an alphabetical sort of vendors would be helpful in identifying the most frequent vendors to one's practice and any duplicate entries in the spread sheet. For monthly comparisons, the rows would be sorted by month. Various codes might be attached to budget categories so that sorting by these codes would yield figures for each category together. Such categories could include, for example, salaries, equipment, materials and supplies, and repairs. Reports for the auditor may look quite different from a report on vendors, even though the two reports might use the same data arranged in different ways.

Rearranging Rows and Columns

This function differs from sorting. It may be desirable to put two related columns or rows next to each other for ease of reference. Historical or projection reports are done this way on the spread sheet. For example, putting one year after another makes it possible to easily compare one year with several years before and after.

Transportation

Sometimes it is important to be able to move information from one spread sheet to another. A spread sheet on which are calculated the volume of business and the number of employees needed to produce that volume plus a 10 percent increase for the next year might be moved to another spread sheet on which a budget for the next year is being constructed. A larger RAM is required to load the programs plus large chunks of data, but moving from one spread sheet to another saves time and reduces vulnerability to error.

Data Interchange Format (DIF) Files

Usually when the user saves a spread sheet file, the whole file is saved. Or, when it is retrieved, the whole file is retrieved. With a DIF, only a section of a spread sheet can be saved. When the DIF file is loaded back into RAM, that section can be placed anywhere on another spread sheet. The DIF files are particularly useful when a section of a spread sheet is used in several different ways on more than one spread sheet. DIF files also allow for the consolidation of data from several spread sheets into one big sheet. Unfortunately, DIF files will not transport formulas for calculations; only numerical entries or numerical values obtained from formulas can be saved in a DIF file.

Setting up the Spread Sheet

When setting up a spread sheet, it is important to plan carefully. Consider the audience who will use it. What kinds of information do they want? What kinds of questions will they ask of it? How is it best to arrange the sheet so that the intended users may look at information they want to look at?

One of the best uses of the spread sheet is the asking of "what if" questions. Identify the "what if" questions to be asked, and determine how they can be answered from the spread sheet. Consider, for example, a spread sheet that displays the patients seen in the practice last month and the income they generated. Now for the questions: What if fees were raised? What if more patients were seen? Suppose that the accounts receivable represent 20 percent of fees charged. What if steps were taken to reduce the accounts receivable to 5 percent? How would doing so affect cash flow? Anticipation of the questions to be asked allows the practitioner to set up the spread sheet in a way that will include helpful data and exclude unnecessary information.

Time should be taken to lay out the general form of the spread sheet before any values or formulas are entered. Label the rows and columns, arrange them to best advantage, and identify where notes and comments are needed. The time spent carefully planning the sheet will be recouped in ease of use and time saved later.

Certain procedures need to be followed carefully and systematically in setting up the spread sheet. Be sure to:

- *Isolate variables*. It is helpful to group key parameters that will frequently be changed into one area of the spread sheet. In addition, reference figure(s), or assumptions, should be put in one cell(s), and those cells should be located together near the upper left corner of the sheet. Grouping together cells to be changed often and reference cells allows easy, quick access to the information without having to move all over the "page." Further, because the spread sheet recalculates from the upper left corner, when those values are changed the whole spread sheet will be recalculated.

- *Focus on key ratios*. The parameters that drive the business are the most important foci of the spread sheet. These are the variables that generate income and expense and are related to productivity. Interest rates for money invested and for money borrowed are two examples of key ratios.

  In identifying and locating variables, assumptions, and key ratios, notice ways in which macro keys or keystroke memory keys can be used when entering information into the spread sheet. Using the macro keys for memorable formulas or keystroke sequences speeds the work and reduces error.

- *Use English*. Overabbreviation makes a spread sheet more difficult to decipher after the user has been away from it a long time. In particular, spread sheets that will be used by several people in the practitioner's office require clear labels and some explanatory notes to avoid confusion.

- *Keep it simple*. The power of a spread sheet can delude the user into believing that every known bit of information must be included. The result is that data that are not necessary to the questions asked will be included just because they are available. Doing so may only serve to clutter the sheet and confuse the user.

  On the other hand, some applications for the spread sheet may be very large, requiring a considerable amount of data and many calculations. It is important to break such a task into smaller parts, each being a miniature spread sheet, and to include all intermediate calculation points. It may be possible to combine all of the calculations into one gigantic formula at the end. However, mammoth equations are subject to error. When error does occur, finding the error is much easier when working with smaller segments of the spread sheet.

- *Use modules.* The smaller segments are modules of a larger construction. Not only do the modules reduce the probability of error and shorten error-tracking time but they also hasten transportation from one part of the spread sheet to another. Even though it will require more memory initially, it is helpful to place modules catercorner to one another instead of parallel, with blank rows and columns between sections (Figure 13–2). Formulas for calculation for each module should be placed in the last blank row or column of the segment. With this arrangement there is vertical and horizontal flexibility for last-minute additions, without having to change the arrangement or location of formulas.

Figure 13–2 Spatial Arrangement of Modules on a Spread Sheet

	A	B	C	D	F	G	H
1	xxxxxxxxxxxx						
2	x	x					
3	x	x					
4	x	x					
5	xxxxxxxxxxxx						
6							
7							
8			xxxxxxxxxxxx				
9			x	x			
10			x	x			
11			x	x			
12			xxxxxxxxxxxx				
13							
14							
15					xxxxxxxxxxxx		
16					x	x	
17					x	x	
18					x	x	
20					xxxxxxxxxxxx		

After the spread sheet has been perfected, the modules can be moved to be parallel to one another, if desired.

- *Check for error*. It is tempting to believe that data and calculations that are "on" the computer are free of error. A common expression among computer users is GIGO—garbage in, garbage out. Formulas must be checked carefully for accuracy in entry, as well as accuracy in logic. That is, formulas must be chosen correctly and written accurately. Many users find it helpful to *use hash totals*: for example, on an expense account, totalling the values both horizontally and vertically helps identify error.

- *Save models*. While developing a spread sheet, it is advisable to save emerging versions at each stage. Each version represents all previous steps plus the most recent additions, yielding a temporal record of the construction process. Such a record permits the user to retrace steps, reconsider assumptions, and find errors.

    Once a layout for a spread sheet is constructed and before entering values, the spread sheet should be saved on diskette as a boilerplate. This "save" records all labels and formulas, without values, as a template for future uses. For example, the boilerplate spread sheet for an expense account would be used each time a new expense account is to be prepared. The boilerplate is loaded, the values for a particular business trip are entered, the recalculation command is keyed in, and the finished expense account is ready to print.

- *Enter values*. Before entering values, columns that are to contain numbers should be formatted for decimal places, rounding, and integer size. Computer operators should check their program manuals for procedure.

Several other entry practices speed the work, make the sheet more useful, and reduce error:

- Turn off the recalculate function during value entry to speed up the process. If the spread sheet recalculates after every value entry, you will have to wait on the program between each entry.

- Put sources of data and other explanations in a column near values. If there is no need for the notes to show on the printed spread sheet, it is possible to format the explanatory column to zero before printing. It will not show on print, but the entries in the column will reappear when you reformat to correct column width.

- Use macro keys to store repetitive keystrokes, fixed or relative. (Refer to previous discussion of macro keys.)

Uses of a Spread Sheet

There are many uses of the spread sheet in the private practice. The spread sheet is a superior tool for keeping clinical research data on single subjects. For a detailed discussion of this application, read Leija McReynolds and Kevin P. Kearns (1983) *Single-Subject Experimental Designs in Communicative Disorders*. Also see Ronald Goldman and Arthur Dahle (Eds.), "High Technology: Implications for Language Disorders," *Topics in Language Disorders,* December, 1985).

Various applications involving financial records and models are of particular importance to the private practice. Some examples are cited below.

Budget

The budget is one of the most important financial tools for any business. If the practice involves more than one person or department, each of those units should develop data regarding salaries by month, expenses in each line item by month, estimated volume of services by month, and an estimate of revenues to be generated by month. These data can be entered on a spread sheet. Examination of individual or department budgets may necessitate adjustments in them. Estimated revenues and expenses can be compared across persons or departments.

To create a corporation budget, the individual budgets are consolidated (by formula). Corporate totals may require further adjustment in the individual budgets; following changes, they can be consolidated again. When final figures are reached, each combination—salaries, expenses, volume, and revenue—should be saved as a separate DIF file (see explanation below) for use in preparing a business income statement and cash flow forecasts. The final budget would include one spread sheet for each department or person reflecting costs (salaries, expenses) and estimated volume of services and resulting revenues for each month; four DIF files of consolidated information; and a summary of corporate totals (the bottom line in each DIF file).

Forecasting Cash Flow

The reader will remember that the original DIF files were constructed with figures by month. Even the consolidation figures were reported by month. A cash flow forecast illustrates when the practitioner might expect to receive revenue and pay expenses so that he or she can determine how much cash on hand is needed to manage the practice. It is critical to have a month-by-month look at the cash situation of the practice.

The cash flow forecast considers monthly expected revenue less expenses. This information has already been generated and saved in the DIF files. Then cash on hand, receipts from the previous month, and interest earned are added. Expenses from the previous month and taxes and interest paid are subtracted. The result is the amount of cash on hand expected for that month. Calculating a cumulative total across months will yield accumulated cash to date. Some cash flow forecasts assume that revenue is received when due. In speech-language pathology and audiology private practice, that assumption may not be true. Third party payers, as well as individuals, are not always prompt in payment. It may be wise to include a percentage of accounts receivable as "doubtful" or not received in any one month and then add values when payment is actually received. Further, expenses may not be level across months or even paid in the month after they are incurred. For example, a separate line item for capital purchases may be added to the cash flow statement. Be sure that depreciation expense in the budget reflects the purchases as they are scheduled. An accountant is the best advisor in adjusting the cash flow forecast to the practice's individual experience and needs. (See Chapters 4, 5, and 9 for further comment on the accountant's role and function.)

This is becoming a more common business activity; the number of private practitioners who are contracting with schools, nursing homes, hospitals, and other human service agencies is increasing rapidly. In order to remain competitive with other potential contractors, careful estimates of the cost of professional and secretarial time, materials and supplies, equipment use time, travel, and indirect costs are needed. More accurate estimates permit careful planning of resource utilization, greater efficiency, and increased profits. In addition, accurate estimates increase agency confidence in the ability of the private practitioner to deliver quality services. Using a boilerplate spread sheet for estimating costs can enable values within the spread sheet to be changed as costs increase or decrease, time requirements change, or the like. The spread sheet will recalculate costs based on the new values. From the cost estimate, a budget can be derived on the spread sheet to be submitted with the contract.

Estimating the Cost of a Contract

Making a decision about the purchase of capital equipment requires information about the original cost of the equipment and the future savings and expenses that the equipment will generate. Analysis of these gains and losses can help you decide whether the purchase of the equipment is a good business decision.

Evaluating the Purchase of Equipment

Because depreciation of equipment is an allowable tax deduction, depreciating equipment can save you money. Moreover, different depreciation methods result in variation of the rate at which items are depreciated, which in turn affects taxes and cash flow. Calculating the depreciation in several ways permits one to identify the method that will achieve the best tax advantage.

Depreciating the Cost of Equipment

If you travel often, maintaining your expense account on a spread sheet is helpful. The calculations by day and category are done automatically, and the expense accounts can be saved on disk for recall at budget, annual report, and tax times. (As pointed out in Chapter 9, expense accounts for professional meetings must be analyzed in terms of the cost of doing business, as well as the need for professional enlightenment and reduced isolation.)

Expense Account

A net worth statement or balance sheet is a summary of the private practitioner's assets and liabilities as of a certain date. The calculations in a net worth statement are minimal, but the spread sheet makes a convenient filing cabinet for the information. Updating the net worth statement every 6 months allows the practitioner to track increases or decreases in net worth and to re-evaluate his or her financial situation. Comparisons of growth in net worth relative to financial goals and investment strategies are important in the private practice. Statements of net worth are also often needed for such financial transactions as borrowing money.

Calculating Net Worth

An income statement shows expenses, revenues, and estimated taxes to give an overall view of financial performance over a given period of time. This is an accounting function that can be generated using the general ledger in standard

Business Income Statement

accounting programs (see the following discussion). The statement can be done on a spread sheet, but it is not the best way of doing so.

ACCOUNTING PROGRAMS

Accounting practices chart the vital signs of a business, including private practices. Anyone whose fortunes rise and fall with private practice should have a keen interest in its accounting aspects. Even though members of the practice may have expertise in this area and computers sitting in their offices, a certified public accountant is a valuable business advisor about the kinds of financial records to be kept, practices and procedures to be followed, and the interpretation of financial information relative to various business decisions. It may even be to the private practitioner's advantage to buy the bookkeeping and accounting services needed from an outside firm, in which case the need for accounting applications will be minimal. On the other hand, doing one's own ''books'' may save money and give one the feeling of more control of the business end of the practice.

Some accounting functions can be done on the spread sheet as described above. Billing, for example, could be prepared from a spread sheet on each patient on which charges and payments are recorded and balances calculated. A practice that has a sizeable volume of accounting, however, is well served by special programs for that purpose.

A number of accounting packages (several programs together with identical commands, file structures, and operating systems) are available for almost any kind of hardware. These packages—*General Accounting,* or *VersaBusiness*—include a general ledger, accounts receivable ledger, accounts payable ledger, payroll register, and inventory control system.

- *Accounts receivable*: This section of an accounting program keeps track of all information about who owes the practice money, and it provides automated billing for past due accounts. It prints statements and provides summary reports. An important feature of accounts receivable is to age the accounts so that overdue accounts can be identified and billed again, or such accounts can be turned over to a collection firm.
- *Accounts payable*: This section is designed to keep track of current and aged bills that the practice owes and to whom. Records on vendors, purchases, and payments and the printing of checks are important functions. Summary reports of transactions are also important in preparing tax information and calculating costs of service.
- *Payroll*: If there are salaried employees in the practice, it is necessary to account for various taxes and contributions made to fringe benefits. The program also prints the payroll checks with all annotations of withholdings and automatic payroll payments.
- *Inventory*: This program may be more important to the merchant who buys and sells goods than to the service provider. Nevertheless, certain supplies are inventoried in speech-language pathology private practice, such as test forms that are used routinely, facial tissues, bathroom towels, copying paper, and

computer supplies. Inventory programs keep track of all items in stock and permit automatic reordering from the vendor when supplies dwindle. Audiologists in private practice may have even greater needs for computer inventory programs, particularly those practices dispensing hearing aids, batteries, earmolds, and/or other products. (See Chapters 8 and 9 for further discussion of inventories.)

- *General ledger*: Balance sheets, income statements, transaction reports, account listings, and a number of other customized reports can be generated from the general ledger. Entries to the general ledger can be made automatically from accounts receivable, accounts payable, payroll, and inventory.

An important consideration in the purchase of accounting packages for private practice is the capacity for entries. Some programs only accommodate 300 entries; others take 15,000 entries. You will want a program which will more than accommodate your present practice, because you should plan for, work for and expect growth.

SPECIALIZED SOFTWARE FOR PATIENT CARE

There are many applications of the computer in the private practice that are related to patient care, rather than to the business end of the practice. Computer-assisted and computer-managed evaluation and instruction programs are being developed at a rapid pace. Special programs for language analysis and cognitive retraining, for example, are available; computerized tympanometry, speech synthesis and other augmented communication systems, and electroacoustical measurements are but a few examples of technology that is already available in the laboratory and clinic. The application of these technologies does not differ in the private practice from any other setting. However, the cost of some may not be justifiable unless the demand in the practice is high. Reviews of specialized software may be found in the journal *Asha,* published by the American Speech-Language-Hearing Association (ASHA), and at various professional conferences and meetings.

REFERENCES

Goldman, R., & Dahle, A. (1985). High technology: Implications for language disorders. *Topics in Language Disorders, 6,* 1.

McReynolds, L.V., & Kearns, K.P. (1983). *Single-Subject Experimental Designs in Communicative Disorders.* Baltimore: University Park Press.

SUGGESTED READINGS

Ammett, A. (1984, July). The two sides of a word processor. *Personal Computing,* pp. 131–145.

Beil, D. *(1983). The DIF File.* Reston, VA: Reston Publishing Co.

Business computer systems. (1984). *5,* 104–106.

Fawcette, J.E. (1984, December). Using spreadsheets to model your business. *Personal Computing,* pp. 70–81.

Fersko-Weiss, H. (1985, July). How to link spreadsheets. *Personal Computing,* pp. 110–117.

Gabel, D. (1984, February). How to buy data-base software. *Personal Computing,* pp. 116–122, 125, 206, 209.

Gabel, D. (1984, March). Starting from scratch with a data base. *Personal Computing,* pp. 104–106, 109–113.

Hogan, T. (1985). Are the biggest sellers the best? *Business Software, 3*(7), 20–28.

Holtz, L. (1985). Merge, and merge again: The fine art of boilerplating. *Business Software, 3*(4), 26–28.

Hughes, G.D. (1984, June). Spreadsheets put you in the driver's seat. *Business Computer Systems*, pp. 22–26.

Jacobson, W. (1984). Choosing and using a data base management program. *Creative Computing, 10*(9), S1–S16.

Kruglinski, D. (1983, October). Database management systems. *Popular Computing*, pp. 117–134.

Lipton, R. (1984, October). Writing the recipe for database success. *Business Computer Systems*, pp. 21–22.

Lockwood, R. (1984). Choosing and using a word processor. *Creative Computing, 10*(12), 126–145.

McCarthy, M. (1984, June). Getting the most out of your spreadsheet. *Personal Computing*, pp. 136–149.

Oliveri, P. (1983, December), Mind your business. *Softalk*, pp. 67–70.

Rubin, C. (1984, January). Touring the on-line data bases. *Personal Computing*, pp. 82–95, 196.

Sehr, R. (1984, August), Saying it with spreadsheets. *Personal Computing*, pp. 79–87.

Walden, J. (1984, October). A new formula for spreadsheets. *Business Computer Systems*, pp. 97–106.

Wallach, W. (1984, March/April). Spreadsheets, feature by feature. *Small Business Computers*, pp. 44–45.

Wolverton, V. (1983). *VisiCalc Advanced Version Worksheets for Business*. San Jose, CA: Visicorp.

Chapter 14

Marketing Strategies from an Audiologic Perspective

Angela Loavenbruck, Ed.D.

The application of marketing concepts and processes to the delivery of audiologic services is a relatively new phenomenon and represents an area with which few audiologists are familiar. Marketing is usually thought of as a tool used exclusively for commercial businesses. It is highly identified with promotion, selling, and advertising—activities that actually represent only one component of a comprehensive marketing program.

Marketing is defined as the analysis, planning, implementation, and control of programs designed to bring about voluntary exchange of products or services with target markets. For audiology, marketing is the performance of an integrated series of activities that directs the flow of services and products from clinician to consumer. A comprehensive marketing program must be thought of as a process the focal point of which is the consumer. The management of marketing processes provides a focus for integrating the efforts of the private practitioner toward an overall goal of consumer satisfaction.

DEVELOPING A MARKETING PHILOSOPHY

Kotler (1975) points out that at least three distinct marketing styles can be identified: (1) aggressive or hard-sell marketing, which emphasizes promotional-type activities; (2) minimal marketing, which emphasizes the quality of a service or product; and (3) balanced marketing, which strives for an effective mix of both marketing elements. In developing the marketing philosophy most useful for the private practitioner, it is helpful to look at the hallmarks and assumptions underlying these marketing styles.

The hard-sell marketing style assumes that consumers will not utilize services or products unless they are approached with a substantial selling and promotional effort. A major tenet of this approach is that consumers can be convinced by the use of various sales-stimulating devices, such as giveaways, promotions, billboards, television ads, and other aggressive sales tactics. In hearing health care, hard-sell marketing techniques have commonly been used by the hearing aid industry and hearing aid dealers. It is a style now being emulated by some audiologists who are dispensing hearing aids, but is a style not easily used to market more comprehensive audiology services. Its lure for the private practitioner can be seen in conference and workshop offerings that stress such topics as "Closing the Sale," "Successful Open Houses," "Telemarketing," and other sales-oriented topics.

The adoption of hard-sell marketing techniques by audiologists is questionable for a number of reasons. It is a style that we, as a profession, have been highly critical of for many years because of its potential for misleading and misinforming the consumer. It is a style that is often offensive to other professionals from whom we may desire referrals and respect. It is a style that reduces us to "giveaways" of our professional services in order to induce consumers to purchase hearing aids, thus emphasizing the product itself, rather than our professional services as the item of value. Finally, and most importantly, the style has not been particularly successful for those generations of hearing aid dealers who have used it in the past. The method has certainly not resulted in a consumer stampede to purchase and use hearing aids. A more creative approach to marketing seems necessary.

Minimal marketing is the style that most professionals have traditionally used. With this approach, it is assumed that demand for audiology services, for example, will grow simply because they are offered and that new clients will search out the service because of word-of-mouth information about its quality. The assumption is that the product or service stands by itself and is recognized by consumers as being superior. This type of marketing fails, however, when consumers are insensitive to or unaware of quality variations or uninformed about the necessity for a particular quality of service, a situation that surely exists for audiology services. Although the situation has improved somewhat, the great majority of hearing-impaired individuals never seek professional help, and many have never even heard of audiology. The minimal marketing approach will never solve the two greatest problems faced by audiologists: low-visibility and lack of consumer knowledge.

Balanced marketing is an orientation that accepts as its key task the determination of the wants, needs, and values of the consumer, followed by the development of a system to satisfy these needs and values. An active marketing research plan is the first step in this process. The data obtained in the marketing research process lead to the identification of the marketing problems that the private practitioner must address and to the development of specific goals for each target market. Promotional activities and strategies can then be developed for each of these markets. The hallmark of a balanced marketing approach is that it begins with the consumer and ends with the satisfaction of consumer needs.

It seems clear that neither the hard-sell marketing philosophy nor the minimal marketing philosophy can adequately serve the private practitioner. This chapter presents a balanced approach to marketing audiology services in a private practice setting. Within the overall objective of delivering quality services and products to hearing-impaired clients, the careful use of balanced marketing principles should facilitate the exchange process central to the successful development of the practice.

The first step in a balanced marketing program is a series of marketing research tasks, including (1) market identification and segmentation, (2) analysis of the needs of the consumers and referral sources within these markets, (3) analysis of competitors and, finally, (4) analysis of the larger environmental issues—federal, state, and local regulations, for example—that affect the practice and its various markets.

BALANCED MARKETING —A COMPREHENSIVE PHILOSOPHY

Marketing Research

Market Identification and Segmentation

The private practitioner must identify and define the major consumer groups and referral sources with which he or she might possibly interact. *Market segmentation* is the process of dividing a market into homogeneous parts so that a specific part can be selected as a target and reached with a distinctive marketing program. The process may take many forms. For example, geographic segmentation may involve simply identifying potential consumers within a certain geographic radius around an office setting. Demographic segmentation may help identify potential consumers in a certain age group or with a certain income level. Psychographic segmentation may attempt to identify consumers with a certain lifestyle, personality, or stage of readiness for accepting the need for some aspect of hearing health care. Underserved or poorly served segments are thus identified and target markets chosen with the highest response and resource potential. The notion of analyzing response/resource potential of target markets is a crucial one for the private practitioner.

For example, senior citizens might be identified as an underserved market in a particular area. However, because Medicare does not pay for hearing-aid-related services, the practitioner might need to segment a group within the overall market that has other resources with which to pay for hearing aids and aural rehabilitative services. Similarly, a particular physician may be willing to make many referrals to a private practitioner, but if those referrals do not have adequate resources to pay for audiologic services, the market segment cannot be served by the private practitioner unless alternative funding mechanisms can be identified.

Analysis of the resource potential of particular market segments may also lead the practitioner to creative approaches to gain access to resource mechanisms. For example, some public funding programs only pay for audiologic services or hearing aids if they are provided in certain practice settings. A contractual arrangement with an approved setting would allow the audiologist to provide and bill for services that could not be billed from a free-standing private office. The importance of "place" of service delivery is discussed further in a later section of this chapter.

Ideally, the careful delineation of target markets allows the practitioner to concentrate marketing efforts on target market segments where a distinctive contribution can be made, where resource potential is high, and where the market is underserved by existing competitors.

For the private practitioner, consumers represent only one group for which a marketing plan is needed. Referral sources are another "market" group that must be subjected to the same type of analysis and segmentation. The marketing goal of reaching more consumers directly, as well as expanding the referral base of the practice, can best be met when marketing planning includes analysis of both consumers and referral sources. Exhibit 14–1 contains a partial list of referral sources with which the practitioner may wish to interact. Each referral source must be analyzed for its response potential—that is, how many referrals will be made—and for the resource potential of the individuals referred. The reader encountered some of these concepts in Chapter 12.

Consumer and Referral Source Analysis

Once the practitioner has identified those referral sources and consumer groups that appear to have the highest response and resource potential, a more detailed analysis of the needs of each group must be made. For both referral sources and consumer groups, a study of our image to them as professionals would be helpful. Are they aware of us as professionals? How do they see the extent and nature of our training and skills? What educational steps would be most successful in raising the familiarity level of these groups with the role of the audiologist in general and the role of the individual practitioner specifically?

The needs of the identified target markets must be analyzed. For consumers, what variables are determinants of the acceptability of various amplification devices and other rehabilitative measures? What factors determine consumer satisfaction with the services and products provided by the audiologist? Is there a difference between the audiologist's notion of consumer needs and the self-perceived needs of the consumer? What tools can be used to answer these questions?

Standardized measuring devices for this type of consumer analysis do not yet exist, and it is unlikely that the individual practitioner could engage in this type of time-consuming research on a large scale. Yet information is vital for the establishment of an effective marketing program. On a smaller scale, the information obtained in the typical case history interview of a hearing-impaired adult and the information gathered from patients subsequent to hearing aid fitting can serve as the basis for a marketing program. Audiologists generally identify which self- or family-assessed specific needs bring clients to their offices, and they generally evaluate to what degree these needs have been met by the services and products dispensed. To develop individual marketing programs, audiologists must attempt to identify the patterns of con-

---

Exhibit 14–1 Referral Markets

Physicians	Speech-language pathologists
Dentists	Audiologists
School nurses	Industry
Nursing homes	Hospitals
Psychologists	HMOs
Home health agencies	Insurance companies
Lawyers	Committees on the handicapped
Nursery schools	Unions
Social service agencies	School districts
Learning disability specialists	Senior citizen groups
School teachers	

sumer problems and solutions found in their practices and then use these data to reach out to others with similar hearing health needs.

For referral sources, needs assessment can be carried out more easily, because direct questions about needs can be asked of them. Why does a particular physician refer patients to the audiologist? Are referrals made only for hearing aid evaluation and fitting, or does the physician need diagnostic audiology services? What criteria are used to determine when referral to the audiologist is made? What aspects of the audiologist's practice are important to particular referral sources? Is rapid scheduling important? Are timely reports important? Are such operational variables as evening and Saturday hours important? Do physicians perceive the need for special tests, such as BSER and ENG? Answers to this type of question help the practitioner delineate which services and products can best meet the needs of particular referral sources.

Competitor Analysis

Once the practitioner has analyzed the various consumer groups and referral sources identified as important markets, the activities and competences of major competitors in these markets must be examined. How do other agencies and/or businesses provide services to markets identified as important to the practice? What strengths and weaknesses are present in the existing service delivery schema? For example, large bureaucracies tend to have difficulty responding quickly to requests for appointments and in timely reporting of results to referral sources. Institutional settings in which audiologists work are likely to have waiting lists or to schedule appointments far in the future. The hearing-impaired person may not see the same audiologist each time in clinic settings, so the services may be viewed as impersonal. Institutional settings also tend to have inflexible hours of operation. They often do not dispense hearing aids so that consumers have to be referred elsewhere for hearing aid fittings and then return to the agency for follow-up, a back-and-forth process that may be regarded as burdensome by the consumer. Hearing aid dealers may be regarded as too commercial and sales-oriented by the hearing-impaired consumer.

Weaknesses identified in competitors should never be used as marketing devices to encourage consumers or referral sources to use the private practitioner's office. Rather, they should be incorporated into a presentation of the positive aspects of the private practice. That is, instead of telling a physician that the community clinic has a 6-week waiting time for appointments, the practitioner would stress that his or her policy is to schedule patients within 3 days and mail a report within 24 hours after the patient visit.

The private practitioner will find that it is important to interact with competitors on many levels. For example, a private practice setting may compete with a community center for referrals, yet need to cooperate and interact with the agency on other issues. The problem of resentment and jealousy of the private practitioner by fellow audiologists or speech-language pathologists is a very real one and one that may need to be addressed openly if cooperative activities are important to the private practitioner.

Environmental Analysis

The final area of analysis in marketing research is an analysis of the "macroenvironment" in which the private practice exists. The impact of various federal, state, and local regulations on the practitioner's ability to provide services to target markets must be assessed. The impact on the private practice of societal and psychological barriers to hearing health care is another important area of study. For example, the lack of Medicare support for hearing health care is a deterrent to the provision of audiologic services to a prime target market. Medicaid legislation in some states is a major enabler to the provision of services, but often only with regulations that severely restrict the participation of private practitioners. The remarkable resistance to hearing aids that continues to be evidenced by many consumers is related at least partially to societal and psychological attitudes toward aging and toward handicaps. All of these factors can have a major impact on the private practice and must be incorporated into the overall marketing plan if the audiologist determines that these factors operate negatively in a particular practice area.

Marketing Problems

Identifying Problems

One of the major purposes of the marketing research process described above is to help the practitioner identify the marketing problems that must be solved. The data obtained allow the audiologist to define marketing goals and tasks that address each marketing "problem." For example, an identified problem might be that hearing-impaired consumers in a particular target market group view hearing aids and related services negatively. The overall goal, then, would be to make the purchase and use of hearing aids and related rehabilitative services more acceptable in the consumers' mind than living with the disadvantage of a hearing loss. A series of marketing tasks would be developed to accomplish this goal, with steps built in to analyze the effectiveness of the tasks.

Identifying Demand States

Kotler (1975) has identified three basic demand states that can exist for a service or a product: underdemand, adequate demand, and overdemand. The underdemand state can be further broken down into negative demand, no demand, latent demand, and faltering demand states. Negative demand is the state in which many market segments dislike the product or service and may pay a high "price" to avoid it. In the no demand state, the market is uninterested, uninformed, or indifferent to an offered service or product. Latent demand is a condition where a market can benefit from a product, but either the product does not exist or its existence is not known to the market. Faltering demand occurs when a demand for a product or service has decreased below its former levels.

The marketing of products and services, such as audiology and hearing aid dispensing services, is at once similar to and different from business marketing. It is in uncharted territory, and little collective wisdom exists. It is reasonable to believe, however, that our marketing task is sufficiently different from business marketing to require fresh thinking and new approaches. One of the major differences is that marketing such services as hearing health care services involves core beliefs and values, rather than simply the more superficial preferences and opinions to which business marketing analysts relate.

For both the product (hearing aids) and services (evaluations, counseling, or therapy) provided in a private practice, underdemand is the state that appears to fit best. Unfortunately, in far too many areas, the marketing problem for the audiologist can be described by saying that we must often deal with a state of negative demand for the product and a state of no demand for the services we offer. These two demand states represent the most difficult marketing problems to solve. If these are the demand states that exist in a particular practice area, the marketer's task is to consider how the rewards of purchasing a negative demand product or service can be increased relative to its perceived negative costs or how to reduce the perceived negative costs.

For some of our referral sources, latent demand may be the best description of the marketing problem faced, i.e., physicians, industries, and schools may need audiologic services, but may not be sufficiently aware of the need. The marketing task in this instance would be to create that awareness using a variety of marketing tools. Specific examples are discussed in the "Marketing Mix" section of this chapter.

Audiologists in private practice must analyze sources of resistance in their various markets. Both consumers and referral sources may have negative attitudes and thus resistance to utilizing the services offered by the practice. Negative attitudes and resistance must be countered by the marketing plan that is devised. *Evaluating Sources of Resistance*

Consumer Resistance. Again, little formal data exist about the hearing-impaired consumer and the factors that encourage some to seek audiologic services and hearing aid fitting while others do not. Even less is known about the knowledge base of the general public with respect to hearing health care, hearing aids, appropriate personnel and their role in hearing health care, hearing loss, and the like. Empirically, however, consumer resistance can be discussed in at least four categories: lack of information and misinformation, negative experiences, psychological fears and expense.

1. *Lack of information and misinformation.* Many hearing-impaired consumers lack even the most basic information about hearing health care. They may never have heard the word "audiologist" until referred to one by their physician. They do not know the difference between an audiologist and commercial hearing aid salespeople. They generally do not understand their hearing loss and why it imposes communication difficulty. They may have been told that hearing aids cannot help "nerve deafness." Many know nothing at all about hearing aids or how they work. Although the visibility of President Reagan's hearing aids has helped, the author continues to encounter far too many consumers who believe that all hearing aids have cords and wires or who are surprised that hearing aids require something to be placed in the ear. Many have unrealistic notions about the benefits of amplification and feel that a hearing aid will solve all their communication problems. This incomplete list of some areas of resistance helps practitioners appreciate the scope of the marketing task before them. It is important for the audiologist to remember that quality services are only marketable if the difference between quality and poor services is apparent to the consumer. For that reason, information about the training and expertise of the audiologist and the relationship between that training and the needs of the hearing-impaired consumer must be built into the marketing plan.

2. *Negative experiences*. Most older people know someone who has purchased a hearing aid and has not been able to wear it. Some have themselves worn aids and discarded them because they were unsuitable. Some may have been turned off by the type of advertising done by commercial hearing aid dealers. Many are openly skeptical about the effectiveness of hearing aids. Such negative experiences and attitudes as these complicate the already difficult task of the practitioner in countering past experiences.

3. *Psychological factors*. These factors represent a powerful source of resistance. Hearing aids are associated with aging or with severe handicaps. People worry that other people will see their aid and know that they have difficulty hearing. They worry about the cosmetic aspects of hearing aids. Basically, everyone wants an aid that is invisible, but will still solve all of their communication difficulties. These psychological factors add significantly to the "costs" of obtaining hearing health care services. In fact, it is this type of cost that makes the hearing-impaired listener particularly resistant to aural rehabilitation services. The psychological cost of using a hearing aid must be accounted for by any marketing effort made by the practice.

4. *Cost factors*. The purchase of one or two hearing aids represents a significant outlay of money for the hearing-impaired consumer. Poor third party coverage, and especially the lack of Medicare reimbursement for hearing aids and related services, causes significant hardship for many individuals. The monetary cost, combined with the heavy psychological cost of hearing aids, is a double resistance factor that must be addressed by a comprehensive marketing plan.

Referral Source Resistance. Many audiology services must be marketed to a variety of referral sources, rather than directly to consumers. Marketing efforts for diagnostic services, such as evoked response audiometry or tympanometry, will always be directed at other professionals. The resistance factors in various referral markets need careful analysis and can be grouped into five general categories: lack of information or misinformation, fear of competition, hearing-aid-related resistance, previously established referral patterns, and bureaucratic barriers.

1. *Lack of information or misinformation*. Referral sources—physicians, social workers, and the like—may lack information about the extent and nature of audiologic services. They may know little about our training. They may have arbitrarily set criteria for the age at which reliable test results can be obtained. They may not realize that audiologists dispense hearing aids; they may be unaware that audiologists provide rehabilitative therapy; they may feel that audiologists are needed only for "difficult" hearing aid fittings and may have their own criteria for what constitutes a "difficult" case. They may assume that private audiology services are very expensive and that therefore hearing aid costs would be higher than those in commercial hearing aid stores.

2. *Fear of competition and jealousy*. A far too common observation by audiologists in private practice is that referrals seldom come from their own professional colleagues. For purposes of referral for hearing aid fittings,

dispensing audiologists are often listed together with commercial hearing aid salespeople. Consumers are frequently advised by nondispensing audiologists to do comparison shopping for hearing aids, rather than told to consider the extent and nature of the training of the dispenser. Fears that the private practitioner will take clients away from the clinic are pervasive. Negative attitudes toward private practitioners are still prevalent in our profession, and those attitudes can interfere with cooperative referral patterns between agency-based audiologists and private practitioners. Physicians may fear that the audiologist is trying to bypass the physician's input. These attitudes must all be actively addressed by the marketing plan.

3. *Hearing-aid-related resistance.* Physicians and other referral sources may lack information or have misinformation about hearing aids and hearing aid candidacy. They may believe that hearing aids are not helpful for losses under 40 dBHL, for high frequency losses, for low frequency losses, or for "nerve" deafness. They may be unaware of advances and improvements in hearing aid fittings. They may approach hearing aid referrals with the same biases as those held by consumers. Physicians, especially non-otolaryngologists, often tell older patients that hearing loss is part of the aging process and must be accepted. They often actively discourage elderly people from considering amplification because of negative experiences that other patients may have had. The marketing plan must include devices that first allow the practitioner to determine the physician's referral policy and then allow systematic efforts to change those policies.

4. *Previously established referral patterns.* When an audiologist opens a practice in an area where long-standing referral patterns already exist for audiological services or hearing aid services, several marketing problems exist. All of the problems related to misinformation discussed in the previous paragraph exist. In addition, referral sources must be made aware of the new practice and of its unique characteristics. The temptation to use "negative" marketing techniques, e.g., pointing out the problems that exist with the current referral pattern should be avoided. Rather, the practitioner must carefully analyze the needs of referral sources and their clients. The marketing program would then be designed to inform referral sources about the advantages offered by the new practice to both them and their clients. These advantages may center around extended hours, evening or Saturday hours, promptly scheduled appointments, timely reports, or other practice management techniques designed for the convenience of referral sources.

5. *Bureaucratic barriers.* The private practitioner frequently encounters situations where various professionals may be perfectly willing and anxious to refer patients, but find bureaucratic or regulatory barriers to private referrals. Federal, state, and local regulations may limit or define strictly where audiologic evaluations may be performed to be eligible for third party reimbursement, and private offices are often excluded. If this type of referral represents a large and important market for the private practitioner, ways to eliminate bureaucratic barriers must be sought. Various contractual relationships with

publicly funded agencies sometimes eliminate reimbursement barriers, because charges are not billed for individual cases. Instead, the audiologist may agree to provide a certain number of hours of service to a particular agency and bill the agency for those hours. The important point here is that, if entry into the reimbursement system cannot be found for a particular market, the private practitioner must devote marketing energy to other more fruitful avenues.

SETTING OBJECTIVES

The identification and analysis of the marketing problems faced by the private practitioner allow the audiologist to set specific objectives for each market that meet the response/resource criteria described earlier in this chapter. Marketing professionals advise that each objective be clearly stated in a manner that allows careful planning of marketing activities and the objective measurement of the effectiveness of the marketing plan. The ultimate objective, of course, is to increase referrals from those markets identified as important to the practice, but interim objectives should be listed that lead to those increased referrals.

For example, if the practitioner has determined that internists see large numbers of older patients and wants to increase the number of referrals for both diagnostic audiology and hearing aid evaluations, objectives might include (1) to increase internists' awareness of the hearing health problems of their elderly patients; (2) to increase internists' awareness of advances in amplification; and (3) to increase internists' knowledge base of audiologic procedures, such as tympanometry and BSER. A marketing plan would be devised for each of these objectives, ideally one that allows the audiologist to measure the effects of each activity toward meeting the overall objective.

MARKETING ACTIVITIES

Having identified various target markets and set objectives for each of these markets, the audiologist's next task is to identify the marketing instruments to be used to reach target markets. Marketing managers classify these activities as the four Ps: product, price, place, and promotion.

Product refers to the total package of products and services to be offered to the consumer or to a referral source. A product is made up of (a) the tangible product (the service or product itself); (b) the core product (what the consumer is really buying, e.g., the hearing-impaired consumer who purchases a hearing aid hopes to be purchasing greater ease of communication; and (c) the augmented product (total benefits and costs incurred by the consumer when the product is obtained). The product/service package delivered to the consumer or referral source varies according to the needs identified by marketing research. For example, for the consumer, what is being marketed is hearing health care and ease of communication. The package includes the hearing aid itself and a host of related diagnostic and fitting services. For a particular referral source, what is being marketed is assistance in diagnostic and management efforts for patients. The package may include a variety of diagnostic procedures, as well as assurance of rapid communication of test results and implications.

Price is the cost the buyer must accept in order to obtain the product. It includes money costs, psychological costs, and energy costs. The marketer/audiologist must consider how the rewards for purchasing the product can be increased relative to costs or how costs can be reduced relative to reward. Placing a monetary cost on a product/ service package, such as audiologic and hearing-aid-related services, is complex. Pricing objectives must be decided; that is, a price may be designed to maximize profit, to recover cost, or to provide incentives to a particular market segment. In this regard, the audiologist might decide to set a fee for the initial audiologic evaluation that simply recovers costs as an incentive to encourage older consumers to consider amplification. The fee for the hearing aid and fitting follow-up services might then be set not only to recover costs but also to make a profit.

Pricing is considered a marketing activity because it is a powerful communication tool to the various publics with which the audiologist in private practice interacts. The importance of price as a marketing activity should give pause to audiologists who offer professional services ''free'' as a way to attract consumers. ''Free'' services may be viewed by consumers as having little value, and recommendations made for hearing aid purchases may be viewed with suspicion when they follow a ''free'' evaluation.

Place refers to the distribution plans developed to make products and services available to various market segments. It means developing an effective hearing health care delivery system. For some market segments, bringing services to them is more efficient than attempting to bring the consumer to a central location. Part of the product may be delivered in one place—screening in a retirement home, for example—whereas the remainder of the services can be delivered at the practice setting. Place refers also to the accessibility of the site for service delivery—its proximity to target markets and referral sources. A marketing campaign should suggest clear steps to be taken in order to obtain offered products or services.

The final ''P'' refers to *promotion* decisions, a blend of persuasive communication instruments that include advertising, public relations, and personal contact. Advertising is any form of paid presentation of products and/or services. Public relations includes any form of unpaid activity designed to promote a favorable relationship with the public. Personal contact or personal selling refers to the overall image created by the individual private practitioner.

The final section of this chapter discusses promotional activities in greater detail. The practitioners' task is to choose an effective blend of activities taking monetary and time costs of various promotional devices into account.

THE MARKETING MIX

Advertising

As discussed in Chapter 9, advertising tools include radio, newspaper, television, posters, sales literature, office brochures, business cards, mailings, and Yellow Page listings. It is an expensive promotional activity and can represent a sizable portion of the practice's budget.

In the author's experience, newspaper advertising, which can take many forms, is not particularly effective. Informational columns can be written about hearing loss, hearing aids, or other aspects of hearing health care. Announcements can be placed that simply list the name of the private practice, the services provided, and the hours. Finally, ads can take the form of more aggressive, hard-sell promotional devices. However, to be even minimally effective, newspaper ads must be repeated regularly and often. The amount and frequency of advertising that is required to make a particular private practitioner a household word are probably beyond the budget means of most audiologists.

The author has experimented with radio advertising aimed at the families of hearing impaired consumers, again with minimal effectiveness. However, printed materials, including business cards, appointment cards, appointment reminder postcards, and informational literature about hearing aids, have proved useful for many purposes. Several business cards are sent periodically to all referral sources along with a letter suggesting that they call if more are needed. Informational literature about hearing aids is given to every person seen for diagnostic audiology prior to hearing aid fitting. Patients are encouraged to share these brochures with their friends and to take more than one.

Probably the single most effective paid advertising is the listing in the Yellow Pages, which is again an expensive form of advertising. A practice can be listed in several places: under Hearing Aids, Audiologists, Speech Pathologists, and Speech and Hearing Clinics. Although none of the author's patients has ever said that he or she called for an appointment because of a newspaper or radio ad, several have said that they got the author's name from the Yellow Pages. In all likelihood, if an individual decided that it was time to get a hearing aid, he or she would check the Yellow Pages before checking to see if any hearing aid ads were in the evening newspaper. Another reason that newspaper advertising may be inefficient is that audiology is simply not a familiar enough discipline to the general or the hearing-impaired public. Local advertising would probably be much more effective if it were done against a background of frequent national, large-scale advertising attempts that served to create a general awareness about audiology and hearing health care in the public. The ASHA and our various state and local professional organizations should be encouraged to budget funds for organized advertising campaigns.

Public Relations   Public relations activities include human interest or informative articles published by a newspaper, public service lectures, workshops, in-services, demonstrations, such community service events as health fairs, and TV or radio public service broadcasts. Although these activities do not usually cost money, they can take a heavy toll on the private practitioner in time and preparation. In the author's experience, public relations activities are an effective and ongoing necessity in the daily running of the practice. Exhibit 14–2 lists some public relations activities that are useful to a private practice. Again, these activities should be designed to address the marketing problems and objectives identified in the marketing audit. It is useful to set a separate goal of engaging in a specified number of public relations activities each month. These activities are an excellent way to keep the private practitioner visible to both selected consumers and referral sources.

Exhibit 14–2 Public Relations Activities

Public library lectures	Radio talk programs
Hospital health tapes	Cable TV programs
Newspaper stories	Inservices
Health fairs	Nursing homes
Letters to editor and editorials	Hospital staff
Newsletters for patients and selected	Nursery teachers
referral sources	Private schools
Hospital lecture series on various	Public school staff
hearing and communication health	Nursery school parents night
topics	Maternity/childbirth classes
Speaking engagements to:	Demonstration days (devices for the hearing
Professional organizations	impaired)
Service clubs	Medical society
Chamber of Commerce	Writing of communication health series for
Dental society	local newspaper
Chiropractors' meetings	Workshops on testing for school nurses
Founding of support clubs for:	Courses for senior citizens at community
Parents of hearing impaired	college or adult education
Parents of disabled	Workshop for nurses in ENT/pediatrician's
Stroke clubs	offices on hearing testing or impedance
Laryngectomy clubs	

Personal Contact/ Personal Selling

Personal selling refers to the overall image created by the private practitioner and the methods used to convey that image personally. It includes attitude, appearance, and demeanor—the atmosphere created by the practitioner's approach to his or her profession. It is the single most important day-to-day promotional activity in which the private practitioner engages. In this regard, the audiologist must decide what personal image should be conveyed and which daily activities will promote the desired image. In general, the private practitioner does well to convey a professional image. It goes without saying that the practitioner must be knowledgeable about every aspect of the practice, but decisiveness and confidence must also be communicated to patients and referral sources. The private practitioner must be personable and involved with the hearing health needs of his or her patients.

To this end, a number of office procedures are helpful. It is important to be straightforward about your procedures and fees. The patient should be made aware of the various treatment options available, but the private practitioner should state his or her recommendations with conviction. Patients have come for advice from a professional, and it should be given. Office staff should be carefully trained about the needs of hearing-impaired people in general, especially the various ways to maximize communication on the telephone and in conversation with patients. Personal touches, such as calling a patient the second day a hearing aid is worn to make sure everything is all right, go a long way toward promoting the practice.

As noted in other chapters, it is useful to call the physician immediately after a diagnostic visit to let him or her know the overall results and then to follow the phone call with a brief, clear, helpful report in the next day or two. It is as important to write reports thanking an audiologist for a referral as it is to thank a physician. Set an example by referring to colleagues for second opinions in difficult-to-test cases or for special skills not available in your practice.

Finally, the most useful and productive attitude to convey is an attitude of joy in one's work and confidence in oneself as a professional. It is critical for the private practitioner to remember that the best promotion for the practice is the day-to-day personal contact with patients and referral sources. These daily activities serve as a foundation and backdrop for all other promotional activities.

SUMMARY

A comprehensive marketing program is essential for the private practitioner. Marketing is not a series of add-on activities, but, rather, represents an overall approach toward the practice's goals. A comprehensive marketing program ensures a consumer needs orientation aimed at generating satisfaction for both consumers and referral sources, thus promoting the long-term health of the private practice.

REFERENCE

Kotler, P. (1975). Marketing for nonprofit organizations. Englewood Cliffs, NJ: Prentice-Hall.

SUGGESTED READINGS

Cooper, P.E. (Ed.). (1979). *Health care marketing—Issues and trends*. Rockville, MD: Aspen Systems Corporation.

Kotler, P., & Zaltman, G. (1971). Social marketing: An approach to planned social change. *Journal of Marketing, 35*, 3–12.

Rothschild, M.L. (1979). Marketing communications in nonbusiness situations or why it's so hard to sell brotherhood like soap. *Journal of Marketing, 43*, 11–20.

Part IV

Personal and Professional Strategies: Advanced Considerations

Chapter 15

Planning for Personal Financial Success

Joseph F. Butler, M.A.

As a successful private practice grows, it develops a separate set of problems revolving around the proper usage of retained earnings from profitable operations. For instance, it is quite normal for a small firm to maintain an amount equal to 1- to 3-months operating expense in its checking account. This amount might provide instant access to pay bills and be used in case of need during unexpected emergencies. However, keeping amounts larger than this in a checking account leads to interest insufficiencies that increase dramatically as those amounts rise. It makes little sense to work hard to obtain such funds in the first place and then to allow that money to become "lazy" in a checking account, which pays a low interest rate compared with other potential investments.

Before considering any financial investment, it is important for the speech-language pathologist or audiologist in private practice to evaluate the need for insurance against unexpected, prolonged loss of "key" personnel. Key staff members are those who actually render the service for which the practice charges its patients; they include the practice owner and such employees whose services are critical to the operation of the practice. In the case of long illness or disablement of any key person, could the practice continue to pay salaries and sustain itself? Because practice income totally depends on services being constantly rendered and key-person term insurance is fairly inexpensive, it would appear to be a wise basic investment. Therefore, first thoughts on investment should be centered on protecting the practitioner against personnel emergencies. Going without such protection, while making other investments, would appear to be an unjustifiable risk.

A second area for preinvestment consideration is that of retirement plans. Both individual retirement accounts (IRAs) and Keogh plans are available to self-employed persons for sheltering income from taxes until age 59½ or older. If possible, setting up either or both of these plans is highly recommended. Not only do they provide convenient tax-free ways to save but also funds in such accounts themselves provide unique investment opportunities. These funds remain under practitioner control for investment even though they are sheltered from taxes. Therefore, once established, such funds can be placed to produce maximum long-term returns, using the same techniques as those employed with other investments.

INITIAL INVESTMENT CONSIDERATIONS

It is the purpose of this chapter to outline various methods and procedures that the practitioner may use to increase the efficient investment of available surplus capital. A word here about minimum amounts to invest. Small investments tend to increase the risk of loss, because they restrict the number of stocks or other securities in a given portfolio. As investment advisor Dr. James B. Cloonan (1984) points out, risk analysis over the past 50 years in stock market activity has shown that "the purchaser of a single stock is taking three times the risk necessary as compared to having a diversified portfolio" (p. 5).

Hence, one should have at least $9,000–$10,000 in surplus capital before attempting to set up an investment program. That much is needed to buy three or more investments in a beginning diversified portfolio, thereby controlling the potential for unsystematic loss that occurs when a portfolio contains only a single investment.

By definition, the term "practitioner" is meant to cover many different types of private practice operators, from those who engage in solo practice or part-time practitioners who operate from their homes, to those who work as part of a clinical team in a medical setting, or still others who maintain highly equipped offices with from 1 to 60 employees. The term "equipment" is used to include reception and inner office furniture, copy machines, computers, typewriters, calculators, tape recorders, audiometers, and all other types of speech-language-hearing clinical instrumentation, including such items as specially equipped vans for screening at industrial plants and school districts.

The following comments about choosing potential investments are not meant to replace the helpful assistance of accountants, lawyers, or certified financial planners. These professionals are generally needed to create forms, documents, or tactical arrangements to fit specific individual requirements, particularly those involving special tax considerations. Instead, this chapter deals with investments in the broader framework of planning.

INVESTMENT STRATEGIES

An important part of beginning an investment program is to decide the strategy to be employed. Neither the size of an investment nor its required term will change a well-founded investment strategy because value is judged on three main axioms:

1. The investment should return the highest interest rate available,
2. . . . in the shortest period of time, and
3. . . . with the least chance of loss within an acceptable risk range.

Operating within these three principles, one of the first steps in establishing a strategy to increase return on invested funds is to set up both short-term and long-term logical goals. Is there a special purpose for which these funds are eventually going to be used? Perhaps the goal might be a comfortable retirement income, a new residence, or other acquisitions. Another logical long-term goal might be to use investment funds to enlarge the physical clinical capacity of an office, thereby increasing its income-producing ability.

In general, accurate analysis is obviously part of long-range investment plans, including the anticipated effect of inflation on costs as well as profits during the time estimated for logical completion of the plan. However, desirable as it is to anticipate these costs, some of them are bound to be difficult to predict accurately. For example, even minor inaccuracies that are projected over a period of years lead to eventual gross errors on which investment plans should not be based. Therefore, long-range planning cannot extend beyond perhaps 5 years without inviting a high probability of unreliable initial assumptions. Still, within a 5-year limit on long-term planning, there is a good opportunity to focus short-term investment activity on the accomplishment of well-analyzed, logical, and targeted long-term goals.

A second point about long-term goals is that they must be flexible. Every goal must be periodically evaluated as to its continuing validity. For example, to maintain a long-term goal assuming a 5 percent inflation rate, when the actual rate may be substantially higher or lower than that, is confusing and misleading. Therefore, a part of long-range goal setting is at least yearly review and error correction to retarget the goal more accurately or perhaps even to change it entirely. As the old saying goes, "Time changes everything," and those who attempt long-term planning cannot ignore it. However, as shall be seen, long-term planning provides the platform for selecting short-term targets.

SHORT-TERM INVESTMENTS

By definition, short-term investments generally are completed within a year or less. There are numerous investment vehicles available with 30-day, 90-day, or annual maturities. Many others can be bought or sold with weekly, daily, or indeterminate short due dates. These are particularly attractive in periods of economic uncertainty, especially when near-term prices are expected to rise. Because short-term funds are not tied up very long, there is minimum time exposure for being at risk for significant loss. Also, when these short-term investments mature, greater economic certainty may exist, or higher interest rates may be available to improve reinvestment yields.

However, drawbacks to short-term investing also must be taken into consideration. As a general rule, the longer an investment takes to return the amount invested plus interest, the higher interest rate such an investment will pay. Conversely, the shorter time an investment takes to return the invested amount plus interest, the lower the interest rate. For example, a 1-year Treasury Bill might pay interest at the rate of 8 to 9 percent, whereas a 30-day Treasury Bill sold on that same day might pay 6 to 7 percent. Therefore, short-term investors who select the 30-day Treasury Bill are either uncertain about the future, or they believe interest rates will rise. Either way, they have an opportunity to reinvest under different risk conditions in a shorter time period. Although they take less chance on being wrong, they receive a lower interest rate for that privilege. On the other hand, long-term investors who select the 1-year Treasury Bill either believe interest rates may go down or that the extra interest that a long-term investment pays is worth the longer-term loss risk.

As a corollary, it should be remembered that almost every transaction requires payment of commission to either a broker or an underwriter. Because short-term investments require more transactions, they cost more than long-term investments in total commissions paid, even further diminishing lower short-term returns. Thus, the investor must consider all aspects of the investment process, including the financial details, and then weigh the rewards against the risks.

PERSONAL FINANCIAL PLANNING AND SETTING LONG-RANGE GOALS

The setting of long-range targets depends to a great degree on thorough knowledge of a person's or practice's present financial status. To this end, it is necessary to take an inventory of current assets and the rate of return they presently produce. Current assets include those items previously described as equipment that are used in the practice to render services to clients. Lists of assets are commonly maintained by a practice's accountant, and when a new piece of equipment is purchased, it is added to the asset list. Assets also include land, buildings, accounts receivable, inventories of stationery and janitorial supplies, and perhaps, unamortized organizational expenses, such as legal costs of forming a corporation. Adding these together provides an up-to-date total of funds invested in the practice. When the total is divided into the amount of net profit generated by the practice during the year, the result is the percentage of return on investment (ROI).

ROI is highly dependent on the combined effect of local, state, and federal tax laws on practice income. This creates a continuing need for legal interpretation of the current and future impact of such tax laws on daily operation of the practice and of investing. For example, regulations affecting depreciation of business equipment were frequently changed via congressional legislation during the 1970s and 1980s. In addition, many local and state legislatures also changed portions of their laws applying to depreciation as an incentive to business and industry to remain in their local area and to update old equipment, thereby increasing the property tax base and helping the area economy grow. When such laws as these are changed, they often offer unique investment opportunities for a practitioner who keeps abreast of them in news reports and then checks with a local attorney or CPA on how best to apply them in an investment plan.

Although seeking legal or financial advice may involve added expense, this kind of advice typically pays for itself by focusing investment attention on the most productive targets, rather than relying on tips from friends, guesswork, or solely on broker recommendations. Also, legal/financial counsel can help a practitioner avoid procedural mistakes that might result in wasted time, effort, or financial loss. In short, the tax advantage of investing in the right target and at the right time is too important to the practitioner's investment strategy to avoid at least some professional help, especially in the beginning.

Once an investment strategy is defined, it requires a systematic approach for effective application. Consider the following example of how a visit with the accountant offers help in carrying out an investment strategy designed to increase present return on investment (ROI):

THE USE OF
SYSTEMS IN
FINANCIAL
PLANNING
AND INVEST-
MENT

1. At the beginning of the meeting the accountant states that the practice produces a rate of 10 percent ROI, or for every $100 invested in practice assets, $10 profit remains each year after expenses.
2. The accountant then recommends that the practitioner use the figure of 10 percent ROI as the target rate against which all other potential investments must be measured. If a potential investment promises to exceed this return, it qualifies for investment under this strategy. If the return is less than 10 percent per year, it does not qualify. To illustrate, suppose that the following situation exists:
   (a) The Standard & Poor (S&P) 500 Stock Index is rising at an annual rate of 7.2 percent.
   (b) One-year Treasury Bills are paying 9.9 percent.
   (c) Long-term government bonds are increasing in value at the rate of 14.5 percent per year.
3. Obviously, the practitioner seeking to improve ROI would not choose investment in a general stock fund, such as the S&P Stock Index, because it currently pays less than 10 percent. Neither would Treasury Bills be chosen because they also pay less than 10 percent. However, long-term government bonds would offer an investment opportunity because they promise a return at current market price of well over 10 percent annually.
4. Not only does the practitioner have investment choices, such as those in (a), (b), and (c) above, but also he or she has the option of added investment in the practice itself that could potentially produce more than a 10 percent annual profit on its cost. Such items as new equipment purchase, additions to the office, and the like can all be judged by the same 10 percent rule for viability in the investment plan.

ROI is only one of many different tests that help qualify various investment options for purchase under the overall investment strategy. As stated previously, each of these investments has its own degree of risk. The higher the risk, the greater the promised return. Therefore, as financial columnist Susan Bondy (1985) wisely points out, an investor needs to do some "soul-searching" as to the level of risk with which he or she can feel comfortable. *Every* investment has some potential for being worth less at the end of the time it is held than it was at the start. The degree of that likelihood (or risk) can, and should be, carefully determined for each of the various investments available to the practitioner.

Typically, risk levels are expressed in terms that compare an investment's historic price volatility to that of the market as a whole. For example, the term "Beta" is used to refer to a stock's price fluctuations compared to those of the total market. If an investment has a Beta rating of 1, it tends to move in price at about the same rate as the total market, which always has a 1 Beta rating. However, if an investment has a Beta of 0.5 or 0.6, it tends to move upward or downward in price at approximately half the overall market average. Low Betas are usually attached to such investments as shares of ponderous blue chip companies. Betas as high as 3 or 4 may be assigned to highly speculative shares of companies with uncertain records in the areas of profits, growth, or both. A higher Beta means a higher risk level, but also a potentially higher rate of return. This is especially true with investments in stock of new or emerging companies offering recently marketed products or services.

There is a secondary risk involved with the purchase of securities. It is the risk of the market itself. The general stock market rises and falls regularly, taking all stocks and their individual Betas with it. Cloonan (1984) points out that approximately 30 percent of the investment risk in stocks is attributable to the general market, and the remaining 70 percent risk is attached to the individual stocks themselves. Thus, the inherent overall risk of stock market investment must be considered, in addition to the particular stock's Beta, in order to form a realistic appraisal of total risk when buying or selling stocks in an investment portfolio.

A third influence on risk is the term of investment. Because, as previously stated, there is less risk in a short-term investment, total risk assessment must also consider the length of time an investment needs to be held in order to create a targeted ROI. For example, there is almost no risk associated with the purchase of short-term Treasury securities bearing maturities of less than a year. The ROI is virtually guaranteed because other interest rates usually do not change radically during such a short period. However, 30-year Treasury bonds have a great deal of risk because other interest rates can change markedly within that space of time. If interest rates rise 3 or 4 percent, the market value of all long-term bonds, including treasuries, will plunge. On the other hand, if interest rates drop, market price for these long-term bonds will soar much higher than the original price, obviously affecting potential returns to investors.

THE INVEST-MENT PORT-FOLIO

The key to avoiding unnecessary risk is diversification of the investment portfolio, i.e. spreading the total investment among many alternative choices. There is no unique universal blending of certain types of stocks, real estate, or long-term versus short-term bonds, to diversify every portfolio ideally. Each investor's personal risk tolerance and tax exposure are sufficiently different to call for special treatment, behooving that investor to adopt systematic methods of portfolio evaluation, particularly at time when major decisions on further investments are made. A flow chart of investment decision making is illustrated in Figure 15–1.

In step 1 of the flow chart, the investor reviews the overall risk level of noninvested cash currently held. Step 2 calls on the investor to check any needs for additional funding from areas, such as emergency cash reserves (3) or regular income (4), that might limit investment of surplus capital at this time. After these are considered, step 5 asks the investor to set a target budget for any unencumbered surplus cash. Then, an assessment is made of market risk level (6), which includes the most recent trends in interest rates (7) and price trends in the market itself (8). This assessment may result in an inclination toward either a short-term or a long-term investment strategy decision in step 9. In step 10, the present portfolio is examined as to the

Figure 15–1 Investment Decision Flow Chart

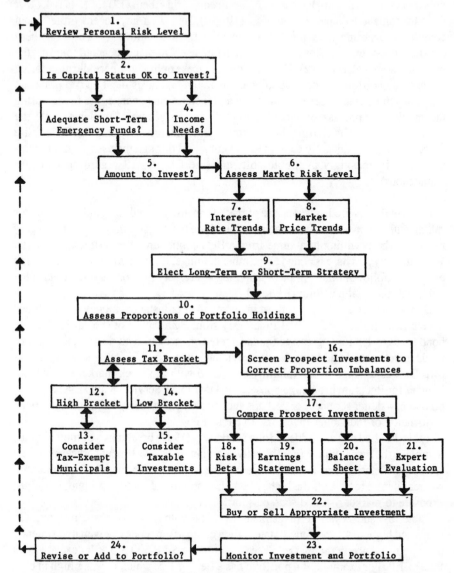

Source: From "Building a Portfolio: How To Answer the Question of Proportions" by J. Markese, 1985, *AAII Journal, 7,* 35. Copyright August 1985 by American Association of Individual Investors. Adapted by permission.

balance of market value between the various investment target categories and the overall portfolio Beta. This step must be taken in conjunction with personal tax considerations, such as (11) the investor's marginal income tax bracket. If additional income will be taxed at 30 percent or more (12), then (13) the investor may wish to consider tax-exempt municipal investments. If under 30 percent (14), then taxable offerings may be better (15) for total investment return. At this point the investor screens the available investment prospects (16) for their ability to correct any imbalances found in step 10, simultaneously comparing them (17) for Beta risk (18), their fundamental financial condition (19, 20), and with any recent professional comments regarding their individual potential for the future (21). After all these considerations, the investor buys or sells the investment that appears to improve the portfolio target balances (22). In the following weeks or months, periodic monitoring of the entire portfolio is continued, including individual investment market price and any change in Beta risk level (23). When and if significant changes are found during the monitoring process or when new surplus cash becomes available (24), the portfolio is revised by starting the investment decision process again (1). This entire process can be significantly expedited and enhanced through the use of a microcomputer and increasingly available software (see Chapter 13 regarding software applications).

The Use of Betas as Decision Guides

Because Beta is used as a measure of risk, it can also be used as a guide to buying or selling within a portfolio. With each new purchase the investor may select the level of risk he or she is willing to assume from a Beta continuum of investment offerings. When the new purchase is added to the other holdings, it changes the Beta value of the overall portfolio. Similarly, sale of a holding with a very high or very low Beta value influences the total portfolio risk level.

Beta values are available for most investments. For instance, money market funds have a Beta of 0.0, and mutual funds vary from Beta values of 0.3 for high-grade bond funds to 1.5 for aggressive funds targeted on growth, with many other types of funds in between. In addition, each individual stock, bond, or other security has its own Beta as a gauge of its volatility compared with the stock market as a whole. Sources for Betas are brokerage houses, the Dow Jones Service, Value Line Service, private newsletter services, or perhaps such individual associations as the American Association of Individual Investors, to name a few.

Table 15–1 adapts and adds to John Markese's (1985) breakdown of mutual funds to provide the reader with a representative continuum of investment choices and their respective Betas. Items 1 and 2 represent the low-risk extreme of the continuum, whereas item 8 represents the highest risk. Investor use of such a continuum to adjust exposure to market risk is discussed shortly.

Table 15-1 shows various investments available with Beta levels ranging from zero to 1.5 and higher. As previously stated, Beta comparison relates a given investment's price performance in the marketplace to that of the S&P 500 Stock Index, always a Beta of 1.0. For example, if a portfolio has a Beta of 1.5, which is rather high in both volatility and risk, this means that the portfolio will on average move up 50 percent more than the market when the market rises, and it will drop 50 percent more than the market during a market descent. On the other hand, a portfolio with a Beta of 0.5 would average 50 percent less movement than the stock index in either direction.

There is also a definite relationship between Beta levels and investment terms. In general, a higher Beta level calls for a longer investment term, whereas low Betas are best for short-term investments. Therefore, during times of economic uncertainty, an investor might move out of an aggressive-growth mutual fund (Beta 1.5) and into

Table 15–1 Continuum of Investment Risk Alternatives by Beta Averages

Investment	Description	Beta Range	Midpoint
Treasury Notes	Short-term obligations of government. No risk. Little price change.	—	0.0
Money Market Fund	Invests in large bank Certificates of Deposit and government/corporate short-term notes. Little risk and negligible price change.	—	0.0
Mutual Bond Fund	Invests in corporate and municipal bonds, the prices of which rise and fall with the market, but much less than do stocks. Low to moderate risk, price change, growth potential, and return.	0.3 to 0.5	0.4
Mutual Income Fund	A mixture of stocks and bonds that pays high dividends, with or without major price changes. Moderate risk and growth potential. Good return.	0.5 to 0.7	0.6
Mutual Balanced, or Growth-Income Fund	A mix of common stocks, bonds, and preferred stocks, targeted at a balance between dividends and capital gains. Moderate risk, price change, growth potential, and return.	0.7 to 0.9	0.8
Mutual Growth or Long-Term Growth Fund	Combination of common stocks and stock options in companies with rising earnings, mostly aimed at capital appreciation, rather than dividends. Statistically often matches the stock market average.	0.9 to 1.1	1.0
Standard & Poor 500 Stock Index	Stock market average price.	—	1.0
Mutual Aggressive Growth or Maximum-Capital-Gain Fund	Shares of smaller companies with high potential for growth, but subject to volatile price change. Also, borrowed money often used to enlarge investment results. Higher-than-average market risk and potential return.	1.1 to 1.5	1.3

Source: From "Building a Portfolio: How To Answer the Question of Proportions" by J. Markese, 1985, *AAII Journal, 7,* 34. Copyright August 1985 by American Association of Individual Investors. Adapted by permission.

---

either a money market fund or Treasury notes (both with Betas of zero), thereby decreasing exposure to risk. When economic prospects begin to improve, the investor might move to relatively higher Beta investments in order to increase the rate of return.

It is axiomatic that portfolios with medium Beta ratings demand less attention from investors than portfolios with high Beta ratings. With high-Beta holdings, there must be very close monitoring in order to stay on track and avoid losses from larger price fluctuations. This is especially true of direct investments from individuals through brokerage houses, such as lot purchase or sale of stocks, bonds, commodities, or options with above-average market volatility. Portfolios with a large percentage of highly volatile securities fundamentally require more investor time in order to manage successful returns and avoid losses.

On the other hand, low-Beta holdings may also demand constant attention by the successful investor. Portfolios dominated by low-Beta investments tend to be conservative and highly liquid, but they produce comparatively inadequate long-term returns. Therefore, although a portfolio may contain some low-Beta holdings for long-term balance, successful investors view a portfolio ruled by low-Betas as merely temporary. Such situations call for additional investor attention to making portfolio changes to adjust the level of risk in order to achieve a better return and possibly to lower the demand on his or her time.

Mutual Funds

Even though successful investing requires a great deal of time, money, and energy to search for the highest paying investment with the least amount of acceptable risk, many people are too busy with their daily occupations to accomplish that task adequately. This fact is probably the biggest reason for the rise in popularity of mutual funds. Mutual funds sell shares to individuals who want to invest in the particular type of security in which that fund specializes. Each fund's share price is set daily by market transactions. Individuals can buy shares from the fund directly or through a stockbroker. The proceeds from such sales are then invested by the mutual fund with the aim of providing periodic dividends and/or an increase in the value of fund shares as a future capital gain to the investor. Thus, after careful selection of the correct type of mutual fund to fit his or her individual need, the investor is relieved of the continual process of investment research.

The advantage of investing in funds, rather than individual securities, is that they are managed by professional specialists who are investment experts about the field in which their particular fund concentrates. These experts charge management fees to the fund for their services. The fees are then passed on to investors as part of the fund's market share price. Some funds charge separate fees for buying and/or selling their shares. These are called "load" funds, with the fee for buying called a "front end load" and the fee for selling termed "back end load." Such fees are similar to commissions paid to brokers for purchase or sale of stock. However, many other funds are termed "no load." No load funds lump together all purchase and redemption fees as part of their operating expense. Therefore, with no load funds, buying and selling fees are integrated as a part of the market share price paid by purchasers and are not paid for separately.

Theoretically, comparison of market share prices between load and no load funds concentrating in the same investment area should show lower per-share pricing for load funds. Yet, this theory has often proved wrong, leading to an increasing trend toward more no load and fewer load funds available for potential investment. Investors would seemingly gain some return advantage by considering only no load funds, avoiding the extra sales and redemption fees.

Both load and no load share prices are quoted daily in major newspapers and *The Wall Street Journal*. During normal stock exchange trading hours, a fund's price per share can usually also be obtained by phoning a toll-free number, or locally it can be secured from a brokerage office.

Another advantage to investment in mutual funds is the ability to switch quickly from one type of fund to another. Many large investment houses feature numerous types of mutual funds, each with a different Beta and rate of return. Some allow a switch from one fund to another by telephone. This is important to investors who wish to modify their levels of risk in order to compensate for changes in the economy or the marketplace. It also enables investors to hold total risk to steady Beta levels by controlling the diversification of their portfolios, if desired. As reference to Table 15–1 demonstrates, the continuum of investment alternatives facilitates this control.

The variety of investment options are almost endless. Therefore, it is wise to set down guidelines regarding the types of investments acceptable to you as the investor and the target distribution ranges for each type in the portfolio. For example, if the investment objective is to maximize income with minimum chance of loss, then allowable investments might include money market funds, bank certificates of deposit, Treasury notes, high-grade corporate bonds, and insured municipal bonds. However, if the objective is highest capital appreciation or to "beat inflation by 5 percent each year," the list of acceptable investments could also include common stocks, long-term bonds, real estate, and other higher-risk options that offer the promise of even greater return.

Setting Individual Risk Levels

After the acceptable investments are decided, target ranges should be set up for the various categories. Doing so apportions the portfolio along the lines of acceptable risk. An example might be to split the portfolio into four areas: The first area would be cash, money market funds, or short-term investments that would average 10–15 percent of the portfolio. The second area could include 15–25 percent intermediate bonds. The third area might contain between 30 and 50 percent stocks, and the fourth area, real estate, could account for 30 to 50 percent of the portfolio. The ranges give some degree of flexibility, but the categories themselves are good guides on which to focus investment activity. The apportionments shown here are probably best described as moderate or medium in risk. High-risk portfolios usually put even greater emphasis on common stock securities, especially those with Beta levels offering potentially more vigorous market movements.

As noted previously, Beta ratings for individual securities are available from a number of sources, such as brokerage houses and investment advisor services. However, one cannot simply average a number of these individual ratings to find the Beta performance of an entire portfolio. Instead, the individual Betas must be weighted, based on their percentage representation (at market value) in the portfolio. For instance, note how this is done in the following example:

No. of Shares	Description	Market Price	Market Value	Per-centage Portfolio	Indivi-dual Beta	Beta % to Portfolio
100	Stock A	24.125	2,412.50	.083861 ×	0.87	= .072959
452.6	Mutual Fund	17.19	7,780.19	.270449 ×	0.62	= .167678
2,500	Money Mkt. Fd.	1.00	2,500.00	.086903 ×	0.0	= .0
400	Stock B	16.625	6,650.00	.231162 ×	1.2	= .273944
100	Bond A	94.25	9,425.00	.327624 ×	0.74	= .242442
3,552.6			28,767.69	.999999	TOTAL BETA	= .757023

The portfolio above is proportioned fairly conservatively compared to the S&P 500 stock index. However, it is well proportioned if the investor is satisfied with the returns at that risk level. The combinations of market values and individual Betas are endless, allowing investors to proportion portfolios to accommodate the risk level they desire or with which they feel comfortable.

Individual Betas seldom change greatly, but if they do it is important for the investor to reapportion the portfolio. In order to avoid errors, it is also important for the investor to do this in a systematic manner. Many options are available for either increasing or decreasing risk and return. Each of these has its effect on other areas of the investor's overall strategy. If options are considered in an orderly manner, it is less likely that they will conflict with such other areas.

Reassessing Risk Levels

As stated earlier, the process of investing involves several logical steps that normally tend to be repeated. That is, most investors monitor the condition of their portfolio on some regular basis. To check its performance only once per year would probably be a costly mistake, because almost any semibalanced portfolio would need changes more frequently than that. However, in-depth monitoring on a daily basis frequently requires more time and energy than many private practitioners can spare.

Establishing Monitoring Intervals

The type of investments in the portfolio often dictates the best time interval for monitoring. Although security prices are reported daily, they are also summarized and reported weekly, monthly, and quarterly. Many companies in which investment might be considered publish quarterly earnings statements that offer financial and other background information. These data often affect the risk level or financial return available to shareholders. Other investments, especially money market funds and mutual funds targeted for income, send investors monthly statements on earnings, dividends, and authorized reinvestments. In short, the selection of time interval for monitoring is important because each examination of the portfolio requires that some sort of record keeping be done. This usually takes time, and the investor must decide how much he or she wishes to dedicate to the monitoring process when investment begins.

In addition to the time that record keeping can take, selection of the interval for monitoring should also take into consideration the allocation of some amount of extra time for communication. Many mutual funds and brokerage accounts offer investors the opportunity to switch risk levels by telephone or by use of personal computers. However, this usually must be done during regular business hours, potentially interfering with the practitioner's everyday workload. Nevertheless, such communication can provide significant increases in return, compensating the practitioner for the added time and perhaps investment in specialized equipment or software required.

The process of either starting a new investment portfolio or modifying an existing one is basically the same. The first step is to analyze existing conditions, both for investment potential and for assessing the market price changes reported on present holdings.

Record Keeping

For the best analysis, it is helpful to develop two types of continuing charts. The first one is an Investment Plan Chart, based on a monthly recording interval, but showing a projected year's predicted income and the months when it should become available for reinvestment. An example of this type of chart is shown in Table 15–2.

The investment plan chart is typically put to practical use during the last week of each calendar month. If the form is properly maintained, as investments are bought and sold, it alerts the user to cyclical income due, such as stock dividends and bond coupon redemptions. It also automatically differentiates short-term from long-term income. However, the main advantage is that it allows the user to look ahead, month by month, to research and plan for reinvestment with no loss of interest income. Therefore, it helps keep the portfolio maximally invested for the greatest returns.

The design of Table 15–2 is such that it can be maintained either manually, using hand-drawn or printed columnar forms, or by a computer, using any type of spread sheet software program. With manual usage, the investor prepares the form for a complete year, leaving extra blank rows for investment changes, which are then posted as they occur. However, if a computer is used, the form can be printed out each month for a permanent record; then the computerized form is modified to show anticipated income up to a year in advance. This is accomplished by deleting the column for the present month (June in Table 15–2), and replacing it with a new column for next year's June in the far-right column, thereby rotating the entire year's income calendar one month forward. Also, a computer enables one to add blank rows in which to insert data about any new investments made during that month and permits individual deletions of a particular investment when it is sold.

The second type of monitoring form is a Portfolio Market Price Chart, on which market prices of investments are recorded regularly each week or month, producing a chronological price record of each holding, as well as the gain or loss for each investment. A history of market prices for other investments that are under consideration for acquisition is also shown. A sample form of this type of chart is shown in Table 15–3.

Often, the Friday closing stock prices each week are used for the purposes of posting to portfolio market price charts. This gives an investor the weekend to do unhurried posting to the chart from the Friday closing prices that are published in all major newspapers, as well as the Monday edition of *The Wall Street Journal*. It also allows the investor time to analyze the chart's display and make decisions about potential investment activity during the following week. Further, it enables the investor to compare portfolio performance periodically with the S & P 500 Index for Beta volatility. Such a chart is also a convenient place to record new purchases or sales by date as they occur, noting commissions or other expenses for later reference when filing income tax returns.

The Use of "Trigger" Rules

Regardless of what the market price charts reveal, or what a seeming army of columnists might indicate about a given investment, there is never a guaranteed method by which to faithfully predict its future price or performance. The risk is always present for loss, as well as gain. Many veteran investors have watched in sad amazement as they held firm to a profitable investment while its market worth

Table 15–2 Monthly Investment Plan Chart

(DATE) ___ Plan for ___ JUNE ___

Investment Income/Expense Sources	JUN	JUL	AUG	SEP	OCT	NOV	DEC	JAN	FEB	MAR	APR	MAY
Municipals (Tax Exempt)												
20 Bond A ... due 7/2001 @ 8.0%		800						800				
15 Bond B ... due 9/2001 @ 6.6%				495						495		
15 Note A ... due June 1 @ 6.9%	16035											
10 Note B ... due Oct. 1 @ 6.7%					10669							
? Sales or Redemptions												
Securities												
100 Stock A .... Dividends		25			25			25			25	
400 Stock B .... Dividends	200			200			200			200		
100 Bond A .... Coupons @ 9.0%		450						450				
100 Bond B .... Coupons @ 9.4%			470						470			
? Sales or Redemptions												
Cash and Short-Term Funds												
*35M Money market fund .... @ 9.0%	263	263	263	263	263	263	263	263	263	263	263	263
*15M Bank savings account .... @ 8.0%	100	100	100	100	100	100	100	100	100	100	100	100
* 5M Bank checking account .... @ 5.2%	44	44	44	44	44	44	44	44	44	44	44	44
* Target balance to maintain												
Expenses												
Federal & state estimate tax due	−400			−400				−400				
† IRA or # KEOGH payments due								†−2000			#?	
NET MONTHLY INCOME TO INVEST (?)	16242	1682	877	702	11131	407	607	−718	877	1102	?	407

Table 15–3 Market Price Chart (Friday Closing Price Postings)

Price Posting Date		Stock A	Stock B	Bond A	Bond B	Stock C	Stock D	Fund A	Bond C	Fund B	Fund C	S&P 500	Portfolio Total
	Name	Stock A	Stock B	Bond A	Bond B	Stock C	Stock D	Fund A	Bond C	Fund B	Fund C	S&P 500	Portfolio Total
	Shares.	100	400	100	100								
	Date Acq.	12/20/84	4/3/85	10/2/83	5/7/85								
	$ Cost	5,482	29,850	10,153	9,024								
4/ 5/85	Price	55.25	74.00	96.93	89.80	22.25	41.00	10.14	89.98	16.53	52.55	182.11	
	Total	5,525	29,600	9,693									44,818
	$+OR−	+43	−250	−460									−667
4/12/85	Price	55.75	74.50	96.98	89.82	22.00	41.00	10.18	90.02	16.50	52.62	183.32	
	Total	5,575	29,800	9,698									45,073
	$+OR−	+93	−50	−455									−412
4/19/85	Price	54.50	75.00	97.10	89.89	22.50	39.75	10.19	90.10	16.49	52.72	182.77	
	Total	5,450	30,000	9,710									45,160
	$+OR−	−32	+150	−443									−325
4/26/85	Price	54.75	75.25	97.30	90.01	22.75	39.25	10.18	90.06	16.46	52.67	183.37	
	Total	5,475	30,100	9,730									45,305
	$+OR−	−7	+250	−423									−180
5/ 3/85	Price	55.50	75.25	97.45	90.24	23.00	39.25	10.16	90.05	16.50	52.48	183.90	
	Total	5,550	30,100	9,745									45,395
	$+OR−	+68	+250	−408									−90
5/10/85	Price	55.63	75.13	97.88	90.28	23.25	39.00	10.14	90.10	16.70	52.65	186.75	
	Total	5,563	30,050	9,788	9,028								54,429
	$+OR−	+81	+200	−365	−4								−88
5/17/85	Price	55.88	75.75	98.05	90.42	23.38	38.50	10.25	90.05	16.80	52.80	186.56	
	Total	5,588	30,300	9,805	9,042								54,735
	$+OR−	+106	+450	−348	+18								+226
5/24/85	Price	55.50	75.75	98.35	91.10	23.50	38.25	10.28	90.00	16.95	52.88	187.25	
	Total	5,550	30,300	9,835	9,110								54,795
	$+OR−	+68	+450	−318	+86								+286

Cash Transfers for Investment

	Beginning Balances	Monthly Additions	Cash Totals	Cash Transfers	Monthly Investment	Ending Balances
Brokerage account	*35,000	16,498	51,498	+ 144	−15,000	36,642
Bank savings account	*15,000	100	15,100	− 100		15,000
Bank checking account	* 5,000	44	5,044	− 44		5,000
	*55,000	16,642	71,642		−15,000	56,642

The Investment Plan for June: .... The securities market seems to indicate a trend toward lower interest rates. Therefore, purchase of high-quality, long-term corporate bonds seems best in order to gain higher interest rates available now. Because bonds are sold in $5,000 increments, $15,000 worth of them will be added to securities. The remaining $1,642 of this month's investment income will stay in the brokerage account as part of the short-term money market fund, earning highest interest, available with next month's income for investment in July.

dwindled drastically within a relatively short period of time. This traumatic process teaches a costly lesson: There are some times when any investment should be sold outright, overriding all other considerations and consequences, in order to minimize loss. Given the truth of the previous statement, the question every investor should ask is, "When should I sell immediately?" The answer lies in the setting of a series of investment price boundaries or rules. When the market price of an investment violates one of these rules, it "triggers" the need to sell it.

Limits should be set by every investor, on the basis of his or her own set of risk rules. Such limits will dictate how far the price of an investment can increase or decrease without being partially or totally removed from the portfolio. Some investors adopt a so-called 20 percent trigger rule to protect against serious loss. This rule states that if the investment's market price drops 10 percent from its highest point, it should be sold. Many apply this rule regardless of how long the investment has been held. The same can be said for typical price-appreciation trigger rules, such as this one: If the price of an investment doubles, half of it should be sold. Applying this rule automatically retrieves 100 percent of the original amount invested while an amount equal to the original investment is retained as part of the portfolio. In this manner, prevention of loss is guaranteed.

Trigger rules are not confined to market price moves. They may be tied to unique measurable conditions within an industry about which the investor has in-depth knowledge. Or, they may be connected to a combined index of several separate indicators that the investor from experience finds to be predictive. Regardless of their origin, it is in the investor's best interest, if possible, to set such trigger rules at the outset of each investment.

Following the establishment of trigger rules, the investor may wish to formalize them by conveying specific instructions to a stockbroker to sell the investment under certain conditions. Such instructions are called "stop loss" orders and are accepted by stockbrokers for automatic execution if the price of the security falls to a predetermined level. This relieves the investor of the burden of intensive price monitoring to prevent loss while permitting unlimited price appreciation. Trigger rules, once established, also should be monitored regularly, so that changes may be made when necessary. Thus, if future circumstances drastically affect an investment's potential, especially considering the long term, such trigger rules can accommodate the changing conditions.

SUMMARY

Over a long period of time, investments can provide a substantial improvement in return over that provided by interest from a normal savings account. Therefore, after both personal and practice debt levels are under control and operational insurance cushions are in place, it is prudent for the successful speech-language pathologist or audiologist to plan a profitable investment portfolio based on risk levels that are subject to one's individual comfort assessment.

Many of the ideas expressed in this chapter may be of assistance in setting a rewarding investment plan in place and maintaining its performance. However, it must be recognized that, because each investor's needs are unique, some suggestions may work well for some individuals, may not be appropriate for others, and may provide still others a mental "springboard" for developing their own system to meet a specific set of investment requirements.

Regardless of which systems or procedures are used, successful investing depends on thorough investigation of each prospective investment before its purchase. After the acquisition, it is equally important to monitor both the value and potential worth of each investment periodically over the term of its holding, measuring its performance against set goals. Finally, profitable investment depends on the willingness to sell at some point in time in order to avoid major loss or claim a rightful gain for the investment risk taken. As the practitioner solidifies the economic gains garnered from a successful practice, what was once investment potential becomes financial reality. Success does indeed breed success.

REFERENCES   Bondy, S. (1985, April 18). Establish objectives on road to profitable investments. *Syracuse Post Standard*, p. B10.

Cloonan, J.B. (1984). A lifetime strategy for investing in common stocks. *American Association of Individual Investors Journal*, 5. (Undated, unnumbered supplement, p. 1–29).

Markese, J. (1985). Building a portfolio: How to answer the question of proportions. *American Association of Individual Investors Journal, 7*(7), 34.

Chapter 16

The Sale or Dissolution of Speech-Language Pathology and Audiology Private Practices

Jeremy Conoway, J.D.

DEFINITIONS

Valuation: The process of attaching a dollar value to a certain asset.

Novation: The substitution by mutual agreement of one debtor for another or one creditor for another, whereby the old debt and liability are extinguished and a new debt and liability are created.

Leasehold Improvements: Structural or cosmetic modifications or additions made to a premises that is subject to a lease. The term normally applies to modifications and improvements made by or on behalf of the tenant.

Basis: The amount reflected in the books of a business as being the initial cost to that business of any given asset. Depreciation is computed using this figure as the starting value.

Book Value: The term applied for the value of any asset reflected in the accounting records of a business. Normally, book value equals the depreciated value of the asset.

The life cycle of any business, most especially professional practice in speech-language pathology or audiology, is characterized by several stages. A wise professional, who is considering the establishment of a private practice first conducts a feasibility study, which examines basic economic, geographic, and demographic data to determine whether or not the geographic area of choice will support a private practice operation. Once the decision has been made to proceed, the business moves into a startup cycle, which is then followed by a marketing cycle. Both of these cycles serve as precursors to an endless reorganization and refinement process that is designed to make the business increasingly more successful and profitable. Most business-oriented texts focus on the areas of startup, marketing, and business operations. For a speech-language pathologist or audiologist contemplating the establishment of a private practice, thorough knowledge of these areas is obviously critical. Likewise, after discounting for luck and good fortune, the sum and substance of what is developed by the private practice entrepreneur during the years of operation and refinement reflect how well these basic business administrative practices have been utilized.

All too often, however, the planning, design, and refinement process neglects to incorporate any contemplation of the ultimate sale of the business. In part, this defect is the product of a mindset that views a private practice as an extension or appendage of the practitioner and fails to comprehend the development of a free-standing entity. No lengthy conversation with a speech-language pathologist or audiologist in private practice will end without some comment about the deprivation and hardship inherent in the startup process. Yet the majority of these successful individuals feel that this pain and suffering was merely the price one must pay to enjoy the benefits of ''being your own boss.'' This mental attitude regarding the value of one's professional efforts is very short-sighted and denies a very important theory of business investment.

Although it is true that the financial and personal rewards of success in private practice are worth the struggle to the practitioner, it does not follow that operational success is the ultimate return on the initial investment. To the contrary, the ultimate return on both a tangible and intangible investment in the creation and development of a private practice can only be realized in a successful sale of either all, or part, of the business enterprise. The monetary and personal considerations enjoyed by a successful practitioner are merely a return against the day-to-day involvement, labor, and risk in that practice. Accordingly, then, it is the sale or transfer of all or a portion of the private practice that allows the professional entrepreneur to realize the real goals of the business experience, which are generally recognized as a return on the investment of resources, labor, and risk. Therefore, this chapter examines in detail the incentives, procedures, and goals of the sale or dissolution process.

The term ''dissolution'' as used in this chapter may be somewhat confusing for those with a legal orientation. Most attorneys consider the word dissolution to apply to a business transaction that results in the death or discontinuance of the business entity. Although this specific occurrence is discussed later, it is not a major theme of this chapter. Indeed, the focus of this material is directed to those circumstances in which a speech-language pathologist or audiologist in private practice undertakes to convey or transfer for consideration all or a portion of the private practice operation.

Areas to be examined include (a) the opportunities created by such a sale or transfer, (b) the factors that must be considered in order to maximize these opportunities, (c) the development of a realistic appraisal process, (d) the factors that make the sale or transfer of a speech-language pathology or audiology private practice unique, and (e) the new area of interest created by the emergence of professional employees who wish to become partners.

ANALYZING MOTI-VATIONS TO SELL

The sale of any business represents an opportunity for the entrepreneur to recognize a return on both the tangible investment of hard dollars and the intangible investment of energy and effort into that business. Unfortunately, all too often individuals seeking to sell either all, or a portion of, a business are motivated by external factors that are not consistent with either good business decisions or maximizing investment potential. There is a cliché about the ownership of boats that suggests that the two happiest days in a boat owner's life are the day he purchases the boat and the day he sells it. This observation is directly relevant to the sale of a private practice, because it calls attention to the fact that all too often the sale of the business is not part of the strategic plan established at the onset, but rather is stimulated by outside events. The seller's instant motivation then becomes a primary consideration in the sale process. Although most individuals involved in selling a business have not had a problem in superficially devising a rationale for wanting to sell their professional practice, the slightest examination below the surface often uncovers a second agenda.

It is important at this point to disclose an assumption underlying this entire discussion. That is, the individual contemplating the sale or transfer of either all or part of a business has, in fact, invested a substantial part of both available assets and energies in the private practice or business enterprise. It is further assumed that, even though the private practice may have been financially successful from an income basis, it has not returned to the investor a rate of return commensurate with the level of risk and energy expended. More specifically, this material would be of little interest to an individual or corporation considering the sale of only one of multiple satellite clinics. Rather, it is specifically directed to speech-language pathologists and audiologists who initiated a free-standing private practice, nurtured it to a point of profitability, and who are now considering the sale of all or part of their private practice for a variety of personal and business reasons.

In the negotiating process, identifying the factors motivating the sale becomes essential in that each rationale for sale brings with it its own mindset regarding the need for the sale. A seller who feels desperate about the sale of a business will not perform well either in negotiations or documentation. Alternatively, a seller who is merely "fishing" for an intelligent buyer who will pay an unrealistic price will, in all likelihood, have long-term problems with the transaction. The following material describes what appear to be the most common motivations for sale and identifies some of the liabilities and vulnerabilities that each create within the sale process.

Spousal Transfer

Women constitute a significant segment within the speech-language and hearing private practice field. Despite the emergence of the two-profession marriage, it is still

still common for professional women to follow their husbands to new locations due to career transfers. It is also likely that an occasional male speech-language or hearing professional may find himself in a similar situation. A sale necessitated by a spousal transfer is often characterized by short notice and a high level of anxiety regarding its timing. It is natural for the seller in this situation to be concerned about the "family" aspects of the move and to fixate inappropriately on the date of the departure of the transferred spouse as the date by which all matters must be finalized. This emotionally based timing sequence generally does not allow the seller to exercise the proper level of care in carrying out the sales transaction. A transaction arising from these circumstances is often characterized by inadequate documentation and, quite probably, a very sloppy transfer of control.

Relocation to Another Work-Setting

Some speech-language pathologists and audiologists involved in private practice come to realize that their personalities are not conducive to the stresses and demands required by private practice. This is not to suggest that these individuals have failed in their private practice; rather, having experienced private practice, they chose to return to agency or industry positions. Such a decision is completely appropriate and, in fact, reflects the unique flexibility arising from an investment in a professional degree and credentials. This same flexibility also permits employment in multiple settings.

Obviously, the acceptance of such a nonprivate practice offer or the exercise of such an option for a portion of those involved in private practice would make perfect sense from the standpoint of both finances and lifestyle. However, a speech-language pathologist or audiologist who is motivated to make this change must exercise a high level of care to ensure that a negative view of private practice is not conveyed that would obviously have an adverse effect on the sale transaction. As in the earlier example, placing an inappropriate high priority on timing can also negatively affect the sale arising from these circumstances.

Professional Burnout

No discussion of career or private practice dissolution would be complete without a reference to professional burnout. Private practitioners responding to this phenomenon seek to leave the field altogether or to move into a different aspect of communication services. Once again, these circumstances can create a mindset that may reflect an inappropriate level of self-esteem and a corresponding negative impression of the value of the business that has been built. The seller in this situation must exercise great care to separate emotional issues from valuation procedures. The private practitioner who faces burnout must, in addition to focusing on his or her mental health, also become sensitive to the effect this condition might have on the value of the private practice as a business and the assets available for sale. The speech-language or hearing professional who continues to operate a private practice several months beyond the point of burnout may discover that a significant depreciation has occurred in the client base of the practice.

Retirement

An increasingly greater number of speech-language pathologists and audiologists in private practice have reached a point of financial success that permits consideration of retirement. For many of these individuals, the sale of the practice represents the primary funding source for their retirement. In that case, the primary objective of the seller may well be a long-range tax-favorable payoff with a heightened concern for the secure future and continuation of the practice. A sale of a private practice under these circumstances carries with it an entirely different set of concerns about timing, funding, and documentation.

Relocation

In direct contrast to the situation of the retiring professional is the successful private practitioner who elects to relocate to a more attractive geographic area. Unlike the retiring professional whose cash flow needs are keyed to living expenses, the primary problem created by relocation relates to the cash needs of the seller who must now go into a new area and reinvest capital.

Although partnerships have either thrived or raged for decades in the legal and medical professions, they are a relatively new experience for private practice speech-language pathologists and audiologists. In increasing numbers, sale and transfer transactions involve the creation of a partnership between the professional and a new colleague or an existing employee. The creation of a partnership can be the best, or worst, business decision made by any entrepreneur.

The discussion to this point has been solely directed to answering the question, "Why is the seller selling the business?" Obviously, there are an endless number of circumstances that could motivate the sale or transfer of a private practice. It is sufficient to say that the first step of the sale process involves analyzing the motivations for the sale and identifying the particular vulnerabilities or strengths arising from those factors. A failure to initiate this inquiry and to analyze properly these factors will almost certainly result in an unsatisfactory sale outcome.

IDENTIFYING BUSINESS ASSETS

Assuming that the speech-language pathologist or audiologist in private practice has now considered the motivations for the sale and has further identified the strengths and weaknesses of his or her position, the next step in the sale process is to determine exactly what is being offered for sale. The proper identification and qualification of assets, both tangible and intangible, is the essence of the appraisal and valuation process.

Real Estate

The first business asset to be examined is the real estate or premises from which the business is operated, and the first consideration is whether the seller owns the property or is merely leasing it. When the seller owns the real estate, whether it is part of the sale transaction is likely to be determined by how much cash the purchaser brings to the transaction. If the purchaser has sufficient funds or credit to include the real estate within the purchase, then the matter can go forward consistent with local custom for real estate transactions.

Alternatively, if the seller is going to retain title to the real estate, then an additional consideration must be made. Is it in the best interest of the business for it to remain in its present location? If so, then it is also in the best interest of the seller to negotiate a lease for the premises with the purchaser as part of the transaction. This option offers the advantage of a built-in, or "captive," tenant for the seller's building, as well as the additional benefit of having the business located in a way to maximize continuity.

If the professional practice is being operated from leased premises, then the lease document must be carefully examined to determine whether or not it can be assigned, or sublet. Many landlords want to use the business transfer as an opportunity to raise the rent. It is advisable for the seller to communicate with the landlord as soon as possible to determine what problems will be caused by sale or transfer of the business.

Generally speaking, most leases are assignable to the new owner. A reassignment agreement is a very important part of the transaction documents. To the extent that the seller will also be providing part of the financing for the new business, it is critical that a reassignment clause appear in the documentation that requires that the purchaser reassign the lease in the event of a default in any of the financing provisions. This clause prevents the problem created when the seller must take the business back, but finds that the real estate in which it is located is not available due to a previous assignment of the lease. The seller also needs to know whether the lease and the landlord will allow for a novation, or exchange of parties, on the event of an assignment or whether the seller will continue to be liable under the lease document after the sale.

The examination of the lease document also offers the seller an opportunity to consider the value of leasehold improvements. Even though the seller may not own the building, a good 5-year lease with extensive leasehold improvements has a definite cash value. The sales transaction offers an opportunity to earn a return on the risk taken in the execution of the lease, as well as the dollars invested in leasehold improvements.

Equipment

The next step in the valuation or appraisal process of a speech-language pathology or audiology private practice is the assessment of the nature, extent, and condition of the equipment being offered for sale. Audiology, in particular, tends to be a very equipment-intensive activity. The value of this equipment depends on its condition, calibration history, and, perhaps most importantly, its age. In recent years the explosion of high technology within the electronics industry has spurred the development of new designs and applications for audiology equipment and has resulted in a high level of obsolescence of previously existing equipment. Early on in the sale process, the seller should contact equipment dealers and discuss with them the realistic value of the equipment being sold. This information not only adds credibility to the valuation process but it also puts the seller in a better negotiating posture. At this point, a determination must also be made whether the seller owns an array of equipment capable of supporting all areas of the private practice or whether the new purchaser will have to make after-sale investments in equipment in order to bring the operation up to current or desired standards.

The early involvement of the seller's accountant is critical in any sale involving depreciable assets. A primary point of negotiation between the seller and the purchaser is the apportionment of the purchase price between depreciable and non-depreciable assets. A wise seller goes into these negotiations with a complete understanding of both "basis" and "book value" so as to escape the very expensive ramifications of depreciation recapture.

Patient Base

Another business asset that must be included in the presale analysis process is the nature and extent of the *standing patient base,* the sum total of those patients who regularly utilize the services of the practice on a direct basis without referral or rereferral. In the case of a speech-language pathology practice, of course, the majority of patients may well come on a referral basis. In an audiology practice, however, the existence of the "user" list may well form the foundation of the goodwill calculation within the business appraisal process. In either event, before the seller enters into negotiations for the sale transaction, a complete analysis must be made of the patient base. An appropriate analysis considers the patient's personal characteristics, the type of services previously delivered, the probability of future services, and the date of last contact. The viability of this resource as a saleable asset might also depend on the level of ongoing communication between the professional and the patient. A patient whose needs have been regularly met and who has received frequent periodic informational mailings can be depended on to look to the practice or facility for continuing care. In contrast, a patient who has neither been contacted nor has requested services for a period of over 18 months is not likely to constitute a viable business asset.

Many sellers, especially in the audiology area, attempt to exploit the patient base before the sale negotiation by various promotional techniques in an attempt to create sales and/or demonstrate the viability of the patient base. Although this option is available to any potential seller, it falls into the same designation as "skimming." If the seller elects to exploit the user list immediately prior to the sale, then the user or patient list ceases to be a viable business asset. In the case of hearing aid sales, this practice can result in the patient list becoming a liability to the new owner, as these individuals return for postfitting service and adjustment.

Although the patient base analysis process yields important information about the viability of the patient base, it does not ensure the successful transfer of that base from one practitioner to another. The development of a sensitive and effective patient orientation program is essential in order to effect this transfer process. This factor suggests, once again, that the successful sale or transfer of a professional practice can be a very time-consuming process.

Existing External Referral Base

The nature and extent of the external referral source base are other critical factors in the valuation and appraisal process. The seller should first examine the nature of any formal referral agreements in effect. How long has the referral source been doing business with the practice? What is the current status of the contract? What income has been produced by the agreement or contract, and is the agreement or contract transferable, both legally and psychologically?

Of even more concern is a review of the informal referral processes. Referral sources and the patient base probably represent the most tenuous asset of any private practice. The personal nature of informal referral arrangements makes their transferability highly vulnerable. A candid assessment must be made by the seller of the probability of the referral source continuing with the new purchaser. Such an assessment may also provide valuable insight into the real interpersonal qualifications of any potential buyer as opposed to those that appear on his or her resume.

The presale assessment of referral sources may well provide the seller with an opportunity to improve the value of this asset through the design of the sale transaction. To the extent that these referrals are personal in nature, then the transfer process may well require that the selling professional coordinate activities with the purchasing professional for a period long enough to transfer successfully these referral sources.

Personnel Management

Another opportunity created by the sale or transfer of a speech-language pathology or audiology practice involves the sale of management expertise. The popularity of franchising in many sectors of the economy over the past 20 years has established that knowing how to get things done is a business asset. A speech-language pathologist or audiologist in private practice who has been in business for several years will have spent an inestimable number of hours organizing, reorganizing, aligning, and re-aligning staff and administrative procedures. Quite often the true investment value of this asset is not realized because the seller has not taken the time to document these procedures in the form of a manual. Likewise, the selection and development of a professional staff are also products of a significant investment in time and energy. Although often relegated to a secondary position under the good-will analysis, the existence of an appropriate staff and smoothly functioning routines can be a primary value in the valuation and appraisal of a professional practice.

Operations and Personnel Manuals

In order for these procedures to have a marketable value, there must be a formal operations manual that sets up procedures, protocol, and routines for all significant business transactions and patient interactions, and a personnel manual that articulates all significant personnel policies. The seller should also review the skills of the professional and administrative staff. This analysis should include not only their qualifications but also their level on the pay scale for the area, what their future potential may be, and whether they are subject to formal employment contracts.

With respect to employment contracts and personnel manuals, employers in several states have been concerned about recent court decisions holding that articulated and formal personnel policies constitute a form of employment contract. The basis of these decisions seems to rest in the idea that, if the employer creates a manual specifying certain procedures and further requires the employee to follow those procedures, then it follows that the employer must follow the procedures, thus creating a form of contract. As a result of these decisions, some employers have issued disclaimers that the personnel manual does not constitute an employment contract. Because of the wide diversity in employment law between different jurisdictions, practitioners would be well advised to seek local counsel. However, for the purposes of this discussion, the existence of a formal personnel manual strongly suggests that the private practice is well managed and is not a "seat-of-the-pants" operation.

Computerization

Another important question is whether the organization to be sold is computer literate. Computer orientation within the business organization, which has been undertaken and financed by the seller, is another saleable asset.

Seller's Continuing Involvement

Although it is true that many purchasers will have their own ideas and procedures about the organization and management of the private practice, experience suggests that these may not be in the best interest of the seller. To the extent that the selling professional is participating in the financing of the sale of the successful practice, it will be critical that this practice continue to run in much the same manner as previously made it successful. There is no substitute for experience and success in professional, administrative, or business procedures. A purchaser whose cash investment allows the seller to walk away is free to experiment at will. However, a seller who must look to the continued success of the business in order to secure the purchase price can ill afford experimentation with the basic procedures of that business.

SCREENING POTENTIAL PURCHASERS

To this point, a presale checklist has been developed that first examines the seller's motivation for selling and next addresses several matters to be considered in the appraisal and valuation of those assets available for sale or transfer. The final step before publicly offering the business for sale is to develop a screening process for potential purchasers. Just as it was critical to the sale process to know the motivations of the seller, it is similarly important to be able to determine, as closely as possible, what are the best interests of any potential purchaser. The following analysis examines likely candidates and assigns considerations appropriate to each.

Local Prospects

The potential purchaser often is a present employee or long-time colleague working in the same community. This situation offers the obvious advantage of familiarity with both the business and the personalities of the individuals involved. The probability for success after the sale is also increased. However, the prospective purchaser's familiarity with the practice may also result in an unwarranted contempt of its valuation and assets. Such a conclusion on the part of a potential purchaser is both inappropriate and short-sighted. Qualified professionals in almost every field make things look "simple," even though a smoothly running business requires complex skills and ongoing monitoring.

Regional Prospects

Another potential purchaser may be a speech-language pathologist or audiologist who owns or operates private practices in the same general geographic area. This type of purchaser is likely to disregard and discount the value of nonphysical assets. The advantage offered by this type of purchaser is his or her access to cash, thus freeing the seller from a long-term financial relationship with the purchaser. Obviously, this potential purchaser is most advantageous for the seller looking for a quick sale and least advantageous for the seller seeking to maximize a return on investment.

Prospects from Other Work Settings

Audiologists and speech-language pathologists entering private practice from academic, public sector, or industry-related positions are also a prime source of potential purchasers. Although some of these professionals will have sufficient cash to buy out the seller completely, more frequently a secured transaction will be necessary, thus necessitating a long-range relationship between the seller and purchaser. The attitudes, work habits, training, and experience of these potential purchasers must be analyzed closely. For those who have lived with the frustration of unrealized potential in salaried positions in highly structured settings, the fantasy of "being your own boss" often obviates the realities of their true professional potentials and energies. The speech-language pathologist whose public school production may have been limited to as little as 13 hours of direct services a week and many, many meetings may be surprised to discover that private practice may require 33 hours or more of direct contact and an equal number of administrative hassles each week. Similarly, an audiologist coming from an industry or academic position may find that day-to-day contact with patients lacks the excitement, glamour, and intellectual stimulation of working with a large group of professional peers.

The development of a *pre-negotiation* screening process designed to determine which potential purchasers are, in fact, eligible on a professional, experiential, and financial basis may well save considerable time and money in the negotiation stage.

ELEMENTS IN NEGOTIATING THE SALE

The negotiation of a business sale transaction is an exacting and professional process. Before starting the actual negotiation process, the seller should have conferred with both his or her attorney and accountant. Every effort should also have been made to develop basic sale parameters about assets to be transferred and contractual provisions that are critical to the seller's best interest. The book, *Getting to Yes* (Fisher, 1981), is an important help in preparing the seller psychologically for the negotiation process.

Using a Broker

A question frequently raised in the sale process is whether to use the services of a real estate broker or other sales professional. At the risk of suggesting that professionals not use other professionals, there is a serious question whether there exists within the general economy sufficient experience in the sale of private practices in either speech-language pathology or audiology to justify paying a commission to a broker. If contact is established with such a professional who claims that experience, one should carefully review this experience, including interviewing the broker's past clients. In most cases, potential purchasers can be reached directly through professional publications and associations. Using these sources, a highly effective effort can be made to contact all potential purchasers with a minimum of effort and investment. Sellers who elect to use a sales agent should be aware of the fact that any misrepresentations made by the agent will create liability on the part of the seller. Indeed, both the seller and the seller's agent are liable for any misrepresentation of the practice or its value.

Determining a Sales Price

Perhaps the most important but difficult step in the sales process is to determine the sales price. Throughout various sectors of the economy, there are basic formulas that can be used in the determination of a sales price for most businesses. Unfortunately, only a handful of speech-language pathology and audiology private practices are sold each year throughout the country and no such basic formula has been developed as yet for these types of practices. There are, however, certain standardized components within any valuation formula that are relevant to the sale of a professional private practice. The first component relates to the market value of all *tangible assets*, including inventory, equipment, fixtures, and leasehold improvements. The second component is what is commonly referred to as the *"good-will" valuation*.

The definition of good will includes several components. It represents the advantage or benefit that is acquired by an establishment in addition to the mere value of the capital, funds, or property employed therein, as a result of the general public patronage and encouragement that the practice receives from constant or habitual patients or customers on account of its local position or common celebrity, or reputation for skill, affluence, or punctuality, or from other accidental circumstances or necessities. In its most basic form, the concept of good will recognizes that there is value to the fact that you are in business, that patients are knowledgeable about your location and services, that they trust your services, and that they return on a regular basis, thus choosing your services over the competition.

Good will as a part of the business valuation formula seeks to place a value on all of the intangible assets and considerations raised in these definitions. In the sale of other professional practices, such as accounting, good will is often expressed in terms of a multiple of annual gross. For instance, it may be said that the value of an established and successful accounting practice may be three times its annual gross. The value of good will in a successful private practice normally exceeds the value of its fixed or tangible assets. Because no uniform formula for the development of a good-will valuation has been created, it is recommended that the seller work closely with a CPA in the development of a common-sense valuation of the specific practice to be sold. Each of the intangible factors raised in this discussion should be carefully considered in arriving at that value. The final sales price will consist of the value of the fixed, or tangible, assets combined with the value placed on good will.

Preparing a Prospectus

The seller is now ready to enter into negotiations with potential purchasers whose eligibility and suitability have already been determined. A wise seller prepares a prospectus that outlines in a favorable yet fair manner all of the asset issues previously discussed. This prospectus should include a history of the practice, an inventory of its equipment, an explanation of its facility arrangements, a description of its patient and referral sources, information relating to staff and procedures, and sufficient accounting information to allow an interested purchaser to determine its financial performance. Great effort must be made to distinguish between objective statements of fact, "puffing," and outright misrepresentations within the prospectus. It is seldom necessary to misrepresent good information about any business. Successful marketing efforts are almost always directed toward the positive aspects of the transaction.

Preparing a Preliminary Sales Agreement

Once a potential purchaser has had an opportunity to examine the prospectus and has indicated an interest to enter into negotiations, the next step is to execute a preliminary purchase agreement. Development of this document recognizes that, following an agreement on the basic deal between the parties, there is a period in which both sides must accomplish a variety of tasks in order to place themselves into position to make the transaction final. These tasks often involve financing, auditing, and inspection. The preliminary purchase agreement establishes the basic parameters of the final transaction. The execution of this document also assists the seller in determining the sincerity level of an eligible purchaser who has passed a previous screening effort. On the execution of this agreement, necessary disclosures of financial information and orientation procedures must also be made. The execution of the preliminary purchase agreement suggests that the parties believe there is at least an 80 percent chance that the transaction will be completed. Normally, this agreement sets forth a date or period of time in which the final transaction is to occur. Assuming that all contingencies within the preliminary purchase agreement are met, the transaction is now ready to move toward final documentation.

The structuring of the various documents necessary for a business sale transaction is a complex and sophisticated undertaking. Although it is advisable to have informed counsel throughout the process, the participation of an attorney is mandatory at this step. The profile of any business sale is like an inverse pyramid, with the weight of the entire transaction coming to rest on the narrow and finely drafted points of the various transaction documents. Some general considerations that must be made in the structuring of these documents are considered below.

Executing the Final Sales Agreement

If the agreement of sale calls for the purchaser to completely pay for or *cash-out* all of the seller's interest, then the transaction becomes relatively simple. Documents necessary to effect the transfer assignment of real estate, leasehold interest, and equipment are the primary considerations. Also important are documents transferring insurance, licenses, and possible third party contracts.

In contrast to the simplicity of the cash sale, however, the complexities of the much more common *secured transaction* are many and exacting. The term "secured transaction" refers to an arrangement wherein the transaction will result in a debt owed by the purchaser to the seller. Although the seller will look primarily to the purchaser for the repayment of this debt or "promissory note," in the event of a default he or she can also look to the value of the security or collateral for the satisfaction of the debt.

Documents necessary to effect this security interest have very precise requirements, and each document plays a specific role in the overall structure of the transaction. Of special importance in this documentation is the concept of *cross collateralization,* which is a drafting technique whereby a default in the terms of one document constitutes a default in the terms of another one. A major emphasis in the drafting of a business sale documents is the protection of the seller in the event of a default by the purchaser. In working with an attorney, the seller should become familiar with these various documents and should assist the attorney in the design and execution of a default model as a process of checking the efficacy of the documentation.

Great effort should also be taken in the documentation of the transaction to identify and limit any and all representations made by the seller to the buyer. *Unwritten "side deals'' between the parties that do not appear in the documentation are to be discouraged at all costs.*

It is not uncommon to find a noncompetition agreement included within the provisions for the sale of a professional practice. These types of provisions have special tax ramifications that should be reviewed with an accountant. Many of these transactions include a workover or consulting provision that requires the seller to stay on-site or in some way physically participate in the business for some period of time following the sale. In the case of a secured transaction, the seller might also wish to document a continuing ''oversight'' function that provides protection against radical change of procedure or operation following the sale.

Executing a Limited Sales Agreement

Rather than an outright sale of substantially all of the practice assets, many private practice speech-language pathologists and audiologists elect to effect a limited sale and the creation of a partnership arrangement. It is critical that the analysis undertaken before entering into this form of business ownership participation include the sum and substance of that analysis undertaken for an outright sale of the business enterprise.

A partnership can offer new and exciting dimensions within the business and practice experience, much of which are expressed in personal, almost emotional, terms. Accordingly, the initial step in any partnership analysis must be to examine one's own personality and professional style. A successful partnership often is more akin to a marriage relationship than a business one. Given this perspective, compatibility of work habits, personal values, and goals appears to be a paramount consideration. A partnership based on the economies of scale is not likely to survive. (See also Chapter 5 in this regard.)

If the proposed partnership can survive the ''marriage'' test, it must next survive the ''business'' test as set forth throughout this chapter. The assets of the selling partner are no less valuable because a partnership is being created to exploit that potential. Quite frequently, friends who become partners are incensed when they find that payment for various assets is expected. Although marriages may be made in heaven, partnerships are created on paper, and every effort must be made to ensure an adequate and complete documentation of the arrangements and agreements between the parties. Primary among these considerations is the amount of capital contribution to be provided by each party, the management controls to be exercised by the partners, the level of professional production expected of each partner, and the nature and extent of reimbursement. A well-drafted partnership agreement anticipates and documents procedures to be followed in the event of the death or disability of a partner and in the event that the partners wish to effect a dissolution of the partnership.

An important final note about partnerships relates to the subject of controlling or majority interest. In partnerships in many professions, the term ''junior partner'' refers to an individual who has been promoted from the status of an employee, i.e., an associate promoted to an equity position within the partnership that is junior to a full or ''senior'' partner. These terms and this concept reflect the fact that partnerships need not be equal in design or function. From a financial standpoint it is quite possible that a promising associate or professional employee simply lacks the funds necessary to negotiate a full partnership interest. Similarly, a disparity in the levels of professional expertise and experience might also give rise to a partnership arrangement in which two or more classes of partnership interest are created. These designations ultimately affect the control and disbursement of profits of the partnership entity.

There are an infinite number of partnership configurations available. An experienced and financially successful audiologist or speech-language pathologist in private practice may be willing to enter into a partnership transaction that transfers a substantial portion of the partnership assets and may be even willing to share partnership profits on an equal basis. However, some professionals may not be willing to share profits equally, nor might it be appropriate to do so. The solution to this dilemma is the creation of a managing partner. The partnership agreement is simply drafted to allow one of the partners to assume the role of managing partner while all other factors remain equal.

SUMMARY

The ultimate sale of a private practice in speech-language pathology or audiology is a phase of the business life cycle that should be designed and anticipated *from its very beginning*. Every effort must be made to ensure that the sale of a private practice maximizes the return on the investment of assets, energy, and creativity made by its founder. The decision to sell a private practice may well require a period of several weeks in which to prepare the business for sale. The hasty and unplanned sale of a private practice is to be avoided at all costs. A careful and complete inventory of all potential assets, both tangible and intangible, must be made in order to maximize the return on investment. The transaction itself must be negotiated and documented in a way that maximizes the level of protection afforded to the seller, especially when the selling professional is planning to participate in the financing of the sale. A well-orchestrated sale transaction ensures the continuity of the practice, which in turn protects the best interests of both the buyer and seller.

REFERENCE

Fisher, R. (1981) *Getting to yes*. Boston: Houghton Mifflin.

Part V

Reflections and Recommendations

Chapter 17

The Private Practice Viewpoint: Personal Reflections from Private Practitioners

Katharine G. Butler, Ph.D.

The recommendations offered by the authors of previous chapters have focused on a number of financial, managerial, technical, and ethical issues in the establishment and enhancement of a private practice in speech-language pathology or audiology. By design, the authors provided information that could be of assistance to a broad spectrum of readers from novice to expert. Although the chapters were not autobiographical in nature, their authors viewed private practice through the lens of their own experiences. Thus, readers may have gained some sense of the authors' perceptions of the scope of private practice, as well as its problems and possibilities.

This chapter is dedicated to making explicit the realities of private practice . . . realities that call for not only an entrepeneurial spirit but a strong sense of ethics as well. It contains the accounts of a number of individuals who consented to reflect on their professional careers in the provision of direct services to those with speech, language, or hearing handicaps. Here the reader may gain a sense of the diversity of private practice, of viewpoints and philosophies, of problems encountered and solved, of practice in cities large and small, and of the delights and difficulties of the intense professional involvement that is the hallmark of private practice. The contributors to this chapter provide a kaleidoscopic view of that involvement. Their offerings may reflect the "small world phenomenon" as well. Although there may be 100,000 practitioners in all work settings (45,000 of whom are ASHA members), speech-language pathology and audiology remains a relatively personalized profession. Strong collegial relationships are established during the years of professional education and in subsequent involvement in local, state, and national professional association activities. Hence, it may be that readers will be familiar with a number of well-known names in the pages that follow.

For reasons that will become self-evident, the "cameo" presentations begin with this reflection.

Paul D. Knight, Glenview, Illinois

Through the several decades since May of 1932 when I opened my office in Chicago, I have tried to find evidence that anyone in our profession preceded me as an entirely independent, full-time, continuously active practitioner in speech-pathology. Never have I been able to identify such a person.

That I was fortunate enough, as a pioneer of this kind, to demonstrate the viability of independent clinical practice—that is, to break first ground in serving many who chose to receive guidance privately, rather than to have it under other available circumstances—has given me much understandable pride. An equal cause for pride and gratification as well has lain in the fact that I could serve as counselor to numerous others who wished to develop their own practices. For some years, I was called on probably because, in the absence of pertinent associational guidelines, I had to learn by doing and to survive in the process.

Then, as ever since, I have attempted through counseling to contribute to an elevated level of informed and disciplined conduct in private practice, conduct that would help to ensure it a respected, integral place in a profession marked by numerous diverse, though tangential interests.

From long experience in developing and maintaining a private practice in speech disorders and in formulating clinical imperatives distinctive to it, some considerations have persisted as especially worthy of serious thought. Prominent among them are these: (1) Private practice is *not* for everyone who might desire to engage in it; (2) no one should attempt to enter independent practice before having read as nearly exhaustively as possible the writings on the subject and sought candid advice from persons who have succeeded as practitioners, and (3) in the course of this reading and in consideration of this advice, one should evaluate personal qualifications for an independent professional venture, which more often than not is a lonely one.

Undeviating answers to such critical questions as the following could determine one's suitability to private practice.

- Am I sufficiently prepared by education and clinical experience to cope with the inevitable hazards of private practice?
- Am I justified in concluding that a Master's degree and ASHA's clinical certification alone constitute sufficient preparation?
- Am I skilled above the average in the use of English, and is my speech well above reproach?
- Do I have more than an ordinary ability to teach, to clarify, and to do it efficiently?
- Do I relate well with people, especially with often unaware, confused, sometimes strong-headed patients?
- Is patience in coping with wavering, resistant, or occasionally regressive clients one of my characteristics?
- Am I eager to continue to learn, and learn, and learn?
- Am I informed in organizing and maintaining all essential records, and am I used by habit to do so?

- Is patience with managerial details one of my well-cultivated traits?
- Do I have specific knowledge about the details of operating a small business?
- Can I afford a creditable office in a reputable, at least predominantly professional building—an office adequately furnished and set up with essential basic materials and equipment?
- Do I have a sufficiently strong financial base to see me through possibly lean times, especially in the first year or so of practice?
- Am I willing to establish a basis for fees consonant with my known abilities as a clinician and readily acceptable to patients as fair compensation for services rendered?
- Am I willing to demonstrate a well-grounded commitment to my profession by serving ASHA and my state and local associations to the fullest extent of my capabilities?
- Am I willing to accept for my personal guidance, and without equivocation, the principles set forth in the ASHA Code of Ethics and to be mindful of ethical codes embraced by related professions?

Some dimensions of an effective clinician in communicative disorders might also include the following reassuring constellation of personal traits, among them:

- unfailing social grace
- obvious honesty
- compassion that never becomes effusive
- empathy in all therapy
- kindness and warmth, even when decisiveness and firmness are necessary (Note: The patient is reassured by the clinician's strength and purpose when neither ever degenerates into rudeness or pontification.)
- a quiet, sure-footed impact in therapy management and in counseling that is born of broad knowledge, experience, and resourcefulness
- an approach to each patient as though *that* person and *that* case were the clinician's *only* concern (Note: A preoccupied manner or evidence of a desire to move on to the next patient can reduce effectiveness in treatment.)
- an over-all assessment of the *person* in one's care, with generous contributions to development of all his or her real abilities and potentialities (Note: Limiting one's activities strictly to treatment of the pathology can be short-sighted.)
- an ongoing cultivation of an insightful pragmatism that touches the heart of the case, built on the immense usefulness of diagnostic testing as the major basis for evaluation
- dissatisfaction with any diagnostic appraisal that seems inadequate, signaling a need for further testing
- a recognition that a pertinent dominant methodology *may* admit of some innovative approaches but that these are never pursued at the patient's expense (Note:

No innovation should be attempted without having in mind a related, more conventional method on which to fall back should the innovation be perceived as confusing to the patient or prove unproductive.)

- continuing devotion to clinical observations and interrelated clinical and theoretical exploration
- a freeing of blocks of time for pursuit of wide-ranging interests, e.g., study, writing, extraprofessional reading, and some travel including investigation of U.S. and foreign clinical facilities
- conservative and cautious, dignified restraint in marketing (Note: "marketing," "selling," and "the market place," terms drawn from the intensely competitive world of business, are offensive to many of our academically and scientifically minded colleagues. Quite aside from this, these terms and the sometimes abominable schemes related to them seem oddly inappropriate when used in *any* professional pursuit devoted to the relief of any form of human discomfort or suffering. In many of these promotional efforts, the emphasis can seem to discerning members of the public to be more on competition and financial gain than on a sincere devotion to health care.)

In my view, much of the foregoing can serve as a rational basis for self-evaluation in undertaking the responsibilities of a private practice in communicative disorders. Obviously, searching, informed, and cautious evaluative thinking on the broad subject of personal assets relevant to engaging in this independent venture is indispensable. Not a few weak practices and failed practices have been attributable to self-seeking, superficial motivations.

In light of all that can be learned about the challenges of private practice, including breadth of education, experiential background, clinical skills, courage, vision, personality qualifications, and business acumen, one would be wise to ponder the implications of two important questions:

1. Do I have what is needed to be and to remain acceptable to referral sources, patients, and their families?
2. Do I have reasonable assurance that I am sufficiently prepared to become a successful independent practitioner in communicative disorders and a credit to private practice and to my profession?

Michael J. D'Asaro, Ph.D., Michael J. D'Asaro, Ph.D. and Associates, Santa Monica, California

A speech pathologist or audiologist contemplating opening a private practice might profit from the consideration of the types of problems that can occur at various stages of an independent practitioner's career. Much discussion is given to preparing oneself for private practice by learning the business management skills necessary for an efficient and profitable enterprise. Most private practitioners learn sooner or later that they are operating a business, as well as conducting a professional venture. In fact, the focus of attention in current short courses and conferences dealing with private practice is almost exclusively on the financial management and productivity of the practice. This was quite evident in the ASHA Telephone Seminar of February 1985 on "Accountability in Health Settings." Without realistic financial accountability, the practice cannot long survive. Without professional and ethical accountability, a private practice is also slated for failure.

CAPITALI-ZATION

The interrelationship between business and professional values can come into conflict early if inadequate attention is given to the financial concept of capitalization. We generally think of capital as an adequate cash reserve to carry us through to the stage where the practice is generating sufficient income to support us. It might also be conceived as income from other sources during our startup period. The optimism of youth may lead us to minimize capital needs, but clinical and professional judgment can be compromised when financial pressure is a strong influence on decisions to be made.

For example, we may limit ourselves to an inadequate work setting as we economize on renting space. We may suffer from subliminal or unconscious conflicting motivations when the time comes to terminate a patient whose termination would cause a large percentage drop in our caseload and income. We may overextend ourselves into areas of minimum competency as we accept a new type of case for treatment instead of more appropriately referring that patient elsewhere.

There is no easy solution to these potential errors of judgment. However, long-range planning before starting a private practice, including planning the transition from part- to full-time employment, anticipating the investment needed to lease and equip a professional office, and anticipating the length of time before income is generated, can help determine the capitalization required.

AFFILIA-TIONS AND ASSO-CIATIONS

Another long-range plan to consider is the possibility of continuing an association with an organization, such as a university, hospital, or other community agency while starting a private practice. In addition to providing a base salary in the early years of a practice, the contact with co-professionals can be a stimulating and enriching experience as stability and identity are reinforced by such an affiliation. With the growth of community agencies funded by the private sector, the possibilities of allying oneself with philanthropic providers of service are multiplying. A volunteer relationship can grow into a fundable program as needs are identified and eventually budgeted.

Further planning around building a group practice with partners, associates, or employees deserves consideration early in one's career, for although a solo practice can be satisfying for the strong individualist, it is a lonely work setting without the easy sharing and conferring that are possible when co-professionals are nearby.

CONSUL-TATIONS

A final concept occurs to me as we consider the growth and expansion of a private practice after its initial stage of development. Although the age of specialization is on us, the private practitioner must be prepared to treat a variety of clients. Although university clinics try to offer diverse experiences to their students through externships and other such programs, we have all found areas in which we have had limited training or clinical experience. Our profession has not yet availed itself of the system widely used by psychologists, psychiatrists, and social workers of working under the paid supervision of a senior clinician when we encounter a patient with a problem with which we have had limited experience. This type of consultation could readily be incorporated into continuing education credit programs. It could utilize the experience of the first generation of private practitioners and other senior clinicians who are approaching retirement and who might be available for part-time employment.

AVOIDING BURNOUT

We have all known clinicians who experience burnout, some so severely that they separate themselves from the profession. Some of the foregoing suggestions are drawn from my own personal experience, and I believe that they have helped me to avoid burnout. Over 30 years of private practice have taught me to appreciate the following:

- diversity of workload provided by outside affiliations, including university, hospital, and philanthropic organizations
- a balance between clinical and administrative activities
- diverse caseload with several areas of specialization
- long-term associations with co-professionals in and out of the office
- access to consultants in our own and related professions.

I still enjoy walking into my own office and meeting the next new patient or working with a returning patient, and I wish the same enjoyment to those who build their own practices.

Donna R. Fox, Ph.D., University of Houston and Kelsey-Seybold Clinic P.A., Houston, Texas

Everyone is interested in being successful, and most individuals entering private practice want to be paid for their services and at the same time practice in a manner that they feel allows for clinical creativity. Rarely, however, am I as a private practitioner asked what I think is necessary for success. Rather, I am asked "How much do you charge?" and "How do you decide what to charge?" Certainly, fiscal responsibility with a balanced budget is one criterion of success, but there are others I believe to be more important. Just as hard work, intelligence, and good training are important ingredients for academic achievement, they are also important ingredients for clinical success. I believe a private practitioner must provide a quality service in the most efficient and effective manner. The patient should have the maximum effect for the least possible expenditure of time and money. The competitive edge of the private practitioner consists of his or her expertise and reputation in delivering outstanding service.

Some years ago I concluded that the environment in which I had more freedom to treat patients with communication disorders was in a private practice. Schools, hospitals, and clinics all had policies that limited what I wanted to do in the practice of speech pathology. Most universities require faculty to teach, to demonstrate for students, and to publish their own research. Universities generally do not pay professors to see patients! Still some of us truly enjoy university teaching, and so for me the solution to this dilemma was to maintain a full-time faculty position and a part-time specialized private practice. Others have reversed these priorities and provided an excellent clinical faculty for university programs.

I, personally, wanted to provide a high-quality clinical service to private patients in an interdisciplinary setting. To do this, I made a series of decisions. First, I chose to join a private medical clinic where I could limit my practice to diagnostic and short-term treatment problems and where I could specialize in patients who had unusual problems and for whom treatment was relatively short-term but management might very well be for long periods of time. In the early years limiting my practice to clefts and/or voice problems was difficult, but over the years consistent referrals from a variety of other professionals have been of great help in doing so.

Another decision I made was to work on a contract basis in this medical clinic. This provided both contacts and the "state-of-the-art" equipment and laboratory facilities to carry out complex studies, when necessary, on patients. Such specialties as psychology, psychiatry, endocrinology, and nutrition were easily accessible. By working for a contracted number of hours for a set fiscal amount I was assured of a cash flow that was not dependent on billing and collecting.

Over the years I have hired various individuals to work for me in this clinic and have established several guidelines. For example, fees generally reflect the time and experience of the personnel. Obviously contractual fees for personnel must be less than the generated income in order to allow for overhead costs, research, and expansion. Although a disadvantage of this system lies in the fact that personnel are being paid while they are not seeing patients, its long-term effect is positive: Records are kept up to date, new materials are studied, and some measure of research can be continued with a private patient population.

The guidelines I have followed for establishing a part-time practice are as follows:

- Work on a contract basis with specific terms.
- Hire personnel on a time basis that is not tied to billing, collections, or profit.
- See all patients oneself for diagnosis and outline of treatment.
- Maintain periodic checks of patient progress (one monthly conference with clinician) and re-evaluate on a 3 to 4 month basis.
- Limit the practice.
- Maintain good inter- and intraprofessional contacts (almost 50 percent of my practice are referrals from other speech-language pathologists).
- Provide follow-up on referrals.

The rewards of combining part-time private practice with university teaching are many. I can demonstrate state-of-the-art practices for emerging clinicians, try out new treatment techniques, research new ideas, and maintain my own clinical skills.

At the same time I am able to continue my own research and teaching career within the university setting. If success is defined as liking what you do and doing what you like well while earning a living, then part-time private practice provides me with a framework for a successful life-work style.

Leola S. Horowitz, Ph.D., Co-Director, Peninsula Group for Speech, Language and Hearing Services, Hewlett, New York

For the speech-language pathologist and audiologist seeking to venture into private practice, the operating maxim should be: Prepare for the unexpected. For example, when our attorney filed for incorporation, we discovered that, because of separate licenses in speech pathology and audiology, we had to form two professional corporations—Peninsula Group for Speech Pathology, P.C., and Peninsula Group for Audiology, P.C. The Peninsula Group for Speech, Language and Hearing Services is a joint venture of these two corporations.

Let me begin with a description of our facilities so that you will have a context within which to evaluate the following comments. Our offices are in a one-floor building known as the Five Towns Medical Center with its own parking and spaces identified for the handicapped. At the outset we decided to create our offices for permanency and expansion. We have a waiting room large enough for small meetings, a group or conference room suitable for small public relations lunches, four therapy rooms, three offices, a fully equipped audiological suite, a secretarial office, and two lavatories. The facilities create a thoroughly professional atmosphere, but also convey a sense of warmth. We provide comprehensive services in speech, language, and hearing, with ancillary services in psychology, learning disabilities, reading, occupational therapy, and other services as requested.

Thus, private practice in a fully equipped office environment may not necessarily reflect the considerations that you might have in an individual practice. Possibly the only common element in different private practice settings might be their philosophy; namely, to offer a necessary and helpful public service to the community that is also professionally and financially rewarding to those who offer the service.

As a director of a university speech and hearing center for many years, I worked with both full- and part-time colleagues in a somewhat protected environment with financial security, secretarial assistance, malpractice insurance, and many eager students for whom it was necessary to create varied clinical experiences through which they could learn. Clearly, there were opportunities to learn how to prepare schedules and budgets and about insurance requirements, to work with other professionals in our own field as well as allied fields, to work with parents, and to experience the many other facets of operating a department and clinical program. There were also constraints within the academic environment, but it certainly was a good training ground for developing a private practice. My two partners also had been involved in teaching, clinical practice, and supervision in the academic setting.

Clearly, there are many avenues to developing a successful practice, but there are also some constants. Among these are patience, hard work, training, optimism, creativity, financial support, and especially faith in one's own ability to be successful. I'll elaborate on some of these.

- *Time span:* Don't be impatient. It takes a long time to develop relationships in the community, but like ripples on a pond, there develops an ever-widening circle of those who know and trust you.

- *Human relations:* One needs to develop and maintain professional and understanding attitudes with other professionals in our field, in allied fields, and with people living in the community.

- *Hard work:* It must be a full-time job. No one ever succeeded in anything on a part-time basis. It requires your heart, your soul, and your body.

- *Financial management:* This is related to the element of time span. One needs to survive the lean years before the good ones arrive. One has to be able to maintain oneself financially and psychologically. One's ego has to be strong to face the fact that there are few clients in the lean years. In addition, as I described in the opening paragraph, as soon as one sees a profit, one will also be confronted with unexpected increases in rent, utilities, secretarial services, maintenance, and insurance costs. In a multiple practice such as ours, the financial benefits to each individual are fewer in the beginning, but the financial burden is also shared.

  Fortunately, from the beginning we established a policy that clients pay us at the time of treatment. A good secretary removes fee payment from the clinical relationship.

- *Professional resources:* A good lawyer is important in advising on agreements, rental contracts, and other problems that arise in setting up a practice. In addition, one's financial affairs will be complicated enough to require an accountant.

- *Public relations:* We have done almost every form of advertising in what we would consider "good taste." We have sent brochures and newsletters; visited the doctors in the area; have had professional people in for lunch; sponsored workshops, and open houses; have spoken to community, parent, and school groups; sent out announcements of new programs and information about our field; have had the mayors of villages in the area proclaim May as Better Speech and Hearing Month; and have advertised in newspapers, community bulletins, the Yellow Pages, and the like. It is difficult to measure the value of such public relations. These activities are costly and time-consuming, but absolutely necessary. We have maintained contact with professionals in our field, which I think is important. We try to do at least one "public relations event" each month.

I would hope that when one reads about our private practice that one gets a sense of the commitment we have made—psychologically, physically, and financially. But for one, I am glad I have invested in the type of practice that has been established with my two partners. The clients are a constant challenge, compelling the clinician to devise new methods, new techniques, and new materials. In short, private practice is not just difficult and challenging, but it also provides constant growth.

Lois V. Douglass, M.A., private practice, Pasadena, California
Private practice was a natural choice for me. My interest in speech-language pathology began with my husband's pursuit of a Ph.D. in the field. Along with the

acquisition of his Ph.D. came close and long-lasting friendships—both with his fellow students and with Lee and Lysa Travis. We became immersed in what speech-language pathology is all about—human relationships.

When our younger daughter reached school age and I sensed there would be more ahead than Camp Fire Guardianship and PTA activities, I began to look for a professional life. An interest in children with speech handicaps and their parents, coupled with open hours in my husband's part-time private practice, made my becoming a speech-language pathologist and partner in my husband's private practice a logical step. My family's needs came first, so attaining my M.A. was 8 years in the doing.

I have now been in private practice for 20 years, with the last 10 years limited to the treatment of children. The feast or famine cycles did not bother me. During the famine, I had more time to give to in-depth study of my clients and more time for further education as I sought answers to my questions. As long as the overhead costs were met, I did not worry about income.

A Ph.D. would have made me a more valuable commodity in the marketplace, but time meant more to me than money. The intensive and extensive commitment a Ph.D. required did not fit into my life. I considered it very seriously, but my husband, children, and a desire to have time for myself kept me from obtaining that degree.

What would I have done differently? Communicating with my colleagues, interfacing with other related professionals, and educating the public would have been higher on my agenda. And I would have taken steps to make my practice more financially rewarding.

I have never regretted my choice of work setting. It has allowed me to set my own schedule, think my own thoughts, do things my way. I could be in charge of my professional life. With my in-depth attention to my clients and their parents and my eagerness to find answers to questions that arose about child development, language delay, and speech disorders, I am (1) still excited about my profession 20 years later as opposed to being burned out and ready to retire and (2) eager to pass on my knowledge and expertise to others (with opportunities to do so as a professor and writer). My insistence that I have more than a professional life has allowed time for my husband and me; time for our children and grandchildren; time for running, piano, politics, and peak climbing. It is a good life!

Robert L. Douglass, Ph.D., private practice, Pasadena, California

One day in 1955, I was examining a lease, a legal document. An act of faith or of foolishness? The lease was a commitment to pay an office landlord what seemed an astronomical sum over a 3-year period and not a client in sight. I gulped, signed, and was in private practice. Well, not exactly. It took time to build a referral base, to work out business procedures, to feel comfortable with telling a prospective client what my fees were.

Thirty years later, I am pleased and impressed at how skillfully our university graduates, with 7 or 8 years of professional experience, begin and build their private practices. It is a declaration of independence. In most workplaces, public schools, hospitals, and health service agencies, clinicians generally become subordinate to prevailing regulations. They are often trapped in an administrative hierarchy where people with little knowledge about our profession control what we do and how we do it. Private practice, to me, represents a significant step toward professional autonomy, an essential advance toward establishing professional identity and respect. Clients are not taken from captive populations. The self-initiation by a client asking for help and the willingness to pay for our services provide the basis for a healthier working relationship. How different would our profession be if our services were provided primarily through private practice?

In addition to financial rewards (and sometimes reverses), private practice provides the opportunity to establish deeper, more meaningful relationships with clients. Only recently has pragmatics been recognized as an important dimension in language. And yet pragmatics is the raison d'etre for what we do professionally. Human communication has meaning and relevance only in the context of human relationships. The effectiveness of therapy can never be determined solely by counting observable behaviors. Changes brought about through therapy are valuable and helpful when a client's relationships with others become more satisfying and rewarding. Often the first meaningful communicative relationship for a client begins with the clinician. The freedom and flexibility of private practice give the clinician control of the time and the conditions of therapy. The extent of change is then determined primarily by the knowledge and skill of the clinician and the motivation and capacity for change of the client. Under such conditions it becomes possible for us to begin to realize our true potential for contributing an essential, indeed, critical, service to communicatively handicapped human beings.

Theodora J. Richards, M.A., private practice, Kalamazoo, Michigan and environs

I began my private practice when I found that no part-time positions were available in my area. Only full-time work was offered in the schools, and the local university had sustained budget cuts. Earlier, I had done summer "fill-in" therapy, and when some clients approached me to work with them privately, I decided to enter private practice on a year-round basis.

First I contacted every speech clinician in the schools that I knew and informed them that I would be offering private therapy. Because my husband, my children, and I live "out in the country" and our home is not designed to accommodate a therapy room, I elected to provide services in the clients' homes. This has worked out very well for me because my house does not have to be spotless, and for my clients' mothers, many of whom work.

Second, I ordered business cards and stationery and purchased a number of diagnostic instruments. I began that summer with two clients. In the fall, I called on the principals of all the private schools in the area and talked with those who were willing to see me, "dressing for success" for each interview. Although I have yet to obtain a client from those interviews, I honestly feel that when you go out and "beat the bushes," somewhere, somehow, something happens. Another client was added in October, and I provided therapy for the child until the family moved away. By summer 1983, my practice consisted of six clients, one of whom was from a home health care agency for which I had worked for several months.

In the fall, three of the six clients remained with my practice. In addition, a school district approached me in October and requested that I provide services to a classroom of autistically impaired pupils. Through the summer I have maintained a practice consisting of seven clients (four children and three adults). At this point, I feel I'm busy enough; my goal of a limited part-time private practice has been achieved.

(Editor's note: Mrs. Richards recently elected to enter a doctoral program in hearing and speech science, effectively reducing for the time being her commitment to part-time private practice).

Kay A. Armstead, Ed.D., director of a general private practice, Morgan Hill, California

Private practice in speech-language pathology has been one of the most satisfying experiences I have had in my multifaceted career in this profession. I began as a speech-language clinician in the public schools and then held the following positions: a supervisor of speech-language clinicians in many types of settings, a university professor teaching academic courses in communication disorders, and, a few years ago, a private practitioner. My practice has changed and expanded from my being the sole clinician conducting therapy myself to employing other speech-language pathologists, with the majority of my responsibilities now being administrative.

In reflecting on these experiences, I am struck with the realization that I felt the same satisfaction in each of these situations. This leads me to believe that the core requirement for attaining a successful practice, no matter the setting, is that you find the profession of communication disorders to be stimulating and challenging. If you enter private practice because you are bored and dissatisfied in other settings, you bring these same feelings to your private practice. On the other hand, if you enjoy working with people, have continuously sought improved approaches to alleviate communicative problems, and give each project you tackle all your energy and attention, you will find success in private practice. Note that success is an ambiguous term and can only be measured by the attitude of an individual. However, there is a tendency to measure success in monetary terms. Though the maintenance of a practice requires that the expenses not outweigh the income, there are other more important qualities of success.

The quality of service is certainly an important aspect of success. A quality service is one in which the major concern is helping a client overcome his or her handicap. The more clients who benefit from a service, the more clients seek that service. This cycle brings about satisfactory monetary benefits. The business world has long understood that emphasis must be placed on the quality of a product. Our product is service. When the prime concern is the dollar, the quality of service suffers. Private practitioners need to devote their labors to exactly what they were trained to do— helping relieve communicative handicaps. This is what brings me satisfaction and success.

Sharlene Goodman, M.A., Executive Director, Newport Language, Speech &
Audiology Center, Inc., Laguna Hills, California

As executive director of one of the largest private practices in California, I have learned a great deal in the past 7 years. Newport Language, Speech & Audiology Center, Inc. (NLSAC) provides speech-language and audiologic services in acute care, rehabilitation facilities, convalescent hospitals, patients' homes, physicians' offices, NLSAC clinics, public schools, and settings of the California Youth Authority.

If you do not wish to be a solo practitioner, you need to decide if and when to employ another clinician in addition to yourself. If you are carrying more than a full caseload, you need to hire a qualified clinician to evaluate and treat patients so that you are not overburdened and will have time to call on other referral sources. Although there are no guarantees, good marketing and public relations should increase your intakes. You need time as you grow to familiarize new employees with your philosophies and procedures, and you need to provide them with continuing professional education so they can deliver the best patient care available. Ultimately, you are responsible for your employees' professionalism and quality of work. Therefore, the most taxing responsibility in a large practice is your selection of personnel and your relationships with them.

It is important to trust the judgment of those whom you hire. You cannot do everything and be everywhere. You become a judge of performance and are faced with hiring, pay increases, and employee termination. I have learned that it is important to review employees on a regular basis and document those reviews, along with any appropriate conferences. It is impossible to be well-liked all the time. As your practice grows, you will need help with interviewing, orientation, supervision, quality care standards, and keeping up with changes in funding and government regulations.

I now know that it is crucial to have professional help with business issues, public relations, and marketing. Other professionals have expertise in these areas. Hiring such experts costs money, but saves time and effort., No matter how bright speech-language pathologists and audiologists are, we do not normally have expertise in business matters.

All in all, I enjoy the challenge of increasing business, marketing new services, and developing new programs. However, I prefer to leave the staffing, quality of care, interviewing, and business issues to other staff members. My goal is to come up with ideas and have others implement them. In the future, I would like to get away from being tied down to the day-to-day running of the practice.

To be honest, I truly miss the concentration on patient care and the one-on-one human interaction in direct patient care. That type of personal involvement does not occur during business operations. When I decided to expand my practice, I did not consciously decide to stop patient treatment: my direct contact with patients gradually ceased as other obligations grew.

Lisa K. Breakey, M.A., private practice, San Jose, California
(Editor's Note: Ms. Breakey was president of the California Speech Pathologists and Audiologists in Private Practice when she wrote the following article, which she entitled "The Solo Practitioner—A Dinosaur?")

Survival as a solo practitioner in a world of ever-growing government regulations and increasing competition may seem as unlikely as were the dinosaur's odds for survival during the Ice Age. Advertisements in professional journals for statewide and even nationwide practices would seem to indicate that the trend in the profession is toward "bigger is better." It must be remembered, however, that the dinosaur's very size led to its extinction.

I have been a solo practitioner, specializing in neurological and surgically based communications disorders for 8 years. And although there have been times when survival seemed to be my only goal, most of the time my practice has been growing, changing, and exciting.

I do not think the solo practitioner is about to become a dinosaur. In fact, a solo practice is becoming even more viable than in the past because it allows flexibility of caseload, control over growth factors, and less responsibility. There are of course disadvantages to the solo practice: feelings of isolation, a ceiling on amount of earnings and expansion, fiscal paranoia and being all things to all people.

However, the disadvantages can be avoided and the advantages emphasized. First, it is important to be part of, and contribute to, your profession. Being a solo practitioner does engender a feeling of isolation. You need peers with whom to discuss cases and impressions. But most importantly, you need the information and the power inherent in a large group.

Second, specialize. Specialization allows control of your caseload and growth factors. It also enables you to limit the amount of information you must assimilate to keep current. Also, many physicians and hospitals prefer to refer to a specialist, a practice that is common in the medical field. Specialization also makes the third point, noted below, much easier to achieve.

Marketing! Marketing yourself and your skills continuously is the basic survival tactic for all the types of practices, but especially so for the solo practitioner. Because you are in competition with larger clinics and practices, you must be able to offer the very best of skills.

Last, avoid fiscal paranoia before you start. Review your budget and decide how much money you need to gross weekly in order to maintain your present lifestyle. Then set that amount as your minimum weekly limit, thereby avoiding most of the usual paranoia produced by the normal fluctuating patient referral. Not all, but most anxiety can be eliminated. Some anxiety is normal when you live under the criteria of "no work—no money." The setting of a minimum limit also allows you to decide when you can take a vacation or sick leave without feeling as if bankruptcy is around the corner.

Remember the story of the three little pigs and the big bad wolf? Build your solo practice of bricks and not straw, and you will avoid both the fate of the pigs and the dinosaurs.

Kathryn Beadle, Ph.D., Mid-Peninsula Speech and Language Clinic, P.C., Clinical Associate Professor of Surgery, Stanford University, Palo Alto, California
(Editor's Note: Dr. Beadle was asked by the editor to contribute a series of reflections on the demands and dangers inherent in private practice. She responded with the following piece entitled "On the Horns of a Dilemma.")

First of all, speech and language therapy is not a field one goes into if one's goal is to become wealthy. It simply is not possible to provide high-quality, state-of-the-art service in private practice and make a lot of money doing it. If you run a one-person office, I believe you can make a good living, but certainly your professional stimulation is limited, no matter how good you are. In addition, no one person can offer all types of services well. I believe that a really good professional private practice should provide intraprofessional collaboration or offer full services within the practice. This, of course, significantly increases overhead costs and inevitably reduces profit. That is why there are so few free-standing speech and language clinics, except for some of the nonprofit types left over from better days when the government and the public sector were more generous.

But if full-service clinics are supplanted by private practices that farm out therapists with varying degrees of skill and training and provide little or no supervision and minimal accountability, how will this affect the profession? The reality is that the bottom line in private practice is not service, not professionalism, not growth and not learning—it is *revenue,* pure and simple. No one seems willing to state this fact and bring it into the open. Yet, this reality leads to what I believe is a profound philosophical dilemma. How do we control it? What begins as economic survival so easily can become materialistic greed. Now, we, too, must say that *time is money,* and good service requires a good deal of time on the part of the professional.

So much of the quality of our services depends on engaging in empathic listening and providing thoughtful explanations. We cannot, unless we wish to emulate attorneys, charge for all these services. Therefore, the danger of eliminating them is ever present.

The *time is money* problem must also be dealt with in terms of professional contributions outside of the practice or business. Few private practitioners can afford to belong to committees that require frequent or prolonged absences from work. Similarly, research and writing are also "nonproductive" in this wonderland of self-employment.

I don't have any answers, only questions. But I do think it is time that we as individuals and as a profession began to ask them. Our future development may well be headed in the direction of private practice, and there is reason to fear that this road could lead to the destruction of the vocational nature of our commitment. The quest to make money and to provide good service must begin with the recognition that these two goals are not comfortable bedfellows.

One answer to survival, of course, is to raise fees to cover the costs of qualified and experienced personnel. These fees must also cover professional involvement outside the clinic if we are to avoid isolation. The question is whether those for whom the field was created can afford such fees. And, do we, can we, will we give them their money's worth?

In terms of commitment, private practice is the most demanding of all of the roads we might choose because it is the most dangerous in terms of self-interest. Do we really believe that anyone with a degree in the field, regardless of ability or experience, can or should do it?

So far, the silence, at least on one side of this question, is deafening.

Candace L. Goldsworthy, Ph.D., private practice, Yuba City, California

For many professionals in the field of speech-language pathology and audiology, going into private practice represents a glamorous, prestigious adventure where you act as your own boss, name your hours and caseload, and realize financial rewards far in excess of typical salaries paid by schools, institutions, or clinics. I would like to caution those considering such an endeavor to examine their motives closely.

From my perspective, private practice should be approached as would any entrepreneur starting a small business. Entrepreneurship refers to the opportunity to pursue independent business careers. Broom et al. (1983) refer to entrepreneurs as "the people who provide the spark and the dynamic leadership for our economic system by taking risks and being innovative" (p. 2). And Nelton (1984), in her description of entrepreneurs' energy, creativity, courage, and zest for what they are doing, refers to such persons as "the stars of the 1980s" and calls this "the age of the entrepreneurs" (p. 22).

Reasons most often given for entering small business vary from the profit motive to independence and freedom to a more satisfying way of life. Realizing these goals requires advanced planning, for it is quite likely that no human or business condition has ever improved through hope alone, but intelligent and thorough planning can minimize failure and optimize opportunities.

An essential aspect of planning before beginning a practice includes a market survey, which is something I did 2 full years before moving to the area in which I began my practice. Consequently, I was well informed about my competition, need for my specialty in the area, and potential referral sources well before I actually began the practice. But planning does not stop when you "open your doors." Planning is a continual and necessary function for a successful business. Such factors as a slow economy or reduced third party payer reimbursement must constantly be dealt with, and there are few if any other ways to deal successfully with such issues except through intelligent advanced planning.

Independence and personal satisfaction are synonymous for me. By setting certain hours in my private practice, I have been free to pursue and accomplish other equally important facets of my professional career. Namely, while operating my private practice I was able to work with a large publishing company to develop my ideas about informal language testing. The result was published in 1982 in the form of the Multilevel Informal Language Inventory (MILI). In addition, I have been able to teach at a nearby university, travel to numerous public speaking engagements, and become actively involved with my state speech, language, and hearing association.

Although it would appear that the freedom to operate independently is a strong motive for entering private practice, there are inherent constraints. The speech-language pathologist or audiologist who does not appreciate or feel comfortable without the support of an organization should be very cautious about entering private practice. In some ways it can be a lonely experience. If you choose to work alone, for instance, you do not have feedback from co-workers. You are ultimately responsible for all aspects of the business. And although you can take credit for the things that work, you must also be willing to take the responsibility for them when they do not. Further, although it is true that when you go into private practice you leave the traditional concept of "having a boss," you, in fact, have as many bosses as you have clients and contracts.

Above all, the new speech-language pathology or audiology private practice venture should be entered into with an acute awareness of the risks, as well as the rewards. Although private practice opens exciting avenues for professional achievement, care should be taken not to short circuit those avenues by failing to understand and follow sound business practices.

Broom, H.N., Longenecker, J.G., & Moore, D.W. (1983). *Small business management.* Cincinnati: South-Western Publishing Co.

Nelton, S. (1984, June). The people who take the plunge. *Nation's Business*, p. 22.

Barbara Samuels, M.A., Director, Center for Communication Disorders, Canoga Park, California

My private practice is an extension of my personal philosophy of patient care. I have long since passed the point where I personally provide all the treatment. In fact, service is being provided by my practice for which I am not even trained nor qualified, but I still maintain interest and direct involvement in all areas of my practice. I want the same high level of patient care provided by my staff that I personally give to everyone I treat. In terms of speech pathology, I am very careful to select staff members whose philosophical approach to patient care is closely attuned to my own. Our staff operates in essentially the same manner regardless of who is treating the patient so that a change in clinician does not result in a radical change in the therapeutic regimen. Although I am not directly involved with the audiology and hearing aid dispensing to patients, many of them know who I am and feel comfortable discussing their problems and concerns with me because they know that I am aware and concerned about their situations.

For my practice, I find it beneficial to permit a new speech pathologist on staff to observe me working with patients for several days and then for me to observe the new staff member with several patients before that individual begins working independently. Subsequently, I do observe even licensed staff, periodically. Whenever problems arise, my staff feels very comfortable about asking me to come into a session to observe and possibly attempt some slightly different approach.

Because my practice is a highly personal thing and because I do feel my responsibility for it, I read all of the notes written by my staff, generally within a week of the time they are written.

In terms of handling employees, I have found that a written agreement between my professional staff and myself is necessary in order to be certain that both parties agree to all of the terms and conditions of employment. The agreement needs to set forth specifically what the employee is expected to do, what the basis for reimbursement is, what the conditions are for terminating the agreement, and whether the employee is allowed to carry out similar activities in any other setting. A section needs to be included that clearly sets forth the physical and geographic constraints against the employee setting up a private practice in the immediate area and attempting to drain away patients and referral sources when the association is terminated. Because of some conditions of third party reimbursement and delayed payment even from individuals, it has proven valuable to me to have an irrevocable assignment clause to cash checks made payable to the employee during the term of employment and after termination. To be valid this agreement does need to be signed in the presence of a notary.

Before employing a professional staff there are certain questions the practitioner must answer, including how much am I willing to teach my staff . . . how much responsibility am I willing to delegate to my staff . . . to what degree do I wish to train future competition? The answers to these questions will assist you in determining how you wish to operate, whether you will employ professional staff, how much or how little you will supervise them, and to what degree you will train them in doing the documentation necessary for third party reimbursement. When I first expanded my practice, I attempted to teach each clinician I hired to complete all of the billing questionnaires and other support documentation required for third party reimbursement. I soon found that I was frustrating both my staff and myself because of the time involved in the training program and the very tedious nature of the documentation required. I also found that frequently by the time someone had really learned how to do the job that individual was ready to start a competing practice or was off to another employment setting. At this point in time my secretary can do a good bit of the necessary documentation independently, and I dictate the remainder. Although this is an annoying drain on my time overall, I find it far less frustrating than the earlier approach.

Ellen Naliboff, M.A., private practice, San Diego, California
(Editor's Note: Ellen Naliboff has chosen to specialize in speech-language cognitive rehabilitation through independent contracting with home health agencies. The following is excerpted from her contribution, entitled "Bending with the Winds of Change."

Private practice requires personal characteristics similar to those needed to attain the CCC. One must have self-confidence, perseverance, flexibility, a high energy level, commitment, tolerance for risk, a high learning curve, initiative, responsibility, and realistic goals. In addition to these, a business plan covering management, personnel, and marketing must be developed to raise money from lenders, creditors, and/or investors.

Marketing is the means to start the cash flowing. Determine who wants the service, where they are, how they may be reached, and who else is offering what other services. The home health care industry is addressing these issues and provides a vehicle to deliver speech-language pathology services. A contract with a home health agency gives you the opportunity to ride their coattails in a sales campaign.

Although a successful marketing program results in more referrals, these new patients will then require more time for planning, treatment, and record keeping. The trap to avoid is failure to maintain the proper records. A clerical support staff is vital to the financial survival of your practice. The simplest answer to this problem is to do the thing you do best and delegate the other tasks to those who do them well. A home health agency provides the "others" (administration, marketing, sales, accounting, clerical staff) if what you do best is provide therapy to patients.

Many changes are occurring in the health care industry due to the prospective payment system of financing patients in general hospitals. As a result, patients are leaving the hospital earlier, but they still require intermittent skilled care. Because speech-language pathology is a covered service of Medicare, it can be delivered in the natural setting of the home. Do remember that the personal computer can be used as a therapeutic tool in a home-based speech-language-cognitive rehabilitation program. Several aphasia and cognitive rehabilitation programs are available commercially. Single-subject studies have shown remarkable improvement with independent use of the computer.

I have found that opportunities exist for teaching nursing staff in the health agencies the depth and breadth of speech-language-cognitive rehabilitation. This is an excellent marketing strategy as the staff members become educated on the signs and symptoms of communicative disorders and the available treatment and then make appropriate referrals.

In conclusion, obtaining independent contracts with home health agencies is my choice of venue for practicing my profession. I limit myself to rehabilitation of adults with acquired communicative disorders because I like clinical work with patients and do not care for the administrative, financial, and sales aspects of a small business.

John M. Samples, Ph.D., private practice, Santa Rosa, California

I strongly believe that speech-language pathologists with a good business background have every opportunity to provide themselves with their own livelihood. You can do it yourself, and you do not have to rely, either emotionally or financially, on any other professional. My philosophy of private practice includes the necessity of providing quality service, holding the highest of ethics and developing good business ability. Private practice is the most exciting area of our field, and it will continue to grow to unbelievable proportions in the future. However, you must not only be committed to work hard but also many years of experience in our field are required to gain the necessary background. This is an investment in something you should know well because it becomes, in essence, your lifestyle. That lifestyle includes becoming a competent and successful businessperson.

My successful strategies include doing most of the work myself, keeping my staff small, getting to know my banker well, and growing slowly. Understanding the intricacies and complexities of a Medicare-certified agency, as well as surviving audits, and the meeting of payroll taxes in today's high technology era are matters that require careful planning. In addition, a private practice should not expand too rapidly, but should be located in an area of major referral sources. On the other hand, the practice must not be allowed to stagnate. One cannot assume that referrals will continue indefinitely without consistent and frequent contacts with both potential and existing referral sources.

Joyce E. Carter, M.Ed., Director, Brookhaven Center for Communication Disorders, Coram, New York
(Editor's Note: Ms. Carter's response to the request for a reflection on the exigencies of private practice indicates the time pressures all private practitioners, without exception, have reported).

I really have not had time to properly reflect on your request and do it justice. I have, however, a small tidbit that you may want to include in your do's and don'ts of office management. New private practitioners tend to spend far too much time on the telephone, resulting in time away from their office hours. The best advice I received was from a friend who, after hearing me on the telephone answering question after question after question from a potential client, warned, ''Don't talk too much! Provide information related to the fee schedule, office policies in regard to cancellation when asked, and so forth, but other questions are more properly answered once the client has been scheduled for an appointment and is in your office.''

Readers who have perused the previous chapters carefully have found considerable consensus between the views expressed by the chapter authors and those whose reflections are included in this chapter. The need to develop the appropriate skills and experience for private practice has been universally expressed. Many of the precepts apply equally well to speech-language pathologists and audiologists, although some differences undoubtedly exist between the two specialties. Authors Hampton, Bevan, and Loavenbruck have shared considerable information in this regard.

In their glimpses of their professional and personal lives, these portraits of private practitioners have highlighted a number of major areas: the diversity of service settings, the differing practices in small versus large communities, the opportunities for self-fulfillment in private practice, the freedom and the fragility of that freedom, the desire for specialization or the definition of one's practice as a general practice and/or a comprehensive service, and, finally, the unremitting requirement that quality of service and ethical behavior should guide the practitioner through the shoals and onto the shores of success.

In summary, the practitioners of today are enthusiastically embracing a professional and personal life that, despite its difficulties, appears to provide the opportunity to exercise greater control over one's life and one's career. For some, the verdict is not yet in. Does the private practitioner have the world on a string . . . or a tiger by the tail?

Chapter 18

An Epilogue: The Cloudy Crystal

Katharine G. Butler, Ph.D.

An epilogue is designed to conclude or round out a narrative. This chapter not only reviews the status of private practice in speech-language pathology and audiology as viewed through the eyes of the authors of the preceding chapters but it also addresses the future of the profession. The authors have shared their thoughts on the presuppositions, the perils, and the prototypical rewards of practice in the private sector. As the thoughtful reader has noted, the current state of the art in private practice as reported here reflects a balance of achievements and disappointments. This raises the questions: What of tomorrow? What might the professional entering private practice find in the late 1980s and the 1990s?

Gazing into the crystal ball, there appear to be a number of possible scenarios. It would appear certain that private practitioners, perhaps more than professionals in other work settings, will be required to respond to the forces of the marketplace in perhaps unforeseen ways. Although the crystal ball is cloudy in regard to the future, it is likely that some of yesterday and today's issues will remain, perhaps in altered form. As historians are fond of saying, to predict the future, one must look to the past.

PROFESSIONAL AUTONOMY

In the 1930s, the founders of the profession in the United States boldly stated that the field would be independent of psychology and of medicine (Van Riper, 1981). A bold declaration for a fledgling profession, to be sure. Flower (1984) addresses the issue from a current perspective when he reports:

> Unquestionably, the medical profession has maintained the pivotal position in the health care system, a position that is assured in all national, state, and local regulations, policies, and practices. Yet, in view of the formidable responsibilities society assigns to physicians, and the equally formidable penalties it levies for abrogations of those responsibilities, their pivotal position is probably appropriate (p. 22).

295

Flower notes, however, that the health care system is increasingly characterized by multidisciplinary participation, and an observer of the current scene could do naught but agree. The question for the future is whether such multidisciplinary participation will eventually include full autonomy for a number of health professionals who currently have not achieved that status.

Within the medical profession, the importance of licensure and specialty certification has long been recognized. Speech-language pathologists and audiologists have also recognized the importance of licensing, but are divided on the worth of specialty certification. Psychology shares with the medical profession the mandate of licensure in every state; it shares with speech-language pathology and audiology a variety of work environments, e.g., education, health, and private practice. In a majority of the states, a license to practice in psychology requires a doctorate, with the exception of certification for master's level school psychologists that is typically granted by the state education agency and required for service in school settings. In contrast, speech-language pathologists and audiologists need not hold a doctorate to practice in any work setting at this time. In fact, as Chapey et al. (1981) have reported, the private practice sector is currently dominated by master's level practitioners. In a survey of 536 private practitioners, they found that 80% held the M.A. or M.S. degree, whereas 19% held a Ph.D. or Ed.D. It has been hypothesized that the absence of the doctoral degree may contribute to the perceived barriers to autonomy and that a significant increase in the number of professionals holding the doctorate in full-time private practice might modify the status differential.

The crystal ball is particularly cloudy on this issue of autonomy. For more than 50 years, it has been a subject of discussion and debate, and it has yet to be resolved. In the past, territorial issues between professions have been best solved on an individual or local basis (Flower, 1984). Increasingly, however, territorial issues are being addressed at the state and national level in terms of state or federal agency rules and regulations, as various professional associations take a more active stance in assisting their members to find solutions to such questions as who may be considered a qualified provider of health-related services.

In summary, although complete autonomy continues to be seen as a highly desired goal by a number of health-related professional groups, speech-language pathology and audiology among them, its elusiveness has not hampered the growth of either psychology or speech-language pathology and audiology in the private sector. This rapid growth may well be sustained over the next several years due to a constellation of factors that include the graying of America; the increase in identified speech, language, and hearing difficulties; greater recognition of the profession by the public; and the like.

THIRD PARTY REIMBURSEMENT: DOROTHY IN THE LAND OF OZ

Dorothy's adventures in the Land of Oz include a walk down the Yellow Brick Road with the Tin Woodsman, the Cowardly Lion, and the Scarecrow. All are frightened when they come to a dark forest. In the classic film of L. Frank Baum's great adventure, Judy Garland, in the role of Dorothy, speaks for the group as she gazes fearfully into the shadows. "Lions and tigers and bears . . . oh, my!" she gasps.

Private practitioners have encountered their share of frightening visages in the thickets of third party reimbursement, proliferating governmental regulations, and denial of payment by insurance companies. The rapidity with which such factors change and their complexity have been alluded to by previous authors. Travel down the Yellow Brick Road of reimbursement requires a firm step with an eye to the curves in the road, as well as understanding of the "deep structure" of HMOs, DRGs, Medicare, HCFA, PPO, JCAH, and so forth.

Because regulations are subject to change and to challenge, the private practitioner of today and of tomorrow will need to keep abreast of activities related to fee-for-service dilemmas. This can best be done by networking with colleagues both formally through state and national professional associations and informally through local and area meetings. In larger states, the state speech-language-hearing associations have expanded their role in third party reimbursement by becoming more active in the public policy arena than in the past. A number of state associations have an office in the state capital and employ personnel whose duties include relating to governmental agencies and to state legislators. Political action has become commonplace, as professionals have come to recognize the importance of influencing state legislation and regulations. This has also occurred at the national level, with the national association focusing much more of its attention on governmental issues that affect private practitioners.

Rising health care costs have been a persistent problem, and governmental strategies to contain those costs have been underway for some time, albeit somewhat unsuccessfully. There is tremendous pressure exerted on many health-related personnel by third party reimbursement sources to contain costs. Consumers of speech-language pathology and audiology services are increasingly denied these services by various insurance programs. Such carriers as Blue Cross and Blue Shield, Aetna Life and Casualty, and Transamerica Occidental Life Insurance Company administer Medicare Supplementary Medical Insurance (Part B) locally for the federal government (White, 1986). As White notes, because the private insurance companies administer the program, it is a specific carrier's *interpretation* of federal Medicare regulations and guidelines that may deny or reduce a claim for services rendered. He adds:

> There has been a major clarification of how inquiries by beneficiaries concerning claims are to be handled by carriers. The Gray Panthers successfully sued the U.S. Department of Health and Human Services (of which HCFA is a branch) over notice and review procedures for Medicare beneficiaries dissatisfied with a carrier's denial of all or part of a claim for services under Part B (p. 4).

In detailing the results of the successful suit, White presents information that is of importance to the consumer and the private practitioner alike. As Chapey et al. (1981) report from their survey of practitioners, medical insurance and Medicare appear to be available to about one-half of the clients seen by those who deliver speech-language pathology and audiology services in the private sector. Those authors also report that the major problems confronting those in private practice "appear in relationship to fees and consistency of income, which in turn seem to reflect problems with third party payment and public awareness" (p. 339).

Suits, such as that mounted by the Gray Panthers, will undoubtedly increase as consumers and service providers attempt to obtain services for the communicatively impaired. Every American is aware of the "graying of America," as those over 65 make up an ever larger portion of the population. In the next several years it is predicted that life expectancy will also significantly increase. As it becomes more common to live beyond 75 or 85, there will be an increased demand for our profession's services because speech, language, and hearing handicaps are frequent in such age groups. One can only hope that services for those handicaps will remain available as health costs continue to soar.

At the other end of the age spectrum, services for the very young have come under fire recently. For example, in December 1985 speech therapy services for children ages 0–3 were endangered in California when "Medi-Cal field officers were notified that speech therapy for children 0–3 was presumed not to be medically effective and that children 3–21 should be referred to the schools for speech and hearing services" (California Speech-Language-Hearing Association, 1986, p. 1).

At least two major issues are involved in the above ruling. The first deals with the general notion of whether intervention with young children is efficacious, a matter that even now can be answered by extant research, both general and specific. As Johnston (1983) commented: "It is indeed the mark of growing professional maturity that we have looked carefully and documented the results of our therapeutic efforts in ways that are replicable, objective and convincing" (p. 53). For infants and pre-school children at risk for language disorders, language intervention is based on a wealth of information from the infant research literature about early "communicative" interactions (Bricker and Schiefelbusch, 1983, p. 244). It may be difficult for those from other disciplines to appreciate fully the current emphases on not only social-communicative exchange as the basis for training speech and language but also the role of the communicative disorders specialist in developing intervention strategies that are shared with a variety of caregivers. A second major issue is the increasingly observed tendency of the health care system and the education system in the United States to each maintain that the consumer of services, in this case a young child, is the responsibility of the other. Indeed, a real Catch-22 is inevitable as services under PL 94–142 are also increasingly subject to reduction at the state and national levels.

In summary, third party reimbursement promises to continue to be a source of difficulty in the foreseeable future. Its importance to the needs of communicatively handicapped individuals requires that a continuous campaign to educate those responsible for setting regulations and policies be supported by both consumers and the profession. There are, indeed, lions and tigers and bears residing alongside the Yellow Brick Road.

Speech-language pathologists and audiologists were unconcerned about potential malpractice suits for a large number of years. That period of the profession's existence is now over, as the chapters in this book by Kooper and Sullivan and Woody make painfully clear. This profession is but one of many to feel the recent impact of malpractice suits.

Fisher (1985) reports that "the American Medical Association in February called for major policy initiatives for physicians, insurers and government to combat what is called a problem of crisis proportions" (p. 6). Daily newspapers report such facts as:

- In the last decade suits against doctors have tripled.

- In that time the average jury award in a malpractice case has risen from $166,165 to $954,858.

- The American Medical Association reports 16 percent of its members were sued in 1984 for malpractice. In this climate, 35 percent of its members told the AMA they have limited the types of cases they will accept (Moody, 1985, p. D1).

- In 1986, the largest medical malpractice judgment in California history ($8.4 million) was awarded to the parents of a 5-year-old girl who is blind, severely retarded, and paraplegic, due to a hospital's failure to diagnose hypoxia at birth (Harris, 1986).

While Moody reported the AMA's identification of the current status of malpractice suits as a crisis, he also reported the converse side of the coin by adding, "Stanley Rosenblatt, a plaintiff's attorney in Miami [stated]: 'The crisis only exists in the pocketbooks of doctors. Doctors are too stupid to realize they are being ripped off by the insurance carriers'" (p. D1). However one may react to that statement, members of the health professions are increasingly concerned about professional liability. Available data would seem to support that concern. For example, Fisher (1985) reports:

> The personal nightmare of malpractice has become real for psychologists only in the past few years. . . . From 1955 to 1965, the first 10 years that the American Psychological Association offered malpractice coverage through its Insurance Trust, there were no claims filed against psychologists, and premiums were stable. But between 1976 and 1981, 266 claims against psychologists were filed with the trust's insurers—an average of 44 claims a year. During the period from 1982 to 1984 the annual rate more than tripled, to an average of 153 claims. . . . Judgments in those same cases . . . multiplied by a factor of eight. (p. 6)

The APA's insurance carrier has reported that the number of claims against psychologists has increased more rapidly in the past 3 years than for any other mental health professionals. Of interest to private practitioners in speech-language pathology and audiology was the insurance carrier's comment that the malpractice crisis in psychology was due, at least to some extent, to the success of psychologists in achieving independent practice status. Malpractice insurance costs have increased six-fold from $50 for $1 million worth of coverage to $300 for $1 million coverage over the past 2 years for psychologists.

In summary, there appears to be no doubt that the "cost of doing business" will be increased for both psychologists and speech-language pathologists and audiologists as professional liability premiums climb, at least presumably, to reflect the increase in malpractice suits. Malpractice awards are increasing, as are property casualty and product liability awards. For example, in 1984 the average product liability court award was slightly more than $1 million; the average medical malpractice award was $950,000 (Tompkins, 1986). Thus, those who deal in any way with products, such as hearing aids, or rent or own property used for professional purposes must safeguard their professional practice and their futures by keeping current regarding liability issues. It is unlikely that the spiral of increased costs resulting from living in a society that has become increasingly litigation-minded will significantly slow, at least in the short term. There may only be long-term partial solutions as professionals, particularly those in medicine, either retire from practice due to high malpractice costs or become highly selective regarding whom they will serve. The new game in town for the health professions may be "professional's choice," rather than "patient choice."

ACQUISITION OF BUSINESS SURVIVAL SKILLS

Those in the private sector have long noted that one cannot begin a practice without a fair measure of basic survival skills, even though, in the past, a fair number of individuals in speech-language pathology and audiology have gone into practice with only a limited repertoire of such skills. Many examples cited in this book reflect that theme.

Conventional wisdom cites the reasons for business failure to include lack of experience in the chosen field, lack of money or undercapitalization, selection of the wrong location, and poor credit-creating practices. All of these issues have been addressed in the preceding chapters. Also, competition from larger and more established practices, may be an obstacle to initiating a practice, particularly in urban or suburban areas where the established private practitioners have been providing services for some time. This factor highlights the need to select the location of the practice with all the care the authors of this book have emphasized.

There are a number of ways, many of them of the self-help variety, to assimilate the necessary survival skills. Certainly information can be obtained from attending state, regional, and national conferences for speech-language pathologists and audiologists or allied professions. If professional time must be devoted to the practice, rather than attendance of conferences, it is possible to gather information from such resources as the Small Business Administration (as identified by Hampton in Chapter 8) or to join the American Management Association (AMA) and one or more of its divisions. The AMA is of particular value as one's practice grows because its Extension Institute deals with such matters as employee productivity, efficiency, and motivation through a formal appraisal process (AMA, 1986). Overall, there is no dearth of material—written, audiotaped, basic or advanced—that can enlighten the prospective practitioner or the seasoned veteran.

Practitioners have frequently noted that their educational preparation did not train them to make the business and administrative decisions necessary to a successful private practice. Some practitioners have chosen to obtain a Master's of Business Administration; others have sought a law degree. Many more have pressed for inclusion of coursework related to business and administration within the confines of a professional doctorate in speech-language pathology and audiology, and even larger numbers have sought to have such knowledge included in master's level programs. Institutions of higher education have responded only slowly to this demand, although many programs in speech-language pathology and audiology have included private practice concerns in a general graduate-level course that previously dealt primarily with the delivery of services in educational and hospital settings.

Graduate programs are hard pressed to provide all the necessary theoretical, scientific, technical, and clinical information and hesitate to pursue instruction in the business-related aspects of professional practice, although some programs have begun to meet this need. There is also significant movement in educational programs to provide instruction in computer-based assessment, intervention, and clinical management procedures. The attainment of computer literacy as a part of both undergraduate and graduate educational programs is an emerging reality. This literacy will be of inestimable value to the practitioner, independent of the work settings elected on the completion of such training.

In summary, there is an acknowledged need for information regarding the management aspects of private practice. This need is being met through a variety of resources: conferences, programs, association membership, coursework, and self-initiated reading. University preparation programs are not only recognizing their responsibility to provide at least a portion of this information but they are also moving rapidly ahead in the area of teaching computer literacy in both research and practice. Students who attain such computer literacy opportunities will find themselves with one of the basic survival skills of the future.

TO MARKET, TO MARKET

Perhaps one's semantic associations with the term "marketing" stem from the childhood rhyme that begins, "To market, to market, to buy a fat pig." If so, the term carries certain repugnant overtones, unrelated to one's preference for pork. Yet there is evidence that marketing is a concept that has been adopted by the health-related professions.

For example, medicine's use of marketing was extolled in a recent article in *The Wall Street Journal* (1985) that described how physicians are utilizing consultants, focus groups, surveys of patients, and demographic studies to enhance their practices. One ophthalmologist reported that he did not take a management course when he was in medical school because that was considered unprofessional. Since then, however, he has taken a few business courses and "has learned about marketing, though he still shies away from the word. He does 'two or three hundred little things' that make his practice successful enough to support a 32-person staff and his own surgery center'' (Bean, 1985, p. 1). Conversely, other physicians express concern that the quality of medical care may drop as physicians increase their concern and interest in marketing, advertising, and business management. The *Journal* concludes that medical marketing is not likely to ''go away,'' but is here to stay.

Psychologists, too, have looked to the future. Recently reported in the *APA Monitor* were the predictions that with the expansion of health maintenance organizations (HMOs), preferred provider organizations (PPOs), and independent practitioner associations (IPAs), there will be more and more enabling legislation passed without regulations (Turkington, 1986). This period of rapid expansion will then be followed by a period of governmental regulation, due to the complaints of consumers hurt during the nonregulatory environment. Turkington reports that psychologists remain concerned about the quality of care, noting that HMOs may interpret federal or state regulations in such a manner as to limit access of consumers to specialized or long-term mental health care. An example provided was that of a youngster referred to an HMO that had a 20-visit limit on mental health care. When told that the child was psychotic and that there was a need for long-term therapy, the HMO authorities ''said that it would be cruel and unusual to stop treatment after 20 visits—so they wouldn't fund any care at all'' (Turkington, 1986, p. 16). On a less contentious note, the need to use a number of avenues of communication to reach the local community, service providers in other professions, public officials, legislators, media personnel, and the general public is frequently advocated by nonacademic psychologists (Maloney et al., 1985).

Speech-language pathologists and audiologists who enter private practice also become particularly concerned with marketing. Such involvement may stem from sheer necessity. In response, the national professional association has developed a number of approaches, including periodic newsletters, such as *Speech-Language Pathology Update*, a publication of its Professional Practices Division that summarizes items of interest to speech-language pathologists in various work settings. State associations also address the need for further information. For example, among 55 sessions to be offered at the New York State Speech-Language-Hearing Association 1986 spring conference, ten discuss items of interest to private practitioners: Malpractice Update; RUGS, DRGs, and PROs; Legal Defense for Professionals; a series on Marketing Yourself; Maintaining Professional Standards in Part-Time Private Practice; and Comparison of Standards for the Practice of Speech-Language Pathology and Audiology in New York State. It is safe to say that a decade ago, or even 5 years ago, no state conference would have provided that much attention to the needs and concerns of the private sector.

In summary, many professions have found it necessary to become more concerned with the marketplace. Private practitioners, as the most vulnerable to the vagaries of independent practice, are attempting to position themselves to maximize their efforts in an increasingly difficult period of time that may move between regulation and deregulation in sometimes mysterious ways.

Previous chapters have stressed the importance of maintaining professional standards and providing high-quality services. The Council on Professional Standards in Speech-Language Pathology and Audiology is engaged in an intensive study of standards (*Asha,* 1985). A 3-year content validity study has been undertaken that will include a study of the knowledge, skills, and abilities required for speech-language pathologists to perform their positions at entry level in order to analyze professional tasks and the basic requirements for the Certification of Clinical Competence, i.e., academic and practicum performance, the National Examinations in Speech-Language Pathology and Audiology (NENSPA), and the Clinical Fellowship Year (CFY). Such a study speaks to a number of interrelated issues that have been addressed in previous chapters:

**PROFES-
SIONAL
STANDARDS**

- the need to define for ourselves, for our profession, for other professionals, and for regulatory agencies the content of our curriculum and clinical practice requirements
- the need to respecify the knowledge, skills, and abilities that are required for the *beginning* practitioner, given the massive changes in the knowledge base over the past several years
- the need to review professional tasks in light of the nationally recognized Certificate of Clinical Competence
- the need to convert such knowledge into state licensure requirements and to achieve licensing in the remaining unlicensed states
- the need to utilize the above information to identify continuing educational requirements, whether they be voluntary or mandatory
- the need to reevaluate the status of specialty certification as one avenue for identifying specific areas of expertise as our understanding of normal and disordered communication expands.

All of the above and more lie in the future.

At the beginning of this brief glimpse into the cloudy crystal, the question was raised about the future for professionals who were considering entering into the private, rather than the public, practice sector. What does the future hold?

Private practice remains an exciting opportunity for those with an entrepreneurial spirit. However, it is just that, an opportunity, and not a self-fulfilling prophecy of success. And although everyone must begin somewhere, it would appear to be foolish to begin a private practice without arming oneself with the necessary knowledge and skills. Undergirding this book is the assumption that the practitioners who desire to enter private practice do so based on a solid academic and clinical background and an experiential past that includes significant experience in assessment and intervention with a large range of communication disorders. Few professionals believe that the necessary skills can be garnered by the close of the clinical fellowship year.

Although the difficulties inherent in entering a competitive environment have been carefully documented, those difficulties are no more nor no less than those encountered by a number of the professions with whom speech-language pathologists and audiologists relate. It is, therefore, incumbent on the individual practitioner to understand both the risks and the opportunities inherent not only in the private practice work setting but in other settings as well, although those settings have not been the focus of this book. To be sure, every setting has its rewards and its difficulties, and private practice is no exception. Only the reader can answer the question: Is it for me?

It is the authors' and editor's hope that this book has served to illuminate this most important question.

REFERENCES

American Management Association. (1986). *The performance appraisal process*. New York: AMA Extension Institute.

American Speech-Language-Hearing Association. (1985). Council on professionl standards annual report. (1984). *Asha 27*, 53.

Bean, E. (1985, March 15). Doctors find a dose of marketing can cure pain of sluggish practice. *The Wall Street Journal*, p. 27.

Bricker, D., & Schiefelbusch, R.L. (1983). Infants at risk. In L. McCormick & R.L. Schiefelbusch (Eds.), *Early language intervention* (pp. 243–266). Columbus, OH: Charles E. Merrill.

California Speech-Language-Hearing Association. (1986, January). *Legislative Bulletin*, p. 1.

Chapey, R., Chwat, S., Gurland, G., & Guillermo, P. (1981). Perspectives in private practice: A nationwide analysis. *Asha, 23,* 335–340.

Fisher, K. (1985). Charges catch clinicians in cycle of shame, slip-ups. *American Psychological Association Monitor, 16,* 6.

Flower, R.M. (1984). *Delivery of services in speech-language pathology and audiology services*. Baltimore, MD: Williams & Wilkins.

Harris, S. (1986). $8.4 million won over birth defects. *Los Angeles Times,* April 16, p. 1, part 2.

Johnston, J.R. (1983). What is language intervention? The role of theory. In J. Miller, D. Yoder, & R. Schiefelbusch (Eds.), *Contemporary issues in language intervention*. Rockville, MD: American Speech-Language-Hearing Association, 52–60.

Maloney, D.M., Fixsen, D.L.L., & Phillips, E.L. (1985). Marketing your product: The psychologist as communicator. *American Psychologist 40,* 961–962.

Moody, S. (1985, December 1). Sickness over lawsuits. *Syracuse Herald-American*, p. D–1.

New York State Speech-Language-Hearing Association. (1986). *The Communicator, 14,* 1–2.

Tompkins, K.L. (1986, March 3). Insurance crisis. *Syracuse Post-Standard*, p. D–1.

Turkington, C. (1986). Marketing. *American Psychological Association Monitor, 17,* 16.

Van Riper, C. (1981). An early history of ASHA. *Asha, 23,* 855–858.

White, S.C. (1986). Insurance notes. *National Association for Hearing and Speech Action, 5,* 4.

Code of Ethics
of the
American Speech-Language-Hearing Association
1986

(Revised January 1, 1986)

The preservation of the highest standards of integrity and ethical principles is vital to the successful discharge of the professional responsibilities of all speech-language pathologists and audiologists. This Code of Ethics has been promulgated by the Association in an effort to stress the fundamental rules considered essential to this basic purpose. Any action that is in violation of the spirit and purpose of this Code shall be considered unethical. Failure to specify any particular responsibility or practice in this Code of Ethics should not be construed as denial of the existence of other responsibilities or practices.

PREAMBLE

The fundamental rules of ethical conduct are described in three categories: Principles of Ethics, Ethical Proscriptions, Matters of Professional Propriety.

1. *Principles of Ethics.* Six Principles serve as a basis for the ethical evaluation of professional conduct and form the underlying moral basis for the Code of Ethics. Individuals[1] subscribing to this Code shall observe these principles as affirmative obligations under all conditions of professional activity.
2. *Ethical Proscriptions.* Ethical Proscriptions are formal statements of prohibitions that are derived from the Principles of Ethics.
3. *Matters of Professional Propriety.* Matters of Professional Propriety represent guidelines of conduct designed to promote the public interest and thereby better inform the public and particularly the persons in need of speech-language pathology and audiology services as to the availability and the rules regarding the delivery of those services.

---

[1]"Individuals" refers to all members of the American Speech-Lanuage-Hearing Assocation and non-members who hold a Certificate of Clinical Competence from this Association.

Source: From *ASHA,* April 1986, pp. 55–57. Copyright 1986 by American-Speech-Language-Hearing Association, Rockville, MD Reprinted by permission.

PRINCIPLE OF ETHICS I

Individuals shall hold paramount the welfare of persons served professionally.

A. Individuals shall use every resource available, including referral to other specialists as needed, to provide the best service possible.
B. Individuals shall fully inform persons served of the nature and possible effects of the services.
C. Individuals shall fully inform subjects participating in research or teaching activities of the nature and possible effects of these activities.
D. Individuals' fees shall be commensurate with services rendered.
E. Individuals shall provide appropriate access to records of persons served professionally.
F. Individuals shall take all reasonable precautions to avoid injuring persons in the delivery of professional services.
G. Individuals shall evaluate services rendered to determine effectiveness.

Ethical Proscriptions

1. Individuals must not exploit persons in the delivery of professional services, including accepting persons for treatment when benefit cannot reasonably be expected or continuing treatment unnecessarily.
2. Individuals must not guarantee the results of any therapeutic procedures, directly or by implication. A reasonable statement of prognosis may be made, but caution must be exercised not to mislead persons served professionally to expect results that cannot be predicted from sound evidence.
3. Individuals must not use persons for teaching or research in a manner that constitutes invasion of privacy or fails to afford informed free choice to participate.
4. Individuals must not evaluate or treat speech, language or hearing disorders except in a professional relationship. They must not evaluate or treat solely by correspondence. This does not preclude follow-up correspondence with persons previously seen, nor providing them with general information of an educational nature.
5. Individuals must not reveal to unauthorized persons any professional or personal information obtained from the person served professionally, unless required by law or unless necessary to protect the welfare of the person or the community.
6. Individuals must not discriminate in the delivery of professional services on any basis that is unjustifiable or irrelevant to the need for and potential benefit from such services, such as race, sex, age, or religion.
7. Individuals must not charge for services not rendered.

PRINCIPLE OF ETHICS II

Individuals shall maintain high standards of professional competence.
A. Individuals engaging in clinical practice or supervision thereof shall hold the appropriate Certificate(s) of Clinical Competence for the area(s) in which they are providing or supervising professional services.

B. Individuals shall continue their professional development throughout their careers.

C. Individuals shall identify competent, dependable referral sources for persons served professionally.

D. Individuals shall maintain adequate records of professional services rendered.

Ethical Proscriptions

1. Individuals must neither provide services nor supervision of services for which they have not been properly prepared, nor permit services to be provided by any of their staff who are not properly prepared.

2. Individuals must not provide clinical services by prescription of anyone who does not hold the Certificate of Clinical Competence.

3. Individuals must not delegate any service requiring the professional competence of a certified clinician to anyone unqualified.

4. Individuals must not offer clinical services by supportive personnel for whom they do not provide appropriate supervision and assume full responsibility.

5. Individuals must not require anyone under their supervision to engage in any practice that is a violation of the Code of Ethics.

PRINCIPLE OF ETHICS III

Individuals' statements to persons served professionally and to the public shall provide accurate information about the nature and management of communicative disorders, and about the profession and services rendered by its practitioners.

Ethical Proscriptions

1. Individuals must not misrepresent their training or competence.

2. Individuals' public statements providing information about professional services and products must not contain representations or claims that are false, deceptive or misleading.

3. Individuals must not use professional or commercial affiliations in any way that would mislead or limit services to persons served professionally.

Matters of Professional Propriety

1. Individuals should announce services in a manner consonant with highest professional standards in the community.

PRINCIPLE OF ETHICS IV

Individuals shall maintain objectivity in all matters concerning the welfare of persons served professionally.

A. Individuals who dispense products to persons served professionally shall observe the following standards:

(1) Products associated with professional practice must be dispensed to the person served as a part of a program of comprehensive habilitative care.

(2) Fees established for professional services must be independent of whether a product is dispensed.

(3) Persons served must be provided freedom of choice for the source of services and products.

(4) Price information about professional services rendered and products dispensed must be disclosed by providing to or posting for persons served a complete schedule of fees and charges in advance of rendering services, which schedule differentiates between fees for professional services and charges for products dispensed.

(5) Products dispensed to the person served must be evaluated to determine effectiveness.

Ethical Proscriptions

1. Individuals must not participate in activities that constitute a conflict of professional interest.

Matters of Professional Propriety

1. Individuals should not accept compensation for supervision or sponsorship from the clinical fellow being supervised or sponsored beyond reasonable reimbursement for direct expenses.

2. Individuals should present products they have developed to their colleagues in a manner consonant with highest professional standards.

PRINCIPLE OF ETHICS V

Individuals shall honor their responsibilities to the public, their profession, and their relationships with colleagues and members of allied professions.

Matters of Professional Propriety

1. Individuals should seek to provide and expand services to persons with speech, language and hearing handicaps as well as to assist in establishing high professional standards for such programs.

2. Individuals should educate the public about speech, language and hearing processes, speech, language and hearing problems, and matters related to professional competence.

3. Individuals should strive to increase knowledge within the profession and share research with colleagues.

4. Individuals should establish harmonious relations with colleagues and members of other professions, and endeavor to inform members of related professions of services provided by speech-language pathologists and audiologists, as well as seek information from them.

5. Individuals should assign credit to those who have contributed to a publication in proportion to their contribution.

PRINCIPLE OF ETHICS VI

Individuals shall uphold the dignity of the profession and freely accept the profession's self-imposed standards.

A. Individuals shall inform the Ethical Practice Board when they have reason to believe that a member or certificate holder may have violated the Code of Ethics.

B. Individuals shall cooperate fully with the Ethical Practice Board concerning matters of professional conduct related to this Code of Ethics.

1. Individuals shall not engage in violations of the Principles of Ethics or in any attempt to circumvent any of them.
2. Individuals shall not engage in dishonesty, fraud, deceit, misrepresentation, or other forms of illegal conduct that adversely reflect on the profession or the individuals' fitness for membership in the profession.

Ethical Proscriptions

Ethical Practice Board
Statement of Practices and
Procedures

(Effective February 15, 1986)

The Ethical Practice Board (EPB) is charged by the Bylaws of the American Speech-Language-Hearing Association with the responsibility to interpret, administer, and enforce the Code of Ethics of the Association. Accordingly, the EPB hereby adopts the following practices and procedures to be followed in administering and enforcing that Code.

A fundamental precept that guides the EPB in the discharge of its responsibility is that an effective Code of Ethics requires an orderly and fair administration and enforcement of its terms and requires full compliance by all members of the Association and all holders of Certificates of Clinical Competence. The EPB recognizes that each case must be judged on an individual basis, and that no two cases are likely to be identical. Thus, the EPB has the responsibility to exercise its judgment on the merits of each case and on its interpretation of the Code.

1.	*EPB:*	Ethical Practice Board
2.	*Association:*	American Speech-Language-Hearing Association
3.	*Code:*	Code of Ethics of the Association
4.	*Certificate(s):*	Certificate(s) of Clinical Competence
5.	*Respondent:*	The alleged offender
6.	*Complainant(s):*	The person(s) alleging that a violation occurred
7.	*Initial Determination:*	Initial Determination by the EPB, subject to Further Consideration and appeal, of the (a) finding, (b) proposed sanction, and (c) extent of disclosure
8.	*Sanctions:*	Penalties imposed by the EPB
9.	*Disclosure:*	Announcement of the final EPB Decision to other than Respondent
10.	*Further Consideration:*	Further Consideration by the EPB of its Initial Determination

A. DEFINITION OF TERMS

11. *EPB Decision:*   Final decision of the EPB after: 1) Further Consideration; or 2) 30 days from the date of notice of the Initial Determination by the EPB if no request for Further Consideration is received

12. *Appeal:*   Written request from Respondent to EPB alleging error in the EPB Decision and asking that it be reversed in whole or in part by the Executive Board

B. INVESTIGATIVE PROCEDURES

1. Alleged violations shall be reviewed by the EPB in such manner as the EPB may, in its discretion, deem necessary and proper. If, after review, the EPB elects to investigate the allegation, the EPB shall notify Respondent of the alleged offense in writing and shall advise Respondent that Respondent's answer to the allegation shall be in writing and must be *received* by the EPB no later than 45 days after the date of the EPB notice to Respondent. Voluntary resignation of membership and/or voluntary surrender of the Certificate(s) shall not preclude the EPB from continuing to process the alleged violation to conclusion, and the notice from the EPB to Respondent requesting an answer shall so advise Respondent.

2. At the discretion of the EPB, the Director of the Professional Affairs Department of the Association's National Office may be informed that Respondent is under investigation by the EPB for alleged violation of the Code and may be instructed that no change in membership and or certification status shall be permitted without approval of the EPB.

3. The EPB shall consider all information secured from its investigation, including Respondent's answer to the allegation, and shall base its Initial Determination on that information.

4. If the EPB finds that there is not sufficient evidence to warrant further proceedings, Respondent and Complainant(s) shall be so advised and the investigation shall be terminated.

5. If the EPB finds that there is sufficient evidence to warrant further proceedings, the EPB shall make an Initial Determination, which includes (a) the finding of violation, (b) the proposed sanction, and (c) the proposed extent of disclosure. In this regard, the final decision of any State, Federal, regulatory, or judicial body may be considered sufficient evidence that the Code was violated.

6. The EPB may, as part of its Initial Determination, order that the Respondent cease and desist from any practice found to be a violation of the Code. Failure to comply with such a Cease and Desist Order is, itself, a violation of the Code, and shall normally result in Revocation of Membership and/or Revocation of the Certificate(s).

7. The EPB shall give Respondent notice of its Initial Determination, with copy to Complainant(s). The notice shall also advise Respondent of the right to request Further Consideration by the EPB and of the right, *after Further Consideration*, to request an appeal to the Executive Board. The procedures to be followed in exercising those rights are described in Sections F and G of this statement.

All notices and answers shall be in writing and considered to be given or furnished (1) to Respondent when *sent*—Certified Mail, Addressee Only, Return Receipt Requested—to the address then listed in the ASHA membership records, and (2) to the EPB when *received* by the EPB.

C. NOTICES AND ANSWERS

Sanctions shall consist of one or more of the following, Reprimand; Censure; Withhold, Suspend, or Revoke Membership; Withhold, Suspend, or Revoke the Certificate(s); or other measures determined by the EPB at its discretion.

D. SANCTIONS

1. The EPB Decision, upon becoming final, shall be published in the Journal *Asha* unless the sanction is Reprimand. In the case of Reprimand, the EPB Decision normally shall be disclosed only to Respondent, Respondent's counsel, Complainant(s), witnesses at the EPB Further Consideration Hearing and/or at the Executive Board Hearing, staff, Association counsel, and the Coordinator of the Professional Ethics Section of the Association's National Office, each of whom shall be advised that the decision is strictly confidential and that any breach of that confidentiality by any party who is a member and/or certificate holder of the Association is, itself, a violation of the Code.
2. In appropriate cases, including when the sanction is Reprimand, the EPB may also determine that its Decision shall be disclosed to aggrieved parties and/or other appropriate individuals, bodies, or agencies.

E. DIS-CLOSURE

1. When the notice of Initial Determination from the EPB states that Respondent has violated the Code and announces a proposed sanction and extent of disclosure, Respondent may request that the EPB give Further Consideration to the Initial Determination.
2. Respondent's request for Further Consideration shall be in writing and must be *received* by the EPB Chair no later than 30 days after the date of notice of Initial Determination. *The request for Further Consideration must specify in what respects the Initial Determination was allegedly wrong and why.* In the absence of a timely request for Further Consideration, the Initial Determination shall be the EPB Decision, which decision shall be final; there shall be no further right of appeal to the Executive Board.
3. If Respondent submits a timely request for Further Consideration by the EPB, the EPB shall schedule a hearing and notify Respondent. At the hearing, Respondent shall be entitled to submit a written brief or to appear personally to present evidence and to be accompanied by counsel. The proceeding shall be informal; strict adherence to the rules of evidence shall not be observed, but all evidence shall be accorded such weight as it deserves. As an alternative to personal appearance at the hearing, the EPB shall afford Respondent the opportunity to make a presentation to the EPB and to respond to questions from the EPB via a conference telephone call placed to Respondent by the EPB. All

F. FURTHER CONSIDERA-TION BY THE EPB OF THE INITIAL DETERMINA-TION

personal costs in connection with the Further Consideration hearing, including travel and lodging costs incurred by Respondent. Respondent's counsel and witnesses, and counsel and other fees, shall be Respondent's sole responsibility. The hearing shall be transcribed in full and, upon request, a copy of the transcript shall be made available to Respondent at Respondent's sole expense.

4. After the Further Consideration Hearing, the EPB shall render its decision and notify Respondent. If evidence presented at the hearing warrants, the EPB may modify the finding, increase or decrease the severity of the sanction, and/or modify the extent of disclosure that was announced to Respondent in the notice of Initial Determination. This decision shall be the EPB Decision, and in the absence of a timely appeal to the Executive Board, the EPB Decision shall be final.

G. APPEAL OF EPB DECISION TO EXECUTIVE BOARD

1. Respondent may appeal the EPB Decision to the Executive Board. The request for appeal shall be in writing and must be *received* by the EPB Chair no later than 30 days after the date of notice of the EPB Decision. *The request for appeal shall specify in what respects the EPB Decision was allegedly wrong and why.*

2. The procedures for a hearing before the Executive Board are described in the *Executive Board Statement of Practices and Procedures for Appeals of Decisions of the Ethical Practice Board.*

H. REINSTATEMENT

Persons whose membership or certification has been revoked may, upon application therefore, be reinstated after one year upon a two-thirds vote of the EPB. The applicant bears the burden of demonstrating that the reason(s) for revocation no longer exist and that, upon reinstatement, applicant will abide by the Code.

I. AMENDMENT

This *Statement of Practices and Procedures* may be amended upon recommendation of the EPB and a vote of the Executive Board. All such changes will be given appropriate publicity.

Index

Note: Pages appearing in italics indicate entries found in artwork.

About the Editor

Katharine G. Butler, Ph.D., Editor, has been involved in the practice of speech-language pathology since receiving her B.A. from Western Michigan University (WMU). She holds a M.A. in Speech-Pathology and Audiology from WMU, an Ed.S. in Psychology, also from WMU, and a Ph.D. in Hearing and Speech Science from Michigan State University. She has been a clinician in rural, suburban, and city public schools, Associate Director of the Constance Brown Society for Better Hearing in Kalamazoo, Michigan, and a supervisor in both public schools and university clinics. She has held credentials as a speech clinician, as a Teacher of the Deaf, and as a School Psychologist. Dr. Butler currently holds licenses to practice speech-language pathology in both California and New York, and the Certificate of Clinical Competence in Speech-Language Pathology.

Initially a faculty member in the Department of Psychology at Western Michigan, she joined the faculty at San Jose State University (SJSU) in 1964. At SJSU she held a number of positions, including Coordinator of Clinical Services, Director of the Speech and Hearing Center, Professor of Speech-Language Pathology and Audiology, and Chairman of Special Education. Administrative service included Associate Dean of Professional Studies in the School of Education, and later, Associate Dean and Dean of Graduate Studies and Research. Since the late 1970s she has served as Professor, Communication Sciences and Disorders, and Director of the Division of Special Education and Rehabilitation. In 1983, she became Director, Center for Research, and Director of the Center for Language Research at Syracuse University.

Among her more than 70 publications are several texts, including *Language Learning Disabilities in School Age Children,* co-edited with Dr. Geraldine Wallach in 1984, and *Childhood Language Disorders,* in 1986. She has served as Editor of *Topics in Language Disorders,* a quarterly journal, since 1979.

Dr. Butler has been President of the American Speech-Language-Hearing Association, the Division of Children with Communication Disorders of the Council of Exceptional Children, the National Association for Speech and Hearing Action, and the International Association of Logopedics and Phoniatrics. She has been President of the California Speech-Language-Hearing Association and currently serves as President-Elect of the New York State Speech-Language-Hearing Association.

She is a Fellow of the American Speech-Language-Hearing Association and of the International Academy for Research in Learning Disabilities, and has received Distinguished Alumni Awards from Western Michigan University and Michigan State University.

About the Authors

Deena K. Bernstein, Ph.D., Assistant Professor of Speech-Language Pathology, Herbert H. Lehman College, City University of New York, teaches undergraduate and graduate courses in language development and disorders and supervises clinical practicum. She is active in state and national professional organizations, continuing education, and teacher training. She is the co-author of *Language and Communication Disorders in Children,* is an editorial consultant for *Language, Speech and Hearing Services in the Schools,* has written several journal articles, and has consulted with local school districts as well as public and private agencies. She has lectured extensively. She holds a B.A. from Brooklyn College, an M.A. from Temple University, and a Ph.D. from CUNY. She has been in part-time private practice for some time. The scope of her practice varies according to her primary duties as a university employee. She has provided diagnostic and habilitative services in a residential (home) office, in clients' homes, and as an independent contractor. Her clients include both adults and children exhibiting a wide range of speech-language disorders, ranging from adult aphasics and severely developmentally delayed children, including the autistic, to the mildly language learning disabled.

Marlene A. Bevan, Ph.D., is Executive Director of the Northwestern Michigan Hearing and Speech Center, Traverse City, Michigan. The Center is a sole proprietorship established in a small midwestern community in 1980 with an emphasis on rehabilitative audiology. As part of her developing practice, Dr. Bevan has coordinated and developed community programming in hearing and speech for several philanthropic organizations as well as for local and state agencies. Prior to establishing her practice, she served as Clinical Director of a United Way Agency and worked in several hospital, academic, and private practice settings. She served as President of the Academy of Dispensing Audiologists and is currently the Chairperson of the State of Michigan Board of Hearing Aid Dealers for licensing and regulation. She has lectured and published in the area of amplification and private practice throughout the United States, Germany, and the People's Republic of China. She received a B.A. in Speech Pathology from California State University, Los Angeles, an M.S. in Communication Disorders from the University of Redlands, and a Ph.D. in Speech and Hearing from the University of Connecticut.

Joseph F. Butler, M.A., has had long experience in the field of telecommunications, having served as producer, film director, chief copywriter, and chief announcer and newsman at WKZO-TV, and as sales representative writer, director, announcer, and newsman at WKZO-AM. He was also sales manager at WKMI, and CEO, President, and Chairman of the Board of WKLZ and WLKM in Michigan. He has been both a manager and a consultant for cable systems, and for individuals wishing to invest in telecommunication properties. As an inventor, he founded Research Development Laboratories in 1963, and holds a patent for a public service promotion device marketed to radio stations nationwide by a major manufacturer. He has been an assistant professor in the S.I. Newhouse School of Public Communications, Syracuse University, since 1980, teaching undergraduate and graduate students in Telecommunication Management. He continues to consult and to invest in a variety of areas, is a member of the American Management Association, and participates in the divisions of Finance, Information Systems, Technology, and Marketing, as well as in the American Association of Individual Investors and the Broadcast Educational Association. He holds a B.S. in Radio-Television from Northwestern University, and an M.A. in Speech Communication from San Jose State University.

Patricia R. Cole, Ph.D., is the owner and director of the Austin Center for Speech, Language, and Learning Disorders, Austin, Texas. She has been in private practice since 1970, and specializes in evaluation and intervention for preschool children with language disorders. She has written a book on treatment service for that population. She is Past President of the Texas Speech-Language-Hearing Association and is a Fellow and President-Elect of the American Speech-Language-Hearing Association. She is active in legislative and other public policy matters that have an effect on persons with handicapping conditions. She holds a Ph.D. from the University of Texas at Austin and has worked as a speech-language pathologist in public schools, as a supervisor of clinical practicum in a university, and as a consultant for numerous education and health care facilities.

Jeremy J. Conoway, J.D., is a partner in the law firm of Brott, Conoway & Kipley in Traverse City, Michigan. His clients include several national associations and he speaks frequently on the subject of leadership and organizational dynamics. His involvement with the speech and hearing profession began in 1972 with his responsibilities as Deputy Executive Director of the California State Board of Medical Examiners, which included the Speech Pathology and Audiology licensure programs. He also served the Connecticut General Assembly as Special Counsel for Health Affairs. His articles on the private practice of speech-language pathology and audiology have appeared in several national magazines. His educational background includes a B.A. in Economics from California State University, an M.B.A. from the University of Maryland, and the J.D. degree from the University of the Pacific, McGeorge School of Law.

Dennis C. Hampton, Ph.D., owns a private practice (Dennis C. Hampton, Ph.D. and Associates) in White Plains, New York, and has been in private practice for more than ten years. He has also been a consultant to Westchester County Medical Center, the New York City Department of Health, the New York State Department of Health and to private industry, as well as serving on the consulting staffs of several hospitals. He is a member of the New York State Speech-Language-Hearing Association and the American Speech-Language-Hearing Association, serving on its national Committee on Amplification and the Task Force on Home Health Care. He has presented workshops and seminars on developing, managing, and marketing a private practice at numerous state and national professional conferences. Dr. Hampton received his Ph.D. in Audiology from Columbia University.

Rebecca Kooper, J.D., is an Audiologist with the Nassau-BOCES Hearing Impaired Program. She holds a B.A. and M.A. from the State University of New York, Buffalo and a Certificate of Clinical Competence in Audiology. She is credentialed as a Teacher of the Hearing Impaired (Deaf) and as a Teacher of the Speech and Hearing Impaired by New York State Department of Education. She has been admitted to the New York State Bar, and hopes to increase her advocacy attempts for the parents of hearing-impaired children in the years to come. She has lectured on a number of occasions regarding professional liability issues in speech-language pathology and audiology.

Angela M. Loavenbruck, Ed.D., has been in private practice for more than ten years, and owns Loavenbruck Associates, P.C., in New City, New York. She and her staff provide audiology and speech pathology services at several locations, including hospital settings, nursing homes, intermediate care and health related facilities, home health agencies, industries, and a free-standing private office. Dr. Loavenbruck was recently made a Fellow of the American Speech-Language-Hearing Association and serves on its Ethical Practices Board. She also serves on ASHA's Task Force on Doctoral Preparation and Task Force on CCC Validation. In 1985, she served as one of nine Professional Affairs Conference leaders for ASHA. In addition, she has been elected Private Practice Delegate for the New York State Speech-Language and Hearing Association. Dr. Loavenbruck was Associate Professor of Audiology at Teachers College, Columbia University, and she is co-author, with Dr. Jane Madell, of *Hearing Aid Dispensing for Audiologists—A Guide for Practitioners*. She holds both an M.A. and Ph.D. in Audiology from Teachers College, Columbia University.

Richard M. Flower, Ph.D., is Professor and Vice-Chairman of the Department of Otolaryngology at the University of California, San Francisco. He has served his state and national associations in numerous capacities, including the Presidency of the California Speech-Language-Hearing Association, the Vice-Presidency for Standards and Ethics and the Presidency of the American Speech-Language-Hearing Association, and is currently Immediate Past President of ASHA. He has long been interested in issues related to the delivery of speech-language pathology and audiology services, and is the author of a recent text entitled *Delivery of Speech-Language Pathology and Audiology Services*. He holds a B.A. and M.A. from San Jose State University and a Ph.D. from Northwestern University.

Mariana Newton, Ph.D., became interested in computer applications as Director of the Speech and Hearing Center at North Carolina State University at Greensboro (1969-1985). She has instituted a number of software programs for administrative purposes in the clinic and has reported on these at the American Speech-Language-Hearing Association conferences on computers. Her clinical interest is in the severely physically handicapped, augmentitive communication systems, and communication problems of the aging. She has served as Vice President for Professional and Governmental Affairs of the American Speech-Language-Hearing Association, 1982–84. She holds a B.A. and an M.A. from the University of Redlands and a Ph.D. from Northwestern University.

Robbin Parish, M.A., is Principal of the Parish School, a private school serving language and learning disabled children. In 1972 she founded one of the first private practices in speech pathology in the state of Texas, and has since merged that practice with her private school, which she founded in 1983. Parish is a member of the American Speech-Language-Hearing Association, and serves on its Ethical Practices Board and as an elected Legislative Councilor from Texas. She is immediate Past-President of the Texas Speech-Language-Hearing Association, Past-President of the Houston Area Association for Communication Disorders, and has served on the Board of The Orton Society. She holds a M.A. in Speech Pathology from Our Lady of the Lake College in San Antonio, Texas, and has attended Sullins College and the University of Texas at Austin.

Carol A. Sullivan, M.S., is in private practice in Garden City, New York, with her husband, Roy Sullivan. Mrs. Sullivan has given numerous presentations regarding the legal and financial aspects of private practice, and currently serves as Vice President for Private Practice of the New York State Speech-Language-Hearing Association. She holds a B.S. from the University of Hawaii, a B.B.A. from California Western University, and an M.S. in Speech, Pathology, Audiology and Deaf Education from the University of Hawaii. She has served as an adjunct lecturer at CUNY and Hunter College, and is recognized for her clinical work in voice disorders.

Robert H. Woody, Ph.D., J.D., is a Professor of Psychology at the University of Nebraska at Omaha. He is also engaged in the dual private practices of law and of clinical-forensic psychology in Omaha, Nebraska and Fort Myers, Florida. In teaching, practice, and research, he focuses on safeguarding the health-care professional from malpractice. He is a Fellow of the American Psychological Association, a Diplomate in Clinical Psychology, ABPP, Forensic Psychology, ABFP, Neuropsychology, ABPN, and Psychological Hypnosis, ABPH. He has been admitted to practice law and is licensed as a psychologist in Florida, Michigan, and Nebraska. His publications include nineteen books and about 300 articles in professional journals. He holds a B.Mus. and an Ed.S. in Psychology from Western Michigan University, and an M.A. and Ph.D. from Michigan State University. He also holds a Sc.D. from the University of Pittsburgh and a J.D. from Creighton University, and has completed a postdoctoral internship at the University of Lond's Institute of Psychiatry. In addition, he holds a postdoctoral Certificate in Group Psychotherapy from the Washington School of Psychiatry.